AF600288

CELEBRITY, FAME, AND INFAMY IN THE HELLENISTIC WORLD

PHOENIX

Journal of the Classical Association of Canada
Revue de la Société canadienne des études classiques
Supplementary Volume LVIII
Tome supplémentaire LVIII

EDITED BY RIEMER A. FABER

Celebrity, Fame, and Infamy in the Hellenistic World

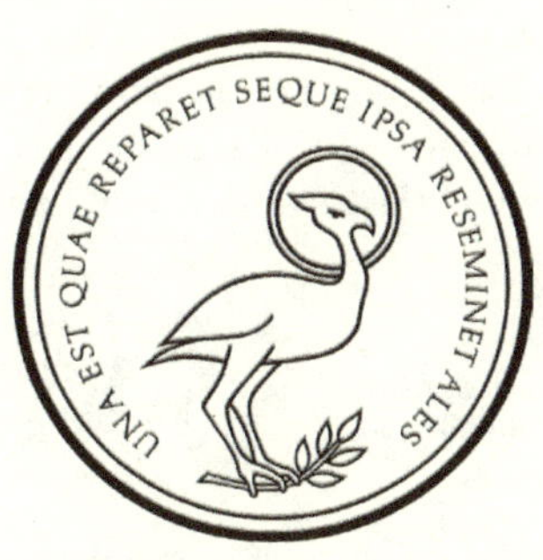

UNIVERSITY OF TORONTO PRESS
Toronto Buffalo London

Toronto Buffalo London
utorontopress.com

ISBN 978-1-4875-0522-6 (cloth)
ISBN 978-1-4875-3179-9 (EPUB)
ISBN 978-1-4875-3178-2 (PDF)

Library and Archives Canada Cataloguing in Publication

Title: Celebrity, fame, and infamy in the Hellenistic world / edited by Riemer A. Faber.
Names: Faber, Riemer A., editor.
Series: Phoenix. Supplementary volume ; 58.
Description: Series statement: Phoenix. Supplementary volume ; LVIII | Includes bibliographical references and index.
Identifiers: Canadiana (print) 20190241292 | Canadiana (ebook) 20190241284 | ISBN 9781487505226 | ISBN 9781487505226 (cloth) | ISBN 9781487531799 (EPUB) | ISBN 9781487531782 (PDF)
Subjects: LCSH: Fame – History. | LCSH: Hellenism. | LCSH: Greece – Civilization – To 146 B.C. | LCSH: Mediterranean Region – Civilization.
Classification: LCC BJ1470.5.C45 2020 | DDC 306.4–dc23

University of Toronto Press acknowledges the financial assistance to its publishing program of the Canada Council for the Arts and the Ontario Arts Council, an agency of the Government of Ontario.

Canada Council for the Arts
Conseil des Arts du Canada

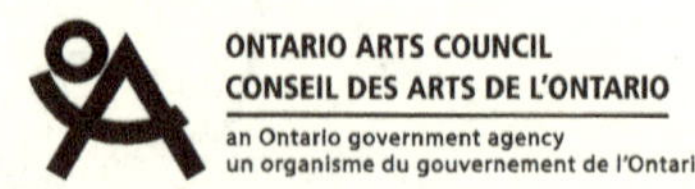

Funded by the Government of Canada
Financé par le gouvernement du Canada

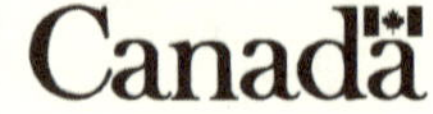

CONTENTS

List of Illustrations vii

Acknowledgments ix

Abbreviations xi

Introduction: Distinctives of Hellenistic Celebrity, Fame, and Infamy 3
RIEMER A. FABER

1 *Fama* and *Infamia*: The Tale of Grypos and Tryphaina 18
SHEILA L. AGER

2 Models of Virtue, Models of Poetry: The Quest for "Everlasting Fame" in Hellenistic Military Epitaphs 37
SILVIA BARBANTANI

3 Can Powerful Women Be Popular? Amastris: Shaping a Persian Wife into a Famous Hellenistic Queen 70
MONICA D'AGOSTINI

4 Remelted or Overstruck: Cases of Monetary *Damnatio Memoriae* in Hellenistic Times? 90
FRANÇOIS DE CALLATAŸ

5 Ptolemaic Officials and Officers in Search of Fame 111
CHRISTELLE FISCHER-BOVET

6 Lemnian Infamy and Masculine Glory in Apollonios' *Argonautica* 135
JUDITH FLETCHER

7 The "Good" Poros and the "Bad" Poros: Infamy and Honour in Alexander Historiography 156
TIMOTHY HOWE

8 Writing Monarchs of the Hellenistic Age: Renown, Fame, and Infamy 172
JACQUELINE KLOOSTER

9 Creating Alexander: The "Official" History of Kallisthenes of Olynthos 199
WALDEMAR HECKEL

References 217

Contributors 245

Index 249

ILLUSTRATIONS

Figures

1.1 Genealogy of Cleopatra Tryphaina 19
3.1 Silver stater (337–305 BCE) from Herakleia Pontika: Dionysos, Herakles 73
3.2 Silver didrachm (300–288 BCE) from Amastris: head of young male, seated Aphrodite 81
3.3 Silver stater (300–288 BCE) from Amastris: head of young male, seated Aphrodite 81
3.4 Silver stater (288/285?–250 BCE) from Amastris: head of young male, seated Aphrodite 85
4.1 Coin of Louis XVI (1789) with cut on neck 92
4.2 Sestertius of Trajan (ca 103–105 CE) heavily defaced 93
4.3 Athenian bronze coin with defaced Pontic symbols 93
4.4 *As* in the name of Aelius Sejanus (31 CE) with erasure of name 95
4.5 Bronze coin (ca 212 CE) with the portraits of Caracalla and erased Geta 95
4.6 Hemistater of Hiketas (278 BCE) with erasure of name 96
4.7 Athenian tetradrachm with Pontic symbols of King Mithridates replaced 96
4.8 Athenian tetradrachm with Pontic symbols of King Mithridates 97
4.9 Tetradrachm of Ptolemy Soter (ca 310 BCE) overstruck on Alexander the Great 98
4.10 Tetradrachm of Timarchos overstruck by jugate portraits of Demetrios I and Laodike 99
4.11 Tetradrachm of Timarchos struck at Seleukeia 100

4.12 Tetradrachm of Bagadat (end of third century BCE?) 101
4.13 Tetradrachm of a king of Persis (?) overstruck by images of Demetrios I and Laodike 101
4.14 Tetradrachm of Tiridates 103
4.15 Tetradrachms attributed to Phraates IV overstruck on Tiridates *philoromaios* 103
4.16 Tetradrachm of Phraatakes and Musa (1 CE) 104
4.17 Overstruck tetradrachm of Vonones I (9/10 CE) 104
4.18 Overstruck tetradrachm of Vonones I (10 CE) 105
4.19 Tetradrachm of Orophernes (158–157 BCE) 106
5.1 Statue of Djedhor, priest of Iat-Maat in Athribis (ca 340–330 BCE) 117
5.2 Statue of Horos of Herakleopolis (ca 340–310 BCE) 119
5.3 Hieroglyphic inscriptions, statue of Horos of Herakleopolis (ca 340–310 BCE) 120
5.4 Colossal statue of Teos I 121
5.5 Colossal statue of Teos II 122
5.6 Statue of Panemerit (ca 125 BCE) 125

Tables

7.1 Accounts of Poros in the Alexander sources 159
8.1 The writings of the Hellenistic kings 180

ACKNOWLEDGMENTS

The essays collected in this volume were presented first in a workshop entitled "Celebrity, Fame, and Infamy in the Hellenistic World," held in Waterloo, Ontario, on 9–11 September 2015, under the auspices of the Waterloo Institute for Hellenistic Studies. Several organizations and individuals supported the project, and I would like to take the opportunity here to thank them. I am very grateful to the Social Sciences and Humanities Research Council for its generosity in funding the research workshop by means of a Connection Grant. Sincere gratitude is expressed also to the Onassis Foundation and, in particular, its director of educational affairs, Dr Maria Sereti, for its generous support of several activities surrounding the event. The foundation is thanked especially for the Onassis Visiting Fellowship awarded to Prof. Waldemar Heckel (University of Calgary), which allowed him to participate in the workshop and to give several lectures to the university community and the general public. At the University of Waterloo, financial assistance was provided by Prof. George Dixon, vice-president for research, and Prof. Douglas Peers, dean of Arts, and I am thankful for their support.

I would like to convey my gratitude to those local individuals who helped in making the workshop a success, in particular my colleagues Sheila Ager, Altay Coşkun, Andrew Faulkner, Craig Hardiman, Ron Kroeker, Maria Liston, Robert Porter, and Christina Vester. Invaluable help in organizing and running the workshop was given by the Institute for Hellenistic Studies' administrative assistant, Brigitte Schneebeli. I thank the following students in the Department of Classical Studies who, by their attention to the details, helped make the workshop a very pleasant experience: Mitchell Elvidge, Geoff Harmsworth, Andrew Kim, Andrew Noakes, and Mojdeh Shahidi.

Not least, I would like to express my sincere gratitude to the research associates of the institute who presented papers and participated in the lively discussions.

The present volume has been published with the help of the Waterloo Institute for Hellenistic Studies and the Faculty of Arts at the University of Waterloo, and I am grateful to these organizations for their financial support. I would also like to express my gratitude to all the contributors to this volume, and to thank them for their collegial collaboration in this project. I am grateful also to the University of Toronto Press and to Suzanne Rancourt, manager, humanitities acquisitions, for their encouragement and support. Special thanks are extended to the anonymous readers of the press for their expert advice and detailed constructive criticism. Finally, I thank the production editor Christine Robertson and her colleagues for their expertise in shepherding the volume to publication.

Riemer Faber
Waterloo, July 2019

ABBREVIATIONS

Abbreviations of classical authors and their works follow the *Oxford Classical Dictionary* (3rd ed.). The following abbreviations also occur in this volume.

BNJ	I. Worthington, (ed.), *Brill's New Jacoby Online*, http://referenceworks.brillonline.com/browse/brill-s-new-jacoby
BNP	H. Cancik and H. Schneider (eds), *Brill's New Pauly Online: Encyclopaedia of the Ancient World: Antiquity* (English ed. edited by C.F. Salazar), http://referenceworks.brillonline.com/cluster/New%20Pauly%Online?s.num=0
CA	J.U. Powell (ed.), *Collectanea Alexandrina*. Oxford, 1925.
CIRB	V. Struve (ed.), *Corpus inscriptionum regni Bosporani*. Moscow, 1965.
CNG	Classical Numismatic Group, Inc. Online, www.cngcoins.com/
EKM	L. Gounaropoulou and M.B. Hatzopoulos, *Epigraphes Katō Makedonias (metaxy tou Vermiou orous kai tou Axiou potamou). Teuchos A'. Epigraphes Veroias.* Athens, 1998.
FGE	D.L. Page, *Further Greek Epigrams*. Cambridge, 1981.
FGrH	F. Jacoby, *Fragmente der griechischen Historiker*. Berlin and Leipzig, 1923–58.
GVI	W. Peek, *Griechische Vers-Inschriften I, Grab-epigramme*. Berlin, 1955.
IC	M. Guarducci (ed.), *Inscriptiones Creticae: Opera et consilio Friderici Halbherr collectae*. 4 volumes. Rome, 1935–50.
ID	*Inscriptions de Délos*. 7 volumes. Paris, 1926–72.
I Didyma	A. Rehm, *Didyma, II: Die Inschriften*. Berlin, 1941.
IG	*Inscriptiones Graecae*. Berlin, 1873–.

IMEGR	É. Bernand, *Inscriptions métriques de l'Égypte gréco-romaine.* Annales littéraires de l'Université de Besançon 98. Paris, 1969.
Inschr. Dem.	W. Spiegelberg (ed.), *Catalogue général des antiquités égyptiennes du Musée du Caire: Die demotischen Denkmäler 30601–31166.* Volume 1. Die demotischen Inschriften. Leipzig, 1904.
IscM	*Inscriptiones Daciae et Scythiae Minoris antiquae.* Bucharest, 1987–.
KILyk	G. Laminger-Pascher, *Die kaiserzeitlichen Inschriften Lykaoniens,* fasc. 1. "Österreichische Akademie der Wissenschaften, Philosophisch-Historische Klasse: Denkschriften" [DAW], 232. "Ergänzungsbände zu den *Tituli Asiae Minoris,* 15. Vienna, 1992.
P.dem.Berlin	W. Spiegelberg, *Demotische Papyrus aus den königlichen Museen zu Berlin.* Leipzig and Berlin, 1902.
PMG	D.L. Page, *Poetae Melici Graeci.* Oxford, 1962.
RC	C.B. Welles, *Royal Correspondence in the Hellenistic Period: A Study in Greek Epigraphy.* New Haven, CT, 1934.
RPC	*Roman Provincial Coinage,* edited by A. Burnet, M. Amandry, C. Howgego, and J. Mairat. Oxford, 1992–.
SB	F. Preisigke, F. Bilabel, and E. Kiessling (eds), *Sammelbuch griechischer Urkunden aus Ägypten.* Strassbourg, Berlin, 1915.
SC	A. Houghton, C. Lorber, and O.D. Hoover, *Seleucid Coins: A Comprehensive Catalogue II. Seleucus IV through Antiochus XIII.* New York, Lancaster, and London, 2008.
SE	M. Alpers and H. Halfmann (eds), *Supplementum Ephesium.* Hamburg, 1995.
SEG	*Supplementum Epigraphicum Graecum.* Leiden and Amsterdam, 1923–.
SGDI	H. Collitz and F. Bechtel (eds), *Sammlung der griechischen Dialekt-Inschriften.* 4 volumes. Göttingen, 1885–9.
SGO	R. Merkelbach and J. Stauber, *Steinepigramme aus dem griechischen Osten.* 5 volumes. Stuttgart, Leipzig, and Munich, 1998–2004.
Suppl. Hell.	H. Lloyd-Jones and P. Parsons (eds), *Supplementum Hellenisticum.* Berlin, 1983. Revised by H.-G. Nesselrath, 2011.
TAM	E. Kalinka (ed.), *Tituli Asiae Minoris.* 5 volumes. Vienna, 1901–.
TrGF	R. Kannicht, S. Radt, and B. Snell (eds), *Tragicorum Graecorum Fragmenta.* Göttingen, 1971–2004.

CELEBRITY, FAME, AND INFAMY IN THE HELLENISTIC WORLD

Introduction: Distinctives of Hellenistic Celebrity, Fame, and Infamy

RIEMER A. FABER

There is only one thing in the world worse than being talked about, and that is not being talked about.

Oscar Wilde

1. Introduction

It is no exaggeration to state that our own age suffers from an addiction to celebrity, fame, and infamy. Nearly every country on earth can boast of someone whose image is recognized instantly around the globe, from Kim Jong Un, the "Supreme Leader" of North Korea, with his inimitable hair style, to Vladimir Putin, flexing his sexagenarian muscles in a training gym. We live in an age when people are famous simply for being famous. Ours is the age of the photo op, the sound byte, and, egotistically, the selfie – an age when a revealing YouTube clip reduces Andy Warhol's dictum to fifteen *seconds* of worldwide fame. And yet our contemporary fascination with celebrity, fame, and infamy also informs our awareness of these social phenomena in antiquity.

The purpose of this introduction is to provide the context for this volume of essays. First we shall briefly characterize the social phenomenon of fame and related concepts in periods of history after the Classical era, identifying some themes common to ancient as well as modern times. The variety of theoretical and methodological approaches pursued in the chapters will be noted. Following a brief survey of the scholarship on the topic from various classical and non-classical perspectives, I will offer some thoughts on the social function of fame and infamy (and related concepts) in order to assist in the exploration this topic as a window providing a better view of social life in the Hellenistic era.

The theme of this collection has been pursued for other periods of European history, but there is no dedicated study of fame in the Hellenistic period. The most recent publication on the subject in classical antiquity appeared in 2015: edited by Rhiannon Ash and others, the volume of essays, entitled *Fame and Infamy*, focuses on the literary representation of personages in historical texts and in the evolution of biography. Philip Hardie's *Rumour and Renown: Representations of* Fama *in Western Literature* (2012) traces the Roman concept of *fama* from early Greek poetry to modern English literature. The personified Rumour, known to classicists especially from the monstrous Fama of *Aeneid* Book 4, undergoes numerous metamorphoses from the time of Vergil to Chaucer and Pope.[1] During the Middle Ages, personal reputation was social capital of such value that both the law courts and the Christian church sought to regulate it, as the essays in Fenster and Smail's *Fama: The Politics of Talk and Reputation in Medieval Europe* (2003) demonstrate. The democratization of Western society that followed the French Revolution, aided by the inventions of mass printing, the photograph, and newspapers, hastened the spread of rumour and renown in literate societies.[2] And so the concept of celebrity evolved into its modern form.

In 2009, the classically trained Tom Payne published a popular book called *Fame: From the Bronze Age to Britney*. In it he sought to explain the modern cult of celebrity by suggesting that, when contemporary celebs such as Britney Spears and Madonna make a very public sacrifice of their own persona, they perpetuate the ancient practice of society offering a sacrificial victim for the sake of the common good. It is *society* that creates and raises up celebrities, only to destroy them and cast them outside the community, like a scapegoat. Think of Britain's Diana, Princess of Wales, or America's Marilyn Monroe. Whether or not Payne's theory sustains critical examination,[3] it is true that (in)famous personages reflect something of the values of the society in which they live and die. One wonders what this observation may mean for the values of our own generation with Lady Gaga (with her outrageous fashion statements), Silvio Berlusconi (and his scandalous *bunga bunga* parties), and most recently Donald Trump, the combed-over populist politician occupying one of the world's highest public offices. Nevertheless, the interpretation of fame and celebrity, and their counterparts ill repute and blame, is as much the assessment of the values of a society as of the famous personages it creates.

The social poetics of celebrity is the premise also of Robert Garland's book *Celebrity in Antiquity: From Media Tarts to Tabloid Queens* (2006). In it he sets out to prove that – in the words of the *BMCR* reviewer – "in many ways the ancient Greeks and Romans created the ideology behind celebrity and have heavily influenced our own ideas of what celebrity is and means."[4] An important, earlier study of fame that influenced several scholars of celebrity in antiquity is Leo Braudy's *The Frenzy of Renown* (1986). Braudy makes the case that celebrity, fame, and infamy are essentially different concepts today than they were before the Industrial Revolution. With its new political and economic context, the Industrial Revolution encouraged the transformation of the classic idea of personal honour. According to Braudy, widespread literacy, the demise of monarchical authority, and the extension of the political franchise led to the modern notion of celebrity (1986: 13). *Modern* fame is predicated on the Industrial Revolution's promise of increasing progress and the Enlightenment's promise of ever-expanding individual will. Modern consumer culture has become intertwined with fame culture to the point that, nowadays, anyone of aspiration feels compelled to present himself or herself in a very public manner (596).

2. Celebrity, Fame, Infamy, and Related Terms

This claim leads one to consider the precise definition of celebrity, fame, and related concepts. Modern studies of the phenomena point out that the English terms for reputation and renown are predominantly of Latin, not Greek, origin (Garland 2006: 5).[5] There are of course Greek approximations of these concepts, such as *axioma* (estimation), *charisma* (magnetic appeal), *doxa* (repute), *epiphaneia* (renown), *kleos* (glory), and *philotimia* (love of honour, ambition). But the Latin terms from which many relevant English derivatives come are more well known: *claritas* (renown), *gloria* (military fame), *laus* (esteem or reputation), *ambitio* (striving for popularity), and, of course, *celebritas*. The fact that several related words, like *philotimia, philoneikia, fama, rumor, ambitio,* and *celebritas* could bear negative as well as positive connotations is indicative of a certain tension in the concepts of celebrity, fame, and infamy in antiquity (Braudy 1986: 17). Not all renown is good renown.

The word "celebrity," when it is used to denote a state of being or a person, is a relatively recent addition to the English language. The *Oxford English Dictionary* attributes it to Samuel Johnson, who in 1751 complained: "I did not find myself yet enriched in proportion to my celebrity." An often-cited modern definition of celebrity is that of the American historian and social commentator Daniel Boorstin, who states: "the celebrity is a person who is well-known for his well-knownness" (1961: 57). The sense of commonness or frequency associated with the Latin *celebritas* carries over into the

English word via the notion of frequent name-dropping. And it seems probable that the Roman concept of *celebritas* arose from the custom of famous men being surrounded by a crowd or mob of bodyguards, the retinue of attendants who are swept along with the personage (Garland 2006: 7). In the concise terms of Leo Braudy's definition, then, celebrity "is made up of four elements: a person and an accomplishment, their immediate publicity, and what posterity has thought about them ever since" (1986: 15).

The Latin word *fama* possesses two central meanings: rumour (including gossip, lying, and truth) and glory or renown. In his book on the Latin language, Varro makes an etymological connection between *fama* and *fari* – the Latin word for "to speak" – and he implies that rumour and renown are produced especially through oral communication and social discourse.[6] The performative function of the speech-act is to communicate some knowledge possessed by groups of undetermined voices (Syson 2013: 29).[7] Thus *fama* may refer to reports of various kinds: accurate, misleading, neutral, scandalous, or positive (Goldhill 1991: 33). But *fama* may also designate renown, widespread acclaim, or "the reputation guaranteed by the wide circulation of someone's name" (Guastella 2017: 5). Though clearly distinct in meaning, these two uses of *fama* share the same means of diffusion – that is, the exchange of information in social contexts.

"Infamy" as a term and concept derives from the Latin word *infamia* (meaning defamation or dishonourable report), a term that was employed especially in rhetorical contexts of portraying the character of a defendant.[8] Besides denoting the loss of certain legal rights as a citizen following the conviction of crime, *infamia* in republican Rome also triggered notions of public reproach and disgrace. As Sarah Bond notes (2014: 2–3), the term often was extended to include censorship of deviant social and – in the late empire – religious behaviour.

The Latinate character of the English terms attests in part to the important role of Roman society in the formation of the modern concepts of celebrity, fame, and infamy. The Roman *cursus honorum*, its fascination with the individual virtues of *dignitas* and *auctoritas*, and the personal focus in historical writings, public monuments, and speeches, attest to the adaptation of Hellenistic concepts of fame and infamy to a different cultural context (Braudy 1986: 61). There existed a strong connection between personal merit and public reward in Rome, especially in the self-aggrandizing oratory of Rome's elite. Oratorical strategies, which included the use of such rhetorical devices as the *laudatio* (testimonial of character), located individual aspirations in the public domain.[9] A complexity of social and moral laws empowered the Roman Republic to determine socially acceptable behaviour, and the good name (*existimatio*) of an up-and-coming public servant depended heavily on reports about him in his social order.[10] To some extent, then, the study of celebrity in the Hellenistic world acknowledges that our perceptions of it may be filtered by Roman social values.

3. Distinguishing Features of Fame in the Hellenistic World

Recent scholarship has shown that notions of celebrity, fame, and infamy provide invaluable access to understanding the accomplishments and ideals that a society admires or disdains among its members (Hardie 2012; Payne 2009; Garland 2006). Indeed, since ancient times the concepts of honour and shame, envy and renown, and reputation and ignominy have controlled public and private behaviour in many societies. These concepts may be traced to Bronze Age cultures of the Mediterranean basin (Peristiany 1966) and have remained in force until at least the decline of the Roman Empire (Flower 2013: 33–78; Thomas 2002; Whitby 1998). The careers of persons such as the Athenian playboy Alkibiades show that the notion of pursuing fame for its own sake (and not for some political motive) is as old as fifth-century Athens. It is clear that the phenomena that form the subject of this volume of essays are not restricted to the Hellenistic era; however, it is especially during the Hellenistic period from 300 to 30 BCE that celebrity, fame, and infamy assumed an irrevocably powerful role.

The Hellenistic era begins and ends with two of the most famous people in the history of the Western world: Alexander "the Great" and Cleopatra, whose very name, "glory of the father," derives from the Greek word "glory" (*kleos*). If we are to believe everything the historians have written about them, the careers of Alexander and Cleopatra meet the modern criteria for celebrity. In the case of Alexander, we may note that he pursued an explicit imitation of a known hero (Achilles); he was an adept self-promoter (dozens of cities and towns were called Alexandria); he carefully developed a public image (e.g., his leonine hairstyle); he was imitated by later aspirants (Pompey "the Great," among others); and he had international appeal (think of his Greek rather than Macedonian persona). Cleopatra, meanwhile, illustrates important requirements for the pre-modern female celebrity: she is someone who did *not* adopt a position that society with its values and prejudices had predetermined for women, and she broke out of the mould of the traditional wife and mother. In general, powerful women in antiquity were connected to powerful males as adjuncts, mothers, wives, or sisters, as the essays by Ager and D'Agostini in this volume note. The carefully stage-managed appearances of Cleopatra, and her manipulation of relations with powerful men, served to maintain the Ptolemaic dynasty and to assure its social control. Labelled the "Tabloid Queen" by Garland, Cleopatra was a brilliant self-promoter and exploiter of "photo-ops" (if nothing more) with politically powerful men.

For Alexander and Cleopatra to reach their astronomic heights of fame and infamy, however, an entire social structure had to be in place. The nature of this infrastructure explains why it is during the Hellenistic period that celebs such as Alexander and Cleopatra became famous. Bosworth (2002) has shown that during this time the interconnections of local communities with larger ruling centres affected communal definitions of reputation and related concepts. In the city-states of the Archaic age, few individuals had reputations that extended beyond the borders of their own community (Garland 2006: 146). In Alexander's empire, the expanding οἰκουμένη was unified by the terrestrial and maritime routes of communication, which aided not only the travel of administrative officials but also the movement of peoples and goods generally. Heckel's essay (chapter 9 in this volume) argues that the carefully controlled written reports of Alexander's movements also travelled westward via these routes.

Another circumstance that fostered the widespread knowledge about people such as Alexander is the self-reflexive character of Hellenistic communities. As Braudy points out, "[Alexander] succeeded beyond previous aspirants in part because he was raised in a society that had become self-conscious of its own inherited values" (1986: 38). What is more, he lived at a critical juncture in history when "older definitions of both public and private behavior were breaking down" (48).

Yet another distinctive of Hellenistic celebrity is the status of the king or queen and the dynasty, which focused greater attention on self-promoting courts via the media of inscription, sculpture, and encomiastic literature. Access to the means of spreading information, the rise of the public spectacle, and the increase in public spaces all contributed to a growing awareness of celebrity, fame, and infamy (Ma 2013: 8; Hazzard 2000). Consequently the widespread promotional use of imagery that begins with Alexander was intended to convey not so much the appearance of the person but rather a series of specific political and social messages for the viewers (Stewart 1993: 59–70). The significance of public reputation for Hellenistic rulers and their officials is explored in the chapters by D'Agostini, Fischer-Bovet, and Klooster in this book.

Taken together, the essays in this volume demonstrate that the following factors, which Garland (2006: 8–9) has identified as defining celebrity and its relation to society, became particularly prominent in the Hellenistic era:

1. Geographical context: The growth of cosmopolitan cities, the rise of urban centres, and the spread and efficiency of communication are all factors that became more powerful in the Hellenistic era.
2. Arenas of social communication: Of course, there had been public assemblies, law courts, and festivals in prior ages, but each of these was used more effectively for political and economic goals.

3. Social status: Up until the past two hundred years, celebrity was attained by royal or aristocratic birth, which provided the economic means necessary for fame. The exceptions to this, also in antiquity, were entertainers, athletes, and professionals. During the Hellenistic period, the fragmentation of the empire created by Alexander resulted in an intensification of propaganda and self-promotion by an increasingly broad range of people.
4. Access to means of disseminating information: This access included commissioned literature, portraiture, building programs, and coinage.
5. Strategic self-representation: In the Hellenistic era, the cultivation of the individual appears to have gained momentum. The individual's style of dress or hair, manner of speaking and social interaction, and even the cultivation of idiosyncratic mannerisms seem to have grown tremendously in this era.

4. Interdisciplinary Approaches to Hellenistic Celebrity, Fame, and Infamy

Our own generation's overdose on celebrity, fame, and infamy is premised in large part on the explosion of social media: traditional means of social communication – which began more than a century ago with the increasing circulation of newspapers, and the invention of the camera, radio, and, later, television (all of which propelled the public hearing and viewing of famous people for an earlier generation) – have been replaced by the world-wide-web of *electronic* media. Some of today's largest corporations were built on our society's need for instant access to the rich and famous: Twitter, Facebook, and Google. Braudy has noted that "as each new medium of fame appears, the human image it conveys is intensified and the number of individuals celebrated expands" (1986: 4).

The point here is that the current explosion of the generators of mass media illuminates the importance of their counterparts in the ancient and, especially, Hellenistic world. From the third to the first centuries BCE, there was an increase in propaganda by means of diverse creative arts in public places: statues, commemorative inscriptions, coinage, literature, monumental edifices, biased biographies, and historical accounts. The Hellenistic era was consciously multi-medial. This development justifies an interdisciplinary approach for defining the nature of celebrity, fame, and infamy in the Hellenistic world. In this volume, the joint examination of how Hellenistic rulers and would-be rulers employed encomiastic literature, portraiture, entertainments, public monuments, and creative artists will serve to bring out the diverse qualities of celebrity, fame, and infamy in the Hellenistic world. Two examples may suffice to illustrate this point.

In his recently published book, *The Hellenistic World: Using Coins as Sources* (2015), Peter Thonemann explores the impact that aspects of globalization, international identity, and cross-cultural political economies and ideologies had on coinage in the Hellenistic world. In treating the role of currency in the creation of civic and cultural identities, the promotion of ideologies, and the Hellenizing role of numismatic iconography in general, Thonemann argues that, in the Hellenistic era, Greek coinage was transformed to take on new social, political, and economic functions. The second example is that of the cult of the artist and the artefact. In her revisionist and provocative book, *The Modernity of Ancient Sculpture* (2012), Elizabeth Prettejohn demonstrates the relationship between artists' personal style and reputation in post-classical times. She argues that the nascent Hellenistic interest in autonomous individuals should not be seen as separate from an increasing awareness of personal style in the period's artistic production. The reputation of Lysippos, the fourth-century artist and sculptor to Alexander the Great, bears witness to the increasing sense of individual spirit in post-classical art that draws our eye not merely to the displayed object but also to the named artist. In short, society's heightened awareness of the image of the individual is reflected in contemporary three-dimensional art that reinforces also the artist's reputation (Prettejohn 2012: 108–23).

In the Hellenistic period, the means of recording fame and infamy were public art, literature, sculpture, coinage, drama, and inscribed monuments. Each of these was carefully employed by the ruling elite of the different Hellenistic kingdoms, and the essays in this volume examine and illustrate their functions in the creation of social, political, and cultural values. The following media have been identified as critical to an understanding of the unique nature of celebrity, fame, and infamy in the Hellenistic world, and each is treated in this collection:

- inscriptions on public monuments (honorific, funerary)
- Greek, Roman, and other historical writings
- stamped coins
- sculptures and other forms of public art
- literary and creative writings, including epic, epigram, panegyric, and drama

5. Theoretical Contexts for the Study of Fame in the Hellenistic World

The multi-disciplinary premise of the volume invokes a diversity of theoretical and methodological approaches to the study of each of these media:

anthropology, social history, and literary and dramatic studies. It would be appropriate, therefore, to offer a few summary comments on the theoretical approaches that have influenced the writing of these chapters and that the contributors have consciously adopted or adapted in their writing. At the risk of being reductionist, one may identify three main streams of theoretical approaches to the topic of the volume: subjectivism, structuralism, and post-structuralism.[11]

Subjectivist accounts of celebrity, fame, and infamy fasten onto the singularity of personal characteristics in the creation of both renown and ignominy (Rojek 2001: 29). Though refined and polished through discipline and practice, and shaped by cultural contexts, it is a person's innate talent that makes her or him a celebrity. The reason audiences were, and are, fascinated by a famous person's appearance, manner of speaking, fashion, or hairstyle, is because these outward appearances may be indicators of the hidden qualities that make them famous. The charisma of the celebrity is inspirational.

The structuralist explanation of the phenomenon concentrates on the relations between human conduct and the social or cultural contexts that inform that conduct (Rojek 2001: 33). Thus, for example, infamy is an expression of universal structural rules that are embedded in a particular culture (Rojek 2001: 33). Taken a step further, organized entertainment, public spectacle, and dissemination via social media reflect a type of social control whereby conduct and standards are shaped and inculcated.

Thirdly, there is the post-structuralist theory of fame and infamy. It focuses not so much on the individual or the social contexts that produce the celebrity but more on the codes of representation through which the famous or infamous image is produced. It moves away from the individual person to the various fields of interest that employ the elements of their fame or infamy (Rojek 2001: 45). In others words, according to the post-structuralist theory of celebrity, what is important are the various forces that use, re-use, appropriate, or reject the famous individual. Different social, political, economic, and cultural forces are at play in the creation of celebrity, fame, and infamy, and what really matters is how the individual character directs the viewer's gaze to the forces at play.

6. The Scope of the Present Volume

This volume of essays arises from a research workshop held at the Waterloo Institute for Hellenistic Studies at the University of Waterloo in September 2015. The purpose of the workshop was to bring together a select group of international specialists in Hellenistic studies and to mobilize a diversity of theoretical and methodological approaches in the study of the media of fame in the Hellenistic era. Sponsored in part by the Social Sciences and Humanities Research Council of Canada, the meeting fostered the transference and cross-fertilization of scholarship through juxtaposing different disciplinary approaches and different case studies. A round-table discussion at the close of the workshop served to further identify and define the unifying themes, distinctives, and approaches in the papers.

As in modern times, so too in antiquity the behaviour of celebrities was scrutinized under the harsh light of society's moral standards. Hellenistic queens in particular were mercilessly condemned if they failed to pass the test of socially approved behaviour, and the alleged actions of the Seleukid queen Cleopatra Tryphaina ensured that she found a place in the annals of Hellenistic infamy. The historiographical portrait of this queen is the focus of this volume's first chapter, "*Fama* and *Infamia*: The Tale of Grypos and Tryphaina," by Sheila L. Ager. Married to the Seleukid king Antiochos VIII, Tryphaina became embroiled in the war between her husband and his half-brother, Antiochos IX. When Antiochos IX's wife – Tryphaina's own full sister, Cleopatra IV – was besieged in a temple, clinging to an altar, Tryphaina ordered that her sister's hands be cut off so that she could be dragged out of the sanctuary and despatched. Within the year, Tryphaina herself was captured by her brother-in-law and executed in turn. The story appears only in Justin and is the only ancient testimonium we have concerning Tryphaina. Ager challenges the veracity of this portrait, and argues instead that Tryphaina was the victim of Seleukid propaganda: perhaps that of her brother-in-law, but even more likely that of her own husband. Ager's treatment of Tryphaina's ill repute (*infamia*) anticipates the subsequent essays by D'Agostini (chapter 3) and Fletcher (chapter 6) on the precarious nature of women's reputations in the Hellenistic era.

With a special focus on military epitaphs, in chapter 2 Silvia Barbantani examines the connection between propaganda and posthumous reputation in a study entitled "Models of Virtue, Models of Poetry: The Quest for 'Everlasting Fame' in Hellenistic Military Epitaphs." Barbantani explores the lexicon of glory and fame in the corpus of Hellenistic military epitaphs within the broader archaic and classical literary traditions, and compares the eulogistic strategies employed by epigrammatists with the ones featured in the best examples of Alexandrian court poetry.

In the Hellenistic kingdoms, the ultimate glory of a military victory belonged exclusively to the king, as stated by encomiastic poetry and dedicatory epigrams. However, not all these epigrams celebrate high-ranking officials and affluent citizens: short verse inscriptions sing the praises of soldiers who apparently were of more modest social rank. The long tradition of the epigram, its pervasiveness in all the areas of the Hellenized Mediterranean, and its versatility as a poetic genre make it an ideal means to explore the survival and the evolution of the concept of *kleos* in the post-classical world.

From the powerful Hellenistic king to the modest citizen-soldier, Greeks obsessed over the legacy of their name. In this regard, grave monuments play a major role, because they reveal for all eternity the desired reputation of the deceased. Not only was the inscription important, but so too was the iconography engraved upon the gravestone. After all, the final image of the deceased was a pictorial construct of codified markers that were intended to immortalize the name, wealth, and/or prowess of the deceased. Much like funerary reliefs, numismatic self-representations of living or deceased monarchs were effective means of conferring and disseminating their public image. An unusual case concerns the numismatic issues from the cities of Herakleia and Amastris in the eastern portions of the Mediterranean world, on the Black Sea. Augmented by the extant writings of the local historian, Memnon of Herakleia, the story of the Persian princess Amastris tells us much about the mechanisms Hellenistic rulers employed to establish and augment their own reputations. She is the focus of chapter 3, "Can Powerful Women Be Popular? Amastris: Shaping a Persian Wife into a Famous Hellenistic Queen," by Monica D'Agostini. Amastris is rather well attested in the area's numismatic production, and also in Memnon's local historiography. As the Achaimenid wife of Krateros, one of Alexander's leading generals, and later married for a time to the local tyrant Dionysios and also to King Lysimachos, Amastris played no small role in the political theatre of the eastern Mediterranean. She became the mistress, *despoina,* of the satrapy, and in that capacity unified the local communities of Sesamos, Kromna, Kytaros, and Tio. In 299 BCE she became the first female *oikist,* founding the eponymous city of Amastris, where she installed her residence. As D'Agostini shows, on her coinage Amastris promoted her queenship not on the grounds of her associations with a powerful husband ruler, but as rooted in her own Persian family lineage. The evidence suggests that Amastris purposefully promoted an image of herself as the founder of her own rule, as the creator of her own dynast, as the architect of her own city, and as the minting authority of her own coins.

If coins were employed to propagate a certain image for political purposes, then the eradication of such images must have appealed to rivals and successful opponents. The condemnation of memory, expressed by the modern term *damnatio memoriae,* reflected the Roman preoccupation with the concepts of memory and fame.[12] In chapter 4, "Remelted or Overstruck: Cases of Monetary *Damnatio Memoriae* in Hellenistic Times?'," François de Callataÿ examines the evidence for the erasure of portrayals of political or military enemies. His study explores the several different ways in which Hellenistic rulers may have sought to impugn or even destroy the reputation of their enemies by damaging representations of them on coins. These include individual alterations of the surface (marks of execration); purposeful alterations of the surface (erasing and countermarks); recalled and overstruck coins; and recalled and remelted coins. There are indeed rare and isolated instances of overstruck coins, such as the tetradrachm of Demetrios and Laodike on the coins issued by Timarchos at Seleukeia on the Tigris sometime after 162 BCE. But these overstrikes were propelled by exceptional and immediate political circumstances and not so much by a desire to erase someone's memory forever. De Callataÿ argues that, generally, systematic monetary *damnatio memoriae* was not practised in Hellenistic times. On the other hand, he observes from the increasing evidence that rulers were not afraid to prolong the currency of coins depicting their opponents, so long as these coins were deemed as legal tender by the beneficiaries, who often were mercenaries.

The role of senior military, political, and civic personnel in promoting the reputation of rulers receives attention in chapter 5, "Ptolemaic Officials and Officers in Search of Fame," by Christelle Fischer-Bovet. She examines the different strategies that local elites serving the Ptolemaic kings employed to maximize their social capital both at the local level and in relation to the royal family. One way of accumulating social capital was obviously through fame emanating from military deeds, but the aim of this essay is to examine a different strategy, in which fame grows from investments in social relations. Fischer-Bovet demonstrates that acts of benefaction toward the local community by Ptolemaic officials belonging to different cultural spheres are an essential mechanism for becoming famous in the Hellenistic period. This is evidenced by the honours granted to them by the community, especially statues, and recorded in honorific decrees and in Egyptian autobiographic inscriptions. The chapter posits that euergetism was not a concept limited to the cultural sphere of only the Greek *poleis*; essential aspects of being a benefactor converged in the Greek and Egyptian cultural spheres. There was a visible homogenization of euergetism and of the honours granted in response to it within the territory of the Ptolemaic empire. More broadly, Fischer-Bovet's study contributes to a post-structuralist theory (as described in §5, above) by illustrating how various forces – ideological, economic, military, and political – all collaborated in effecting fame.

Celebrity, fame, and infamy in the Hellenistic age may also be examined from the perspective of creative literature that describes or prescribes contemporary social values. In her essay "Lemnian Infamy and Masculine Glory in Apollonios' *Argonautica*" (chapter 6), Judith Fletcher explores the theme of fame and infamy in surviving Greek versions of the myth of the

Lemnian women in order to understand how the literary representation of them deviates from and yet conforms to the construction of women's reputation generally and of the Lemnian gynaecocracy in particular. The refusal of leading women to conform to societal expectations of feminine behaviour is a key theme of the story of relations between Hypsipyle, queen of Lemnos, and Jason and the Argonauts. Like all cultural products, literature about the Lemnian women reflects the ideology and values of the society that produced it.

Certainly, as Dee Clayman suggests (2014: 36–8), the mythical Lemnians' union with the Argonauts, whose descendants founded Cyrene, might evoke the Cyrenean wife of Ptolemy Euergetes, Berenike II, who arranged the death of her first husband. Berenike's possible identification with Hypsipyle might account for Apollonios' humanizing treatment of the Lemnian queen and her concerns with a bad reputation (*kaka ... baxis*, *Argonautica* 1.161–2). Nonetheless Apollonios' manipulation of the story reveals the extent to which infamy can be controlled by its bearer, and reaffirms a conventional symmetry between masculinity and glory. For all Hypsipyle's attempts to control her own reputation, the best she can achieve for the Lemnian women is obscurity rather than infamy. Thus while it may be true that, between the classical and Hellenistic periods, cultural norms regarding women's visibility changed, and although women's public identities and relationships to power afforded new possibilities for negotiating the politics of reputation, traditional stereotypes nevertheless retained a certain currency.

Our own age is keenly aware that the public perception of the personal character of political leaders is premised on truthful reporting and honest self-representation. In chapter 7, entitled "The 'Good' Poros and the 'Bad' Poros: Infamy and Honour in Alexander Historiography," Timothy Howe examines how Arrian, in his *Anabasis Alexandri* – which employed Ptolemy I of Egypt as an important source – presents two Indian kings named Poros as exemplars of good and bad kingship. These character portrayals may be traced to a study penned by Ptolemy I as he was legitimating his own control over Egypt during the Diadoch Wars. Howe suggests that, in presenting these opposite figures, Arrian is responding to Ptolemy's propaganda about kingly behaviour in which kings should keep their word. Near Eastern empires, including Ptolemaic Egypt and Seleukid Syria, generated their authority not only through loyalty and submission, but also through projections of kingly truthfulness. Consequently, royal lies and the truth become important historiographical *topoi*. Because he kept his word, Ptolemy intimated that he himself was a good king like Alexander, while others such as Darius III, Bessos, and the Bad Poros were not, because they lied. As a result, the concept of Ptolemaic truthfulness becomes tangible, and of high repute. Even if it were answered by counter-propaganda, the "kingly truth" serves to generate the loyalty, submission, and omniscience on which Hellenistic kingdoms relied. Howe concludes his study by suggesting that, in the fourth century BCE, a new type of kingship emerges, one that looks not to the Homeric world for exemplars of social and moral values associated with rulers, but to the Bronze Age kings of the ancient Near East.

The self-representation of rulers through their *own* writings is the special focus of the study by Jacqueline Klooster, "Writing Monarchs of the Hellenistic Age: Renown, Fame, and Infamy" (chapter 8). To be sure, Hellenistic courts attracted highly trained poets and prose writers with the aim of increasing the prestige of the court and its kings. Excellent and innovative poetry, like Kallimachos' *Aitia*, as well as panegyrics helped spread the renown of the royal patrons. The same is true of the celebrated libraries of these monarchs. This would seem to indicate that Hellenistic kings were looking for a very specific type of celebrity among the Greek intellectual elite by enhancing their cultural capital. However, rulers could also contemplate promoting this image through writings of their own. Klooster asks the fundamental question whether literary activity per se was considered a fitting pursuit for a Hellenistic king. Following a historical survey of the phenomenon of writing kings and statesmen in antiquity in order to sketch some parameters determining the appreciation of literary activities, Klooster goes on to analyse why some Hellenistic kings, including the Ptolemies, the Attalids, and Seleukids, wrote literary works. Offering a survey of the genres in which Hellenistic rulers composed, Klooster observes a correlation with the accompanying stimulation of literary and scientific pursuits at the Ptolemaic court. She concludes that it was a risky undertaking for rulers to write, for it could result in either praise or blame.

This volume concludes with a study by Waldemar Heckel of the reputation of Alexander the Great as developed by one of his biographers: "Creating Alexander: The 'Official' History of Kallisthenes of Olynthos." The accounts in the ancient sources of Alexander's military reputation while he was alive changed considerably after he died; consequently, modern portrayals of Alexander also range from that of savage warrior to promotor of brotherly love. Kallisthenes of Olynthos, the more or less official historian of Alexander's campaigns, presents a special case. Being present with Alexander, Kallisthenes was in a position to know how events unfolded, and also how Alexander himself wished his exploits to be recorded and interpreted. Narrating the events with a view to Greek readers in the West rather than the people conquered eastward, Kallisthenes records the *Alexandrou Praxeis*, or "deeds of Alexander," not so much for the troops but for the home front. Examining the extant fragments of the *Alexandrou Praxeis* and echoes of

Kallisthenes' accounts in the writings of later historians, Heckel probes the evidence for Kallisthenes' place as historian in relation to his flattering and politically motivated contemporaries, and does so from the perspective of establishing and preserving Alexander's reputation. It considers especially the various accounts of Parmenion (at Gaugamela), Alexander at the Persian gates, and the infamous *proskynesis*. In so doing, this chapter makes several observations concerning the criteria that may be applied to determine a consistent historical representation of Alexander and his fame by Kallisthenes.

NOTES

1 On *fama* in the *Aeneid*, see also Clément-Tarantino 2016.

2 On democritization as a factor in promoting reputation, see the essays in Berenson and Giloi 2010.

3 For a critical review of the book, see Mary Beard, *Guardian*, 26 July 2009, at www.theguardian.com/books/2009/jul/26/fame-tom-payne, accessed 20 May 2016.

4 A. Scaife, *BMCR* review, http://bmcr.brynmawr.edu/2007/2007-02-49.html, accessed 9 June 2016.

5 See also Greindl 1938 and Thomas 2002.

6 Varro, *De lingua Latina* 6.55: *ab eodem verbo fari fabulae … dictae: … hinc fama et famosi* ("from the same word *fari* are derived *fabula* (gossip), *fama* (hearsay), and *famosi* (much talked of)"). For further discussion, see Guastella 2017: 54–7.

7 See also Kyriakidis 2016: 1–27.

8 See Guastella 2017: 82–3.

9 See, most recently, the essays in Smith and Covino 2011.

10 On *existimatio*, see Yavetz 1974.

11 This summary of theoretical approaches is based on Rojek 2001.

12 Thus Varner 2004: 2.

1

Fama and *Infamia*: The Tale of Grypos and Tryphaina

SHEILA L. AGER

Moral judgement of the rich and famous was as popular a pastime in antiquity as it is today. Celebrities were held up as moral exemplars, for good or ill, and their *fama* – "reputation, rumour, gossip, public opinion" – was a channel through which society could restate and confirm its most fundamental values.[1] The egregious breaching of a given society's morals was thus a clear recipe for *infamia* – "ill fame, bad repute, disgrace" – and royalty was no exception in this regard: a prevalent view of the later Ptolemies, and their cousins the Seleukids, was that most of those who met a terrible fate clearly had it coming. That opinion is still shared by many today: as Peter Green says, "If the word 'degeneration' has any meaning at all, then the later Seleucids and Ptolemies were degenerate: selfish, greedy, murderous, weak, stupid, vicious, sensual, vengeful, and … suffering from the effects of prolonged and repeated inbreeding."[2] We can read the tale of this Ptolemaic and Seleukid game of thrones and collectively gasp in delighted horror at the vicious antics of this gang of despicable fiends as they rape, murder, and dismember their way through their nearest and dearest.

This chapter explores the significance of royal reputations in the context of a minor incident in late Seleukid history, involving the ruler Antiochos VIII "Grypos" and his Ptolemaic wife Cleopatra Tryphaina.[3] My aim is to examine our received historiographical portrait of Tryphaina through a more critical lens, and to suggest that the portrait may owe more to the propaganda of others than to the actions of Tryphaina herself. The *fama* of queens in general was fragile: women in particular were mercilessly condemned if they failed to pass the test of socially approved behaviour, and the alleged actions of Cleopatra Tryphaina ensured that she found a place in the annals of Hellenistic infamy.[4] John Mahaffy saw in her "such

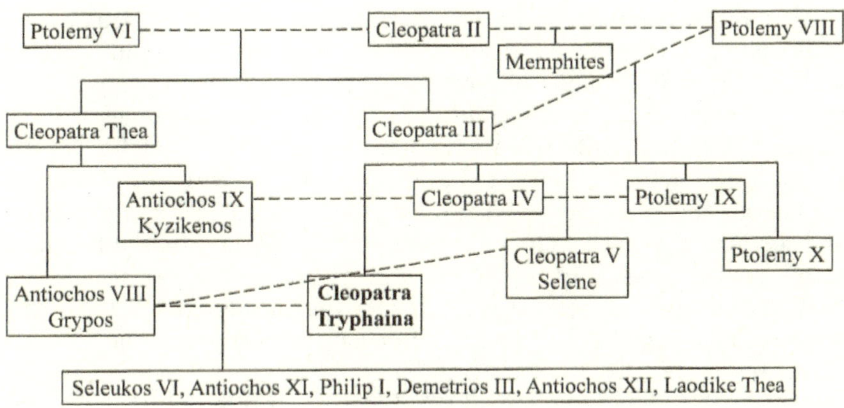

Figure 1.1 Genealogy of Cleopatra Tryphaina

[a] picture of depravity as [would] make any reasonable man pause and ask himself whether human nature had deserted [this woman] and the Hyrcanian tiger of the poet taken its place."[5] Other scholars describe her as "terrible," "nasty," "violent," "jealous," "furious," "vindictive," "ruthless," and "implacable."[6] All of these judgements are based solely on a brief chapter in Justin (*Epitome* 39.3), wherein the stubborn and merciless Tryphaina has no redeeming features whatsoever. Not only does she fail to meet the standards of behaviour for Hellenistic queens – who by this time were associated with various positive attributes such as altruism and benevolence[7] – she fails the simple test of ordinary human compassion.

In order to place Tryphaina in her context, we have to make certain deductions and assumptions. She was almost certainly the eldest of the daughters of Ptolemy VIII and Cleopatra III, and was thus born around 141 or early 140 BCE.[8] We know nothing of her prior to her marriage to the Seleukid prince Antiochos VIII "Grypos" around 124 BCE, but we should assume that her childhood was spent with her parents. That would mean that she would have left Alexandria with them when the tensions between her aunt, Cleopatra II – who was also her grandmother – on the one hand, and her father and mother on the other, led to the temporary exile on Cyprus of Ptolemy VIII and Cleopatra III and their children, around 131 BCE, when Tryphaina would have been about nine years old. (The genealogy of Cleopatra Tryphaina appears in figure 1.1.)

We first hear of Tryphaina in the context of the reconciliation of her father with his powerful sister Cleopatra II, an event that took place sometime between 30 January and 9 July 124 BCE.[9] Justin tells us that, as was so often the case in the later history of the Ptolemies and the Seleukids, the external relations between the two kingdoms were inextricably intertwined with the internal dynamics of each. By about 150 BCE it had become customary for Ptolemaic rulers to intervene in the dynastic struggles of the different branches of the Seleukid house, supporting one candidate for the throne against another.[10] Prior to his death in 145, Ptolemy VI had married his eldest daughter, Cleopatra Thea, first to the Seleukid Alexander Balas and subsequently to Demetrios II.[11] As the Ptolemaic house itself fractured along dynastic lines, with Cleopatra II competing for power against her brother Ptolemy VIII, both sides in the Ptolemaic struggle looked to different Seleukids for support. Cleopatra II first looked for support from her erstwhile son-in-law, Demetrios II, recently returned from a decade in Parthian captivity, but he proved unhelpful, and Cleopatra was forced to take refuge with her daughter Thea in Syria as of 128. In the meantime, Ptolemy VIII had formed an alliance with Alexander Zabinas, precisely in order to hamper Demetrios, who was ultimately defeated and murdered.[12] In 124, Ptolemy reversed his policy, abandoning Zabinas because the latter was allegedly behaving too independently; throwing his support behind Demetrios' son Antiochos VIII would thus have necessitated a reconciliation with Antiochos' mother, Cleopatra Thea, and his grandmother Cleopatra II. The tool of the marriage alliance was employed again as Ptolemy married his daughter Tryphaina to her cousin Antiochos in 124/3 BCE.[13]

Tryphaina thereupon entered a Syrian court that was dominated perhaps less by her husband than by her strong-willed aunt, Grypos' mother, Cleopatra Thea; Grypos himself was still youthful, perhaps around eighteen or nineteen years of age.[14] Since the death of Grypos' father Demetrios II in 125 and Thea's subsequent alleged murder of her own elder son, Seleukos V,[15] Thea and Grypos had been joint rulers. The famous jugate coinage of the pair is unusual in having the female figure in the foreground, although there are precedents for it.[16] It is generally accepted that the foregrounded individual is the dominant one in a pair, and that hypothesis seems to be borne out not only by the legend on the coinage – which puts Cleopatra's name first – but by the literary sources on Thea: she is described as domineering and power hungry, killing one son and plotting against another. When Grypos came home from hunting one day, Thea offered him a cup of wine; since such thoughtful behaviour was unusual for his mother, Grypos' suspicions were aroused, and he insisted that she drink the wine herself. Naturally it was poisoned, and thus ended the career of Cleopatra Thea.[17]

It is interesting that we have no record of a formal Ptolemaic protest at the murder of Thea. Over a century earlier, the murder of a Ptolemaic princess – the ill-fated Berenike Syra – at the Seleukid court had provided a rationale for a full-scale war (the Third Syrian War). In the case of Thea, sheer pragmatism may have been a factor: at this stage, around 121 BCE, the rulers in Alexandria still had their hands full resettling domestic affairs in the wake of the conflict between Ptolemy VIII and Cleopatra II. In addition, Thea was the daughter of Ptolemy VIII's rival, his brother Ptolemy VI, and Ptolemy VIII was thus under less compulsion to avenge her than he might have been if she had been his own daughter. Moreover, it was Grypos who was Ptolemy VIII's ally, and it would have been expedient for the Ptolemaic court to accept at face value Grypos' claim of self-defence. Cleopatra II was evidently willing to let the murder of her daughter go unavenged, no doubt because she had already seen the dangers inherent in any conflict with her brother.

We have no way of knowing, other than conjecture, what life was like for Cleopatra Tryphaina while her aunt/mother-in-law Cleopatra Thea was still alive. Tryphaina might have had the title *basilissa*, but she would surely have been considered to be subordinate to the "real" *basilissa*:[18] Thea is entirely dominant in the epigraphic and numismatic record, where Tryphaina is all but invisible. It is far from impossible that, as Grace Macurdy conjectured, Thea herself might have felt threatened by Tryphaina's new position at court; if so, she might have tried to rule her daughter-in-law (as her son) with an iron fist.[19] Daniel Ogden also suggests animosity between the two queens, pointing out that Thea and Tryphaina were from opposing branches of the Ptolemaic line (the descendants of Ptolemy VI *versus* the descendants of Ptolemy VIII). Ogden also insinuates that Tryphaina might have persuaded Grypos to have Thea put out of the way.[20]

After Thea's death, Tryphaina would have become the primary royal female, but we still hear nothing about her in either the literary or the epigraphic sources in these years, nor did she ever appear on Grypos' coinage. He continued to mint coinage after his mother's death, but his own portrait is the only one to appear on these coins.[21] Grypos had probably chafed under his mother's rule, and it does not seem that he was willing to elevate another woman to a status similar to that enjoyed by Thea. Seleukid coinage had not in the past featured the female members of the line very much: certainly far less so than Ptolemaic coinage. Both Laodike IV and Laodike V had appeared on coins, and Cleopatra Thea herself was featured in several different spectacular issues.[22] After his mother's death, Grypos evidently intended to reassert the male authority – both in the household and in the kingdom – that had previously been the predominant visual characteristic of Seleukid imagery.

Aside from the notice in Justin that Tryphaina was married to Grypos by her father, and a brief comment in Eusebios confirming that Philip I was her son, the only passage about her in the ancient record is Justin's grim and gory account of Tryphaina's savagery toward her sister Cleopatra IV.[23] Once again, affairs in Alexandria had an impact in the neighbouring kingdom. Ptolemy VIII had died in 116 BCE, leaving the throne to his widow Cleopatra III and whichever of their two sons she preferred. This set the stage for the rivalry between the two sons, Ptolemy IX and Ptolemy X, as well as a power struggle with their mother. One of the casualties of this dynastic tension was the marriage between Ptolemy IX and his sister Cleopatra IV, one of the very few sibling marriages in Ptolemaic history said to have been based on love. Cleopatra III forced them to divorce, and Cleopatra IV left Egypt. Initially going to Cyprus, she then set sail for Syria, complete with a small army, probably in 114 BCE.[24] In Syria she performed an act described by Daniel Ogden as *auto-ecdosis*: she offered herself in marriage to Grypos' half-brother, Antiochos IX Kyzikenos.[25] As in Egypt, so in Syria: the two sons of Cleopatra Thea were rivals for the throne, and Cleopatra IV's opportune arrival boosted her new husband's chances, especially since she brought not only herself but military support. She did not of course represent the official policy of Alexandria, but it is possible that she might have allied herself with her brother Ptolemy X, currently ruling in Cyprus; Ehling suggests that Ptolemy X could have hoped for an alliance of himself, Cleopatra IV, and Antiochos IX against his brother Ptolemy IX and Antiochos VIII (and of course Tryphaina, though Ehling does not attribute any personal significance to her in this coalition).[26]

In the course of the fighting between the two Seleukid half-brothers, Justin embeds an account of fierce rivalry between the two Ptolemaic full sisters; he is the only one to record the participation of the two queens in these events.[27] In the spring or summer of 112 BCE, Grypos' forces had retaken Antioch, where Cleopatra IV had sought refuge in a temple.[28] What followed is best described in Justin's own words:

Now equal to his brother Grypos in military strength, Kyzikenos opened hostilities against him, only to be defeated and put to flight. Then Grypos proceeded to besiege Antioch, the city where Kyzikenos' wife Cleopatra was to be found, and when it was captured Tryphaina, the wife of Grypos, ordered that highest priority be given to hunting down her sister Cleopatra. Not that she wished to help her when taken prisoner; rather it was to ensure that she escape none of the miseries of captivity. For Tryphaina believed that it was from feelings of jealousy towards herself that Cleopatra had entered this kingdom rather than any other, and that she had declared herself her sister's enemy by marrying her sister's foe. She then accused Cleopatra of introducing foreign armies into the dispute between the brothers, and also of marrying outside Egypt against her mother's wishes, after she had been repudiated by her brother. For his part, Grypos begged Tryphaina not to force him to do so dreadful a deed. None of his ancestors, he said, amidst so many wars domestic and foreign, had ever unleashed his wrath on women after a victory; their sex itself sufficed to spare them the perils of war and the cruelty of the victors. And in the case of this particular woman there was also, apart from the code of ethics observed by all combatants, a blood relationship, for the woman who was the object of her vindictive fury was her own sister, his cousin, and the aunt to the children whom they shared. To all these family ties he added his reverence for the temple in which Cleopatra had sought refuge, saying that he needed to be all the more respectful of the gods since his victory derived from their favour and support. Furthermore, by killing Cleopatra Grypos would in no way impair Kyzikenos' strength, nor indeed would he bolster it by giving her back to him. But the more stubbornly Grypos refused to give way, the more the sister was fired with a womanly doggedness,[29] for she thought all these words derived not from human compassion but from sexual attraction. She therefore summoned some soldiers and sent a group of them to kill her sister. They entered the temple; unable to drag her out, they hacked off her hands while she clung to the statue of the goddess. Then, cursing her assassins, Cleopatra expired, enjoining revenge for her death on the deities who had been violated. (Justin *Epitome* 39.3.4–11; Yardley translation, slightly modified)

Justin, who likes to see evil people get their comeuppance, is pleased to announce that, not long after this, probably in 110/09, Tryphaina herself was captured by the forces of her husband's enemy and was executed in order to "appease the shades of his dead wife."[30] Thus ended the career of Cleopatra Tryphaina.

The flavour of the story is typical of many recorded by Justin, such as the Argead Eurydike's plots against her husband and sons or Ptolemy Keraunos' slaughter of the children of his half-sister and wife Arsinoë II.[31] Royalty repeatedly engages in intrafamilial violence in Justin, and it suited Justin's moralizing and rhetorical outlook to amplify such incidents. This is not to say, however, that Justin actually fabricated out of whole cloth the numerous colourful tales that dominate his work. He may have chosen to underscore some events that he found recorded in Trogus and downplay others, as it suited his own purposes, but there is no reason to suppose that what Justin says about Tryphaina was not already to be found in Trogus.[32] As for Trogus' own sources on the later Seleukids, Poseidonios of Syrian Apameia is a prime candidate. Born around 135 BCE, he would have been a young man at the time of the wars between Antiochos VIII and Antiochos IX, and probably would have had access to at least some sources with direct links to the court.[33] A moralizing writer himself, Poseidonios had an interest in the role of passion as a determinant in human behaviour; Tryphaina's irrational and impassioned response to Grypos' measured and logical reasoning, and the sacrilegious aspect of Cleopatra IV's murder, would certainly have seemed to him an excellent *exemplum*.[34] Poseidonios, who might have been critical of Antiochos IX and his addiction to giant puppets, may have seen Grypos as the better king, and the tale in Justin certainly presents him in the best possible light.[35] The tale of the two sisters, then, was surely to be found already in the Hellenistic tradition, and its dramatic and moralizing aspects would have appealed greatly to both Trogus and Justin.[36]

While Hellenistic historiography was no doubt the original source of the story of Grypos and Tryphaina, there may also have been a source closer to home that helped to shape Trogus' and/or Justin's presentation of the tale: Livy.[37] In Book 1 of his history of Rome, Livy describes the downfall of the Tarquin dynasty: the tyranny of the last king, Lucius Tarquinius Superbus, and the wrongs committed by his son Sextus Tarquinius against the Roman matron Lucretia led to the overthrow of the Etruscan royal house. Lucius' reign also began with a crime: the murder of his predecessor, Servius Tullius. Servius was Lucius' father-in-law, twice over, since Lucius had married both of his daughters (both named Tullia) in succession. Lucius' brother Arruns also married one of the Tullias. The structure of the story – two brothers married to two sisters – mirrors the Seleukid marital pairs of Grypos and Tryphaina, and Kyzikenos and Cleopatra IV. This similarity is enhanced by the enmity between the sisters and that between the brothers: Tullia A, married to the gentle Arruns, despises both her husband and her sister, Tullia B (married to the ambitious Lucius), for her lack of drive and *muliebris audacia* (*Epit.* 1.46.6). Tullia A begins an affair with her brother-in-law Lucius, and between them they despatch Tullia B and Arruns, and marry each other.

Beyond the structural parallels (which naturally are far from exact), Trogus/Justin may have found inspiration particularly in the portrayal of Tullia A's character. While Livy presents Lucius Tarquinius as hot-headed, ambitious, and violent, he stresses throughout that it was his second wife who "goaded on his restless spirit."[38] She brought to the marriage all the *muliebris audacia* that had been lacking in her sister: "it was the woman who took the lead in all the mischief," she "inspired the young man with her own temerity," she refused to allow him "any rest by night or by day," "she excited the young man's ambition," and so on.[39] Not only does she harangue and browbeat her husband, as does Tryphaina, she also takes independent action: after the murder of Servius, Tullia drives to the Curia and calls her husband out in order to be the first to proclaim him king (1.48.4). In spite of their mutual bonds of passion and ambition, it seems that this is too much even for Lucius, who tells his wife to go home. Although the situation itself is not analogous, Tryphaina's independent action in summoning the troops herself is reminiscent of Tullia's behaviour here. Finally, Livy surmises that Tullia's most grotesque crime – driving her carriage over her father's dead body in the street – was inspired because she was "crazed by the avenging spirits of her sister and her husband."[40] In Justin, Kyzikenos murders Tryphaina as a sacrifice to the spirit of Tryphaina's dead sister.

There are several elements in Livy's account of the last Tarquins that could have influenced the flavour of the story of Tryphaina in Trogus/Justin.[41] None of this is to say that Livy inspired either Trogus or Justin to create a Seleukid Tullia *ex nihilo*. As stated above, there is no reason to suppose that the account of the sororicidal Tryphaina was not already there in the Hellenistic sources; but it is possible that Livy's presentation of Tullia could have assisted in heightening the drama of the Tryphaina story.

To return to Justin's account: Tryphaina's deed is surely one of the worst committed by any Hellenistic queen – one almost has an image of Tryphaina herself wielding the blade that cut off her sister's hands. The horror of her actions is accentuated by her husband's pleas to show mercy to her sister: Grypos argues with Tryphaina on the grounds of the rules of warfare; the blood relationship; reverence for the gods; and simple pragmatism. Tryphaina rejects all these thoroughly good and logical reasons – and this magnificent rhetoric – with a typically female response: her hatred for her younger sister becomes compounded with sexual competition. As Bevan put it, "Tryphaena suspected him of a guilty passion for Cleopatra, and her vindictiveness was whetted by a furious jealousy."[42]

Sexual jealousy and fear of displacement by another woman as drivers of female action are persistent literary *topoi* in antiquity. Hermione's jealousy leads her to persecute Andromache in Euripides, while Sophokles' Deianeira inadvertently murders her husband Herakles in an attempt to reclaim his affections from Iolë. In Hellenistic historiography, Cleopatra Thea provides a fine example: when her husband Demetrios II was taken by the Parthians, he was held in apparently honourable captivity for a decade, a captivity that included a brand new Parthian wife named Rhodogoune. Appian remarks that it was because of Thea's jealousy of Rhodogoune that she married Demetrios' half-brother, Antiochos VII, and, upon the return of Demetrios to Syria, rejected her first husband and ultimately contrived his murder.[43] Female sexual jealousy can thus be deadly, whether to the rival woman or to the male object (or to both, in the case of the Lemnian women's murder of their unfaithful mates and of the women their men had taken up with).[44] The crimes committed by jealous women are among the most horrific in Greek myth (which features a pretty wide array of criminal acts): Medea's murder of her own innocent children is but one example of the infamous behaviour inspired by female suspicion and resentment.

Of course, one thing that this picture ignores is that female "jealousy" in the context of a Hellenistic court (or anywhere else in antiquity) was directly linked to female security and status concerns. Objecting to Bevan's vilification of both Tryphaina and Cleopatra IV, Grace Macurdy points out that "[i]t should be noted that Tryphaena's 'dearest object' was to prevent her husband from marrying her sister and not abstract 'fratricide.'"[45] The fear of displacement was not unrealistic: pleasing or being useful to their men was one of the few ways in which women could hope to arrange or influence their own lives, and the loss of that connection could certainly threaten a woman's status and security. Cleopatra II's position was undermined by her brother-husband Ptolemy VIII's marriage to her daughter Cleopatra III – but it is next to impossible to imagine that Cleopatra II's conflict with her brother and her daughter was driven by actual sexual jealousy. All that said, I think it likely, in the case of Cleopatra Tryphaina and Cleopatra IV, the allegation of Tryphaina's sexual jealousy (or a more realistic fear for her own status) is just another example of the common *topos*.[46] It is simply one facet of the larger account of the argument between Grypos and Tryphaina, and there is reason to doubt the historical accuracy of this entire account. Too many things in Grypos' lengthy and heartfelt *oratio obliqua* and Tryphaina's response to it rouse suspicion. Yet oddly enough, very few scholars query this version of events,[47] and no author that I am aware of challenges the conventional view that it was Tryphaina, not Grypos, who pulled the trigger. In particular, Justin's comment about Tryphaina being sacrificed to the *manes* of Cleopatra IV has proven to be an eternally popular tagline in the accounts of modern writers.[48]

Among the suspect pieces of information in this passage are Tryphaina's actions upon her rejection of her husband's pleas: why does she bother browbeating Grypos in the first place if all she has to do is summon the soldiers and give the command herself? And are we to imagine Grypos standing around helplessly instead of countermanding her order? Even if these troops were loyal to her personally, it seems impossible that they would obey her order if it were directly revoked by the king.[49] We might also ask, how did this presumably private exchange find its way into the history books? This is an important point that is addressed further below.

For the moment, perhaps the most egregious incongruity is the character portrait of Grypos himself. His arguments suggest a chivalrous concern for women in times of war; deep respect for blood and family relationships; reverence for the gods; and, in the end, a prudent rationality that is in direct contrast to the impassioned fury of his wife. The man is shocked at the idea of killing a woman and killing a blood relative, especially when that woman has sought religious sanctuary. Killing her would be a direct affront to the gods, to whom Grypos modestly attributes his own victories thus far in the struggle between the brothers.

And yet, this is a man who, a decade before, had murdered his own mother. Grypos was also alleged to have attempted to poison another blood relative, his half-brother Kyzikenos, and was certainly not above fighting a war with him.[50] So his mouthing of loving familial sentiments and respect for women does not ring particularly true here. Nevertheless, there is reason to suppose that Grypos was sensitive about his reputation, his *fama*, in this regard, particularly with respect to the allegations of mother-murder, given that he adopted the title *Philometor* as one of his official epithets.[51] It might seem the greatest of ironies that a mother-killer should adopt such a title,[52] but it does show that Grypos was concerned about his public image. Muccioli argues that Cleopatra Thea was a significant figure in the realm even after her death, and that Grypos would have wanted to signal his filial piety as an ideological and political glue for the dynasty.[53]

How then did the argument between Grypos and Tryphaina make its way into the history books? There is no reason to suppose that someone in the chain of sources from Poseidonios to Justin simply made it up; the original source could only have been one of the parties themselves. It is probably safe to conjecture that it was not Tryphaina, and that leaves only Grypos. If we ask the question of *cui bono*, the finger also points at Grypos: Poseidonios or Trogus or Justin may have embellished some of the details,[54] but it is very likely that a version of events that exculpated Grypos and scapegoated Tryphaina was highly useful to the former. We may compare the version of the events surrounding the death of his mother, Cleopatra Thea, which also exonerates Grypos, at least to some extent; his adoption of the title *Philometor* would have been intended to have the same effect. Here too there is reason to be suspicious that it was Grypos' own propaganda machine that manufactured the tale of Thea's attempted poisoning of Grypos himself.[55] He is hardly likely to have issued official bulletins about the death of Thea or the murder of Cleopatra IV, but he could easily have made his version of events known through informal channels.

One thing that seems undeniable is that Cleopatra IV did perish at the hands of her husband's enemies. The version that Justin presents blames Tryphaina; but if we speculate that Grypos was the driving force here, we should then ask, why would Grypos kill Cleopatra IV? His objections to the act on the grounds of chivalry, blood bonds, and piety can be dismissed reasonably easily, but he also presents a pragmatic argument: there was no need to kill Cleopatra IV since it would neither disadvantage Antiochos IX to have his wife dead nor advantage him to have her returned alive. The argument is weak, and one possible answer could lie in the military support Cleopatra had brought with her from Cyprus: Huß suggests that these troops were loyal to her, rather than to Antiochos IX.[56] Grypos may have hoped that, with her death, the troops would be demoralized and unwilling to continue under the allegedly not very charismatic Antiochos IX. He may also have hoped that, in killing Cleopatra IV, he was severing his brother's connections to any further Ptolemaic support from Ptolemy X, while he himself remained in the good graces of his mother-in-law, Cleopatra III, particularly if he pushed the onus onto his wife.

Why would Grypos bother spreading *fama* – here in the sense of "rumour" – that scapegoated Tryphaina for the death of Cleopatra IV? As far as we can tell, there had been no protest from Ptolemaic Egypt when he killed his mother Cleopatra Thea (perhaps he had been careful to disseminate his own version of events immediately). The current victim, however, was both daughter and sister (and ex-wife) to the current Ptolemaic rulers, Cleopatra III and Ptolemy IX. But Cleopatra IV had clearly resented her mother's interference in her life, and her departure for Syria was evidently not sanctioned by Alexandria. Cleopatra III, who ruthlessly manipulated the lives and marriages of her children, does not strike one as the type to forgive a disobedient daughter, so why should Grypos be concerned what anyone thought about the death of Cleopatra IV?

The answer to this question may lie in the field of public relations: as we have seen, Grypos was clearly concerned with his public image and his own *fama*. He was engaged in an ongoing civil war with his brother, and no doubt would have been keen to deflect any cause for complaint about his behaviour among his subjects. Moreover, some years after the deaths of both Cleopatra IV and Tryphaina, Grypos once again found himself in a position where he was happy to have Ptolemaic support, specifically the assistance of his erstwhile mother-in-law, Cleopatra III. This support was symbolized by yet another marriage with a Ptolemaic princess: Cleopatra V Selene, the last of Cleopatra III's three daughters. Even if Cleopatra III cared nothing for her sister Thea or her daughter Cleopatra IV, both Cleopatra III and Grypos might have been sensitive to possible accusations of a slipshod approach to the security and well-being of Ptolemaic princesses in Seleukid Syria.[57] Tryphaina, who was conveniently dead, made a handy scapegoat for Grypos, whose concern for his own reputation would have overridden any disquiet he might have felt about harming hers.

The suggestion made here – that Tryphaina may not have been responsible for the savage murder of Cleopatra IV – need not mean that she was a loving sibling who begged her husband to spare her sister's life (though it is tempting to imagine that the arguments put in Grypos' mouth might actually have been Tryphaina's instead). Growing up in the Ptolemaic household of Cleopatra III and Ptolemy VIII would not have been very conducive to the establishment of normal family affect, the alleged love between Ptolemy IX and Cleopatra IV notwithstanding. From the perspective of both Grypos and Tryphaina, his brother was a rebel and her sister a moral and material supporter of rebels.[58] After all, when she left Egypt, why could Cleopatra IV not have sought asylum with Tryphaina and Grypos, rather than marrying their enemy? The answer presumably is that, once she was barred from becoming queen in Egypt (and perhaps Cyprus), she wanted to be queen in Syria. For her to fulfil that ambition meant that her sister Tryphaina had to lose her own status, and possibly her life. It would not be surprising if Tryphaina was not overly well disposed toward her sister; that does not necessarily mean that she was the implacable virago of Justin.

If we doubt the version of events found in Justin, can Tryphaina's infamous reputation be rescued? She certainly seems to have been intensely loyal to her husband and to his interests. And we can state unequivocally that she was a superb queen on the dynastic front: she presented her husband with not one but five potential heirs, in addition to a daughter. Each one of her sons went on to claim the diadem, which says something about the state of affairs in the Seleukid kingdom in these years. Her daughter, Laodike Thea, also represented a dynastic advantage; she was married to Mithridates I of Kommagene and became the mother of Antiochos I Theos, the creator of the *hierothesion* at Nemrud Dağı.[59] Of all the later Ptolemaic royal women (with the exception of her own mother, Cleopatra III), Tryphaina was the only one to enjoy a single and extremely fruitful marriage to one king (she was also the only one *not* to break tradition by engaging in *auto-ecdosis*). No Hellenistic queen, except perhaps Laodike III, the wife of Antiochos III, bore more sons to a single ruler. Perhaps Tryphaina and Grypos even worked together to instil dynastic solidarity and loyalty in their children: Philip I and Antiochos XI are unique in the Seleukid line for the male jugate coinage celebrating their joint rule.[60] This suggestion cannot be pushed very far, however: as Daniel Ogden points out, full sibling rivalry re-emerged in this generation, a sign of the extreme fragmentation of the Seleukid kingdom as it staggered toward its final demise.[61]

Beyond her loyalty and fecundity,[62] Tryphaina herself, once we excise the story of her murderous rage against her sister, becomes a very shadowy figure with no distinctive personality. But it may be precisely that which indicates that she was in fact a very good queen by the standards of the day, since it is usually queens who "misbehave" who tend to make it into the tabloids (Tryphaina certainly was never accused of sexual misbehaviour, but few Hellenistic queens were, as Grace Macurdy recognized long ago). Royalty prefers to control its own image, something that has become much harder to do in the age of mass media. After the extremely public career of his mother, Cleopatra Thea, Antiochos VIII may have been determined to suppress the female presence in the Seleukid dynasty, and aside from Justin's account we have no evidence – numismatic, epigraphic, or literary – that indicates that Tryphaina was anything other than willing to go along with his royal program.[63] Grypos thus imposed "un-famousness" as well as infamousness on his wife: unlike her predecessors, Tryphaina was not (apparently) celebrated in art, coinage, inscriptions, literature, or other media during her life and reign. And once she was dead, she may have become a convenient scapegoat for her husband, whose interests lay in preserving his own good name. Far from being the vicious Hyrkanian tigress of Mahaffy, the tragedy of Tryphaina is that, of all the Ptolemaic princesses, she may have been one of the few who sublimated her own power, wealth, and ambitions to those of her husband – in return for which he endowed her with an eternal legacy of infamy.[64]

Appendix: The Name/Titulature of Cleopatra Tryphaina

No ancient source gives Tryphaina the dynastic name "Cleopatra," but there is reason to believe that she did hold this name, probably from birth. Both of her sisters – Cleopatra IV and Cleopatra Selene – bore the name, and it is reasonable to suppose that Tryphaina, as the eldest daughter, would also have been given what was by now the leading female name in the Ptolemaic dynasty. There is a possibility that both Cleopatra IV and Cleopatra Selene were given the throne name "Cleopatra" when they married Ptolemy IX, but neither of them acted as his primary co-regent (their mother Cleopatra III saw to that); moreover, we know of no other name for Cleopatra IV, which suggests that she at least was named Cleopatra at birth. The full name Cleopatra Tryphaina is also attested as the name of Ptolemy XII's wife.[65] If the restoration of the name "Cleopatra" at the Nemrud Dağı monument does refer to Tryphaina, it would demonstrate that she bore that name; unfortunately, the evidence is thin and speculative.[66]

Despite Muccioli's view that "Tryphaina" came to be a proper name among the Ptolemies, it seems best to see it as an epithet.[67] "Tryphon" was an informal epithet associated with several Ptolemaic kings – Ptolemy III, Ptolemy IV, and Ptolemy VIII – in reference to their luxuriant mode of living and their display of wealth and magnificence.[68] Despite the fact that the Ptolemies clearly intended to create such a dynastic self-presentation, the term itself seems to have been for the most part non-official and frequently pejorative. It is almost exclusively found in the literary sources; the two exceptions are a demotic papyrus from Thebes and a demotic inscription from Memphis, both referring to Ptolemy VIII.[69] These documents date to the years 132–30 BCE, and Nadig suggests that Ptolemy VIII may have used the epithet Tryphon officially at this time as part of his struggle with his sister Cleopatra II.[70]

If so, it is not impossible that Ptolemy VIII, the only ruler for whom at least semi-official use of the epithet is attested, might have chosen to give his eldest daughter the feminized version[71] – perhaps on the occasion of her marriage to Antiochos VIII? This was the first inter-dynastic marriage between Ptolemies and Seleukids in over twenty years: Ptolemy may have wished to underscore his own magnificence and generosity in giving his daughter to her Seleukid husband, just as Ptolemy II, over a century earlier, had bestowed an enormous dowry on his daughter Berenike when he sent her as a bride to the Seleukid ruler Antiochos II.[72]

NOTES

1 Hardie 2012: 21, 43.

2 Green 1990: 554–5.

3 See the appendix for a discussion of Cleopatra Tryphaina's name/titulature.

4 The Latin *fama* can mean (among other things) a good or a bad reputation, or a positive or a negative public opinion; *infamia* is unambiguously negative.

5 Mahaffy (1898: 214), speaking of both Tryphaina and, rather unfairly, her sister Cleopatra IV (cf. Macurdy 1932: 3). The Hyrkanian tiger appears in *Aeneid* 4.365–7 but was also an image used repeatedly by Shakespeare (*Macbeth, Hamlet, Henry VI Part 3*).

6 Mahaffy 1895: 408; Bevan 1902: 254; 1927: 328; Bellinger 1949: 68, 101; Green 1990: 547; Whitehorne 2001: 135; Ehling 2008: 220.

7 On the role and image of Hellenistic queens, see, among others, Savalli-Lestrade 1994, 2003; Bringmann 1997; Roy 1998; Bielman Sánchez 2003; Widmer 2008; Carney 2011; Caneva 2013, 2014a.

8 For her birth year, Bennett n.d.; see also Hölbl 2001: 203; Huß 2001: 615. Cleopatra IV was probably born ca 138/135, and Cleopatra Selene ca 135/130 (Bennett). The assumption that Tryphaina was the eldest is based on the fact that, when the time came for a dynastic marriage, she was the one chosen. Against this assumption, we might conjecture that, in the Ptolemaic house, an eldest daughter might have been reserved for a (presumably more prestigious?) brother-marriage, but we have no evidence for such a practice. As the eldest, Tryphaina would have been around sixteen at the time of the marriage; this seems a reasonable age for her to have become a royal bride.

9 Huß 2001: 615.

10 For a discussion of Ptolemy VI's Syrian policy, see Seibert 1967: 85–9; Hölbl 2001: 192–4; Huß 2001: 583–9; Muccioli 2003; Ehling 2008: 154–64; Grainger 2010: 334–50.

11 Josephus *AJ* 13.80–2, 13.103–20; *I Maccabees* 10.51–8, 11.1–3, 11.8–12; Diodoros 32.9c.

12 Josephus *AJ* 13.267–9; Justin *Epit.* 39.1.

13 Justin *Epit.* 39.2.3. Seibert 1967: 90; Huß 2001: 615; Nadig 2007: 12, 209–12; Ehling 2008: 213; Grainger 2010: 388.

14 Ehling 2008: 213 (Grypos born between 143 and 141).

15 Livy *Per.* 60; Appian *Syr.* 69; Justin *Epit.* 39.1.6. Re death of Demetrios II in the spring/summer of 125 BCE, see Ehling 2008: 211.

16 On Thea and Grypos: *SC* nos. 2259–62, 2265, 2267–73, 2276, 2277; cf. Laodike IV and her son (*SC* no. 1368) and Cleopatra Thea herself and Alexander Balas (*SC* nos. 1841, 1843–6, 1860). For later Seleukid examples of jugate portraiture, see the coinage of Antiochos XI and Philip I (*SC* nos. 2435–9) and Cleopatra Selene and Antiochos XIII (*SC* nos. 2484–6). See also Le Rider 1986; Houghton 1987 and 1988; Meyer 1992/3.

17 Appian *Syr.* 69; Justin *Epit.* 39.2.7–8; see Ehling 2008: 214–15, who suggests Poseidonios as the original source. On the *topos* of poisoners having their own plots turned against them, cf. the story of Darius III and his vizier Bagoas, as told by Diodoros (17.6).

18 In Egypt, both Cleopatra II and Cleopatra III held the title *basilissa* at the same time; Cleopatra II, whose name always precedes that of her daughter, may have been able to assert her seniority.

19 Macurdy 1932: 99. Whitehorne (2001: 162) thinks that Cleopatra Thea should "by rights" have stepped aside and allowed Grypos to rule alone with Tryphaina by his side.

20 Ogden 1999: 153.

21 *SC* nos. 2278–300, 2302–14, 2316–43.

22 *SC* nos. 1318, 1332, 1368, 1371, 1407, 1421, 1422, 1441, 1477, 1683, 1684, 1686–9, 1691, 1840, 1841, 1843–6, 1860, 1861, 2258; see Ager and Hardiman 2016.

23 Eusebios Porphyry *BNJ* 260 F 32 (28); Justin *Epit.* 39.2.3 and 39.3.1–12.

24 The dates of Antiochos IX's rebellion, the vicissitudes of the war between the half-brothers, and the marriage of Cleopatra IV and Antiochos IX are challenging, but not of primary importance to this chapter, which follows the chronology set out by *SC* (drawing on the work of Houghton and Müseler 1990; Houghton 1993; and Hoover 2007). Antiochos VIII and Antiochos IX each appear to have had three separate periods of reign at Antioch, the city in which the drama was played out: for Antiochos VIII, 121/20–spring/summer 113; spring/summer 112–11/10; 109–96; for Antiochos IX (who would have begun his invasion in 114/13), spring/summer 113–spring/summer 112; 110/9; ca 96–5. Since Cleopatra IV joined Antiochos IX at a point when he had already had some initial success in his invasion of Grypos' kingdom (*SC*: 521), and since

she lived long enough to bear him one child (she was probably the mother of Antiochos X), it is likely that she married him some time in the latter half of 114 BCE.

25 Ogden 1999: 154. For another example of *auto-ecdosis* (Amastris), see D'Agostini's chapter in this volume.

26 Ehling 2008: 220–4. Ehling attributes *RC* 71, a letter from a King Antiochos to Ptolemy X about the freedom of Seleukeia in Pieria, to Antiochos IX rather than Antiochos VIII (Austin 2006: 222).

27 Richter 1987: 199–200.

28 Numismatic evidence shows that Grypos was forced out of Antioch and fled to Aspendos in 113. He retook Antioch in spring or summer of the following year (112): it was at this point that Cleopatra IV was captured and killed. By 110/9, Antiochos IX had retaken the city and executed Tryphaina. See Houghton 1993; Hoover 2007: 284–6; *SC*: 521, 535.

29 *Sed quanto Grypus abnuit, tanto muliebri pertinacia accenditur* (Justin *Epit.* 39.3.10).

30 *Nec multo post repetita proelii congressione victor Cyzicenus uxorem Grypi Tryphaenam, quae paulo ante sororem interfecerat, capit eiusque supplicio uxoris manibus parentavit* (Justin *Epit.* 39.3.12).

31 Justin *Epit.* 7.4–5; 24.2–3.

32 Bartlett (2016: 137) argues that a comparison between Trogus' *Prol.* 39 and the content of Justin's book 39 suggests that Justin chose to highlight and emphasize the rivalry between the sisters much more than Trogus did (in comparison to the other material covered in book 39). This does not mean, however, that the full version of Justin on the two women was not to be found already in Trogus (or in the preceding Hellenistic historiography, which was likewise moralizing, dramatic, and rhetorical).

33 Malitz 1983: 258; Ehling 2008: 33.

34 Timagenes of Alexandria, who would have used Poseidonios for his work *On Kings*, is also a possibility, though Malitz and Richter think that Trogus relied directly on Poseidonios rather than an intermediate source (Malitz 1983: 55–6; Richter 1987: 200, 213; see also Primo 2009: 174, 210). On psychology and emotion in Poseidonios' writings, see Bringmann 1986.

35 Malitz 1983: 299; Richter 1987: 200.

36 Ehling (2008: 221), who sees the account as stemming from Poseidonios, points out that there is a clear Roman influence on the presentation: the description of Kyzikenos sacrificing Tryphaina to the *manes* of his dead wife is certainly Roman in its language, but Greeks too were familiar with the general concept of making sacrifices to the dead.

37 "Livian influence [in Trogus] is deep and pervasive" (Yardley 2003: 20). Yardley does not identify any links between Livy 1.46–8 and Justin *Epit.* 39.3.4–11,

though he does flag *par ... viribus* as a favourite Livian phrase (Justin *Epit.* 39.3.4, the opening of hostilities between Grypos and Kyzikenos: *par igitur iam viribus fratris Cyzicenus proelium committit ac victus in fugam vertitur*; Yardley 2003: 47, 74).

38 Livy 1.46.2 (Loeb translation).

39 Livy 1.46.7–9; 1.47.1, 6 (Loeb translation); compare the *muliebris pertinacia* of Tryphaina (Justin *Epit.* 39.3.10).

40 *Amens agitantibus furiis sororis ac viri*: Livy 1.48.7 (Loeb translation, which says in error "her sister and her sister's husband").

41 We know that Trogus dealt at least with the beginnings of the Tarquin dynasty: *Prol.* 43.

42 Bevan 1902: 254.

43 Appian *Syr.* 68.

44 See Judith Fletcher's discussion of the Lemnian women and female infamy in chapter 6 in this volume.

45 Macurdy 1932: 3; Macurdy's fuller account, however, imputes all the rage to Tryphaina that Justin does (165). See also Ehling (2008: 220–1), who comments on the precariousness of a woman's position at court.

46 One has to ask on what occasion Grypos could possibly ever have seen Cleopatra IV so as to become sexually attracted to her. If she had taken sanctuary in a temple, she presumably was not yet in the clutches of either Tryphaina or Grypos.

47 Bartlett (2016: 136) also notes this.

48 Bevan 1927: 328; Macurdy 1932: 165; Green 1990: 550; Whitehorne 2001: 135; Hölbl 2001: 207; Huß 2001: 637; Ehling 2008: 221.

49 Dumitru (2016: 262) suggests that these troops might have been among those dispatched by Ptolemy VIII to support Grypos at the time he married Tryphaina. It is possible that, in Trogus' account, Tryphaina departs and summons the soldiers privately; perhaps it is Justin's compression of Trogus that makes it look as though Tryphaina summons the soldiers while still in her husband's presence.

50 Grypos allegedly forced Zabinas to drink poison and (also allegedly) tried to poison his half-brother Kyzikenos (Justin *Epit.* 39.2). He also was said to have composed a poem on poisonous snakes (Galen *De Antidotis* 2 [Kuhn 1827 ed. vol. 14: 185, 201]; Pliny 20.100 [264] is often referenced here, but it is clear that Pliny was thinking of Antiochos III).

51 Muccioli 2003: 115 and 2013: 23, 247–8. The epithet *Philometor* appears only on a small set of bronze coins issued at Antioch in Seleukid Era 202 (*SC* no. 2308), but is also attested in Eusebios (Porph. *BNJ* 260 F32.23) and in a few Delian inscriptions (*ID* 1549–52).

52 Cf. Pausanias' comment on the irony of Ptolemy IX Soter II bearing the title *Philometor*, when "no other king was so hated by his mother" (1.9.1).

53 Muccioli (2003: 115; 2013: 23, 247–8).

54 Yardley (2003: 175–6), who believes Justin's *Epitome* was written ca 200 CE, sees some of Justin's language here (notably *muliebri pertinacia* [39.3.10] and *mandata violatis numinibus ultione sui decedit* [29.3.11]) as influenced by sources later than Trogus, such as Seneca and [Quintilian] (*Decl.* 299). But language is only the medium, and this says little as to whether Justin did or did not find the story already whole in Trogus (moreover, it was suggested above that *muliebri pertinacia* may have been inspired by Livy's *muliebri audacia*). If Livy's Tullia did have any influence on the portrait of Tryphaina, then it is likely that Justin already found a well-fleshed version of the tale in Trogus.

Bartlett (2016: 137) argues that the fact that the story is entirely missing from the Prologue to book 39 is significant, but this is not persuasive. There are many such examples when we compare Justin's *Epitome* to the Prologues; moreover, the Prologues themselves represent the work not of Trogus himself but of yet another unknown excerptor with his own agenda. The following examples will suffice: the Prologues of books 26 and 27 make no mention of the actions of Berenike II, Laodike I, or Berenike Syra; the murder of Ptolemy III and Berenike II by their son is not referenced in Prologue 30; Prologue 38 makes no mention of the marriage of Cleopatra II and Ptolemy VIII, the murder of her son, the rape of Cleopatra III, or the murder of Memphites. As for the Prologue to book 39, aside from missing the enmity of Tryphaina and Cleopatra IV, it also misses Cleopatra Thea and her murder. Some of these incidents (though not, alas, the conflict between the sisters) made their way into the *Periochae* of Livy's lost books; this certainly suggests that the stories were current in the Augustan period. The author of the *Periochae* seems in general to have been slightly more willing to reference the actions of royal women than was the author of the Prologues.

55 See Whitehorne 2001: 162–3; Ogden 1999: 153; Winder 2017: 391–2; and cf. Macurdy 1932: 100. Winder suggests that Kyzikenos subsequently used Grypos' own strategy against him, manufacturing a tale of attempted poisoning as a justification for making war against Grypos (2017: 392–3).

56 Huß 2001: 637.

57 Every Ptolemaic royal woman we know of who married into the Seleukid dynasty died a violent death. Will (1982: 448) suggests the possibility that Cleopatra III was in fact acting to avenge Tryphaina by supporting her widower against his half-brother, though it seems rather late in the day for her to have taken up this cause. The war of 103–1 BCE was largely a Ptolemaic civil conflict played out in the battlefields of Syria; see Van't Dack et al. 1989; Grainger 2010: 393–402.

58 See Grainger 2015: 142.

59 Dörner 1996; Jacobs 2000; Strootman 2016. Tryphaina's descendants can be traced into the second century CE: Sullivan 1990: 570–2.

60 *SC* nos. 2435–9. This is the first time we see the name Philip in the Seleukid house, perhaps a sign that Grypos and Tryphaina were looking back to the Macedonian past and saw themselves as the parents of a new dynasty.

61 Ogden 1999: 157–8.

62 One common positive attribute of Hellenistic queens was euergetism, often in the form of benefactions to Greek cities (on the euergetism of Amastris, which included the founding of a city, see D'Agostini's chapter in this volume). We find no evidence for such behaviour by Tryphaina; but most of our information about queenly euergetism comes from the Greek cities of Asia Minor, to which the Seleukids no longer had access in the late second century. The lack of evidence for Tryphaina in this respect could thus be a source problem.

63 The only appearance of Tryphaina in epigraphy is a very uncertain one from the ancestor galleries at Nemrud Dağı (the monument raised by her grandson, Antiochos I of Kommagene), where the name [Κλεοπάτ]ραν has been restored; see Dörner 1996; Jacobs 2000.

64 Some of the arguments presented here were briefly adumbrated in Ager 2020.

65 *SB* III 6027.

66 The monument was dedicated to the ancestors of Antiochos I of Kommagene, the grandson of Tryphaina through her daughter Laodike Thea; Dörner 1996; Jacobs 2000; Muccioli 2013: 186 and 299; Strootman 2016; *SEG* 50 1382.

67 See also Otto and Bengtson 1938: 50. Cleopatra Tryphaina, the wife of Ptolemy XII, is never called "Tryphaina" alone.

68 Nadig 2007: 61–6; Muccioli 2013: 185–7. See Tondriau 1948 for a discussion of *tryphē* as a dynastic signature of the Ptolemies.

69 *P.dem.Berlin* 3113; *Inschr. Dem.* Cairo 31110.

70 Nadig 2007: 65–6. See also Otto and Bengtson 1938: 47–51.

71 In his discussion of the *Beiname* Tryphon, Nadig does not mention the feminine form Tryphaina.

72 Porph. *BNJ* 260 F43.

2

Models of Virtue, Models of Poetry: The Quest for "Everlasting Fame" in Hellenistic Military Epitaphs

SILVIA BARBANTANI

1. Introduction: The Glory of the King and of His *Philoi*

Since the dawn of the Greek poetic tradition, male individuals were granted eternal fame mainly for their successful martial activities against humans, gods, or monsters. It was only later that literary, euergetic, and athletic achievements were added as immortalizing factors. Things did not change in the Hellenistic age. Of the war-themed epic poetry of the Hellenistic period (many of which were notorious for their poor quality already at that time), only a few titles and fragments survive.[1] More-refined poets chose mainly to celebrate other aspects of royal ideology: as a sponsor of the *poeta doctus*, the Hellenistic ruler or *basileus* might receive from him a hymn as a γέρας ("a gift of gratitude"), even without accomplishing heroic deeds. Encomiastic literature in honour of Ptolemaic rulers develops the themes of ὄλβος ("prosperity"), power and success which focus on a timeless here and now: the king is a god or a god-like creature, and therefore the praise relates to his inherent qualities and to his dynastic heritage rather than to his specific, individual enterprises. Theokritos commences *Idyll* 17, which he wrote as an encomium for Ptolemy II, with an implicit comparison between the king and the ancient heroes who performed καλὰ ἔργα ("marvellous deeds") and deserved to be celebrated by good poets. Then the poet quickly assimilates the ruler with a god worthy of a hymn (*Idyll* 17.5–8),[2] and implicitly identifies himself with the ancient poets, knowing καλὰ εἰπεῖν, how to compose marvellous songs. References to military deeds are quite generic in this encomiastic poem. Ptolemy Philadelphos was more inclined to diplomacy and scholarly interests than to military deeds; nevertheless, Theokritos celebrates him as an excellent spearman (according to the example of Alexander the Great and his model Achilles),[3] in keeping with the Greek and Egyptian *topos* of the similarity between father and son in the context of a solid dynasty (see *Idyll* 17.56–7, 103). As Richard Hunter has noted, in this poem the omission of a section about the *res gestae* of the *laudandus* is understandable in light of the Egyptian ideology in which the very fact of a king maintaining order inside his kingdom is a glorious enterprise – the maintenance of the cosmic balance, or *ma'at* (on *maat*, see Selden 1998 and Stephens 2003).

In *Idyll* 16.42–59, Theokritos advertizes himself as the (potential) personal Homer and Simonides to Hieron of Syracuse, warning his prospective sponsor that immortality would not be achieved merely through riches and success.[4] Only the poet is truly able to bestow *kleos;* and only as a patron of poets could the tyrant reach the same level of fame and glory as the Homeric heroes. Theokritos presents himself as a poet able to confer upon Hieron the fame and glory that Pindar had granted to his Sicilian predecessor of the same name, when he praised his sponsor as both a victorious fighter and a patron of the arts (*Pythian* 1). The lesson was well learned by the first Ptolemies, who, as creators of the Library, posed as both promoters of new scholarly talents and keepers of the entire Hellenic cultural tradition: Ptolemy II is referred to as φιλόμουσος ("Muse-lover," i.e., supporter of the arts) in Theokritos *Idyll* 14.61. However, the Lagids also marketed themselves as heirs of Alexander and of the mythical conquerors and civilizing heroes and gods (especially the Argead Herakles, and Dionysos). The two activities are combined, at the same level of importance, in the anonymous epigram *Supplementum Hellenisticum* 979.6–7, where Ptolemy IV Philopator is said to be "excellent with the spear and in the activities of the Muses."[5] The idea that consorting with those who exercise poetry and culture is in itself a way to be remembered after death, and to gain a portion of immortality, was already clear in Sappho's fr. 55 Voigt (to an uncultivated rival): κατθάνοισα δὲ κείσῃι οὐδέ ποτα <u>μναμοσύνα</u> σέθεν/ἔσσετ' οὐδὲ †ποκ'† ὔστερον· <u>οὐ γὰρ πεδέχῃις βρόδων/τῶν ἐκ Πιερίας</u>· ἀλλ' <u>ἀφάνης</u> κἀν Ἀίδα δόμωι/φοιτάσῃις πεδ' ἀμαύρων νεκύων ἐκπεποταμένα.[6] On the other hand, military success was considered a natural requirement for keeping peace within a country, and this created the right conditions for the royal display of patronage in every field of the arts and sciences. The combination of cultural excellence and military power as providers of honour and fame was by no means confined to royal ideology. The Hellenistic elegy praising Halikarnassos states that that city received its honour, or τιμή, from its good relations with the gods and from a long list of poets and men of letters who were born and raised there; the city's involvement in military activities is mentioned only briefly at the end of the elegy.[7]

Military victory (control over a spear-won land) (Barbantani 2007: 69) was the clearest sign of divine favour, the κῦδος, or "temporary power," bestowed by the gods on the chosen heroes in Homer (Benveniste 1969: II.57–69);[8] therefore it was a fundamental element of legitimation for the *basileus*, like his agonistic victories, extensively praised in the *Hippika* by Poseidippos.[9] In war, the responsibility of victory was ascribed to the king, but never without protection from above. In Kallimachos *Hymn* 4.171 Ptolemy Philadelphos and Apollo are joined in a "common battle" against the Galatians; divine collaboration in military victory, in the form of the gods' *eunoia* or *pronoia*, is acknowledged in Hellenistic official inscriptions (Barbantani 2011 and 2007: 69). Any accomplishment achieved by the kings' φίλοι ("friends") or generals automatically became a prerogative of the king himself, as shown by the epigram found in Apollonia (Souza, Cyrene's harbour), dedicated by a Cyrenean officer as a *geras* to King Magas after a victory.[10] Not all the king's φίλοι behaved like this, however: as a reward for his military exploits, the citizens of Tlos honoured Neoptolemos, a Ptolemaic στρατηγός in Pisidia and also a priest of the royal cult in Alexandria, with a statue probably modelled on the Alexander *Aichmephoros* by Lysippos (*SGO* IV 17/11/02) (Barbantani 2007). In the epigram there is no trace of the Ptolemies: the general proudly celebrates his own merits as "barbarian-slayer" with the expression κῦδος ἐμοῦ δόρατος, "glory of my spear" (l. 2). This Neoptolemos could be identified tentatively as the experienced general praised in the encomiastic elegy *Supplementum Hellenisticum* 969.[11] At line 4, we find an interesting Hellenistic update of the *topos* of the eternity of fame: the δόξα, the fame achieved through military victory, will be eternal because it is fixed "in books" (ἐν βύβλοις δόξαν ἀειρα[άμενος?) – the same rolls of papyrus that are personified in Theokritos *Idyll* 16.5–12. Oral poetry was already a vehicle of eternal fame in Homer, Theognis, and Pindar,[12] but, in the Hellenistic period, "poetry" is not meant exclusively for oral performance: *kleos* will survive through the ages thanks to the copy process of bookrolls.

The values that encomiastic poetry attributes to the king's courtiers (technically defined as φίλοι ["friends"] and συγγενεῖς ["relatives"]), but also to his mercenaries, are the same as those attributed to their master. Among the epitaphs from Hassaia (necropolis of Apollinopolis Magna / Edfu), composed by a certain Herodes for the members of a distinguished family (second century BCE),[13] the second one, for Apollonios (Bernand *IMEGR* no. 5), celebrates his military prowess and his glory, which is actually a reflection of the glory of his father, both as a συγγενής of the king and as a warrior. As we have seen in Theokritos *Idyll* 17, the similarity between father and son is meant as a compliment for both, and is a guarantee of loyalty and stability within the dynasty and the court.[14]

[Πατρ]ίδ' ἐμὴν συνγνοὺς καὶ τίς τίνος εἰμὶ προσελθώ[ν],
[ξ]εῖνε, σὺν εὐτυχίηι στεῖχε δι' ἀτραπιτοῦ
εἰμὶ γὰρ εὐκλειοῦς Ἀπολλώνιος ὁ Πτολεμαίου
κοῦρος, ὃν Εὐέρκται μίτρᾳ ἐπηγλάισαν,
συγγενικῆς δόξης ἱερὸν γέρας· εὔνοια γάρ μιν
βαῖνε καὶ εἴσω γᾶς ἄχρι καὶ ὠκεανόν.
τοὔνεκα κἀμὲ πατρὸς καλὸν κλέος εἰσορόωντα
τῆς αὐτῆς ψαύειν θυμὸς ἔθηγ' ἀρετῆς,
καὶ πατρίδος καλῆς τὸν ἐπάξιον ἑσμὸν ἑλέσθαι,
αἰπ{υ}είας Φοίβου τῆσδ' ἱερᾶς πόλεως,
πατρὸς ἐμοῦ γνωτοῖσι συνεκπλεύσαντα φέριστε
ξεῖνε, ὅτε σκάπτρων ἦλυθ' Ἄρης Συρίην.
καὶ γενόμην εὔνους, γλυκερὰν τηρῶν ἅμα πίστιν
καὶ δορὶ καὶ τόλμᾳ πάντας ἐνεγκάμενος.
ὡς δ' ἐμὲ Μοῖρ' ἐδάμασσε βιοκλώστειρα, τί σὲ χρὴ
τοῦτο μαθεῖν, νόστου μνησάμενον γλυκείου
ἡλικίης ἀκόρητον, ὅτ' ọὐδὲ φίλων ἐνέπλησα
θυμὸν ἐμῶν τέκνων, ὧ̣ν λίπον ἐν θαλάμοις;
ταῦτα μαθών, ὦ ξεῖνε, λ̣έγοις πατρὶ τῶι κτερίσαντι,
'σαυτὸν μὴ τρύχειν μνησάμενον βιότου'
καὶ σοὶ δ' εὐοδίης τρίβον ὄλβιον εὔχομαι εἶναι
πρός γ' ἔτι καὶ τέκνοις σοῖσι φιλοφροσύνοις.
Ἀπολλώνιε χρηστέ, χαῖρε.
Ἡρώδου.

Having learned of my homeland, of my identity and of
my father,
O stranger, proceed further on your path with good fortune.
For I am Apollonios son of the illustrious Ptolemy
whom the Euergetai honoured with a diadem,
sacred prerogative of the glory of the "relatives." His goodwill
made him proceed inland, and as far as the Ocean.
Therefore, looking to the noble glory of my father,
I was seized by the desire of attaining the same virtue,
and of choosing the worthy swarm of my beautiful homeland:
this high, sacred city of Phoebos,

and sailed out together with the acquaintances of my father,
o excellent stranger,
when Ares of the sceptres came to Syria.
And I was benevolent, preserving sweet loyalty, and, at the same time
surpassing all with my spear and my boldness.
How Moira, who spins human destinies, tamed me, why should you learn this? I was remembering the sweet homecoming,
still hungry for my youth, without fulfilling my desire to see my children,
whom I had left in their chambers. Having learned these things, stranger,
I hope you can say to my father, who buried me:
"Do not torture yourself, remember the human destiny,"
and I pray that you can tread a prosperous path of good fortune,
and with you your loving children.
Noble Apollonios, greetings!
(Composed by) Herodes.

The value (ἀρετή), and consequently the glory (*kleos*), of a professional soldier is enhanced by the reputation and the power of the leader for whom the heroism is displayed; therefore, if relevant, the name of the "employer" is often advertised in military epitaphs. An example is the epitaph of Praxagoras, a Cretan officer (*GVI* 1076.3–4, Cyprus, third century BCE):[15] Πραξαγόρας δ' ὄνομ' ἔσχον ἐπικλεές, ὃν πρὶν ἐπ' ἀνδρῶν/θήκατο Λαγείδας κοίρανος ἀγεμόνα ("My name was Praxagoras, and I bore it with glory, since the Lagid king established me as a commander of men"). The key expression Λαγείδας κοίρανος stands out in the centre of the last pentameter, preceding the military title attributed by the *basileus* to Praxagoras: his name has become ἐπικλεές ("famed, glorious") as a consequence of his being hired by Ptolemy as commander (ἀγεμόνα). Likewise, in the epigram *SGO* I 01/09/07 (Kaunos), the Rhodian Antileon is honoured by his grateful fellow citizens because he has loyally served the "kings descending from Bacchus" (the Ptolemies), and his good reputation as an individual officer has rebounded on the civic community:[16]

[Ὁ δῆμ]ος ὁ Καυνίων
[Ἀν]τι[λέον]τα [Με]νάνδρου·
τοὺς ἀγαθοὺς [ὑμν]εῖν ὀλ[ίγ]ος πόνος, ἁ δὲ παρ' ἀστῶν
τιμὰ καρύσσ[ει πα]ντόσ[ε] τὰς χάριτας.

ὅσσα δ' ἔχω λα̣[λέει]μ, [φίλ' ὅμ]ως καλὰ καὶ φίλα δάμωι,
ἀτρεκὲς ἔγ μ[ου ἔπ]ος πεύθεο τᾶσδε λίθου·
τὸν δορὶ πόλλ' [ἀνύσαν]τα καὶ εὐ[κ]λέα σὺμ βασιλεῦσιν
Βακχιάδαις π[όντο]υ̣ [κ]α̣ὶ χ̣θ̣ο̣ν̣ὸ̣ς̣ ἁ̣γεμόσιν
Ἀντιλέοντα λέγω ̣τ̣ο̣ι ἐ̣π̣ι[κ]λέο[ς] υἷα Μενάνδρου,
ὄ̣λβιος, εἰ τοσσ̣ῶ̣νδ' ἀ̣ν̣τ̣έ̣τ̣υ̣χ' ε̣ἰς γεράων·
ὃς δὲ καὶ ἐξανύ̣σ̣α̣ς [ὑ]μ̣ν̣[ηθ' ἔ]ο χεῖρας ἐπ' ὄλβου
ὤρεξεν, μεγάλ̣ο̣ις ἀθανάτοισι φίλος.
(Integr. Peek 1980, except v. 5 [καμόν]τα Merkelbach, [ἀνύσαν]τα Peek)

The people of Kaunos
to Antileon son of Menander:
It is an easy task to celebrate brave men, and honour, arising from his fellow citizens,
everywhere proclaims the feelings of gratitude for him.
The equally pleasant and friendly things that I have to declare to the people,
you will know directly from me, this stone:
I mean him who accomplished many glorious deeds with his spear, together with his kings
descended from Bacchus, lords of sea and land,
Antileon, the son of the glorious Menander.
Fortunate, if he had a share in so many prizes;
Although he accomplished so much, [he never] laid his hands on riches,
therefore he is dear to the Great Immortals.

The epigram opens with with the epinician *topos* of Honour (τιμή, the positive evaluation of the officer by his community, παρ' ἀστῶν) taking on the duty of Fame, and announcing like a herald (καρύσσει) the deeds of the addressee. However, there is also the awareness that such fame will be preserved and transmitted to posterity by the stone whereon the verses are inscribed (l. 4). Along with φήμη or φάτις ("report," "news" of victory),[17] which often appears in encomiastic poems praising a victor (in war or in any other sort of competition), we find occasionaly some other synonym like βάξις[18] ("fame," "reputation," "rumour," "news," but elsewhere the word has also the meaning of "oracular voice"). Such is the case of the epitaph for Apollonios of Pantikapaion (Black Sea/Tauric Chersonnese, ca 50 BCE),[19] where, with the death of the man defined as "a model for virtue" (l. 9),[20] all other elements of his character disappear except the fame of his valour, which survives beyond the tomb.

Ἀπολλώνιος Ἀπολλωνίου,
χαῖρε.

σὺ μὲν πρὸς Ἅδην ἀστένακτος ἔδραμες,
λιπὼν {ν} ἀήταις πνεῦμα θουρίᾳ χερί,
ἡ σὴ {ι} δ' ὅμευνος δακρύοις ἀναστένει,
ἀπροσδόκητον πένθος εἰσδεδεγμένη.
τεὸν δ' ὄλωλε κ<ά>λλος ἔσζβεσται χάρις,
φρόνησις ἔπτη, πάντα συνφορᾶς γέμει·
ὁ τῆς γὰρ ἀρετῆς μοῦνος ἐκλάσθης κανών.
ἀλλ' εἰ σὲ κλωστὴρ Μοιρέων ἐρόμβισεν,
πρὸς δεινὸν ἔγχος βαρβάρων νενευκότα,
<ν>ῦν οὐ κελαινὸς οἶκος, ἡρώων δὲ σὲ
ἕξουσι σηκοί· σοὶ γάρ, ὡπολλώνιε,
καὶ πρόσθε σεμνὴ βάξις ἦν τεθημένη
καὶ νῦν θανόντι πᾶσα κοσμ<ε>ῖται χάρις.

Apollonios son of Apollonios, greetings.
You ran to Hades without complaint,
Leaving your spirit to the winds, with courageous hand.
Your wife wails with tears,
having received grief unexpected.
Perished is your beauty, extinguished is your charm,
your wit is gone, everything is full of misfortune.
You, the only standard of virtue, are broken.
But even if the spindle of the Moirai has spun you around,
fallen before the terrible spear of the barbarians,
You will be kept, not in the house of darkness, but in the
Enclosures of the Heroes; you, O Apollonios,
had a venerable reputation even before now,
and now that you are dead, every grace adorns you.

2. Military Glory in Epigrams for Common Soldiers

Let's move a little further down the social ladder. Homer (still defined in a Hellenistic epitaph as "herald of the valour of the heroes and prophet of the gods," ἡρώων κάρυκα ἀρετᾶς μακάρων τε προφήταν, *IGUR* IV 1532.1 = *Anth. Pal.* 7.6.1), is the first to express the belief that eternal fame, ἄσβεστον κλέος,[21] or κλέος ἄφθιτον,[22] acquired with *arete*, can survive after death. Some requisites, however, are necessary: in particular, a σῆμα (the burial place of the hero), and tales conveying the memory of his deeds to posterity.[23]

The use of Homeric references to enhance the idea that poetry can bestow immortality on a mortal is common practice not only among court poets but also among anonymous professional versifiers composing epitaphs for common soldiers.[24] Military epitaphs frequently refer to Homer and to other elegiac or epic martial poetry, mainly recycling the same formulae without much variation, as for example καὶ ἐσσομένοισι πυθέσθαι ("so that even posterity will know").[25] See, for example, the epigram celebrating the statue of the commander and satrap Zamaspos, elected by Fraate IV (37–2 BCE), found in Susiana:[26] ἔστασαν μνήμαις ἄφθιτον ἐσσομένοις ("erected [a statue] immortal for the memory of the posterity," l. 10).[27] Poetry is actually the sole means not only to preserve *kleos* through time, but also to convey it across space – an ability that makes it superior to immovable monuments and statues (the *semata*) (Pindar *Nemean* 5.1–3). Promises of promotion to heroic status through poetry are updated in the Hellenistic period, with the development of book culture, and with the growth, in quantity and quality, of epigrammatic poetry inscribed on *semata,* or funerary monuments. Simple soldiers, unlike their officers and kings, could not commission an epic poem or a full-length encomium to immortalize their acts of valour. In the classical period, the most fortunate could count on their families for short epitaphs, while others hoped that their civic communities would commission professional poets to compose epigrams for the *polyandria* where their bodies were destined to rest anonymously. At the beginning of the third century BCE, the so-called *Sylloge Simonidea* offered a model for epic praise of the dead in a short inscriptional form. Attributed to Simonides but probably later, *Anth. Pal.* 7.251 repeats the Homeric principles in miniaturized form.[28] The two main Simonidean reference pieces for the Hellenistic poets, however, are not epigrams but the elegy to Plataia[29] and the lyric *encomion* for the fallen at the Thermopylae, which elaborates on the connection between *sema* and *kleos.*

Simonides, *Elegy for Plataia* fr. 11.13–21 West[2]

Τοί δὲ πόλι]ν πέρσαντες ἀοίδιμον [οἴκαδ′ ἵ]κοντο
   ]ωων ἀγέμαχοι Δαναοί [
οἷς ἐπ' ἀθά]νατον κέχυται κλέος ἀν[δρὸς] ἕκητι
   ὃς παρ' ἰοπ]λοκάμων δέξατο Πιερίδ[ων
πᾶσαν ἀλη]θείην καὶ ἐπώνυμον ὁπ[λοτέρ]οισιν
   ποίησ' ἡμ]ιθέων ὠκύμορον γενεή[ν.
ἀλλὰ σὺ μὲ]ν νῦν χαῖρε, θεᾶς ἐρικυ[δέος υἱέ
   κούρης εἰν]αλίου Νηρέος· αὐτὰρ ἐγώ[
κικλήισκω] σ' ἐπίκουρον ἐμοί, π[ολυώνυμ]ε Μοῦσα,
   εἴ περ γ' ἀν]θρώπων εὐχομένω[ν μέλεαι·
ἔντυνο]ν καὶ τόνδ[ε μελ]ίφρονα κ[όσμον ἀο]ιδῆς
   ἡμετ]έρης, ἵνα τις [μνή]σεται ὕ[στερον αὖ
ἀνδρῶ]ν, οἵ Σπάρτ[ηι τε καὶ Ἑλλάδι δούλιον ἦμ]αρ
   ἔσχον] ἀμυνόμ[ενοι μή τιν' ἰδεῖν φανερ]ῶ[ς.

[And so] the valiant Danaans, [best of warr]iors,
    sacked the much-sung-of city, and came [home;]
[and they] are bathed in fame that cannot die, by grace
[of one who from the dark-]tressed Muses had
the tru[th entire,] and made the heroes' short-lived race
a theme familiar to younger men.
[But] now farewell, [thou son] of goddess glorious,
[daughter] of Nereus of the sea, while I [now summon] thee,
i[llustriou]s Muse, to my support,
[if thou hast any thought] for men who pray:
[fit ou]t, as is thy wont, this [grat]eful song-a[rray]
[of mi]ne, so that rem[embrance is preserved]
of those who held the line for Spart[a and for Greece,]
[that none should see] the da[y of slavery]. (Tr. M. West)

Simonides, fr. 531 *PMG*
Τῶν ἐν Θερμοπύλαις θανόντων
εὐκλεὴς μὲν ἁ τύχα, καλὸς δ' ὁ πότμος,
βωμὸς δ' ὁ τάφος, πρὸ γόων δὲ μνᾶστις, ὁ δ' οἶκτος ἔπαινος·
ἐντάφιον δὲ τοιοῦτον οὔτ' εὐρὼς
οὔθ' ὁ πανδαμάτωρ ἀμαυρώσει χρόνος.
ἀνδρῶν ἀγαθῶν ὅδε σηκὸς οἰκέταν εὐδοξίαν
Ἑλλάδος εἵλετο· μαρτυρεῖ δὲ καὶ Λεωνίδας,
Σπάρτας βασιλεύς, ἀρετᾶς μέγαν λελοιπὼς
κόσμον ἀέναόν τε κλέος.

The dead at Thermopylae:
glorious is their fortune, *fair* their fate,
their tomb an altar, instead of laments fame, their pity acclaim.
Such a shroud mould and
time which conquer all will not obliterate.
This burial place of good men chose for its dweller the glory
of Greece. Leonidas himself testifies to this,
king of Sparta, who left a great ornament
of courage and eternal glory. (Tr. A.D. Morrison)

What will not perish or decay is not only the ἐντάφιον (a *sema*, which could be historically the place of a yearly ritual of commemoration) but the *kleos* of their *arete*, thanks to the memory preserved by the community as well as by poets like Simonides himself. The author of the epitaph for Epigonos (*SGO* I 02/14/11, Laodikeia on the Lykos, Phrygia, first century BCE) probably has Simonides in mind, along with Sophokles (*Ajax* 714: πάνθ' ὁ μέγας χρόνος μαραίνει, "Powerful Time withers everything") and Homer (*Il.* 18.117–18: οὐδὲ γὰρ οὐδὲ βίη Ἡρακλῆος φύγε κῆρα, / ὅς περ φίλτατος ἔσκε Διὶ Κρονίωνι ἄνακτι ..., "not even strong Herakles could avoid his destiny,/although he was much dear to lord Kronides Zeus"), tempering the Iliadic pessimism about the transience of life with faith in the survival of *Arete* over Time: the *mnemeion* (l. 1) is purely a monument, a *sema*, while the *mnama* ("memory," l. 9) of Epigonos' virtue will outlive him and his tomb.

Οὐκ ἄλλου, παροδῖτα, τόδε μνημῆον [ἐσαθρεῖς],
  ἀλλ' οὗ τὰν ἀρετὰν οὐδ' ὁ χρόνος μαρανε[ῖ]
Ἐπιγόνου, πρωτῆα παρὰ ζωοῖσι λιπόντος
  σωφροσύνας μορφᾶς θ' εἵνεκα θειοτάτα[ς]·
οὔτε γὰρ ὁ κτίνας Πριάμου παῖδ' Ἕκτορ' Ἀχιλλεύ[ς]
  οὔθ' ὁ τὰ λέκτρα φυγὼν τοῦ πατρὸς Ἱππόλυτος
τοιοίδ' οὐκ ἐγένονθ̣' οἷο[ς] γένετ' Ἐπίγονος π[αῖς]
  Ἀνδρέου εὐγενέτα πατ[ρ]ὸς ἴσου βασιλε[ῖ].
ἀλλ' ὁ μὲν Ἐπίγονος μνᾶμα ζωιοῖς δια[μίμνει]·
  οὐδ' Ἀχιλλεὺς δ' ἔφυ̣γε̣ν μοῖρ[αν] ἀ̣ὶ Θέτιδος ...

This monument that you see, passerby, is of none other
than Epigonos, whose virtue Time will not corrupt;
he left among the living the preeminence
of temperance and divine beauty.
Neither Achilles, the one who killed Hektor, son of Priam, nor Hippolytos
who avoided his father's bed, were like Epigonos, son
of Andreas, noble son of a father equal to a king.
But Epigonos leaves a lasting memory among the living;
not even Achilles, son of Thetis, escaped the destiny ...

Epigrams of outstanding quality, or attributed to famous poets, were certainly a status symbol. In antiquity, however, the majority of epitaphs consisted of just a few words recording the basic anagraphic data and including, occasionally, a mention of the good reputation obtained by the deceased; see, for example, *GVI* 601 (Paros, first century BCE):[30] Διφίλου οὗτος ὅδ ἐστὶ τύπος τοῦ Διφίλου υἱοῦ, / ὃς καὶ ἐπὶ σ<τ>ρατίης δόξαν ἔχεν μεγάλην ("This is the image of Diphilos son of Diphilos, who had great fame in the army"). Only in the Hellenistic and Roman period do epitaphs tend to become longer, sometimes including extended narratives with the biography of the dead.[31] We register the case of exceptional individuals (like Philopoimen, mentioned above) who were granted an epitaph at public expense, starting with the famous Simonidean case of a *mantis*, Megistias (*Anth. Pal.* 7.677). See also the example of Kleodemos, who likewise was honoured with a Simonidean epitaph (*Anth. Pal.* 7.514): αἰδὼς καὶ Κλεόδημον ἐπὶ προχοῇσι Θεαίρου / ἀενάου στονόεντ' ἤγαγεν εἰς θάνατον/Θρηικίῳ κύρσαντα λόχῳ· πατρὸς δὲ κλεεννὸν / Διφίλου αἰχμητὴς υἱὸς ἔθηκ' ὄνομα ("Shame of retreat led Kleodemos, too, to mournful death when on the banks of ever-flowing Theaerus he engaged the Thracian troop, and his warrior son made the name of his father, Diphilus, famous," Tr. W. Paton). So, too, the case of the Scythian Menecharmos (*IScM* I 171 Scythia Minor, Istros, fourth century BCE); although here *kudos* is integrated only in lacuna, the personification of *Arete* reminds us of Bacchylides 1.159–60:[32] δῖ' Ἀρετὰ κλυτόφαμε, θεῶγ γ[ένος ἐκγεγαυῖα], / ἔξοχα ἐτίμησας τόνδε σε φ[ιλάμενον]/εὐσθένεος Μενέχαρμον· ὃ[ν ἐν δαῒ κῦδος ἑλέσθαι] / μαρτυρεῖ ἥδε πάτρα τῶιδ[ε τίουσα λίθωι] ("Splendid Arete of glorious name, of divine origin, you honoured above all this man, Menecharmos son of Eusthenes; that he obtained glory in battle is attested by his fatherland, who paid homage to him with this stone").

Family and *polis* often unite in commemorating a fallen youth, as in the case of the prematurely deceased Neon, whose *stele* was paid for by his father Theokles, but adorned by the *polis* with ἀειμνήστοισ[ι] … ἐπαίνοις ("eternal eulogies").[33]

Πολλά σε ἔπαινος ἐπευκλεΐσεν νεότητος ἐν ἀκμῇ
παῖδα μὲν ὄντα Νέ<ω>ν κοσμιότητι τρόπων,
ἥβῃ δ' αὐξηθέντα νόμων πατρίων θεραπείᾳ,
ἐν συνόδ<οις> ὅ<τ'> Ἄρης ἀντιπάλους συνάγοι,
ἱππομαχο<ῦ>ντα· ἀρετῇ γὰρ ἐτόλμησας στεφανῶσαι
πατρίδα καὶ προγόνους· μνῆμα δὲ σῆς ἀρετῆς
στ[ῆσε] πατὴρ Θεο[κ]<λ>ῆς. ἀειμνήστοισ[ι] δὲ ἐπαίνοις
κόσμησε ἥδε πόλις καὶ κατὰ γῆς φθίμενον.

Praise gave you plenty of fame in the bloom of youth
when you were still a child, Neon, for the grace of your manners;
when you grew up as a young man in the respect of the laws of the fore-fathers,
in the clash when Ares gathers the adversaries
you fought on horseback: with your valour you dared to crown
your homeland and your ancestors. This memory of your valour
did your father Theokles build; with eternal eulogies
this city adorned (you) even dead below ground.

The epigram is a short but clumsy and grandiloquent encomium, underlining (like the epigram for Eugnotos we shall see below) the equestrian rank of Neon (l. 5). The word ἔπαινος is repeated twice (ll. 1 and 7), and so is ἀρετή (ll. 5 and 6): the generic "praise" for the noble manners of the well-bred and educated child Neon is upgraded into "eternal eulogies" when the boy grows into a heroic young man and prematurely dies. The adjective ἀείμνηστος may refer either to the eternal persistence of the encomiastic funerary inscription or to periodic commemorations of the fallen soldier; cases of official "heroization" of a citizen, with a special cult decreed by the community, are common in the Hellenistic and imperial period (Barbantani 2016). The remark that the young man fell following the *patrios nomos* (ancestral norm), thus honouring his father and other forebears, is another commonplace since Tyrtaios.

Compare this epitaph with the Hellenistic funerary inscription in elegiacs for Phanias son of Antipater *SGO* I 02/06/08, from Stratonikeia (Karia):

Σοὶ τύμβον μάτηρ τεῦξεν [....] κεδνοῦ
  Φανία Ἀντιπάτρου κοῦρε θεοῖσιν φ[ίλε]
Πλούτων δὸς καὶ ἐκεῖ νεκύων λ[ιμένα]ς ἀσαλεύτους
  οὐ φθιμένων μακάρων δ' ἄγαγε [εἰς ἠλύσιον?]
<u>καρύσσει δὲ πάτρα τὸ τεὸν κλέος ὀψ[ιγόνοισιν]</u>
  καὶ θνάσκων ζωᾶς ἀντέπορες χά[ριτας.

Your mother prepared for you a tomb …
  Phanias, son of the venerable Antipater, boy dear to the gods.
Plouton, grant (him) also here the unshaken [harbour] of the dead,
  guide him to [the Elysium?] of the unperishable Blessed.
<u>Your country will herald your glory to the future generations</u>
  and you, dying, received gratitude for having lived.

Here too, the homeland of the deceased,[34] personified (possibly because public money was spent to help the mother in commissioning the epitaph), takes the role of Fama (or, in factual terms, of the poet himself) in advertising the virtue of the deceased to the posterity, with a different formula from the common Homeric one we have already discussed: καρύσσει δὲ πάτρα τὸ τεὸν κλέος ὀψ[ιγόνοισιν].[35] The same word recurs in another funerary poem (Peek, *GVI* 1513, Knossos, second century BCE), where an anonymous, optimistic epigrammatist foresees that the endeavours of the suitably named young warrior Tharsymachos,[36] an aristocratic Cretan cavalryman, would become a legendary subject of future epic songs (l. 4):

Θαρσύμαχος Λεοντίω.
οὐδὲ θανὼν <u>ἀρετᾶς ὄνυμ'</u> ὤλεσας, ἀλλά σε <u>φάμα</u>
  <u>κυδαίνουσ'</u> ἀνάγει δώματος ἐξ Ἀΐδα,

Θαρσύμαχε· τρανὲς δὲ καὶ ὀψιγόνων τις ἀείσει
μνωόμενος κείνας θού[ριδ]ος ἱπποσύνας,
Ἐρταίων ὅτε μοῦνος ἐπ' ἠ[νε]μόεντος Ἐλαίου
οὐλαμὸν ἱππείας ῥήξαο φοιλόπιδ<ο>ς,
ἄξια μὲν γενέταο Λεοντίου, ἄξια δ' ἐσθλῶν
ἔργα μεγαυχήτων μηδόμενος προγόνων.
τοὔνεκ[ά] σε φθιμένων καθ' ὁμήγ<υ>ριν ὁ κλυτὸς Ἅδης
ἷσε πολισσούχῳ σύνθρονον Ἰδομενεῖ.

Tharsymachos son of Leontios.
You have not lost the glory of your valour, not even after your death,
but the fame which honours you brings you up from Hades' chambers,
Tharsymachos. Someone of the later generations will sing about you,
recalling that impetuous chivalry,
when near windy Elaion you, alone among the Cretans,
broke a squadron during the battle of the cavalry,
in your effort to accomplish deeds worthy of your father Leontios.
Therefore among the assembly of the dead illustrious Hades
established you as a companion of the throne of Idomeneos
patron of the city. (Tr. A. Chaniotis, adapted)

In the Tyrtaios-echoing epitaph of the Athenian Chairippos (*GVI* 40; *IG* II^2 5227a, 287/6 BCE) the *polis* is said to have provided for his statue and tomb (*sema*) as a reward for his sacrifice and reminder of his glory (*kudos*) (ll. 3–4):

Τλῆτε νέοι, πόδα θέντες ἐναντία δυσμενέεσσιν
θνήισκειν, αἰδόμενοι πατρίδα καὶ γο[ν]έας·
καὶ γάρ σοι, Χαίριππε, καταφθιμένωι μ[έ]γα κῦδος
εἰκόνα δημοσίαι τε εἵσατο σῆμα πόλις,
ἡνίκα Μουνιχίας ὑπὸ τείχεσι δούλιον ἦμαρ
[ῥ]υόμενος πρὸ φίλης πνεῦμα ἔλιπες πατρίδος.

Young men, endure to plant your feet opposite to the enemy
and die. Thus show how you honour your country and your parents.
And to you, Chairippos, who died, the city at public
expenses dedicated a statue, great honour,
because under the walls of Mounichia you left your life
for your country, saving it from slavery. (Tr. R. Lattimore)

When the family could not help, or was too far away to help, *politeumata,* associations of soldiers, could pay for a funerary stela for their members, thus preserving their memory and their good fame: Teleutia, chief of a garrison, had his sepulture and epitaph paid for by his fellow soldiers (Atrax, Pelasgiotis, Thessaly; ca 350–300 BCE) (Moretti 1975: 73–5, no. 100):

Σῆς ἀρετῆς μνημεῖα Τελευτία ἐνθάδε φρουροὶ
  στῆσαν ἀποφθιμένωι μνῆμα τόδ' ἀθάνατον·
εἰ δ' ἀρετῆς ἕνεκεν θνητῶν ὤικτειρέ τιν' Ἅιδης,
  οὐ τἂν ἐξέλιπεν φέγγος ὅδ' ἠελίου.

As a memory of your valour, Teleutia, here the members of the garrison
erected to you, deceased, this immortal monument of remembrance.
If Hades could mourn for one of the mortals for his valour
this one would not have left the light of the day.

The epitaph echoes some of the *topoi* of the epigram for Neon, and the one for Epigonos, especially the anxiety of remembrance, and the hope in the persistence of the *sema* as a tool for the durability of memory (l. 1: σῆς ἀρετῆς μνημεῖα; l. 2: μνῆμα τόδ' ἀθάνατον).

While in the *docta poesis* the immortality of fame is strictly linked to the quality and skills of the poet, and therefore to his name, in the case of epitaphs for individual military men we rarely know the author;[37] nonetheless, the concept that poetry, even anonymous and even in the small turn of an epigram, has the power to save and spread the fame of the heroic deeds as much as a full-length epic poem is often repeated.[38] Like the oral epic poets of old, the stone "sings" the praise of the man who fell in battle; so declares Anyte in the literary epitaph *Anth. Pal.* 7.724.3–4:[39] ἀλλὰ καλόν τοι ὕπερθεν ἔπος τόδε πέτρος ἀείδει, / ὡς ἔθανες πρὸ φίλας μαρνάμενος πατρίδος ("But the stone above you sings this beautiful verse, how you died fighting for your beloved country"). Following a concept well known to Sappho (the rival will not be remembered), the epitaph for Archos, from Sikinos (Kyklades),[40] suggests, as a way of consolation, that the deceased is already dwelling among the heroes[41] and enjoying the honour of a laudatory epitaph, while the shrewd enemy who killed him is condemned to the worst fate a Greek warrior (epic or real) could imagine – that is, to be ignored by poets and therefore by posterity: worse than infamy (the enemy in this epitaph is not even mentioned by name!) is silence.[42]

> [Ἐν μακάρων τ]εμένεσσιν ἐν ἡρώοισί τε, Ἄρχε,
> [ναίεις, ἁ δ' ἀ]ρετὰ λάμπει ἐν ἁμερίοις
> [δαλοῦσ' Αἰνήτ]ου υἱέ, τό τευ κράτος· οὐδ' ὁ δολόφρων
> [ἐχθρὸς ποι]ητοῦ μέλπετ' ἀπὸ στόματος,
> [ἀλλά τυ· εὐί]ππων γὰρ Ἄρης φίλος· ἁ δὲ Θόαντος
> [νᾶσος ἐρίστ]ερνος θυμὸν [ἔθαλ]πε πατρὸς
> ... c.10 ... ταστο ... c.10 ... ου τολματὰ

> You [dwell] in the dens of [the Blessed] among the heroes, Archos;
> [your] valour shines among the mortals,
> [manifesting], O son [of Ainetos], your might; nor will the
> fraudulent
> enemy be sung by the mouth of a poet,
> [but you]; Ares is friend of those who possess good horses.
> [The Island ...] of Thoas warmed the soul of your father ...

The reference to the enemy δολόφρων (rarer than δολοφραδής, and often used by Nonnos, Oppian, Sophron, Quintus Smyrnaeus, and Byzantine authors) could be a realistic reference to an ambush where the young man died, as in the epigram for the Aitolian Skorpion, possibly by Poseidippos (Poseidippos *Dubia* 31 Fernández-Galiano; Thermos, ca 284–1 BCE);[43] most probably, however, it is a literary allusion to the Iliadic Dolon (*Iliad* 10) or, according to others, to the deceitful Odysseus who tricked Ajax:[44] one may compare Asklepiades *Anth. Pal.* 7.145.1–4 (epitaph of Ajax), where *Arete* personified represents Ajax: ἅδ' ἐγὼ ἁ τλάμων Ἀρετὰ παρὰ τῷδε κάθημαι / Αἴαντος τύμβῳ κειρομένα πλοκάμους, / θυμὸν ἄχει μεγάλῳ βεβολημένα, εἰ παρ' Ἀχαιοῖς / ἁ δολόφρων Ἀπάτα κρέσσον ἐμεῦ δύναται ... ("By the tomb of Ajax on the Rhoetean shore, I, Virtue, sit and mourn, heavy at heart, with shorn locks, in soiled raiment, because that in the judgment court of the Greeks not Virtue but Fraud triumphed ..."; Tr. W.R. Paton). The young man belongs to the equestrian aristocracy and probably received, as did other contemporary fallen citizens, heroic honours from his community.

We have seen earlier that victory is a key element of encomiastic poetry, but this epigram seems to contradict this assumption. *Kleos* – a good reputation and a glorious name remembered by posterity – is linked primarily to success; however, in military epitaphs the behaviour of the deceased, independent from the outcome of his heroism, is already a guarantee of *kleos* and of the respect of the community. An outstanding case is the epigram for Eugnotos of Akraipha (*GVI* 1603), an encomium for a defeated man:

Τοῖος ἐὼν Εὔγνωτος ἐναντίος εἰς βασιλῆος
  χεῖρας ἀνηρίθμους ἦλθε βοαδρομέων,
θηξάμενος Βοιωτὸν ἐπὶ πλεόνεσσιν Ἄρηα·
  οὐ δ'ὑπὲρ Ὀγχηστοῦ χάλκεον ὦσε νέφος·
ἤδη γάρ δοράτεσσιν ἐλείπετο θραυομένοισιν,
  Ζεῦ πάτερ, ἄρ<ρ>ηκτον λῆμα παρασχόμενος,
ὀκτάκι γάρ δεκάκις τε συνήλασεν ἰλαδὸν ἵππω[ι],
  ἥσσονι δὲ ζώειν οὐ καλὸν ὡρίσατο,
ἀλλ'ὅγ' ἀνεὶς θώρακα παρὰ ξίφος ἄρσενι θυμῶι
  π[ήξ]ατο(?), γενναίων ὡς ἔθος ἀγεμόνων·
τὸμ μὲν ἄρ' ἀσκύλευτον ἐλεύθερον αἷμα χέοντα
  δῶκαν ἐπὶ προγόνων ἠρία δυσμενέες·
νῦν δέ νιν ἔκ τε θυγατρὸς ἐοικότα κἀπὸ συνεύνου
  χάλκεον [εἰκ]ον' ἔχει π[έτ]ρος Ἀκραιφιέων.
ἀλλά, νέοι, γίνεσθαι κατά κλέος ὧδε μαχηταί,
  ὧδ'ἀγ[αθ]οί, πατέρων ἄιστεα[ρ]υόμενοι.

This is what Eugnotos was like when he came to the rescue,
facing the numberless troops of the king,
having whetted the Boiotian Ares against greater numbers,
but he did not drive the bronze cloud above Onchestos.
For indeed he was defeated, alone among snapping spears,
father Zeus, presenting an unbroken courage,
for eight times and ten he drove forth by squadron with cavalry,
and he did not think it right for one defeated to live,
but, removing his breast-plate, he struck with male heart
against his sword (?),
as is the custom for noble leaders.
In fact, the enemy gave him back unstrapped,
pouring free blood, for the mounds of his ancestors;
and now, the rock of Akraphians has him, from his daughter
and his wife, as bronze image in his likeness.
But, young men, thus in glory become fighters,
thus become brave men, defending the city of your fathers.
(Tr. J. Ma)

His glory did not originate in victory, or in a sacrifice which led to victory, as is usual, but in self-sacrifice (he committed suicide once he saw himself trapped) as he faced the overwhelming troops of Demetrios the Besieger (291 BCE). If, as we have seen, serving under a king was considered an asset in the quest for *kleos*, the prestige of the enemy and his superior power makes the defeat of a soldier more heroic. The epigram was conceived as a companion piece to an equestrian statue of Eugnotos, as aptly pointed out by John Ma.[45] The hero of the *polis* is represented as a knight, evoking the funerary monuments of the *equites* from classical Athens (or Hellenistic Bithynia) but also the equestrian monuments of the kings (a famous statue of Alexander-Founder on horseback stood in Alexandria), with which the unfortunate fighter is equated. The final verses are particularly Tyrtaic.[46] Suicide apart, Eugnotos' fate is similar to that of Hektor, the paradigm of the unfortunate hero obtaining immortal glory even in the defeat, who became one of the Homeric characters most frequently offered as a model for deceased soldiers in Hellenistic and Roman Asia Minor.[47] Hektor, minutes before being slaughtered by Achilles, expresses his hope of gaining eternal glory (*kleos*) among future generations (*Iliad* 22.305–6: μὴ μὰν ἀσπουδί γε καὶ ἀκλειῶς ἀπολοίμην, / ἀλλὰ μέγα ῥέξας τι καὶ ἐσσομένοισι πυθέσθαι ["may I not die without a struggle and without glory, but accomplishing some great deed for the future generations to know"]), hope that was fulfilled by the survival and the wide reception of the Homer poems not only in antiquity but also in modern times.[48]

As we have seen, in the individual epitaphs from the Mediterranean Greek-speaking *poleis*, a fallen youth is generally presented as a glorious model of patriotism to the contemporary and future citizens, upholding the values of his ancestors. In the majority of inscriptional epitaphs for soldiers, it is clear that the cost of *kleos* was often premature death, according to the epic example of Achilles. See, for example, Damagetos *Anth. Pal.* 7.438.2–3 = Peek, *GVI* 1464 (Achaia 220–17 BCE): χαλεπὸν γὰρ Ἀχαιικὸν ἄνδρα νοῆσαι / ἄλκιμον, εἰς πολιὰν ὅστις ἔμεινε τρίχα ("It is hard to find a brave Achaian who had survived till his hairs are grey"; Tr. W. Paton, adapted). The main reference, before Simonides, is obviously Tyrtaios.[49]

Tyrtaios fr. 12.23–37 West
αὐτὸς δ' ἐν προμάχοισι πεσὼν φίλον ὤλεσε θυμόν,
  ἄστυ τε καὶ λαοὺς καὶ πατέρ' εὐκλεΐσας,
πολλὰ διὰ στέρνοιο καὶ ἀσπίδος ὀμφαλοέσσης
  καὶ διὰ θώρηκος πρόσθεν ἐληλάμενος.
ὸν δ' ὀλοφύρονται μὲν ὁμῶς νέοι ἠδὲ γέροντες,
  ἀργαλέωι δὲ πόθωι πᾶσα κέκηδε πόλις,
καὶ τύμβος καὶ παῖδες ἐν ἀνθρώποις ἀρίσημοι
  καὶ παίδων παῖδες καὶ γένος ἐξοπίσω·

οὐδέ ποτε κλέος ἐσθλὸν ἀπόλλυται οὐδ' ὄνομ' αὐτοῦ,
 ἀλλ' ὑπὸ γῆς περ ἐὼν γίνεται ἀθάνατος,
ὅντιν' ἀριστεύοντα μένοντά τε μαρνάμενόν τε
 γῆς πέρι καὶ παίδων θοῦρος Ἄρης ὀλέσηι.
εἰ δὲ φύγηι μὲν κῆρα τανηλεγέος θανάτοιο,
 νικήσας δ' αἰχμῆς ἀγλαὸν εὖχος ἕληι,
πάντες μιν τιμῶσιν, ὁμῶς νέοι ἠδὲ παλαιοί, …

Moreover he that falleth in the van and loseth dear life
to the glory of his city and his countrymen and his father,
with many a frontwise wound through breast
and breastplate and through bossy shield,
he is bewailed alike by young and old,
and lamented with sore regret by all the city.
His grave and his children are conspicuous among men,
and his children's and his line after them;
nor ever doth his name and good fame perish,
but though he be underground he liveth evermore,
seeing that he was doing nobly and abiding in the fight
for country's and children's sake when fierce Ares brought him low
But and if he escape the doom of outstretched Death
and by victory make good the splendid boast of battle,
he hath honour of all, alike young as old … (Tr. J.M. Edmonds)

But instead of lingering on the very common Tyrtaic *topoi*, let's see some variants of the epigrams celebrating military *kleos*. One very frequent variant is the association between the virtues manifested by the deceased in time of peace and his military prowess: the fame for being a good citizen equals the fame arising from military prowess. In the epitaph for the Cretan Theagenidas (*IC* II xxiii 22, Creta, Polyrrhenia, first century BCE),[50] all the repertoire of the Hellenistic warrior-citizen funerary encomium is displayed:

A.1 Θεαγενίδας/Πασινόω. B.1 Αἰτίμεια/Πίθω.
C.1 ἔτλαν καὶ πολέμου βαρυαλ<γ>έα ἶσα ἥρωι
 ἂν μίμνε[ι]ν ἐπέλα[χ]ον, δουριβαρῆ κάματον,
κ[ἄ]<λ>λως αἰ[χμη]τῶν προγόνων κλέος ἔ<σ>χον ἄμεμφ[ές],
 δόξαν ἐλ<ὣ>ν πινυτὰν ἔξοχα σωφροσύναν·
προσφιλὲς ἀνυσάμαν ἐμ πατρίδι πὰρ πολιητῶν
 κῦδος ὁ Πασινόου, ξεῖνε, Θεαγενίδας.
εἰ δέ με δακρυχαρὴς Λάθας ὑπεδέξατο κευθμὼν
 ἀλλ' ἀρετὰ περάτων ἀντία κῦρ' ἀνιῷν.

Theagenidas son of Pasinoos – Aitimeia daugther of Pito.
I endured like a hero the hardships of war, everything
that was destined for me to suffer, the hard work of the spear;
and I got the irreproachable fame of my warrior ancestors,
having the reputation of being exceptionally wise and temperant.
I got glory and affection from my fellow citizens in my homeland, O stranger,
I, Theagenidas, the son of Pasinoös. And if the underground abode of Lete,
who takes pleasure in tears, welcomed me,
my virtue reaches to the boundaries (of Earth).

Here we find the following themes: 1) the assimilation with a hero (often resulting in a real cult established by the family or the *polis*); 2) the mention of the spear, the Homeric and Alexandrian symbol of *arete*; 3) respect for the military tradition of the ancestors (Crete has always been, like Karia, the better place for mercenaries); 4) the well-rounded character of the citizen, temperant and wise, in addition to his being a good soldier; 5) the love and veneration his fellow citizens show him, as a result of his character and skill as a soldier.

The epigram for Nikasichoros (Opous, Lokris, after 229 BCE; Poseidippos, *Dubia* 33 Fernández Galiano; *IG* IX, 1:270) is probably a companion piece for a statue:[51]

Πατρὸς ἀριζήλοιο Πολυκρίτου υἷα σὺν ἵππῳ
    δέρκεο, Βοιωτῶν ἀρχὸν ἀεθλοφόρων·
δὶς γὰρ ἐνὶ πτολέμοις ἁγήσατο τὰν ἀσάλευτον
    νίκαν ἐκ πατέρων τηλόθεν ἀρνύμενος,
καὶ τρίτον ἱππήων· Ὀπόεντα δὲ πολλάκι τάνδε
    καὶ χερὶ καὶ βουλᾶι θῆκε ὀνομαστοτέραν.
ἐν δὲ ἀρχαῖς ἀχάλινος ὑπ' ἀργύρου ἔπλετο πάσαις,
    ἀστῶν εὐνομίας θέσμια παρθεμένων·
τῷ καὶ ἀείμναστον Νικασιχόρῳ κλέος ἔσται,
    πίστις ἐπεὶ πάντων κοίρανος ἁγνοτάτα.

Watch the son of the noble Polykritos, mounted on horseback,
leader of the victorious Boiotians;
twice in war he guided them, preserving, far away,
the unshaken victory inherited from his fathers,
and a third time as a commander of cavalry. Often he made this city, Opous,
more renowned with the work of his hand and of his mind.
In all his appointments he was never bridled by the greed of money,
for his fellow citizens laid the foundations of Good Government.

Therefore the glory of Nikasichoros will be eternal,
since loyalty is the purest leader of all.

The name of his father, evidently an already famed member of his community, is placed first, while the name of the deceased comes last, his glory justified by the deeds summarized in the short poem. Again, we have the mention of heroic behaviour in tune with the glory of the ancestors, the idea that the good renown of the individual citizen, in war and in peace, enhances the glory of his city, and the concept that the Homeric ἀείμναστον κλέος or eternal renown has been gained not only through martial actions but especially through loyalty and generosity toward the community. It is worth noting that also a court elegy, Kallimachos' *Epinician for Sosibios* (fr. 384.57–8 Pfeiffer), underlines generosity toward the subjects and loyalty toward the king as key elements that make a royal *philos'* glory complete. The *iunctura* καὶ χερὶ καὶ βουλᾶι ("with his hand and his judgement") is very common in epitaphs and has many variants, such as καὶ βουλᾶι καὶ χερσίν.[52]

Military glory sometimes is shared between father and sons. Military epitaphs, reinforcing the common values of the community in times of danger, often underline that the fallen youth dutifully observed the tradition of the father in serving the *polis* as a soldier. We have drawn attention earlier to the Simonidean epigram for Kleodemos (*Anth. Pal.* 7.514), who, with his heroic death, made his father glorious (κλεεννὸν). Ptolemy and his son Menodoros died together and received a common epitaph (Bernand *IMEGR* nr. 4 = *GVI* 1149) (Barbantani 2007: 112–13; Barbantani 2014: 314–15). Ptolemy proudly names his son (3–8, 11), who, like him (according to the Ptolemaic dogma of the similarity of father and son), has been a bold warrior, an αἰχμητής, holding the flag of his battalion. Ptolemy recalls the "illustrious gifts" he gave to his homeland, including also his role of gymnasiarch.

Ἀγεμόνα Πτολεμαῖον, ὁδοιπόρε, τῆιδέ με κεύθει
  τύμβος, ἀνὰ κρατερήν φυλόπιδα φθίμενον,
παῖδὰ τε Μηνόδωρον ἐνὶ πτολέμοισιν ἀταρβῆ
  καὶ θρασὺν αἰχμητὴν σημοφόρωι κάμακι,
εὖτ' ἐπὶ δυσμενέεσσι Μακηδόνι σύν στρατιώτῃ,
  τοῖο τόθ' ἀγεμόνων, θούριον ἆγον Ἄρη·
δήϊα δ' ἐν προμάχοισι καὶ ἄσπετα φῦλα κανόντας
  ἀμφοτέρους Ἀίδας ὠμὸς ἐληΐσατο.
κλεινὰ δ' ὑπὲρ πάτρας θάνομεν θρεπτήρια δόντες,
  γυμνασιάρχος ἐν αἷ καὶ τὸ πάρος γενόμαν,

πολλάκι τ' ἐμ πρυλέεσσιν]ἀρήιος, ἔνθα δὲ βουλᾶς
χρῆμα, τὸν ἐκ πραπίδων αἶνον ἐνεγκάμενος.
[ἀλλ]ὰ σύ, καρτερέ, χαῖρε καὶ ἐμ φθιμένοις, Πτολεμαῖε·
[ὅν τε προσ]αυδήσας, υἱό<ν>, ὁδῖτ', ἄπιθι.
(14: integr. Bernand)

Here, O passer-by, the tomb encloses me,
commander Ptolemy: I died in a mighty battle;
and there is also my son Menodoros,
never trembling in the wars, courageous warrior holding the flag-bearing pole,
when against the enemies, with the Macedonian troops
of which I was then the commander, I guided the furious Ares;
having killed innumerable enemies, while fighting in the front ranks,
cruel Hades took both of us.
We died after giving glorious gifts for our homeland
where previously I was also gymnasiarch,
often valiant among the infantry, and when it was time to give advice, I received the praise for my wisdom.
O mighty Ptolemy, I salute you even among the dead;
speak to his son, passer-by, and then leave.

Most frequently, as in the case of Kleodemos, the son leaves his parents behind, casting over them the light of his *kleos*. When, on the contrary, a deceased young father leaves relatives behind, his children are obviously the first recipients of their parent's glory. A paternal good fame is an important social requirement, as much as a good heirloom. For example, Τιμέας (Timeas), the son of Euthydamos of Ithaka (who has already Fame, τιμή, in his name), is the heir both of his father's material patrimony and of his "spiritual inheritance," immortal fame *GVI* 102 = *IG* IX, 1:658 (second century BCE):

Τήνω τοι τόδε σᾶμα τὸ λάϊνον, ὦ <ξ>έν', Εὐθυδάμ[ω],
ὅς ποκ' ἐν ἀμφιάλωι πρᾶτος ἔ<γ>ε<ν>τ' Ἰθάκαι
καὶ βουλᾶι καὶ χερσὶν ἐς Ἄρεα. Τιμέαι δὲ παιδὶ
ἔλλιπε καὶ κτῆσιν καὶ κλέος ἀθάνατον.

This tombstone, O stranger, is the one of Euthydemos,
Who once in Ithaka surrounded by the sea was first
for his counsel and his military action. To his son Timeas
He left his possession and his immortal fame.

Notable is also the *iunctura* already mentioned above, here in the form καὶ βουλᾶι καὶ χερσὶν (l. 3).

We have already noted that *kleos* in funerary epigrams is not necessarily dependent on the success of the military action. It is important to stress that *kleos* belongs also to someone whom a Tyrtaic enthusiast would stigmatize as unheroic. The Egyptian scribe Ammonios, a young clerk prematurely deceased, although bravely facing the enemies (ll. 10–11), did not die ἐμ προμάχοισι ("in the first ranks"), like the Ptolemy mentioned here above and many other warriors in the fictionalized heroic narrative of the funerary epigrams, but, more commonly, "in the middle of the army." Just for dying in battle, however, he earned κλέος με[γ]ακυδές ("illustrious fame"), becoming a hero to his family and even receiving a private cult (Bernand *IMEGR*, 64, Alexandria, second/first century BCE).[53]

Χρὴ μέν σε προλιπόντα καλὸν φάος ἠελίοιο
καὶ γραφίδος τέχνας οὐ τελέσαντα γέρας
στέργειν δακρύσαντας ἐπ' ἤματι τῶιδε, φέρ<ι>στε,
ὧι σε πικρὸς Μοιρῶν ἐσφετέριξε μίτος.
ἄρτι γὰρ ἐς πέμ[π]τον σε καὶ <ἰ>κοστὸν λυκάβαντα
ἱσταμένη βιοτᾶς ἅρπασε βασκανίη
οἴκων ἐξ ἰδί[ων], Ἀμμώνιε, συγγενέσιν μὲν
οἰκτρότατον [λύ]πας ἀμφιβα[λ]οῦσα γόον,
σοὶ δὲ κλέος με[γ]ακυδὲς ἐπήρατο· πατρίδα σῴζων
κάτθα[ν]ες, ἀντιπάλων ἀντίος ἱστάμενος,
καὶ δορὸ[ς] οὐκ ᾔσχυνας ἀριζάλοιο τίναγμα,
ψυχὰν δὲ στρατιᾶς ἄμμιγα συγκατέθου·
τοὔνεκά σ' ἡρώεσσι τετιμένον, οὐχὶ θανόντα
κεκλόμεθ' ἀλλὰ θεοῖς ἶσα καταχθονίοις
ἁγνοτάταις <σ>πονδαῖσι ποθινοτάταισί τε λοιβαῖς
κλῄζομεν, ἀρχαίοις ὡς πάρος ἐστὶν ἔθος·
πᾶσι δ' ἀίμνηστος γίνοι φίλος· ἀγχόθι δή σου
λήθη παρμίμνοι χῶρον ἀν' εὐσεβέων.

It is necessary that you, since you have left the beautiful sunlight
and had not the privilege of being accomplished in the scribal art,
love those who cry for you, O good man, since the day
when the cruel thread of the Moirai took possession of you.
Envy, in fact, standing up against your twenty-five years
of life, has just abducted you
from your own house, Ammonios, drowning your parents
in a miserable lament of pain;

but she procured you illustrious fame. You died saving your homeland,
standing up against the enemies,
and you did not fear the blow of famous spear,
but you lost your life in the middle of the army.
Therefore you are honoured among the heroes, and we do not call you dead,
but we invoke you like we do with the infernal gods with the
purest libations and offerings full of longing,
according to the custom of our ancestors.
May you be remembered as a friend by everyone; may Oblivion
dwell with you, in the Land of the Pious ones.

It would be an error also to think that *kleos* would follow only young warriors who died more or less heroically in battle. More realistically, good renown is the prize also for surviving until old age.[54] Seasoned soldiers extol in their epitaphs, as part of their glory, the comforting advantages of a successful career, the ability to take care of their wife and children, providing them with status and with a family tomb (the dovecote tombs of the Near East).[55] Exceptionally rich in "glorious terminology" is the short epigram *SGO* IV 22/20/1 (Caesarea Eitha) commissioned by Diomedes, *eques romanus* who belonged to *Legio III Cyrenaica*, for a statue and relief commemorating his valour, very likely part of his funerary monument:

Ἱππέα κύδιστον Διομήδεα δέρκεο, ξεῖνε
τάγματι Κυρήνης στρατιήν τ' ἀσκοῦντ' ἐπιτίμον
ὃς θέτο [προ]φρ[ονέως] ἀρετῆς μνήμη, ἀνεγείρας
αὐτῷ καὶ τέκνοις κῦδος τόδ' ὁρώμενον ἐσθλόν.

Look to the illustrious cavalryman Diomedes, stranger,
who completed his honourable military service in the *Legio Cyrenaica*.
Readily he made memory of his valour, building
for himself and his children this noble sign of honour to be seen.

In the first line he puts his rank, "illustrious cavalryman"; then, as many Roman soldiers, he declares to have completed his *militia* (military duties) with honourable discharge; finally, unashamedly, he states to have built the monument as a memory of his own valour, also on behalf of his children, who would certainly profit (and not only economically) from the statue of their father, a monument that is to be seen as the embodiment of his honour.

I have remarked earlier in this chapter that, in Ptolemaic court poetry, the praise and glory related to scholarly activities, or to the protection of scholarly and poetic activities, often are accompanied by martial *kleos*. The same happens in many epitaphs for Hellenistic soldiers, praised, like the self-conscious Archilochos, both as servants of Ares and as recipients of the gifts of the Muses. Most of the time, the first virtue praised in their epitaph is the intellectual, not the martial, one.[56] In general, these are funerary poems for young men of the Hellenistic *poleis* (either in mainland Greece or in Asia Minor) who were educated in the gymnasium, and are meant to reinforce, with the praise of the intellectual and physical education provided to the civic elite by the gymnasium system, a fundamental cultural and social institution of Greek civilization, especially when the *poleis* fell under control of the Hellenistic kings and of the Roman empire. One of the most interesting is the epitaph for the poet-soldier Sopolis (*IG* IX, 1² 2:314), probably deceased around 191 BCE, during an attack of the Aitolians and the Seleukid troops of Antiochos III on the Akarnanian city of Thyrreion:[57]

[…] όφαννтε Ἐμιναύτα Λέων|ος.
χαίρετε
καὶ λόγον αὐξήσαντα καὶ ἐν λιγυαχέσι Μούσαις
κεκριμένον κρύπτει Σώπολιν ἅδε κόνις,
Θυρρείου ναετῆρα, μεγαυχήτοιο Λέοντος
κοῦρον, ἀμωμήτου σωφροσύνης κανόνα·
ὃν πᾶς μὲν φιλέεσκεν, ὑπερφιάλων δὲ πρὸς ἐχθρῶν
[ὤ]λετο φοινίξας ἀπροτίοπτον Ἄρη·
[ἀ]λλ' εἰ καὶ νέος ἦλθεν ὑπὸ ζόφον, οὐ μὲν ἀσάμως
[τὰν] ἀρετὰν λẹίπει ζῶσαν ὑπ' ἀελίωι.

[…] ofantes of Eminautes(?) of Leon
farewell
This dust hides the man who glorified the word, the one who
was chosen among the clear-sounding Muses, Sopolis.
He was a citizen of Thyrreion, son of the highly famous Leon,
a model of irreproachable temperance.
He was loved by everybody, but died at the hands of arrogant
enemies, coloring with his blood unsightly Ares.
But even though he went to the darkness so young, he leaves
behind him, not without signs, the valour living under the sun.

The first virtue declared by the poem is the gift of the Muses (apparently, both as a poet and as a rhetor), not Sopolis' military *arete*. A conflation of moral and aesthetic evaluation appears at line 4: besides being a poet, the deceased is presented as a "model of irreproachable temperance," ἀμωμήτου σωφροσύνης κανόνα.[58] Only the second part of the epitaph is devoted to Sopolis' military prowess and to the signs of *arete* he left behind; ambiguously, οὐ μὲν ἀσάμως and ἀρετὰν ... ζῶσαν ("not without signs," "living valour") may be interpreted in this context both as a generic reference, as usual, to the *sema* and to the epitaph praising the young man, or to other proofs of Sopolis' multi-talented short life, perhaps his poems.

3. The Memory Remains

I have presented some examples of how the concept of Fame is elaborated in Hellenistic military epitaphs and is intertwined with the personal character of the deceased and with the values of the community. As I have hinted in the last paragraph, in some of the epitaphs for young Hellenistic soldier-members of the gymnasium, the military *kleos* is coupled with the practice of poetry, as if the protection given by the Muses could guarantee a longer-lasting fame to the deceased. Even for uncultivated or modestly educated soldiers, fame could be provided by professional poets or amateur versifiers (their friends or relatives) with a poetic epitaph on their tombstone (Barbantani 2019). Poetry, however, is mainly perceived as persistently linked to the material support, the stone. It was an obsession of ancient epigrammatists,[59] and also of more recent poets dealing with funerary poetry, to preserve by material support the fading memory of the deceased.[60] A particularly lucky case is the one of Asklepiodotos, a benefactor from Aphrodisias (ca 480 CE) whose epitaph, lamenting that "Long time wears away even stone" actually survived until the twenty-first century both on stone and on "paper" (i.e., the *Palatine Anthology*: *Anth. Pal.* 9.704).[61] For once, the wish that, even when the marble was eroded by the passing of the time, the κλέος ἀθάνατον (variation on the Homeric ἄσβεστον κλέος) would survive, has been fulfilled; generally, however, the only Hellenistic epitaphs preserved in literary anthologies are the ones composed by famous authors such as Anyte or Damagetos. Kings and courtiers, meanwhile, continued to hire the best scholars and poets to secure for themselves "eternal fame in books." For the Ptolemies, at least, the sheer fact of sponsoring poets who would become "classics" like Homer and Simonides in the future was a motivation for *kleos* that was as strong as obtaining military victory.

NOTES

1 E.g., the epic on Alexander the Great; see Barbantani 2017; Taietti forthcoming; Ziegler 1988.

2 Theokritos probably has in mind Simonides' elegy for Plataia, with its hymn to Achilles; Theokritos *Id.* 17.5–8: "The heroes who of old were sprung from demigods, when they had accomplished noble deeds (καλὰ ἔργα), found skilled poets to honour them; but I who know how to praise (ἐπιστάμενος καλὰ εἰπεῖν) must sing of Ptolemy; and songs are the meed even of the immortals themselves" (Tr. A.S.F. Gow).

3 See Barbantani 2017, with further bibliography.

4 Theokritos *Id.* 16.42–59:

... And leaving that rich store, unremembered [ἄμναστοι] would they have lain long ages among the hapless dead had not a bard inspired, the man from Ceos, turned his varied lays to the lyre of many strings and made them famous among the men of later days [εἰ μὴ θεῖος ἀοιδὸς ὁ Κήιος αἰόλα φωνέων / βάρβιτον ἐς πολύχορδον ἐν ἀνδράσι θῆκ' ὀνομαστούς / ὁπλοτέροις]; and even the swift steeds lacked not their meed of glory that brought them from the holy games the crown of victory. Who would have known ever the chieftains of the Lycians, or Priam's long-haired sons, or Cycnus, maidenlike of skin, if poets had not sung the battle-cries of men of old [εἰ μὴ φυλόπιδας προτέρων ὕμνησαν ἀοιδοί;]? Never had Odysseus won lasting fame [δηναιὸν κλέος ἔσχεν], who wandered six score months through all the world, and came alive to farthest Hades, and escaped from the cave of the baleful Cyclops; never would the swineherd Eumaeus have been named, nor Philoetius, busied with the cattle of the herd, nor the great-hearted Laertes himself, had not the minstrelsy of an Ionian bard profited them. From the Muses comes good report to men, but the possessions of the dead are wasted by the living [εἰ μή σφεας ὤνασαν Ἰάονος ἀνδρὸς ἀοιδαί. / ἐκ Μοισᾶν ἀγαθὸν κλέος ἔρχεται ἀνθρώποισι, / χρήματα δὲ ζώοντες ἀμαλδύνουσι θανόντων].

And 73–5: "... That man shall be who shall have need of me for his poet when he has done such deeds as great Achilles wrought, or dread Aias, on the plain of Simois where stands the tomb of Phrygian Ilus" (ἔσσεται οὗτος ἀνὴρ ὃς ἐμεῦ κεχρήσετ' ἀοιδοῦ, / ῥέξας ἢ Ἀχιλεὺς ὅσσον μέγας ἢ βαρὺς Αἴας / ἐν πεδίῳ Σιμόεντος, ὅθι Φρυγὸς ἠρίον Ἴλου) (Tr. A.S.F. Gow).

5 *Suppl. Hell.* 979.6–7: ὄλβιοι ὦ θνατῶν εὐεργέται, [οἳ] τὸν ἄριστον / ἐν δορὶ καὶ Μούσαις κοίρανον ἠρόσατε ("O fortunate benefactors of the mortals, you who sowed the seed of a king excellent in the spear and in the (arts of the) Muses." See Barbantani 2001: 54, and 2007: 72.

6 "But when you die you will lie there, and afterwards there will never be any recollection of you or any longing for you since you have no share in the roses of Pieria; unseen in the house of Hades also, flown from our midst, you will go to and from among the shadowy corpses" (Tr. D.A. Campbell). The concept is expressed in a contrastive way. Of course similar wishes for immortality were expressed also by many other Greek and Latin authors, such as Ennius

(*Ep.* 2.5: *Volito vivos per ora virum,* "I fly alive on the lips of men" and Horace (*Exegi monumentum aere perennius … non omnis moriar,* "I have erected a monument more lasting than bronze … I shall not die entirely," *Odes* 3.30.1, 6).

7 Isager 1998: 6–9: l. 3: τῆς Ἁλικαρνασσοῦ τί τὸ τίμιον; ll. 43–54: list of writers; ll. 55–60: ἄλλους τ'ἐξ ἐσθλῶν ἐσθλοὺς τέκε· μυρίος αἰὼν / οὐ τελέσει δόξης πείρατα πάντ' ἐνέπειν, / πολλὰ μὲν ἐν χέρσωι κάμεν ἀγλαά, πολλὰ δὲ πόντωι / ἐσθλὰ σὺν Ἑλλήνων ἡγεμόσιν φέρεται· / εὐσεβέων πάντιμον ἔχει γέρας, ἔν τ'ἀγαθοῖσιν / ἔργοις κυδίστων ἀντέχεται στεφάνων ("And she bore other noble sons of noble fathers; Time the infinite shall never cease to tell of the deeds by which they won their fame. She has done many glorious deeds on land, and at sea has won many a noble prize with the commanders of the Greeks. The guerdon of the righteous, that brings all honours, is hers, and by means of her noble doings she lays claim to the most glorious of garlands," Tr. H. Lloyd-Jones).

8 On *kudos* in Homer and in archaic and classical poetry, see Greindl 1938: 49; Nagy 1979: 63–4 (IV); Stecher 1981: 74n90; Sider 2011. By the fifth century BCE, *kudos* is a quality associated with abstract or personified values, like *arete* (Bacchylides 1.159–60); in the Hellenistic period it becomes a synonym for *kleos* ("renown, fame, glory") (in Theokritos *Id.* 22.218, it is the poet, Homer, who gives *kudos* to the Dioskouroi). *Kudos,* in the sense of *kleos,* appears very frequently in encomiastic and funerary epigrams, from the late classical and Hellenistic period to late antiquity, to indicate the glory of the *laudandus,* and it does not refer exclusively to military deeds. For a comparison with the Neoptolemos epigram (below, p. 39), see the epitaph for the second-century BCE Arcadian leader Philopoimen in Pausanias 8.52.6: τοῦδ' ἀρετὰ καὶ δόξα καθ' Ἑλλάδα, πολλὰ μὲν ἀλκαῖς, / πολλὰ δὲ καὶ βουλαῖς ἔργα πονησαμένου, / Ἀρκάδος αἰχμητᾶ Φιλοποίμενος, ᾧ μέγα κῦδος ἔσπετ' ἐνὶ πτολέμῳ δούρατος ἁγεμόνι ("Throughout Greece are renowned the virtue and fame of this man, who accomplished many deeds with his strength, and many with his wisdom, the Arcadian warrior Philopoimen; great glory followed him in war as a commander of the spear").

9 A full bibliography on military victories as legitimization of rulers may be found in Barbantani 2012.

10 [ἀσπ]ὶς Ἐνυαλίωι πρέπον ἄνθεμα καὶ φάλαρα ἵππων / ποικίλα· τὰν Νίκαν δὲ ἀνθέμεν Εὐπόλεμος / φατὶ Μάγαι βασιλῆϊ καλὸν γέρας, ὄφρα ὑπὸ τᾶιδε / σκῆπτρά τε καὶ λαοὺς καὶ πτολίεθρα σαοῖ ("A shield is a convenient offer for Enyalios and so are horses' ornate / cheek-pieces; but Victory, Eupolemos / declares to have dedicated to king Magas as a beautiful gift / so that he can preserve his sceptre, the people and the cities"). Cf. Poseidonios *Ep.* 74 A.–B.; the combination of military and athletic victory also appears in Attalid epinician epigrams; see, e.g., Arkesilaos *Suppl. Hell.* 121; Barbantani 2012. On the Cyrenean epigram, see Chamoux 1958; Fantuzzi and Hunter 2004: 392.

11 See Barbantani 2001: 73–115.

12 Theognis 1.236–52:

I have given thee wings to fly with ease aloft the boundless sea and all the land. No meal or feast but thou'lt be there, couched 'twixt the lips of many a guest, and lovely youths shall sing thee clear and well in orderly wise to the clear-voiced flute. And when thou comest to go down to the lamentable house of Hades in the depths of the gloomy earth, never, albeit thou be dead, shalt thou lose thy fame [οὐδέποτ' οὐδὲ θανὼν ἀπολεῖς κλέος], but men will think of thee as one of immortal name, Cyrnus, who rangeth the land of Greece and the isles thereof – crossing the fishy unharvestable deep not upon horseback mounted but sped of the glorious gifts of the violet-crowned Muses unto all that care to receive thee; and living as they thou shalt be a song unto posterity so long as Earth and Sun abide [ἀλλά σε πέμψει / ἀγλαὰ Μουσάων δῶρα ἰοστεφάνων. / πᾶσι δ', ὅσοισι μέμηλε, καὶ ἐσσομένοισιν ἀοιδή / ἔσσηι ὁμῶς, ὄφρ' ἂν γῆ τε καὶ ἠέλιος]. (Tr. J.M. Edmonds)

Pindar *Nem.* 5.1–5: οὐκ ἀνδριαντοποιός εἰμ', ὥστ' ἐλινύσοντα ἐργάζεσθαι ἀγάλματ' ἐπ' αὐτᾶς βαθμίδος / ἑσταότ'· ἀλλ' ἐπὶ πάσας / ὁλκάδος ἔν τ' ἀκάτῳ, γλυκεῖ' ἀοιδά, / στεῖχ' ἀπ' Αἰγίνας διαγγέλλοισ', ὅτι / Λάμπωνος υἱὸς Πυθέας εὐρυσθενής / νίκη Νεμείοις παγκρατίου στέφανον ("I am not a sculptor, to make statues that stand motionless on the same pedestal. Sweet song, go on every merchant-ship and rowboat leaving Aegina, and announce that Lampon's powerful son Pytheas won the victory garland for the pancratium at the Nemean games").

13 See Barbantani 2014; Garulli 2008: 634–7.

14 See Van't Dack et al. 1989: 84–8 for the dating of the epigram after 103/102 BCE; on the epigram, see Barbantani 2007: 113–14 and 2014: 303–4.

15 See Barbantani 2014: 310–11 on this epigram and on another, Seleukid, example of the combination "fortune of the employer–glory of the employee" (Peek *GVI* 1286 = *SGO* I, 01/20/35).

16 For a commentary of the epigram, see Barbantani 2007: 110–11.

17 See Barbantani 2001: 89, 96–7.

18 "Oracular voice," e.g., in Aeschylus *PV* 663; Sophokles *Trach.* 87; "report, rumour," Mimnermus 15; Theognis 1.1298; Sophokles *Aj.* 494, *El.* 642, 638, 1006; Euripides *Hel.* 224 (LSJ).

19 Peek, *GVI* 1471; *CIRB* 119; *SGDI* 5558; *SEG* LV 2005 nr. 866 (with commentary); Gavrilov 2005; Obryk 2012: 67: B16 (on the warrior's fame in general see Obryk 80–4).

20 On the use of the word "canon" in encomiastic epigrams, see Barbantani 2018.

21 See Ecker 1990: 34–40; 189–94.

22 For the Indo-European formula, *sravas aksitam* ("unperishable glory"), see Benveniste, 1969: 2. 58–9; Finkelberg 1986; Nagy 1981; Volk 2002.

23 Ἄσβεστον κλέος and burial (all tr. by A.T. Murray): *Od.* 4.584: χεῦ' Ἀγαμέμνονι τύμβον, ἵν' ἄσβεστον κλέος εἴη ("I heaped up a mound to Agamemnon, that his fame might be unquenchable"); *Od.* 24.80–4: ἀμφ' αὐτοῖσι δ' ἔπειτα μέγαν καὶ ἀμύμονα τύμβον / χεύαμεν Ἀργείων ἱερὸς στρατὸς αἰχμητάων / ἀκτῇ ἔπι προὐχούσῃ, ἐπὶ πλατεῖ Ἑλλησπόντῳ, / ὥς κεν τηλεφανὴς ἐκ ποντόφιν ἀνδράσιν εἴη / τοῖσ', οἳ νῦν γεγάασι καὶ οἳ μετόπισθεν ἔσονται ("And over them [i.e., the ashes of Achilles and Patroclus] we heaped up a great and goodly tomb, we the mighty host of Argive spearmen, on a projecting headland by the broad Hellespont, that it might be seen from far over the sea both by men that now are and that shall be born hereafter"); *Il.* 16.456–7: ἔνθά ἑ ταρχύσουσι κασίγνητοί τε ἔται τε / τύμβῳ τε στήλῃ τε· τὸ γὰρ γέρας ἐστὶ θανόντων ("And there shall his [i.e., Sarpedon's] brethren and his kinsfolk give him burial with mound and pillar; for this is the due of the dead"). Posterity: *Il.* 6.357–9: οἷσιν ἐπὶ Ζεὺς θῆκε κακὸν μόρον, ὡς καὶ ὀπίσσω / ἀνθρώποισι πελώμεθ' ἀοίδιμοι ἐσσομένοισι ("On whom Zeus hath brought an evil doom, that even in days to come we may be a song for men that are yet to be"); *Il.* 22.305–6: μὴ μὰν ἀσπουδί γε καὶ ἀκλειῶς ἀπολοίμην, / ἀλλὰ μέγα ῥέξας τι καὶ ἐσσομένοισι πυθέσθαι ("Nay, but not without a struggle let me die, neither ingloriously, [305] but in the working of some great deed for the hearing of men that are yet to be"); *Od.* 24.93–4: ὣς σὺ μὲν οὐδὲ θανὼν ὄνομ' ὤλεσας, ἀλλά τοι αἰεὶ / πάντας ἐπ' ἀνθρώπους κλέος ἔσσεται ἐσθλόν, Ἀχιλλεῦ ("Thus not even in death didst thou lose thy name, but ever shalt thou have fair renown among all men, Achilles").

24 See Barbantani 2014, 2018, and 2019. According to Derderian (2001: 89–91) formulaic expressions drawing from a common poetic tradition (Homer, elegy, lyric poetry) are concentrated in epitaphs for "exceptional deaths" (especially those relevant for the community, such as the sacrifice of soldiers), because formulae appeal on a common cultural ground, underlining the interrelation between the individual and the group. As I tried to show in several publications, however, epitaphs for individual soldiers, especially from the Hellenistic period onwards, sometimes stand out for their original style and vocabulary. On the influence of poets other than Homer on professional epigrammatists see Garulli 2012: 379–82; Tsagalis 2008: 262–76.

25 See above note 23. Kaibel 527.5–6 (Beroia, Macedonia, third century CE?) = *EKM 1. Beroia* 400; *IK Klaudioupolis* 78.4 (Bithynia, Imperial period): μνήμην ἀνθρώποισι καὶ ἐσσομένοισι πυθέσθαι ("memory even for future men to know"); *KILyk* I 306 (Lykaonia, Lystra, Imperial period), l. 18 = Peek, *GVI* 569.18: ἄσ]ματα καλὰ φράσουσι καὶ ἐσσομένοισ[ι πυθέσθαι] ("[others] will know beautiful songs, to be renowned also by posterity"). Cf. *SGO* I 01/05/02.

26 *SGO* III 12/03/03 (Susa, 9/8 century BCE or 2/3 century CE); *IK Estremo oriente* 214, pp. 118–19; Merkelback-Stauber 2005: 405; *SEG* 7.13.

27 The theme of the eternal memory left to the posterity and the use of the non-technical word like *stratiarchos* coexist with the specific term "satrapes" and with the detail of the hydraulic works he sponsored.

28 [Simonides] *Anth. Pal.* 7.251: ἄσβεστον κλέος οἵδε φίλη περὶ πατρίδι θέντες / κυάνεον θανάτου ἀμφεβάλοντο νέφος·/ οὐδὲ τεθνᾶσι θανόντες, ἐπεί σφ' ἀρετὴ καθύπερθε/ κυδαίνουσ' ἀνάγει δώματος ἐξ Ἀίδεω ("These men having clothed their dear country in inextinguishable glory, donned the dark cloud of death; and having died, yet they are not dead, for their valour's renown brings them up from the house of Hades," Tr. W. Paton). On the anxiety of the Homeric hero, Hektor, over the survival of his *kleos* in the distant future, see Bouvier 2002: 51–4, 207–13.

29 "Encomiastic" military elegy in the Archaic and classical period commemorates the dead and serves as a *parainesis* for the living; thus Boedeker 1995: 221: "The elegies of Tyrtaeus, … performed according to Philochorus (*FGrH* 328 F216) in informal contests at Spartan communal meals, include verses on the κλέος and immortality of warriors (Tyrtaeus 9.31–2 Gentili-Prato). But unlike the Plataea elegy, Tyrtaeus 9 celebrates Spartan military virtue in general, describing the kind of man who receives κλέος, rather than memorializing any individual(s) specifically."

30 = *IG* XII, 5 300 and addenda p. 313.

31 See Barbantani 2014 and 2019.

32 Bacchylides 1.159–60: φαμὶ καὶ φάσω | μέγιστον κῦδος ἔχειν ἀρετάν; *Anth. Pal.* 7.254.1–2 (Simonides): χαίρετ᾽ ἀριστῆες πολέμου μέγα κῦδος ἔχοντες, / κοῦροι Ἀθηναίων, ἔξοχοι ἱπποσύνῃ ("Hail, ye champions who won great glory in war, ye sons of Athens, excellent horsemen"); *Anth. Pal.* 16.349.56: διπλόον οὔνομα τοῦτο, τόπερ λάχε χάλκεος ἥρως / οὗτος, ὁ τεθρίπποις κῦδος ἑλὼν ἀρετῆς ("The two names that belonged to this brazen hero, who won the meed of valour in the chariot-races," Tr. W. Paton).

33 Peek, *GVI* 1504 (Oreos / Histiaia, Euboea; not before the third century BCE); cf. Addenda, Peek, 177; Kaibel 1878: 209; *IG* XII.9 1195; *IG* XII, supp.198, 1195; Barbantani 2014.

34 On the Horatian theme *dulce et decorum est pro patria mori* in Hellenistic epigrams, and on the disconfession of it in modern war poetry, see Barbantani 2016, esp. 213–14.

35 This other word for "posterity" is still Homeric, and connected with fame: ὀψιγόνων ἀνθρώπων (*Il.* 3.353: a lesson to be taught for the future generation to learn); *Il.* 7.87: καί ποτέ τις εἴπῃσι καὶ ὀψιγόνων ἀνθρώπων (Hektor dreams that the *sema* of Menelaos, in case he would kill the Achaian hero, in the future would prompt the occasional traveller to remember his own *kleos*). Cf. Kallimachos *Hymn* 4.175: ὀψίγονοι Τιτῆνες.

36 He died in Messenia about 183/2 BCE; see Barbantani 2014: 317–18. *IC* I.viii 33; cf. *IC* I.xvi 48 = *SEG* XXVIII 749.

37 The topic is discussed in Barbantani 2019.

38 On the power of poetry to preserve fame, see also the chapter by Klooster in this volume.

39 Cf. ὁ πέτρος αὐδᾷ in the new epitaph from Aphrodisias, in Chaniotis 2009; Peek, *GVI* 1729.4: ἀείμνηστον γράμμα λαλεῦσα πέτρη and *SGO* 05/01/42 = Peek, *GVI* 1745, Smyrna 245, a funerary inscription in elegiacs for Hermias, dead on Mt Tmolos: 1 [ὀ]στέα μὲν κρύπτει Τμῶλος νεάταισιν ὑπ' ὄχθαις / Ἑρμίου, ὀγκωτὰ δὲ ἀμφιβέβακε κόνις / [τ]ηλεφάης· ξεστὰ δὲ πέτρα καθύπερθε ἀγορεύει / [τ]ὸν νέκυν ἀφθόγγωι φθεγγομένα στόματι. (cf. Simias *Anth. Pal.* 7.193) / 5 τοῦτο δέ οἱ κενέωμα τάφου ποθέοντες ἑταῖροι / Σμύρνης ἀγχιάλοις χεῦαν ἐπ' ἀϊόσιν.

40 See Peek, *GVI* 1515; *IG* XII, Suppl. 183; Sikinos, second century BCE.

41 About the imagery of the Island of the Blessed and the deceased as heroes, see Barbantani 2016; Wypustek 2013: 65–95. See also Quadrino 2010: 73, who tentatively identifies the "*heroa*" as a particular sepulchral area of Sikinos, an *heroon* later reused as a church. She also integrates the name of the father as "Ainetos" (55).

42 On the importance of condemning a rival to eternal oblivion by the non-mention or removal of his name, see the chapter by de Callataÿ in this volume.

43 = *IG* IX, 1^2 1:51 = Moretti 1975: 41–2, no. 85; see further bibliography in Barbantani 2014: 324–5. This cavalry officer was the victim of a vile and unheroic surprise attack (ll. 1–3): ἄλσει ἐνὶ χρυσέῳ σε βοαδρομέοντα σὺν ἵππῳ / [Φ]ωκίσι Τείθρωνος κτεῖνεν ὑπὸ στεφάναις / δυσμενέων κρυφθεὶς ἄφατος λόχος ("in a golden grove, when you were rushing on horseback to help the Phokians, under the hights of the Teithron, an unknown squad of enemies killed you in an ambush": the cowardice of the enemy does not impound the valour and the heroic status of the deceased (ll. 3–4: ἄξια πάτρας, / ἄξια δ' Οἰνειδᾶν μησάμενον προγόνων ("accomplishing deeds wothy of your homeland, of your ancestors Oeniades").

44 See Quadrino 2009.

45 See Ma 2005. On the funerary monuments in the cities, see Herrmann 1995 and Ma 2013.

46 Cf. Tyrtaios fr. 10.15–17 West: ὦ νέοι, ἀλλὰ μάχεσθε παρ' ἀλλήλοισι μένοντες, / μηδὲ φυγῆς αἰσχρῆς ἄρχετε μηδὲ φόβου, / ἀλλὰ μέγαν ποιεῖτε καὶ ἄλκιμον ἐν φρεσὶ θυμόν, / μηδὲ φιλοψυχεῖτ' ἀνδράσι μαρνάμενοι ("You young men, keep together, hold the line, / do not start panic or disgraceful rout. / Keep grand and valiant spirits in your hearts, be not in love with life – the fight's with men!" Tr. M.L. West).

47 E.g., Peek, *GVI* 1521 = *CIRB* 136, Pantikapaion, first century CE; *GVI* 689.1–8 = *TAM* IV, 1 322 (Bithynia, second century CE): l.3 Ἑκτόριον π[αράδειγμα πόλει, κύδους ἰσ]όμοιρον "I was an Hektorean example for the city, sharing with him

a glorious fate"; *SGO* I 10/02/28 (Caesarea-Hadrianopolis, Paphlagonia, second century CE). See Barbantani 2016.

48 Ugo Foscolo, the final verses (296–9) of *I sepolcri* (1807): "E tu onore di pianti, Ettore, avrai, / ove fia santo e lagrimato il sangue / per la patria versato, e finché il Sole / risplenderà su le sciagure umane." The unfortunate heroic Hektor is also the moral conscience and the protagonist of Jean Giraudoux's pièce *La guerre de Troie n'aura pas lieu.*

49 For the Homeric and Tyrtaian *topos* of the "death in the first line" in epitaphs, see Barbantani 2014.

50 See Martinez Fernández 2006: 206–10.

51 See Barbantani 2014: 316–17.

52 The *iunctura* is inspired by *Il.* 16.630 (ἐν γὰρ χερσὶ τέλος πολέμου, ἐπέων δ' ἐνὶ βουλῇ ["The end of war is in the hands, the end of words in discussion / council"]) and *Od.* 16.241–2 (ὦ πάτερ, ἦ τοι σεῖο μέγα κλέος αἰὲν ἄκουον, / χεῖράς τ' αἰχμητὴν ἔμεναι καὶ ἐπίφρονα βουλήν ["O father, I always heard of your great renown, that you were a warrior with your hands and wise in giving advice"]). Cf. Pindar *Pyth.* 4.72–4, *Nem.* 8.7–8, and see further Garulli 2012: 341–5.

53 See Barbantani 2014: 325, 320, and 322–3 for the *topos* of the "first ranks"; Barbantani 2016: 201–4.

54 See, e.g., the epitaph for the Lykian Osses and Manossas (Barbantani 2014: 318–19), who fell in old age; they are not only brave in combat for their προστασίη similar to Ajax, but also εὐκλεές for their temperance and honesty. The theme of well-deserved wealth is common to Hellenistic and Roman epitaphs for veterans: the connection between *kleos* and *sophrosyne* is to be found in epitaphs since the fourth century BCE (see Tsagalis 2008: 158–60). Likewise, the Cretan mercenary, who was buried on the island of Telos, Dodekanesos (*GVI* 1811.1–4,Telos, second century BCE), managed, in spite of his perilous life, to reach an old age "of good fame" (εὐκλειὲς γῆρας, l. 6; all Crete "praised" him as top archer, literally, "for his good aim," l. 5: [α]ἴνεσε καὶ Κρήτα πᾶσα κατ' εὐστοχίαν), and was taken not by Ares, like many soldiers, but by the Homeric Chronos ὁ πανδαμάτω[ρ] (l. 7). Looking back with a mixture of pride and modesty to his military career, Kimon underlines his being πιστὸς ἀεὶ προμάχεσθαι, trustworthy, loyal, and courageous, as a main feature of his character (see Barbantani 2014: 319–20).

55 I discuss some epitaphs for family tombs, very frequent in the Hellenistic and Roman East, in Barbantani 2019: 171–2.

56 I have treated this topic in Barbantani 2018.

57 The epigram of Sopolis is discussed thoroughly in Barbantani 2018: 298–301.

58 In antiquity, the term "canon" had a generic ethic-aesthetic meaning of "norm, model to imitate, reference"; see Oppel 1937.

59 See Barbantani 2019.

60 "Row after row with strict impunity / The headstones yield their names to the elements" (Allen Tate [1889–1979], "Ode to the Confederate Dead"); Foscolo, *I Sepolcri* 39: "e serbi un sasso il nome."

61 *SGO* I 02/09/05; see Barbantani 2019: 173–4. The *arete* of the euergetes survived also in the memory of his community thanks to the monuments he had restored: 1 [λ]άμπει κ(αὶ) φθιμένοις ἀρετῆς φάος, οἳ περὶ πάτρη[ς] / πολλὰ πονησάμενοι ξυνὸν ἔθεντ' ὄφελ[ος.] / Ἀσκληπιοδότωι λόγος ἥρμοσεν, ὧι πόλις ἥ[δε] / οἷάπερ οἰκιστῆι τόνδ' ἀνέθηκε τύπο[ν.] / 5 τήκει καὶ πέτρην ὁ πολὺς χρόνος· ἀλλ' ἀ[ρετάων] / Ἀσκληπιοδότου τὸ κλέος ἀθάνατον, / ὅσσα καὶ οἷα πόρεν γέρα πατρίδι τοῖς ἐπὶ π[ᾶσιν] / καὶ τόδε μετρείσθω ξυνὸν ἔρεισμα θό[λου.] ("The light of virtue shines even for dead men, who, undertaking many labours for their country, established general benefits. The saying fits Asklepiodotus, for whom this city has dedicated this statue as for a founder. Long time wears away even stone; but the fame of Asklepiodotus' virtues is immortal, the number and kind of privileges which he obtained for his country. In addition to all these, let this adjacent structure of the vaulted chamber be counted as well" Tr. C. Rouché).

3

Can Powerful Women Be Popular? Amastris: Shaping a Persian Wife into a Famous Hellenistic Queen

MONICA D'AGOSTINI

Extemplo Libyae magnas it Fama per urbes,
Fama, malum qua non aliud velocius ullum.

Aeneid 4.173–4

The well-known verses of Vergil introduce the equally well-known description of the allegory of *Fama*, the personification of the rumour that spreads among the people over the tragic affair of Dido and Aeneas. The mythical queen, like most historical royal women in ancient literature, is the passive object of her reputation and fame, or rather infamy, which grows beyond her control and regardless of her will.[1] Yet, as mentioned by Riemer Faber, "different social, political, economic, and cultural forces are at play in the creation of celebrity, fame, and infamy, and what really matters is how the individual character directs the viewer's gaze to the forces at play."[2] The successors of Alexander the Great engaged in shaping their own image of *Basileis* via inscriptions, coins, literature, sculpture, and symbolic actions. Hellenistic rulers and statesmen became increasingly aware of the relevance of self-representation to convey political and social messages for their audience (i.e., the armies and the elites and establishment of the newly formed Hellenistic kingdoms). Unique among them is the case of the *Basilissa* Amastris of Herakleia, currently the first woman, at least in the history of the Greek Mediterranean and Near East, publicly identified by means of agency and appearance as the political, economic, and administrative royal authority. Amastris engendered and managed her own fame in order to consciously increase the popularity of her rule. To grant support and confer legitimacy on the new Hellenistic institutions, she made herself and her *Basileia* vessels of innovations that reflected the interests not only of the conqueror but also those of the native cultures, which had to accept them. She employed various media strategies at a local level to confer upon the new political and administrative structures the popularity that they needed in order to be effective. Such media strategies are rather well attested in the numismatic production, as well as in the local historiography; a detailed impression may be gained specifically from the account of Memnon of Herakleia, whose writing I introduce in the next section.

1. Photios, Memnon, and Nymphis

Unfortunately, not much is known about Memnon (*FGrH* 434) of the city-state of Herakleia on the Black Sea, author of a historical work of at least sixteen books, and probably twenty-four (Desideri 1967: 373–4.).[3] Thanks to the *Excerpta* of Photios I, the patriarch of Constantinople, it is still possible to read the account of the events from the mid-fourth to mid-first century BCE in the summary of Memnon's books 9–16. Mainly concerned with local history, the *Excerpta* of Memnon nevertheless offer a unique historiographical perspective on the local impact of the outcome of Alexander's conquest and of the Successors' Wars.

The *Excerpta* of book 11–13 (or 14), delivered in chapters 4–17 of Photios' *Excerpta*, provide an uninterrupted account of the events between Alexander's conquest of the area until the aftermath of Curupedion and the death of Ptolemy II – that is, from ca 334 until early 246 BCE. This section of Memnon's work employs as a source the writings of Nymphis of Herakleia. The most famous ancient local historian of the area, Nymphis lived in the first half of the third century BCE and belonged to one of the families exiled from Herakleia by the tyranny (Billows *BNJ*, s.v. "Nymphis [432]"). His democratic and anti-tyrannical background is shown in the surviving fragments of his works, which are, according to the Suda (s.v. "Nymphis"), *On Herakleia* (Νύμφις, Περὶ Ἡρακλείας) and *On Alexander and on the Diadochoi and Epigonoi* (Περὶ Ἀλεξάνδρου καὶ τῶν Διαδόχων καὶ Ἐπιγόνων). The first work concerned the history of Herakleia at least until the end of the Herakleiote tyranny in 281 BCE, probably including also the return of the citizens exiled under the tyranny, including Nymphis. The latter work probably reached to the death of Ptolemy II in 246 BCE and provided a reconstruction of early Hellenistic events with a "more balanced and impartial" perspective toward Hellenistic kings (Mathisen 1978: 71–4).

Due to the consistency in Memnon's account – even after the interpolations of Photios – regarding the Hellenistic events from Alexander's conquest (F 1.4) until the accession of Ptolemy III to the throne (F 1.17), it is likely that Memnon employed both works of Nymphis as sources. It is no coincidence that the information focusing on Herakleia became more sporadic after 281/80, when it is supposed that *On Herakleia* ended, leaving Nymphis' general history *On Alexander and on the Diadochoi and Epigonoi* until the digression on Rome (F 1.18) as the main source for Memnon's books 13–14.

2. Herakleia at the Time of the Hellenistic Conquest

Saprykin (1997: 143–4) stressed that the tyranny of Timotheos and Dionysios over Herakleia is an example of "proto-Hellenism," which he defines as "[a] typical feature for outlying Greek countries which is connected with a peculiar way of their historical development, caused by a confluence of Hellenic *poleis* with native societies. It had brought to life a specific form of government which differed from former *polis* organization and was close to monocratic rule like a power of Hellenistic kings."

Although Alexander's conquest is described as having allowed the empowerment of dynasts such as Dionysios who had been subjected to Persian power, at first glance there seems to be no trace of political or administrative innovation after the conquest. The proto-Hellenistic structures appear not to have been subjected to evident changes by the conquerors: despite the many requests from the exiled to be readmitted to Herakleia and to establish a democratic constitution in that city, both Alexander and Perdikkas left the rule in the hands of Dionysios and did not introduce any political change (Memnon *BNJ* 434 F 1.4.1–3.).[4] According to Memnon, the tyrant took advantage of both the Persian defeat by Alexander and of Perdikkas' death to reinforce his rule (Muccioli 2011).

Dionysios' growing strength is supported by the numismatic evidence. In these years, Herakleia began minting new silver staters; similar to the previous ones, they were of a local standard and showed a standing Herakles and the profile of Dionysos. However, instead of Dionysios' name being together with that of his brother and predecessor, Timotheos, the staters bore the name of only the ruler Dionysios (figure 3.1) (Mørkholm 1991: 95–6; Erçiyas 2003: 1411–12). Notably, Dionysios was the first ruler to have his name on a city issue, after Themistokles in Magnesia on the Meander. Moreover, the presence of Dionysios on Herakleia's issues after the Macedonian

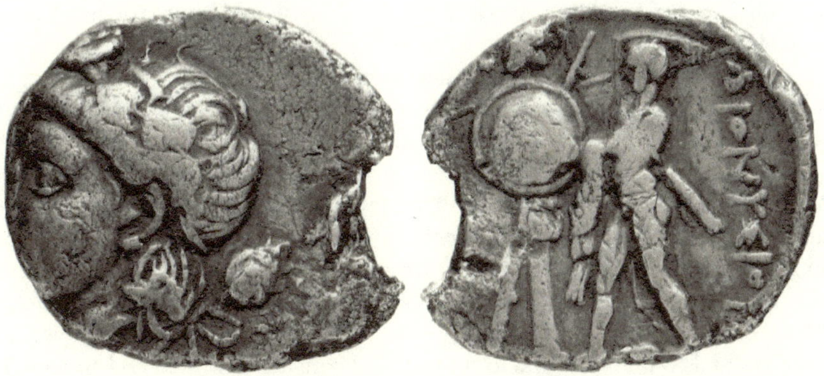

Figure 3.1 Silver stater (8.85 g), 337–305 BCE, from Herakleia Pontika. *Obverse:* Head of Dionysos, left, wreathed with ivy, thyrsos behind. *Reverse:* ΔΙΟΝΥΣΙΟΥ, Herakles standing left, wearing lion skin over left arm and sword in sheath, attaching spear and shield to a trophy of arms.

Bibliothèque nationale de France, département Monnaies, médailles et antiques, Fonds général 595: http://catalogue.bnf.fr/ark:/12148/cb41810142d.

conquest also corroborates the lack of political interference in the city by both Alexander himself and his general Perdikkas.

3. Amastris and the Value of a Persian Wife

The first trace of direct interest in the politics of Herakleia was shown by one of Alexander's leading generals, Krateros.[5] The Macedonian *philos* had been wed by his king in Susa to Amastris, the Achaimenid princess daughter of Oxathres (= Oxyathres), and niece of Darius III (Diodoros 20.109.7; Arrian, *Anabasis* 7.4.5; Brosius 1996: 78 and 184). When Alexander commanded Krateros to lead back to Macedon a part of the army and take charge of Macedonia, Thrace, Thessaly, and Greece, he brought his Persian wife with him to his western homeland, contrary to what had been done by the rest of the army (Arrian, *Anabasis* 7.12.2). The aforementioned sources underline that marrying the noble Amastris conferred prestige upon Krateros: it confirmed his position of authority in the *Basileia* that was second only to that of Hephaistion, who married Darius III's daughter Drypetis, the sister of Alexander's wife Stateira (Carney 2000: 108–9).[6] Amastris clearly had explicit symbolic value, or rather was "symbolic capital" for Krateros as the living embodiment of Alexander's emotional affection and political trust

(O'Neil 2002: 172). After Alexander's death, it would thus not have been possible for the *diadochos* to separate himself from his bride without raising questions about his loyalty to the deceased king.

Maria Brosius (2016) has extensively explored the social, economic, and political roles of Persian women, also examining specifically the agency of the Achaimenid royal women. In her research, the scholar studied the Achaimenid Persepolis Fortification Tablets (PF), which are ancient Persian cuneiform administrative texts, mostly in Elamite. They deliver information on the chancellery and administration of the Achaimenid empire between 506 and 497 BCE (Briant, Henkelman, and Stolper 2008). Building on this documentary evidence, Brosius demonstrated that Persian royal women were trained to manage land and estates of considerable size and to control villages and towns across the empire.[7] After being married, they preserved their economic independence, which they used to support themselves and to "pursue the welfare of their family" (Brosius 1996: 187). Even if they had no formal political power, they belonged to the king's entourage, and they could act as mediator between the king and the nobility (Brosius 2016).

The relevance of Macedonian-Persian weddings contemporary to Amatris' has been stressed by Gillian Ramsey (2016a), who has recently explored that of Seleukos I with Apame.[8] The Milesian honour decree of 299 from Didyma (*I. Didyma* 480), dedicated by the commander Demodamas and his army to the queen Apame as thanks for her support and benevolence, reflects this active role of the queen as political facilitator.[9] It thus shows that Seleukos reinforced his marriage with a noble Iranian woman by adding a diplomatic aspect to the economic one. Apame had been raised according to Persian custom to attend managerial duties and economic enterprises;[10] hence, her economic and political connection with the Baktrian-Sogdian area contributed to her husband's acquisition and control of the region, ultimately conferring upon her a precious and unique diplomatic value.[11] As Ramsey (2016a: 96) states:

> In addition to the possible economic concerns regarding confiscated dowries, the political activity of the wives must be considered, since they were all powerful princesses and daughters of satraps, not a group of helpless war captives. They would have expected to use their marriages to restore access to hereditary lands and rights, and this activity would be far more likely to alienate their Diadoch husbands, whose political ambitions lay elsewhere. (2016a: 96)

As a Persian royal woman, Amastris too had been raised to assume managerial duty, and she was an economic and diplomatic asset to anchor the Macedonian rule over the acquired areas, as Apame was for Seleukos

I. Therefore when Krateros married Phila, the daughter of Antipater, in order to enter into an alliance with her father, he also saw the opportunity of remarrying Amastris to the local tyrant Dionysios and expanding his influence as well as that of the *diadochoi* (Diodoros 18.18.7).[12] It is unclear whether Amastris had inherited land and estates from her family of origin on the occasion, but Krateros did provide her with a sizeable dowry in order to wed her to the Herakleian tyrant:

> When Alexander had departed from among men, Krateros inclined towards Phila, the daughter of Antipater, and Amastris, with Krateros' consent, was given in marriage to Dionysios. (5) From that time his rule was to a great extent enhanced both by the endowment of wealth which had accrued from his inter-marriage and of his personal love for the beautiful. (Memnon *BNJ* 434 F 1.4.4–5)

In betrothing Amastris to Dionysios, Krateros acted as his former wife's *kyrios*, her legal guardian, a role customarily played by the closest male relative. According to the Athenian legal system, the woman usually was under her father's or brother's supervision until her marriage, and then, if she was widowed, she would be served as guardian by her son.[13] *Kyrioi* took a less active role in the Hellenistic period, especially in the Near East and in Egypt, both in the local communities and in the Hellenic ones.[14] The encounter of different traditions and the frequent changing of the economic and administrative circumstances affect the application of the institution of the *Kyría/Kyreia*, which became more of a contingent solution than a bureaucratic necessity (Ramsey 2016b).[15] Therefore Krateros provided the economic security Amastris needed to be wedded because he aimed to establish his political connection with Herakleia through Amastris. He acknowledged the diplomatic value of her symbolic capital, which Apame had too.

On this occasion, Herakleia entered the *diadochoi*'s political sphere as the main centre for the control of the Hellespont area, and henceforth Dionysios' political action was bonded to the Hellenistic conquerors. After Krateros' death, Dionysios' loyalty went to Antigonos. The bond between the two rulers was reinforced through an *epigamia*: Dionysios wed his daughter to the Macedonian governor of the area, Antigonos' nephew Ptolemy (Memnon *BNJ* 434 F 1.4.6). Consequently, Antigonos gradually strengthened his connection to Herakleia and Dionysios: the satrap took part in the campaigns and wars of the *diadochoi* on Antigonos' side, acting as a *philos* of the king. From the literary sources, he also appears to have acquired the title of βασιλεύς (Memnon *BNJ* 434 F 1.4.8; Diodoros 20.109.7); nevertheless, the name of Dionysios disappears from the coins, and it is replaced by the city name, suggesting an actual weakening of the independence of the ruler from the Hellenistic *diadochoi*.

4. Amastris and the Shaping of Hellenistic Queenship

As mentioned, while she was the wife of Dionysios, Amastris had economic autonomy and likely contributed to the inclusion of Herakleia in the influence of the *diadochoi*; nevertheless, during those years, as was usual for Persian women, she appears not to have had an actual, formal political role or royal function. This clearly changes after the death of Dionysios, as Memnon states: "On the point of death he appointed this woman as mistress of all he possessed and, together with some others, as guardian of the children who were just infants" (Memnon *BNJ* 434 F 1.4.8).[16] Amastris acquired a public political role, since she was left as mistress, *despoina*, of all the regions ruled by her deceased husband, as well as guardian, *epitropos*, of the dynastic succession of her three children, Amastris, Klearchos, and Oxathres. The Persian princess was put in charge of the administration, the diplomacy, and the military power of the satrapy, with the support of Antigonos: "Even after his departure from among men the affairs of the city tended no less towards prosperity since Antigonos provided for both the children of Dionysios and the citizens in no cursory fashion" (Memnon *BNJ* 434 F 1.4.9).[17]

There is no other evidence of wives of kings being named guardians or successors to rule at this time in a Hellenistic context: if Persian royal women certainly had an informal authority, they had no formal and public ruler image. Moreover, at this time, if Hellenistic queens, such as Phila, Apame, and Stratonike, were increasingly being incorporated formally into many public aspects of the monarchic rule, especially diplomatic protocols and royal cults, such appointments were mainly in support of their husbands' policy and diplomacy.[18] In becoming mistress of the satrapy, Amastris had no precedent to turn to for shaping the image of the formal political power entrusted to her; she devoted the following years to creating the image of the female royal authority, setting a Hellenistic precedent.

5. *Auto-Ecdosis*

At the beginning of the fourth war of the *diadochoi* in 303/2 BCE, Lysimachos crossed into Asia, and, in order to strengthen his position against Antigonos, he sought an understanding with the ruler of the satrapy, Amastris, as narrated by Memnon (Landucci Gattinoni 1992: 134–48; Franco 1993: 140–3; Müller 2013a):

When he turned his thoughts to other matters, Lysimachos once more took charge of the affairs of Herakleia and of the children and he even made Amastris his wife. In the beginning he loved her exceedingly but when trouble befell him he left her in Herakleia while he himself was engaged in pressing matters. After no length of time when he had rested from his many labours, he summoned her to Sardis and continued to love her just the same. (Memnon *BNJ* 434 F 1.4.9)[19]

As noticed by Sheila Ager, "it is certainly clear that royal weddings could not have taken place without some initial formal agreement between the parties, an agreement that might specify the size of the dowry, and might also formulate the terms of a treaty" (2017: 166). And as we have seen above, in the previous marriage of Amastris to Dionysios, the terms of the treaty were formulated by Krateros, who acted as her *kyrios* and provided for her dowry. Conversely, in this specific case, no father, brother, or husband negotiated the *ecdosis* of Amastris or economically supported her.[20] The status of *despoina* of Herakleia might have granted her independence from the male guardianship and allowed her autonomously to take a military and diplomatic initiative. Although the ruler likely consulted with her *philoi* about the terms of the *epigamia,* she chose to betroth herself to Lysimachos and acquired further international recognition of her political authority in the area.[21]

On his side, Lysimachos, in marrying the ruler herself, pursued a rather invasive infiltration policy in the region. Since the *diadochos* aimed to build an empire on the Straits, which would control both shores of the Black Sea, Herakleia was no longer just another regional capital but was meant to be one of the capitals of the empire together with Sardis, capital of Asia Minor (Franco 1993: 140–2). Consequently, Herakleia was more than an important ally for the control of the area; it was the main Asiatic port on the Black Sea of Lysimachos' empire. Memnon's insistence on the extraordinary love bonding the two rulers is evidence of the public attention given to the new couple and to the fame engendered and experienced by this new alliance: the emotional connection and familial harmony between them was exceptional from the beginning, and, after a moment of temporary separation due to pressing matters, the strength of their love reunited Amastris to Lysimachos again in Sardis. The importance of familial love and harmony in the image of Hellenistic dynasties has been investigated recently by Sabine Müller (2016: 127).[22] As she observes:

The public staging of harmony, unity and mutual love in the royal family was a key factor in the legitimization of the Hellenistic dynasties. In ancient sources, there are traces of this ideology of a dynastic idyll. We hear about royal siblings deeply caring for each other, kings and queens in love … The dynastic harmony theme had a multi-faceted meaning. First, it transported the message that the ruling house stood solid as a rock guaranteeing for a safe rule that was not troubled by inner-dynastic strife causing social wars. A dynasty united in harmony promised peace, wealth and a good life for the inhabitants of the empire. In addition, the image provided a warning for potential foreign rivals for the throne implying that there would be no chance to interfere. The ruling family united in love and mutual respect was invincible.

The advertised love Lysimachos felt for Amastris also presented the Herakleian ruler as worthy of the admiration, desire, and affection of the Hellenistic king. It is hence arguable that the public promotion of the reciprocity of love between the royal couple advertised the image of the wife of the king as valuable to the king himself; the reciprocity thus underscored the position of the wife as joint ruler with her husband.[23]

6. Self-Promotion: City Foundation, Eponymy, and Minting

Around 299 BCE, Lysimachos, due to foreign politics, married one of the daughters of Ptolemy I Soter, Arsinoë, and Amastris returned to Herakleia, remaining a political ally of the Macedonian king and likely acting as local ruler for him (Landucci Gattinoni 1992: 164–7).[24] Memnon's fragment yields evidence of the political actions undertaken by Amastris following the establishment of this new political situation:

> But later he [Lysimachos] transferred his love to the daughter of Ptolemy (her name was Arsinoë) and he gave cause to Amastris to divorce him, and she left him and returned to Herakleia. When she had arrived there she founded Amastris and united the people together to make of it one city. (Memnon *BNJ* 434 F 1.4.9)[25]

Such political actions are confirmed by Porphyry: "For Kappadokia, Armenia, Bithynia, Herakleia, Bosphoros and other provinces withdrew from the power of the Macedonians and established different kings for themselves" (Porphyry *BNJ* 260 F 41). The Herakleian ruler left Lysimachos' court and moved back to her satrapy, where, alone, she re-established and reinforced her presence in the area. Amastris unified the people of Sesamos, Kromna, Kytaros, and Tios, becoming the *oikist* as well as the eponym of the city of Amastris, where she installed her residence.[26]

Starting with Kassandros' inauguration of Thessalonike for his wife, already by the fourth century BCE kings founded and refounded cities and named them after Hellenistic royal women. At almost the same time as the foundation of Amastris, Seleukos had named three cities after his Persian wife Apame. Among them was the Apameia that, together with Laodikeia,

Antioch, and Seleukeia in Pieria, formed the Seleukid Tetrapolis: Seleukos marked the names of the royal couple and of the king's parents on the land of the new Seleukid centre, and involved the royal women in the representation of power in the territory on which it was exerted (Carney 1988 and 2000: 207–9; Cohen 1995: 101–5; Ogden 1999: 119; Widmer 2016). Nevertheless, Amastris is the only known case of a royal woman founding and naming her own city.

Conversely, such a practice was rather well established among male rulers since Philip II became *oikist* and the eponym of Philippi in 356: there he reproposed the heroic tradition of the mythic Greek city-founders and eponyms, resorting to heroic elements while shaping and establishing his kingship.[27] Following his example, Philip's son Alexander made the act of founding and naming cities one of the characteristics of his conquest.[28] This practice was adopted consistently and enhanced by the Epigonoi when they established their kingdoms (Marasco 1983).[29] In particular, in the founding narrative of royal propaganda, the king not only founds and names the cities of the territory he conquers, but he also actively concocts the urban planning (Leschhorn 1984: 338–9).[30] By unifying and connecting several smaller towns or villages, and creating a new political and administrative entity, the Hellenistic ruler borrows elements of the founder-hero to implement the image of the king-architect. As the coeval Hellenistic *Basilissa*, Amastris also actively and physically created her own kingdom, shaping the land as the territorial incarnation of the royal identity.[31]

Amastris in 299 BCE replicated this ruling strategy at a local level, in her territory: not only did she found and name the city of Amastris, but she actually created it by unifying four pre-existing cities through *synoikismos*. The ruler gave them a collective administrative, economic, and political centre in Sesamos, where she built her acropolis, as beautifully described by Strabo:

> After the Parthenios River, then, one comes to Amastris, a city bearing the same name as the woman who founded it. It is situated on a peninsula and has harbours on either side of the isthmus. Amastris was the wife of Dionysios the tyrant of Herakleia and the daughter of Oxathres, the brother of the Darius whom Alexander fought. Now she formed the city out of four settlements, Sesamos and Kytorum and Kromna (which Homer mentions in his marshalling of the Paphlagonian ships) and, fourth, Tios. This last, however, soon revolted from the united city, but the other three remained together; and, of these three, Sesamos is called the acropolis of Amastris. (12.3.10)

Amastris financed the urbanization and monumentalizing with her own newly minted coins (de Callataÿ 2004; Erçiyas 2003: 1420–1). She issued silver and bronze coins employing the Herakleian weight coin system (Gorini 2002), while in Herakleia the mints of the city adopted the Attic-weight tetradrachm, besides the local standard staters.[32] Amastris' silver staters and bronze issues and their iconography have been explored thoroughly by de Callataÿ (2004). On the obverse of the bronze and silver coins is the head of a youth, identifiable as Mithras, rather than as Amastris herself or an Amazon, wearing a Persian headdress with wreath. On the reverse, the issues bear Amastris' name with the title of *Basilissa*, ΒΑΣΙΛΙΣΣΗΣ ΑΜΑΣΤΡΙΟΣ. The bronze exemplars have only a bow in its quiver, while the silver coins show a leaning sceptre and a veiled and enthroned Aphrodite on the left, holding Eros, who presents a wreath (with visible leaves, as suggested by Catharine Lorber) to a radiate head of Helios (figure 3.2). In an alternative series, the reverse Aphrodite has a cylindrical crown, a *polos*, and, instead of Eros, a Nike crowns either her or her title, while Helios is no longer present (figure 3.3).

The young male with a Phrygian bonnet – Mithras – openly recalled the Persian ancestry of Amastris and was consistent with her choice to adopt the Persian weight as standard. Although the ruler was wife of two Macedonian *diadochoi* and of a Greek dynast, Amastris chose not to promote the legitimacy of her claim by building primarily on her Greco-Macedonian connection. Her queenship was instead promoted as rooted in her family lineage, in her descent from Oxathres, the brother of Darius, as it is obsessively repeated by the literary sources (Diodoros 20.109.7; Arrian *Anab.* 7.4.5; Strabo 12.3.10; Memnon *BNJ* 434 F 1.4.4). Similar to what was done by kings, between the family of origin and the family by marriage, Amastris openly grants prominence to the former.

The reverse of the coin has been interpreted convincingly as Aphrodite.[33] There are several instances of Hellenistic royal women and consorts identified with Aphrodite and often honoured with civic cults, starting with Phila Aphrodite (Athenaios 255c).[34] Scholars have suggested that this association was due to the attribution to the royal women of the goddess' sexuality and domesticity – valuable qualities for the wife-mother of the king (Carney 2000: 220–5; Ramsey 2016a). Nevertheless, in the Seleukid environment, Aphrodite with less domestic features appeared also in association with queens; in particular, Panagiotis Iossif and Catharine Lorber (2007) have related the military victory of Nikephoros to the goddess, exploring the association of at least two Seleukid queens, Stratonike and Laodike III, with the militarily victorious Aphrodite.[35] Not accidentally, in the Iranian East, Aphrodite had been related to the Iranian deity Anahita, also goddess of fertility, waters, and sea conveyance, who additionally had bellicose features and gave aid against the enemy.[36] Most important, Anahita was the divinity

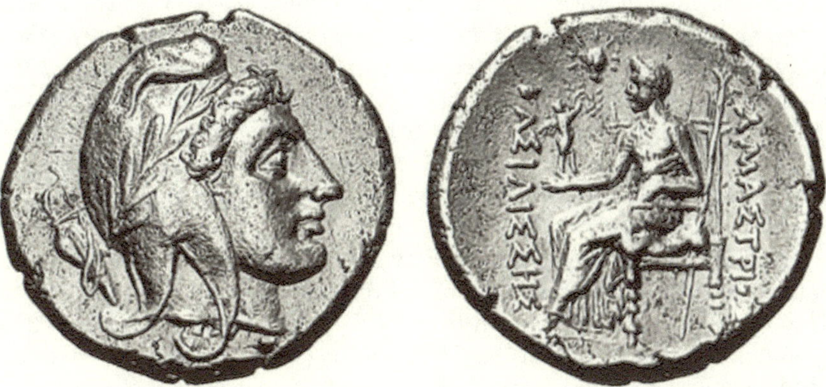

Figure 3.2 Silver didrachm (9.67 g), 300–288 BCE, from Amastris. *Obverse*: Head of young male with no beard, right, wearing Persian headdress with wreath; bow in quiver behind. *Reverse*: ΑΜΑΣΤΡΙΟ[Σ] ΒΑΣΙΛΙΣΣΗΣ, veiled Aphrodite seated on a throne, left, holding Eros bearing a wreath to the head of Helios; sceptre leaning against throne.

Auction 275 (22.09.2011) lot 3674 www.acsearch.info/search.html?id=1087716
Photo courtesy of Gerhard Hirsch Nachfolger www.coinhirsch.de/.

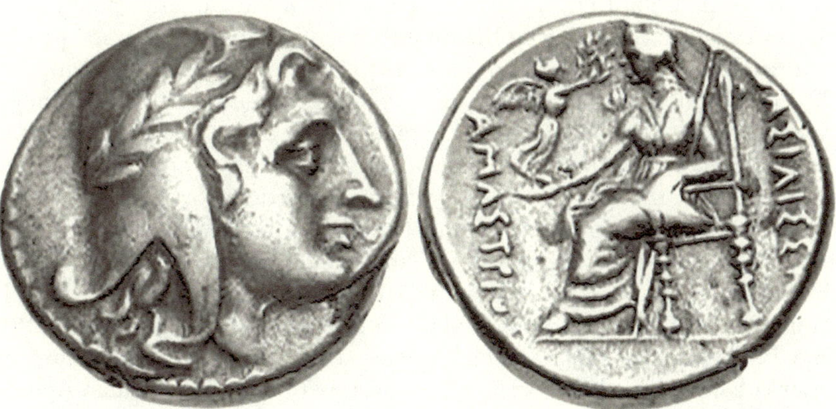

Figure 3.3 Silver stater (9.71 g), 300–288 BCE, from Amastris. *Obverse*: Head of young male with no beard, right, wearing Persian headdress with wreath. *Reverse*: ΒΑΣΙΛΙΣΣ[ΗΣ] ΑΜΑΣΤΡΙΟΣ, Aphrodite seated left, holding (lotus-tipped?) sceptre, and Nike, who crowns her with wreath.

CNG Auction 94 (18.09.2013) lot 401 (cf. www.acsearch.info/search.html?id=1682667)
Photo courtesy of Classical Numismatic Group, Inc. www.cngcoins.com/.

responsible for the investiture of kings, as she enthroned the Achaimenid kings, and was thus closely connected with royalty and legitimacy (Hanaway 1982; Muccioli 2016). Therefore, the crown-bearing Nike and the *polos* associated with Aphrodite/Anahita on Amastris' coins portrayed the militant goddess of victory, responsible for enthroning monarchs. This image likely aimed to induce the people of the satrapy to identify the victorious goddess with the successful queen, who clearly was making a statement of the legitimacy of her rule.[37]

Additionally, the astral iconography of the staters portrays the veiled enthroned Aphrodite while sustaining Eros who offered Helios the wreath. The presence of and interaction between Helios, Aphrodite, and Eros long ago induced Imhoof-Blumer (1883: 229) to suggest the interpretation of the goddess as Aphrodite Ourania. In fact, Anahita, as well as the Asia Minor Aphrodite, was also ascribed the celestial features of Ourania, as wife of Helios.[38] By suggesting the identification between Amastris and the goddess, the coin might ultimately present the queen as offering herself as the astral wife of the celestial god Helios, symbol of male kingship itself.[39]

7. The Name of the Famous Queen

The Achaimenid royal women did not play any part in religious ceremonies (Brosius 1996: 199). Nevertheless, the role of founder and eponym of a city was connected closely to the establishment of honours, if not a proper cult, to commemorate the creation of the city itself by its *oikist* (Muccioli 2011). The cults for the founder are very well attested for Hellenistic kings, celebrating them as *oikist* and name giver of the city.[40] The cult attributed to the founder the role of protector of the city as well as *ktistes* of the rule (Marasco 1983). Thus, the absence of divine honours for Amastris as the founder of her eponymous city would be rather unusual. This would be even more peculiar considering that de Callataÿ (2004) has shown that the image on Amastris' coins portrayed an actual statue of the goddess in the city, indicating the presence of a shrine for the cult of Amastris' Aphrodite. It thus may be argued that religious celebrations existed, either as *timai* or proper ruler cults: they likely associated the queen with her divine avatar, Aphrodite, creating one of those symbioses well attested for Hellenistic queens.[41]

The religious ceremonies for Amastris as *oikist* and protector of the city were a novelty required for shaping the new queenship as politically visible leadership. She crafted and promoted an image of herself and her *fama* as the founder of her own rule, the creator of her own dynasty, the architect of her own city, and the minting authority of her own coins. However, Amastris did not present herself as a king; instead she borrowed from Hellenistic kingship those features useful to shape her female leadership without eliminating the male component while sublimating it to a symbolic level. She adopted the Greco-Macedonian title of *Basilissa* on her coins but gave a new meaning to it. Increasingly attested since Phila, wife of Demetrios I Poliorketes, used it in the fourth century, *Basilissa* designated Hellenistic royal women, daughters, mothers, sisters, and wives of kings. This female title appeared related to a *Basileos* mainly to indicate the female relatives of the king or the female members of the royal court (Carney 2000: 169, 225–8; Muccioli 2013: 80–1). If in the Persian context it did not identify any political function,[42] in Hellenistic times the title appeared mainly in inscriptions relative to religious contexts, inducing Carney (2011) to highlight that, "like the female title, female cult seems to suggest the need to understand power as both male and female, though hardly equally divided." The female title thus was understood mainly in relation to the male counterpart from which the *Basilissa* derived her status.

With regard to Amastris, the absence of any reference to a male authority from whom she would derive her title is puzzling. It is rather uncertain whether Dionysios actually bore the title of *Basileos*, as is attested only in the literary tradition (Memnon *BNJ* 434 F 1.4.6). On the one hand, the title does not appear on any of his coins; on the other, he never had any authority over the city of Amastris. Additionally, it is very clear that Amastris was not considered as Lysimachos' *Basilissa*, since she had administratively detached herself from her former king and husband Lysimachos, while still politically cooperating with him.[43]

Amastris is the first Hellenistic ruler to employ the title *Basilissa* outside religious contexts, and the first to publicize it on coins. Building on her ancestry, Amastris claimed the title for herself on her issues, picturing Helios himself as the only male entity. She attributed to the *Basilissa* the new features of her queenship, and, borrowing from the new contemporary Hellenistic monarchic examples, she created a whole new idea of female regality wherein the *Basilissa* could and did formally exert political, military, economic, and administrative authority.

8. The Epilogue: Posthumous Fame

Amastris' queenship lasted beyond the coming of age of her sons, who were appointed leaders in Herakleia and successors to the mother in her *Basileia*. The two princes, hoping to take over the throne, killed their mother and queen, drowning her at sea after she had boarded a ship. Following the murder of the *Basilissa*, Klearchos and Oxathres welcomed Lysimachos into the region, expecting their rule to be acknowledged by the king. However, instead of welcoming their succession, Lysimachos sentenced the two princes to death, confirming that Amastris was governing the area either as his ally or his local ruler. The king took direct control of the area; he proceeded to include the former *Basileia* of the queen in his kingdom by confiscating the wealth and giving a democratic constitution to Herakleia, at first. Nevertheless, soon afterwards he gave the region to his wife Arsinoë, confirming the relevance of the area: the new *Basilissa* controlled Herakleia through a garrison and a minister, probably an *epistates* named Herakleides of Kyme (Memnon *BNJ* 434 F 1.5.2–3).[44]

The memory of the fame of Amastris and of her great *Basileia* was celebrated and broadcasted by Lysimachos, as preserved by Memnon (*BNJ* 434 F 1.5.4): "When Lysimachos had returned to his own realm he held Amastris in praise. He admired both her ways and how her kingdom was strengthened in size, greatness and power. While he exalted Herakleia, he included in his praises both Tios and Amastris which she had founded and named after herself."[45]

According to Lysimachos' tribute to Amastris, the ruler's greatness and positive fame was not linked to her domestic skills, her motherly attitude, her behaviour as loving wife, or her piety toward the gods. The praise for the royal woman, the *Basilissa*, was that she enriched and enlarged her kingdom and ruled it powerfully. Thus, the queen is celebrated in the literary tradition, and her iconography is preserved by Lysimachos on the coins of her city after her death – but with the addition of an eight-rayed star on the obverse, interpreted as evidence of her probable divinization (figure 3.4).[46] On this matter, the narrative of Amastris' death offered the ideal background for her divinization: it cannot be interpreted as coincidence that the *Basilissa* died at sea, on board a ship, as if she were reconnecting herself to her divine avatar Aphrodite/Anahita, goddess of water and sea and of naval transportation.[47] The peculiar and symbolic way Amastris was killed yielded likely material for a popular narrative, circulated and promoted by Lysimachos himself, while he was taking control of the *Basileia* and entrusting it directly to his wife and *Basilissa* Arsinoë. The fame of the *Basilissa* Amastris transcended her *Basileia* and her life, appealing to the younger successor, who subsequently claimed the area for herself. Without venturing to explore the complex life and fame of the future Arsinoë II, Philadelphos of Egypt, it might however be worth noting that a third-century hymn to Arsinoë-Aphrodite, preserved in a second-century BCE papyrus, attributed to the *Basilissa* both the role of patroness of a city and of mistress of the sea (and of the navy) (*P. Lit. Goodsp.* 2, I–IV; Barbantani 2005). It would be difficult not to detect in these roles the echo of Amastris' experience, whose fame might have inspired the queenship(s) of her successor, Arsinoë.[48]

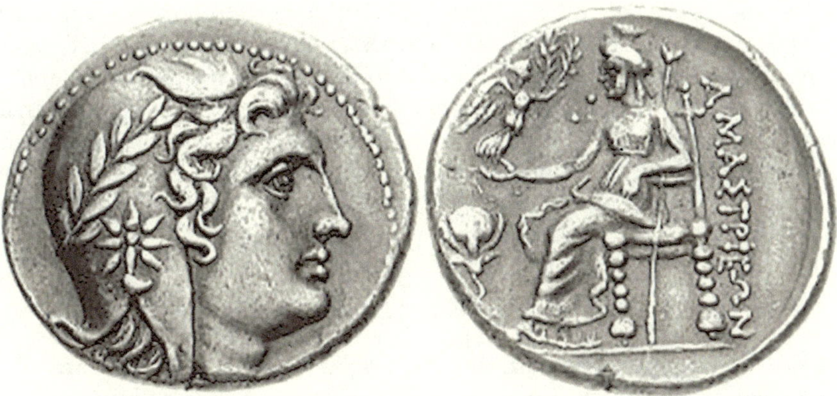

Figure 3.4 Silver stater (9.54 g), 288/285?–250 BCE, from Amastris. *Obverse*: Head of young male with no beard, right, wearing Persian headdress adorned with laurel wreath and eight-rayed star below. *Reverse*: Aphrodite seated left with *polos*, holding Nike, who crowns her with wreath, in extended right hand, and in left arm cradling lotus-tipped sceptre and resting on throne; rose bud to left, ΑΜΑΣΤΡΙΕΩΝ to right.

CNG Mail Bid Sale 78 (14.05.2008) lot 751 (cf. www.acsearch.info/search.html?id=472427). From the Sunrise Collection. Ex Robert Schonwalter Collection (Triton V, 15.01.2002), lot 1400; Coin Galleries (18.08.1978), lot 282; Coin Galleries (20.04.1961), lot 132; Ars Classica 14 (2.07.1929), lot 298.

Amastris' experience was, to some extent, an isolated experiment. The peculiarity of her personal background and of the metamorphic historical context around her allowed her to move between cultures and to manipulate the social conventions to create a new political profile. By means of appropriation of the title and functions of *basileus* in her actions (as *oikist*, as administrative and diplomatic authority) and in the representation of her rule (in her numismatic issues as well as in Lysimachos' praise of the greatness and power of her kingdom), Amastris not only crafted her own *Basileia* but she also shaped her own fame. She was no victim of someone else's rumour on her *Basileia*: she consciously directed the viewer's gaze to the forces at play to create her political support. While inventing new procedures, she stressed her connections with the past local tradition; while experimenting with a political alternative to Hellenistic kingship, she enhanced the connections and similarities with the state model of Alexander's successors.

Her independence, her ability to move interculturally, and her apparent conscious self-advancement (and self-preservation) likely inspired later experiences, yet belonged specifically to Amastris' anomalous cast and essence. As a consequence, on the one hand, at least for the next hundred years, no woman would be able to control her own agency and appearance as Amastris had; on the other, some functions that she attributed to the *Basilissa* would never be replicated.

NOTES

1 See Ager on Tryphaina in chapter 1 of this volume. I am grateful to Catharine Lorber and the two anonymous readers for the Press for their kind and meaningful feedback on this paper.

2 See the introduction to this volume.

3 For a recent summary of our knowledge of Memnon, see Paganoni 2015; see further Keaveney and Madden 2015.

4 On Herakleia and its tyranny, see Burstein 1974: 75–7; Saprykin 1997: 131–57; Bittner 1998. Throughout this chapter, citations of the Greek text of Memnon, and the English translation of it, derive from Keaveney and Madden 2015.

5 On Krateros, see Heckel 1992: 107–33.

6 Among other officers who kept their wives after Alexander's death is the famous case of Seleukos, who spent the subsequent years in the East and built his empire on his wife's homeland. Similar are the cases of Alexander's *philos*, the navarch and historian Nearchos, and the Greco-Persian noble Barsine. On the Susa wedding and the decisions defining Alexander's policy in 324 and 323, see Olbrycht 2016.

7 Brosius 1996: 123–9: "Greek and Near Eastern sources give ample evidence that royal women of the Achaimenid household could control land holdings within the empire. These lands are known to have been located in the Persis and Babylonia, as well as in Media and Syria. Over a continuous period of almost one hundred years royal women are reported to have been estate holders." See in particular the case of Irdabama, discussed in ibid., 129–44.

8 See also Olbrycht 2016.

9 *I. Didyma* 480 ll. 1–7: Λύκος Ἀπολλοδότ[ου εἶπεν·] | περὶ ὧν προεγράψατο εἰς τὴμ βουλὴν Δημοδάμας Ἀρ[ιστείδου,] | ὅπως Ἀπάμη ἡ Σελεύκου τοῦ βασιλέως γυνὴ τ[ιμηθῆι,] | δεδόχθαι τῆι βουλῆι καὶ τῶι δήμωι· ἐπειδὴ Ἀπά[μη ἡ βα] | σίλισσα πρότερόν τε πολλὴν εὔνοιαν καὶ προ[θυμίαν] | παρείχετο περὶ Μιλησίων τοὺς στρατευομένου[ς σὺν] | [τ]ῶι βασιλεῖ Σελεύκωι.

10 On Apame, see also Widmer 2016. On agency and image of third-century Hellenistic royal women, see D'Agostini 2016; on women in the Hellenistic age generally, see Ramsey 2016b.

11 See also Robert 1984.

12 See Carney 2000.

13 One of the readers for the Press notes that Perikles acted as *kyrios* for his first wife's remarriage, with her own consent, according to Plutarch, *Per.* 24.5.

14 I have found no Macedonian attestation of male guardianship (*Kyria*) of adult women. The term is, however, attested in relation to the tutorship of children. On the coeval use of the term for territorial administrative appointment in Macedonia and Seleukid Asia Minor, see Capdetrey 2007: 284–6; D'Agostini 2013. See, in general, Cudjoe 2010; Le Bohec-Bouhet 2006.

15 For later use of the term, see in general Evans Grubbs 2002: 34–7.

16 Μέλλων τελευτᾶν ταύτην τε τῶν ὅλων δέσποιναν καταλιμπάνει καὶ τῶν παίδων κομιδῆι νηπίων ὄντων σύν τισιν ἑτέροις ἐπίτροπον.

17 Οὐδὲν δὲ ἧττον καὶ μετὰ τὴν ἐκείνου ἐξ ἀνθρώπων ἀναχώρησιν τὰ τῆς πόλεως πρὸς εὐδαιμονίαν ἐφέρετο, ᾿Αντιγόνου τῶν τε παίδων Διονυσίου καὶ τῶν πολιτῶν οὐ παρέργως προνοουμένου.

18 On the concurrent experimentation with the title and image of *Basilissa* for Stratonike I, see Michel 2017; Widmer 2019. On the public role of the *Basilissa*, see Carney 2000: 165–9; Widmer 2016: 17–34. See also Savalli-Lestrade 1994; Carney 2011.

19 Ἐκείνου δὲ πρὸς ἕτερα τὰς φροντίδας τρεψαμένου, Λυσίμαχος πάλιν τῶν περὶ ῾Ηράκλειαν καὶ τῶν παίδων ἐπεμελεῖτο, ὃς καὶ ῎Αμαστριν ποιεῖται γυναῖκα· καὶ κατ᾽ ἀρχὰς μὲν λίαν ἔστερξε, πραγμάτων δὲ αὐτῶι προσπεσόντων, αὐτὴν μὲν ἐν ῾Ηρακλείαι λείπει, αὐτὸς δ᾽ εἴχετο τῶν ἐπειγόντων. Εἰς Σάρδεις δὲ μετ᾽ οὐ πολὺν χρόνον, τῶν πολλῶν πόνων ῥάισας, μετεπέμψατο ταύτην, καὶ ἔστεργεν ὁμοίως.

20 On the *auto-ecdosis* of Cleopatra IV, see the chapter by Ager in this volume.

21 Compare Cleopatra Thea and Antiochos VII Sidetes, and Arsinoë II and Ptolemy Keraunos; see also Vatin 1970: 98.

22 See also Schmitt 1991; Carney 2013: 37; van Bremen 2003: 328.

23 See also Carney 2011.

24 On Lysimachos' second marriage, see Dmitriev 2007 and Carney 2013: 30–7. Interesting observations were made in this regard by Branko van Oppen in his paper "Amastris: The First Hellenistic Queen," presented at *The Eleventh Celtic Conference in Classics*, University of St Andrews, 11–14 July 2018.

25 Ὕστερον δὲ πρὸς τὴν θυγατέρα (2) Πτολεμαίου τοῦ Φιλαδέλφου (᾿Αρσινόη δὲ ἦν τὸ ὄνομα) τὸν ἔρωτα μεταθείς, διαζυγῆναι τὴν ῎Αμαστριν αὐτοῦ παρέσχεν αἰτίαν, καὶ καταλιποῦσαν τοῦτον καταλαβεῖν τὴν ῾Ηράκλειαν. Ἐγείρει δὲ αὕτη παραγενομένη, καὶ συνοικίζει πόλιν ῎Αμαστριν.

26 Tios reclaimed its autonomy rather soon.

27 Asheri 1996; Boddez 2016, with detailed bibliography on the relation to Hellenistic heroic and divine cults. Notably, the heroic cult could be attributed only posthumously.

28 On Alexander's colonization, see in particular Fraser 1996 and Briant 1998.

29 See Leschhorn 1984: 223–88, and specifically on Lysimachos' foundations and colonization, 254–7.

30 On the foundation narratives, see Kosmin 2014: 211–18.

31 Capdetrey 2007: 67: "Ce mode d'expression du pouvoir royal montre … que la royauté hellénistique pouvait être une royauté territorial s'incarnant dans un espace constitutif de l'identité royale."

32 The adoption of the double standard in Herakleia, while Amastris issues exclusively coins of local weight, might be connected with the international vocation of Herakleia as a port, a city centred on trade, different from the administrative capital of the area of Amastris.

33 For a complete summary of the *état des questions*, see de Callataÿ 2004.

34 On this topic, see specifically Carney 2000: 220–5 (with bibliography) and 2011. See also Barbantani 2005 on the use of the association of Aphrodite with Ptolemaic queens from Arsinoë II Philadelphos.

35 On the military attributes of Aphrodite, see Budin 2003: 273–82 and Pironti 2005; on the cult of Seleukid queens, see Ager and Hardiman 2016; on Stratonike, see Ramsey 2016a; on Laodike III, see Widmer 2008.

36 On this syncretism, see Hanaway 1982 and Piras 2004.

37 See Perassi (2014) for the resemblance of the Hellenistic queen portraits to Aphrodite's features.

38 On Aphrodite Ourania, see in particular Pirenne-Delforge 2005.

39 On the use of the *epiclisis* "Ourania" for Hellenistic queens, see Bigwood 2004 and Muccioli 2013: 325–6.

40 For a complete, annotated collection of the attestation of the founder cult in Hellenistic times, see Leschhorn 1984: 202–333 and 339–434. Muccioli (2011) also explores the possibility of religious cults in Herakleia for Klearchos. See also Boddez (2016) on the relation between divine cults and city foundation.

41 On the cult for royal women in early Hellenism, see Caneva 2012 and 2014a. See also Carney 2000: 218–19.

42 See Brosius (1996: 18–20) on the Persian use of the term, which is even more broad than the Hellenistic one: "a Greek term used to identify certain women as members of the royal court or ruling house" (184).

43 After Lysimachos' wedding with Arsinoë, the queen's son Klearchos, ruling Herakleia for her, became a *philos* of the *diadochos* and campaigned with him against the Getae: Memnon *BNJ* 434 F 1.5.1–2.

44 On Lysimachos' policy toward Herakleia and the city of Amastris after Amastris' death, see Franco 1993: 143–53.

45 Λυσίμαχος δὲ τὴν ἰδίαν ἀρχὴν καταλαβών, δι᾽ ἐπαίνων μὲν τὴν Ἄμαστριν εἶχεν, ἐθαύμαζε δὲ αὐτῆς τούς τε τρόπους καὶ τὴν ἀρχήν, πρὸς ὄγκον καὶ μέγεθος καὶ

ἰσχὺν ὡς ἐκρατύνατο, ἐξαίρων μὲν τὴν Ἡράκλειαν, μέρος δὲ τῶν ἐπαίνων καὶ τὴν Τῖον καὶ τὴν Ἄμαστριν, ἣν ἐπώνυμον ἤγειρεν ἐκείνη, ποιούμενος·.

46 See de Callataÿ 2004 and Iossif and Lorber 2007.

47 On the narrative about the violent deaths of Hellenistic queens and their relevance for dynastic legitimacy, see Savalli-Lestrade 2015. On the divinization of Hellenistic monarchs, see the volume by Gnoli and Muccioli (2014), in particular the contributions by Landucci Gattinoni, Caneva, and Iossif. In the same volume, Ballesteros Pastor focuses on the fusion between the Hellenistic and Iranian tradition in the divinization of Mithridates Eupator.

48 On Arsinoë II and her relation with Amastris, see Carney 2013, in particular 37–43. On her cult, eponymous foundations, numismatic issues, and royal image among the many contributions, see Carney 2013: 106–24.

4

Remelted or Overstruck: Cases of Monetary *Damnatio Memoriae* in Hellenistic Times?

FRANÇOIS DE CALLATAŸ

1. Introduction

This book is about celebrity, fame, and infamy. Because coins are often described as the most common medium to propagate images in ancient times, they seem to form the best support to spread glory and celebrity. The line is thin between propagation and propaganda, and there is considerable literature about how rulers took advantage of this unique opportunity to communicate with their subjects. Recent research, however, has downplayed the effectiveness of such a propagandistic role for coins. Beyond the fact that the word "propaganda" itself has been subject to debate, the disagreement between opposite views is wide. "At one extreme," writes Andrew Burnett, "it can be thought that coins are really only economic objects, and that the designs placed on them are just incidental: they were chosen by a minor government department and were little noticed and generally misunderstood by a population that was largely illiterate or incapable of comprehending their subtle symbolism. At the other extreme, it can be thought that the emperor himself was interested in choosing the designs used on his coins to promote the various features of his reign which he wished to bring to the attention of the whole population." We might characterize these opposing views as the "economic" and the "propaganda" functions, even though the word "propaganda" is usually avoided nowadays, in favour of milder terms like "message" or "persuasiveness.'"[1]

In comparison with past decades, the current trend is to minimize the propaganda purpose coins may have served in ancient times. As there is a growing consensus that the first beneficiaries of Greek and Roman coins were soldiers, coin propaganda first should be considered as aimed at this specific audience. But, for the issuer, it was much more important to convince users to accept a currency than it was to dabble with images. Trust is indeed the fundamental concept of monetary matters. For Hellenistic kingdoms, Andrew Meadows and I have demonstrated repeatedly how victorious rulers were not embarrassed to use civic coinages – hence "pseudo-civic" – or even to strike coins with the image of their enemies.

In contrast with the vast literature about coins that propagate fame, this chapter deals with infamy. As far as we can judge, there is not a single case in the thousands of different Greek coin types that would have been deliberately conceived to stigmatize a person or a group. On the other hand, some coin issues were deliberately altered or removed from circulation by the new authority in charge with the idea to attack the memory of the person so immortalized.

Damnatio memoriae, a Latin phrase not recorded in ancient literature (it first appeared during the last third of the seventeenth century), here is defined simply as cancelling every trace of a public person who is proclaimed an enemy of the state, in order to obliterate his or her memory.[2] From a numismatic point of view, this was never easy to accomplish, since it required calling back coins that had been dispersed through circulation.[3] Realistically, the chances of achieving true eradication of an abominated currency were greater with small coinages not yet dispersed on a large scale.

It is not always easy for modern experts to decide on the nature of what they see, and, even more, of what they don't see. For those who look at coins, the possibility of dealing with a *damnatio memoriae* arises in different forms.[4] These forms could affect the surface of the coins or their very existence. If only the surface, they could be the result of some individual marks of execration or an official decision taken at some political level. More dramatically, coins could disappear by being massively overstruck or melted down.

2. Individual Surface Alterations: Marks of Execration

Execration marks should not be confused with test cuts that have been made to verify the alloy (frequent on Hellenistic silver coins), nor with graffiti. One commonly identifies them as deep cuts on sensitive areas, most generally the portrait. Sometimes historical circumstances reinforce the presumption of execration, as, for example, with the French silver écus of Louis XV and Louis XVI found in a hoard buried after 1792 at Châtelet (Belgium), out of which a considerable proportion present cuts on the neck of the king (figure 4.1).[5]

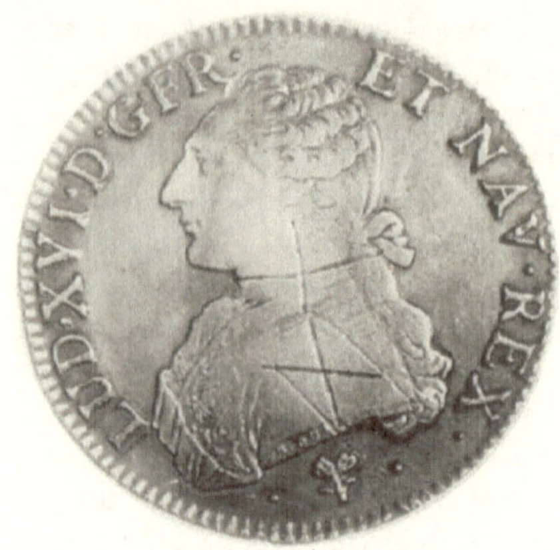

Figure 4.1 Coin of six *écus* of Louis XVI struck at Bayonne in 1789 with cut on his neck. (Callataÿ 1994a, pl. XXVIII, no. 228).

This type of phenomenon is rare for ancient coins and – to my knowledge – never organized into a pattern. We are left instead with what appear as individual initiatives for which it is nearly always hard to decide about the depth of political concern. At that individual level, idleness and inconsistency may have caused such disfiguration, as with a sestertius of Trajan (figure 4.2), one of the few emperors nearly unanimously praised by commentators and historians and about whom it seems more desperate than useful to suggest that "these marks may have been made by someone, perhaps a former Dacian prisoner or other victim of the war, to express their dissatisfaction at the subjugation of their homeland."[6]

Rare for Roman coins, these kind of cuts are even rarer for Greek coins. Commenting on an issue of Athenian bronze coins with the Pontic symbols (two crescents and an eight-rayed star), Jack Kroll argues for a quick demonetization, explaining some surface marks as "to void them as legal tender" (figure 4.3).[7] The fact that this issue has been demonetized is in itself questionable, but it is nearly certain that the cross chiselled on the cheek of Athena is an individual gesture.

3. Intentional Surface Alterations: Erasing or Countermarks

Admittedly a rare phenomenon, too, erased legends or portraits are well documented for the Roman world, in particular for the name of Sejanus (Lucius Aelius Seianus, prefect of the praetorian guard), which was carefully

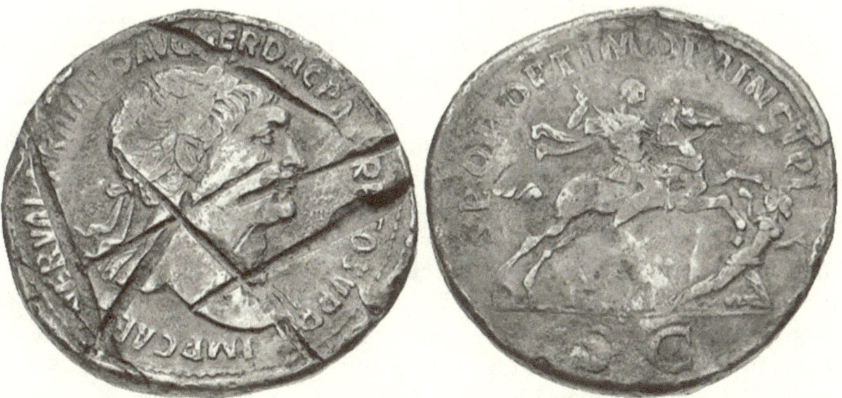

Figure 4.2 Sestertius of Trajan issued in Rome (ca 103–105 CE) and heavily defaced.

Classical Numismatic Group (hereafter CNG), Electronic Auction 349, 22 April 2015, 398 (27.51g).

(CNG – © Coinarchives.com).

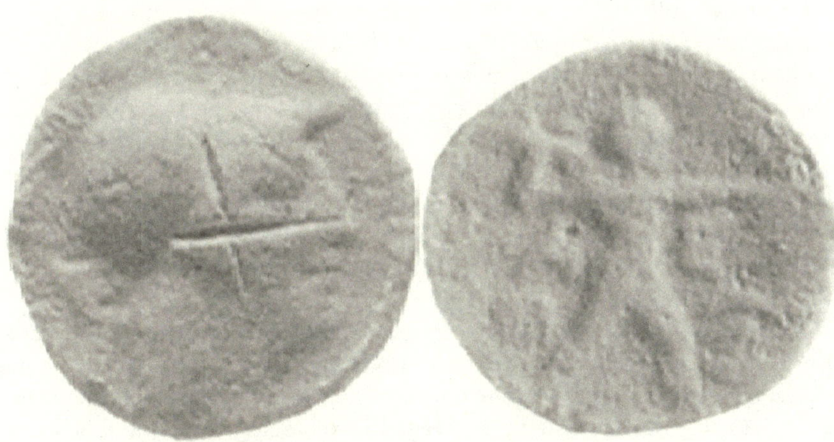

Figure 4.3 Athenian bronze coin with Pontic symbols defaced with a chisel mark (X) on the obverse.

(Kroll 1993, 74, no. 97h, pl. 9).

removed (figure 4.4) after the failure of his conspiracy against Tiberius (31 CE), and the name or the portrait of Geta, which was altogether deleted after he was killed by his brother Caracalla in 212 CE (figure 4.5).

These large bronze coins are spectacular and have been reproduced in many historical writings, but it is important to note that such intentional erasing action concerns only a limited number of all the coins struck in the name of Sejanus or Geta. Only bronze coins are affected and furthermore only in specific geographical areas: Bilbilis Augusta (near Tarraco in Spain) for Sejanus, and Asia Minor for Geta.[8] It has been noted that, for Geta in Asia Minor, only approximately fifty occurrences are known out of a much bigger number of coins on which nothing has been erased.[9] So, if they were done purposefully and linked with the general *damnatio*, such marks never were decided at the highest level but rather were only partially applied at a local level.

Considering the full picture of Roman coinages, erasures remain somewhere between very and extremely rare.[10] For many execrated figures such as Antony or Maxentius, there is a noticeable contrast between the high ratio of erasing on inscriptions and the nearly non-existent ratio for coins.

Cases of re-engraving of Greek coins are well attested (although the need for a general survey remains), but these are concentrated on control-marks and have nothing to do with *damnatio memoriae*.[11] Cases of political erasing are nearly unknown.[12] Among the few exceptions is a die of gold staters for the tyrant Hiketas at Syracuse, where, after his fall in 278 BCE, his name has been carefully deleted at the exergue on the die itself (figure 4.6).[13]

Another possible exception is provided by a unique Athenian tetradrachm in the names of King Mithridates and Aristion for which the typical Pontic symbols of two crescent and an eight-rayed star (in the right field of the reverse) have been replaced by a flat countermark with a headdress of Isis (figures 4.7 and 4.8). While it seems right that the purpose of the countermark was to erase the Pontic symbols, it is hard to understand why the name of King Mithridates (ΒΑΣΙ/ΛΕ – ΜΙ/ΘΡΑ – ΔΑ – ΤΗΣ) was left untouched.[14] Furthermore, it is again an isolated occurrence (one coin out of the seven known for this variety).

These two first categories (execration marks and erasure of the type) affect the surface of coins that may, however, continue to circulate. If one has to judge based only on them, one may conclude that neither the Romans nor (even less so) the Greeks ever succeeded in achieving what could be called a monetary *damnatio memoriae*. But such a conclusion would be premature, since it is much more efficient to completely transform the coins than to modify their surface locally. Coins could be transformed into metal by

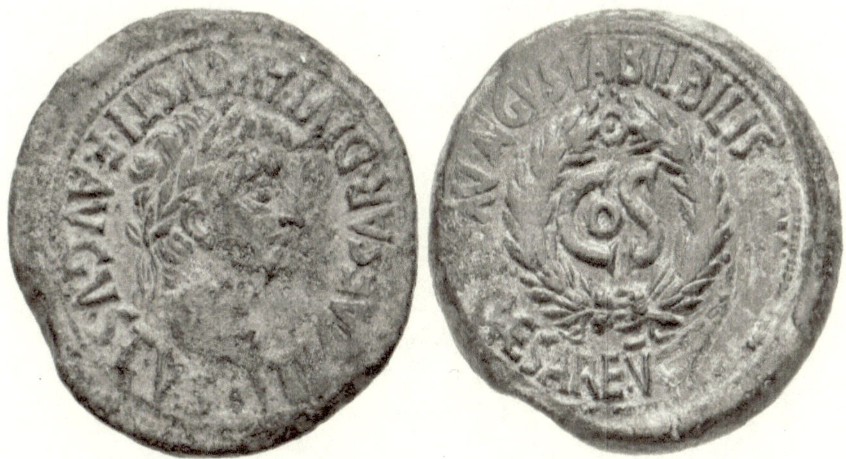

Figure 4.4 *As* in the name of Aelius Sejanus struck at Bilbilis in 31 CE, whose words AELI(o) SEIAN(o) have been erased.

(*Triton* XVIII, 6 January 2015, 869 – © Coinarchives.com).[15]

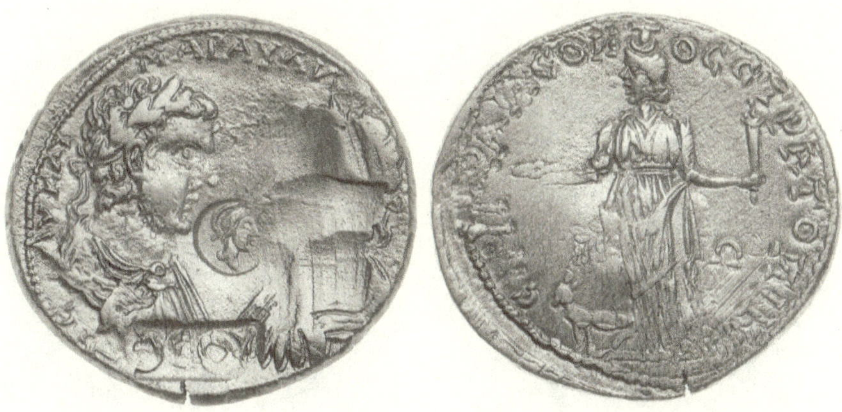

Figure 4.5 Large bronze coin (ca 212 CE) with the portraits of Caracalla and (erased) Geta, struck at Stratonicea.

(Ira and Larry Goldberg, 72, 5 February 2013, 4173 [19.47g] – © Coinarchives.com).[16]

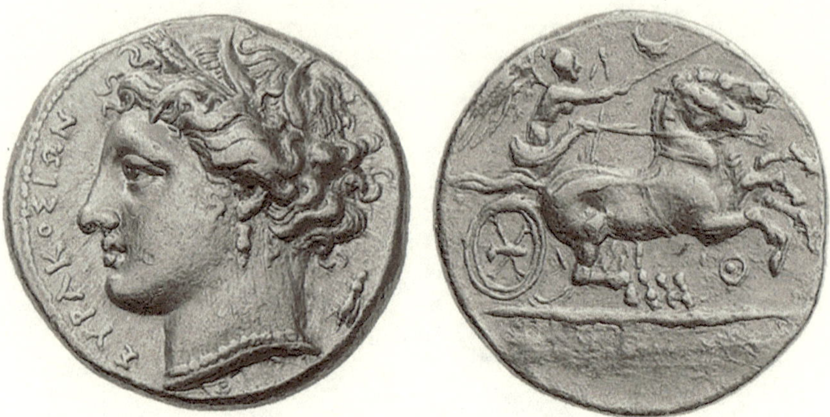

Figure 4.6 Hemistater of Hiketas issued at Syracuse, whose name has been erased (278 BCE).

(*Nomos* 8, 22 Oct. 2013, 58 [4.25g] – © Coinarchives.com).[17]

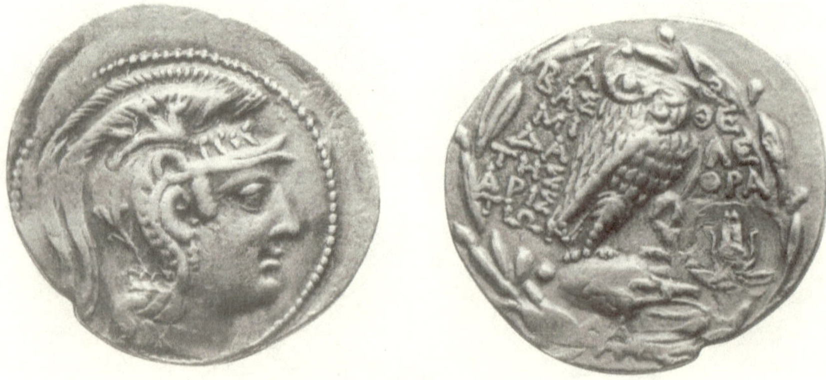

Figure 4.7 Athenian tetradrachm in the name of King Mithridates, whose Pontic symbols have been replaced by a headdress of Isis.

(de Callataÿ 1997, pl. LII, nr. F).[18]

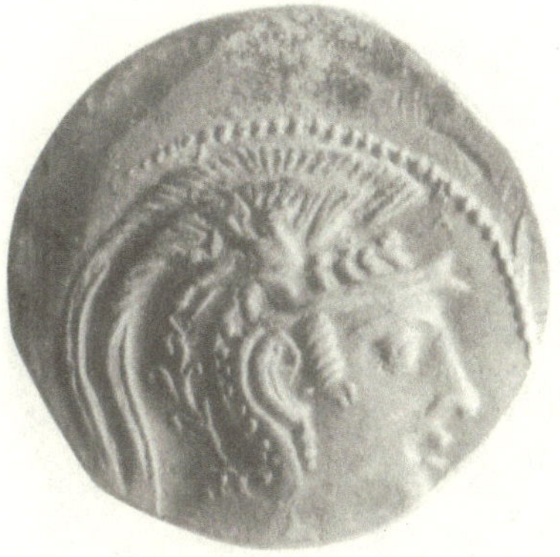
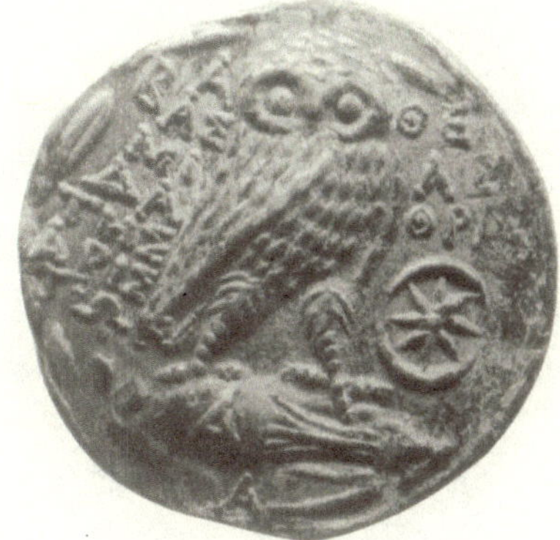

Figure 4.8 Athenian tetradrachm in the name of King Mithridates with the Pontic symbols of the crescent and the eight-rayed star.

(de Callataÿ 1997, pl. LII, nr. G).[19]

being melted down, or into other coins. To transform coins into other coins, the normal way to proceed – as the Delphic amphictiones did in the 330s BCE – is to melt them down in order to strike again. However, this process is longer and more expensive than to use ancient coins directly as blanks and to overstrike an old currency to produce a new one.

4. Recalled and Overstruck Hellenistic Coins

Coin overstrikes are a great resource for numismatic research since they provide fundamental keys for establishing the relative chronology and they allow identification of the movement of coins – their circulation (as hoards) as well as, more importantly, how they died – that is, how they were retrieved from circulation.[20]

Recognizable overstrikes concern a very small number of all Greek coins, much less than 1 per cent – more in the range of one out of a thousand. Any detected overstrike is in fact the result of an imperfect action. A prejudicial question, then, is: for any detected overstrike, how many more do we have to imagine for which the undertype left no trace at all? Georges Le Rider, in a 1971 essay that is still the best reading on the topic, argues for a limited coefficient.[21] To make the undertype disappear entirely is not an easy task. Subsequent research confirms the presumption, as overstrikes are not randomly dispersed through the full sequence but often limited to the coins struck with one or a bunch of connected obverse dies.[22]

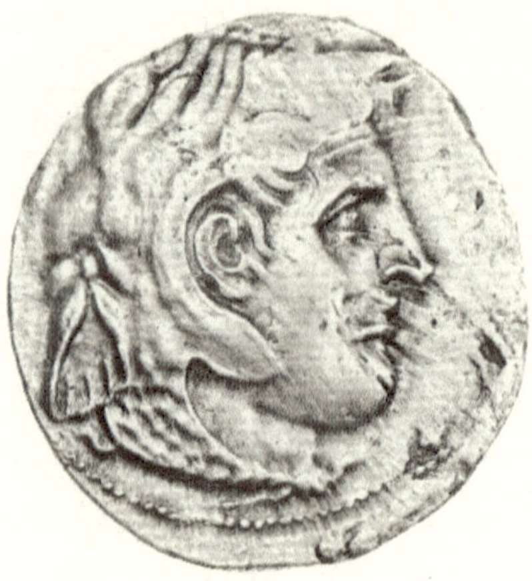
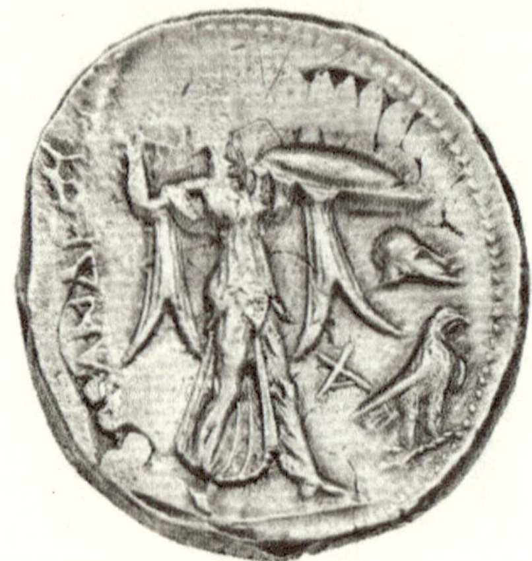

Figure 4.9 Tetradrachm of Ptolemy Soter (Alexandria, ca 310 BCE) overstruck on Alexander the Great.

(MacDonald 2007, 190, no. 243 [15.69g]).

Do we have examples of massive overstriking in Hellenistic times on coins issued by defeated rulers? At first glance, there may well be three instances: a) once for the Seleukids with the usurper Timarchos, and twice for the Parthians, with b) Tiridates, the only king who dared to proclaim himself on his coins *philoromaios*, "friend of the Romans," and c) Vonones, who overstruck the coins bearing the name of his hated stepmother, Musa.

But before we deal more specifically with these exceptional cases, it is worthwhile to make some general comments. Coins of Hellenistic rulers were not overstruck more frequently than the average. We do not have a single case of overstrike for most royal Hellenistic coinages such as the tetradrachms of the Bithynian and the Pontic kings, or those in the name of Philetairos issued by the Attalid kings, or the drachmas and the tetradrachms of the Kappadokian kings.[23] Except for Timarchos, Seleukid coins, too, present very few cases of overstrikes.[24] Real patterns of overstrikes affect, for the silver, only Ptolemy I, and for the bronze, only Tigranes and the Indo-Greeks.[25]

In Egypt it turns out that, when Ptolemy I Soter decided to create his own currency, he massively reused the tetradrachms in the name of Alexander the Great (figure 4.9).[26] The irony is thus that Ptolemy, who tried to keep alive the memory of the Macedonian conqueror more than anyone else, is the only one who effectively removed his images on a large scale.

What motivated Ptolemy was to quickly produce his own currency.[27] Tetradrachms of Alexander the Great not only were the only coins available in large quantities at that moment in Egypt, but also had to be removed

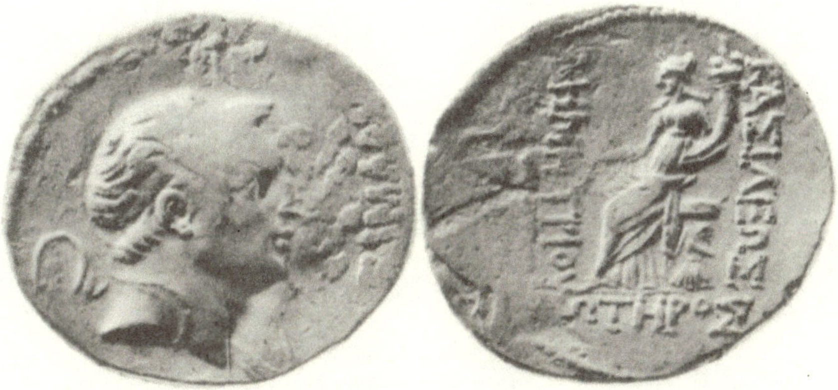

Figure 4.10 Tetradrachm of Timarchos overstruck by jugate portraits of Demetrios I and Laodike.

(Vienna, Kunsthistorisches Museum [16.30g]; Le Rider 1965, 142, pl. XXVII, D).

from circulation in order for Ptolemy to create a closed monetary economy with an obligation of exchange at the borders. So financial reasons prevailed twice. With this example in mind, let us consider now the only three cases for which a pattern of many overstrikes could best be represented as a kind of monetary *damnatio memoriae*.

5. Demetrios and Laodike on Timarchos at Seleukeia on the Tigris (after 162 BCE)

Very few cases of overstrikes have been detected for silver Seleukid coins.[28] In sharp contrast with this general pattern, a group of tetradrachms issued at Seleukeia on the Tigris in the name of King Demetrios and with the jugate portraits of Demetrios I and Laodike is characterized by several cases of overstrikes on the coins of the usurper Timarchos (figure 4.10).

Georges Le Rider provides two reasons for this phenomenon, stating that is was "because it was necessary as quickly as possible to cause the monetary traces of the usurpation to disappear and because it was urgent to put a new currency into circulation."[29] In a footnote he adds:

> About examples of that kind, one has used the words "overstrikes for political reason," as if the overstrike held a special virtue in the cases of *damnatio memoriae*. In my view, only the urgency of removing the currency of the defeated king and to put a new currency into circulation explains the use of overstrike, which

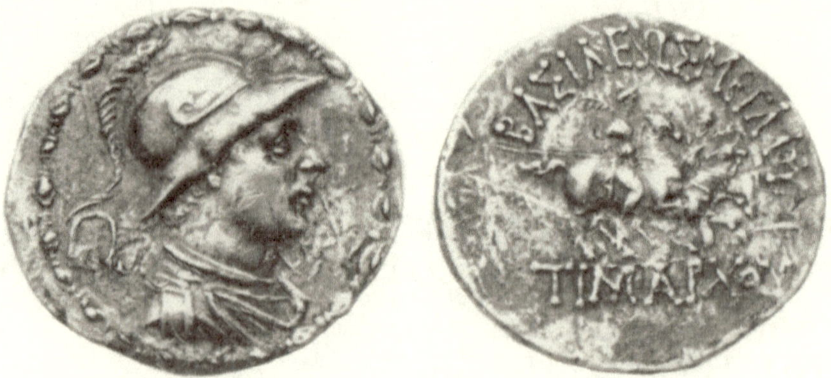

Figure 4.11 Tetradrachm of Timarchos struck at Seleukeia.

(Houghton 1979, 214, no. B).

is not always as effective as we would have liked, since it sometimes leaves the types and the name of the one who has been prohibited below those of the winner. Melting them down would have been much safer if one has had the time to do a normal issue.[30]

Arthur Houghton has devoted a paper to these overstrikes, in which he argues that Timarchos, to whom two tetradrachms attributed to Ekbatana were known so far, also struck tetradrachms at Seleukeia on the Tigris.[31] Commenting on the only coin known for Seleukeia (figure 4.11), he writes that their rarety "is not surprising, given the brief period of its production and the fact that Demetrius evidently ordered the recall and overstriking of all of Timarchos' tetradrachms during his campaign to reclaim the eastern provinces from the usurper."[32]

So, until now, we have only three tetradrachms of Timarchos that were not overstruck to compare with at least the same number on which his types can be surely recognized under Demetrios and Laodike at Seleukeia on the Tigris (figure 4.10). It is tempting indeed to maintain that Demetrios intentionally sought to delete the monetary traces of his enemy. However, what complicates this simple scenario is the fact that tetradrachms of Demetrios and Laodike also have another type of overstrike, which looks similar to the one of Bagadat of Persis (figure 4.12).[33]

On figure 4.13, one may recognize the type of a headdress with a strong chignon to the left on the obverse, while a fire altar is visible on the reverse of other overstrikes.[34]

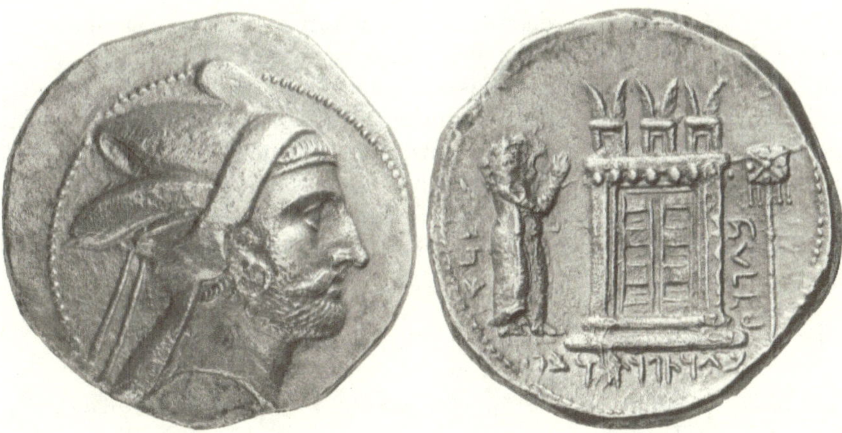

Figure 4.12 Tetradrachm of Bagadat, king of Persis (end of the third century BCE?).

(*Numismatica Ars Classica* 100, 29 May 2017, 173 [16.27g] – © Coinarchives.com).

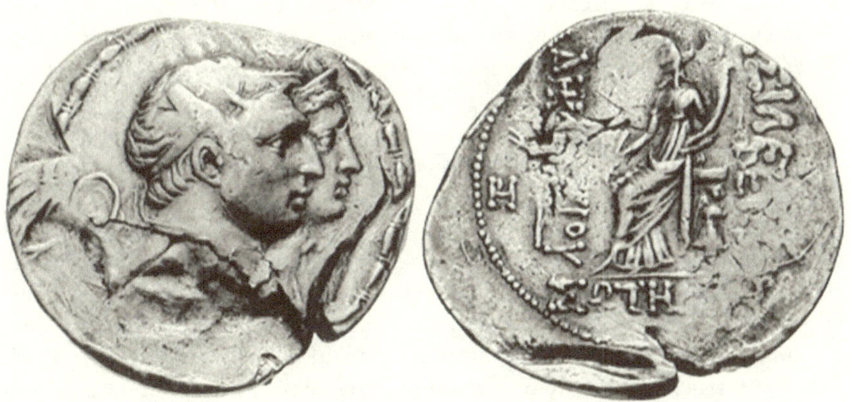

Figure 4.13 Tetradrachm of a king of Persis (?) overstruck by images of Demetrios I and Laodike.

(CNG, MBS 64, 24 Sept. 2003, 391 [16.20g] – © Coinarchives.com).[35]

While it is difficult to determine the undertypes on the coin shown in figure 4.13 (leaving open the fascinating possibility of dealing with an entirely unrecorded coinage), it is absolutely clear that they are not those of Timarchos. Thus we are left with the idea that Demetrios restruck what he could, not targeting only the coins of his defeated enemy. This is close to what Georges Le Rider argued: Demetrios was in a hurry to put his own coinage into circulation. In so doing, he eliminated a good part of the freshly struck tetradrachms of Timarchos – but more as a result than for a non-economic purpose.[36]

6. Phraates IV on Tiridates "Philoromaios" (in 25–24 BCE)

The only two other cases of the kind are to be found with Parthian kings. Tiridates was the only one of all the Parthian kings who was foolish enough to proclaim himself the friend of the Romans (*philoromaios*) on his tetradrachms (dated from March to May 26 BCE).[37] Not surprisingly, these tetradrachms are extremely rare nowadays (figure 4.14).[38]

As identified a century ago, some of these coins were quickly overstruck by Phraates IV.[39] But for a long time the magnitude of the phenomenon was not fully appreciated, until the study of a hoard provided rich new evidence: out of the 356 tetradrachms attributed to Phraates IV, twenty-two present traces of overstrike. Out of these twenty-two, no fewer than six have surely been overstruck on Tiridates *philoromaios* (figure 4.15),[40] while it is likely to have been the case for eleven and potentially for twenty-one.[41] So, just as for tetradrachms of Timarchos, it turns out that also tetradrachms of Tiridates *philoromaios* are more attested today as undertypes than as true coins. As far as Hellenistic royal coinages are concerned, here we possibly have the best case of immediate recall for political reasons.

7. Vonones over Phraatakes and Musa (in 10–11 CE)

Parthian numismatics offer a second and last example of large restriking of tetradrachms in troubled circumstances. The young Vonones, whom his stepmother, Musa, forced into exile and who grew up in Rome, was at a certain point installed on the throne by the Romans. His reign did not last long, but long enough to strike dated tetradrachms in his name (8–12 CE), which were overstruck repeatedly on those in the name of the king Phraatakes and the queen Musa (joint reign: 4 BCE–2 CE) (figure 4.16).

Among the tetradrachms struck in the name of Vonones, a fair proportion shows signs of overstrike. At least in six cases, the undertype can be identified as the one of Phraatakes and Musa (figures 4.17 and 4.18), but that may be the

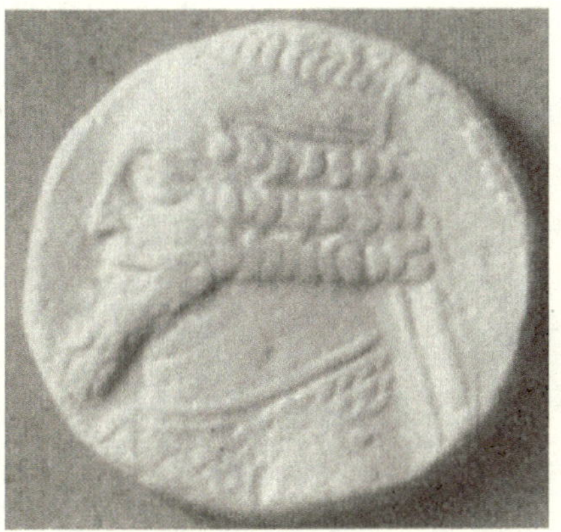

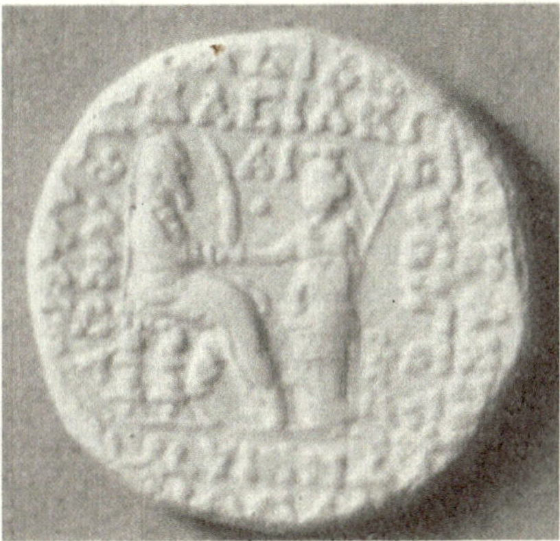

Figure 4.14 Tetradrachm of Tiridates with the legend *Autokrator Philoromaios* at the exergue.

(Bern, Historisches Museum [13.85g – see de Callataÿ 1994b, pl. XX, 4]).

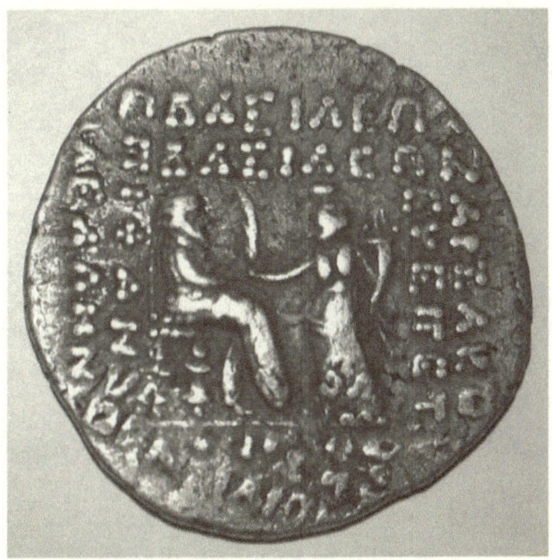

Figure 4.15 Tetradrachms attributed to Phraates IV overstruck on Tiridates *philoromaios*.

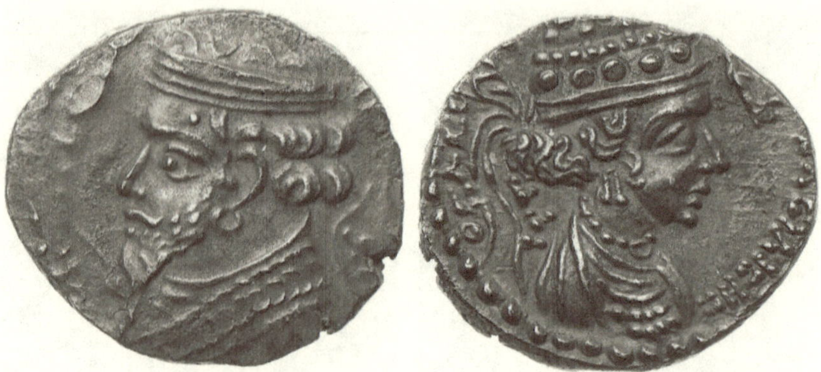

Figure 4.16 Tetradrachm of Phraatakes and Musa, Seleukeia on the Tigris, 1 CE.

(New York Sale, XXXIV, 6 Jan. 2015, 245 [12.52g] – © Coinarchives.com).

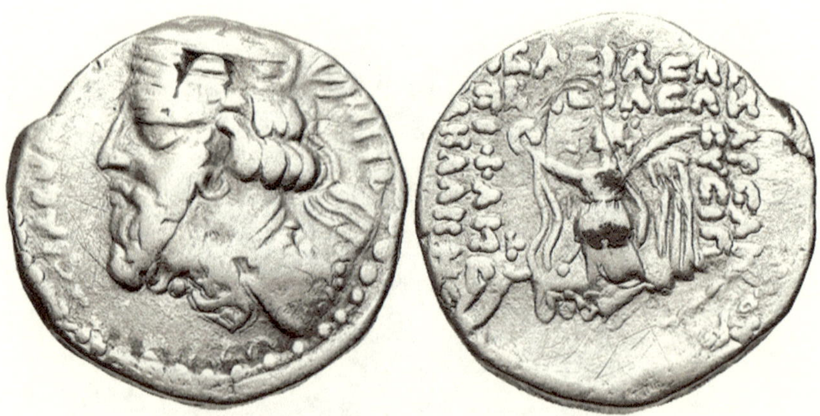

Figure 4.17 Tetradrachm of Vonones I, Seleukeia on the Tigris, 9/10 CE, over Phraatakes and Musa.

(CNG, EA 397, 17 May 2017, 264 [13.99g] – © Coinarchives.com).

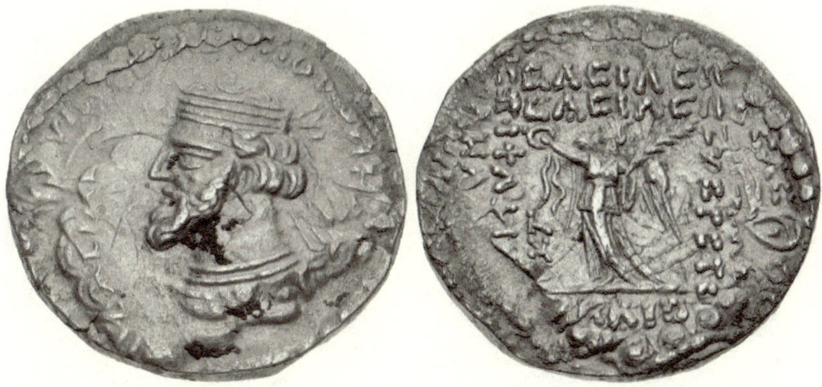

Figure 4.18 Tetradrachm of Vonones I, Seleukeia on the Tigris, August 10 CE, over Phraatakes and Musa.

(CNG, 102, 18 May 2016, 696 [11.47g] – © Coinarchives.com).

case with many more as well.[42] Here again, it is likely that some intentionality was involved in restriking coins that contained the head of Musa.

8. Recalled and Remelted

Lastly, it is possible in theory that some coinages left no trace at all, having been totally recalled and successfully melted down. Since, by definition, they left no trace, our best chance to identify such instances is provided by coinages known by one or two specimens and for which circumstances point to a possible political explanation for their actual rarity.

Out of the at least 20,000 Greek issues, a few are known by one or two coins, as is the case with the unique Aitna tetradrachm, the alleged "Mona Lisa" of ancient coinages. Speaking of Hellenistic royal coinage, we may think of the unique tetradrachm of Mithridates V Euergetes or the two tetradrachms with the portrait of Eumenes II. But in both cases, one is at pains to explain why their successors should have any reason to attack their memory (quite the opposite instead).

Focusing on usurpers, for which there was no shortage in Hellenistic times, it may well be that our best and only case are the beautiful tetradrachms of the Kappadokian Orophernes, dear to Constantine Cavafy, who dedicated to them one of his most praised poems (figure 4.19).[43] Today, they are known

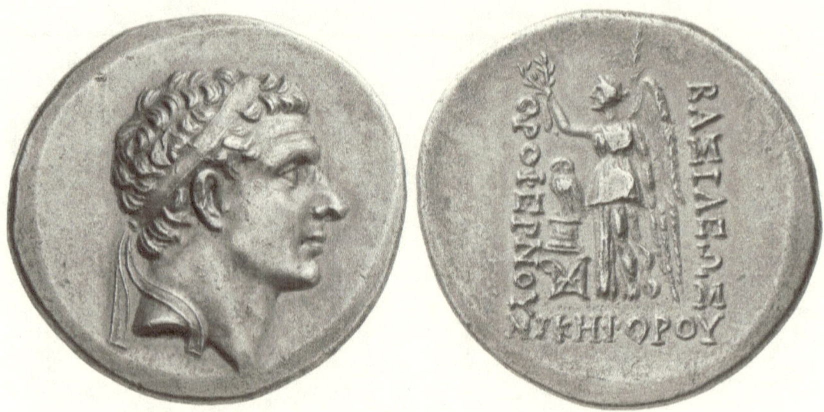

Figure 4.19 Tetradrachm of Orophernes struck at Priene (?), 158–157 BCE.
(*Numismatica Ars Classica* 106, 9 May 2018, 331 [16.53g] – © Coinarchives.com).

by a small number of pieces, all of them apparently coming from the same hoard found in the base of a temple at Priene (*IGCH* 1323) – that is, in the very city where he grew up as a hostage before he was encouraged by the Seleukids to seize the Kappadokian throne. [44] It is hard to say whether this coinage ever circulated, or whether it concerns a foundation deposit of coins that never entered into circulation.

On the one hand, we should be cautious not to turn the absence of proof too quickly into the proof of the absence. On the other hand, the amount of recorded hoards (around 5,000 for the Greek coinages, of which about 1,000 are royal Hellenistic coins) offers some growing confidence about the unlikelihood that much is missing. It would be fascinating to build a graph that records how many totally unknown coinages (not varieties) have appeared every decade during the past century. We may guess a decreasing and very limited number nowadays.[45]

Regarding royal Hellenistic tetradrachms, a unique coin of Mithridates V Euergetes, king of Pontus, was first published in 1976, while a unique coin of Ariarathes IV, king of Kappadokia, was first reported in the 1990s.[46] In both cases, historical circumstances make it unlikely that these coinages were prematurely withdrawn from circulation in a form of execration.

On the whole the full panorama of royal Hellenistic silver issues proves to be very scanty if one looks at possible cases of *damnatio memoriae*. We may wonder if such was ever the case for the Romans. For the Greeks, it is worse: there is virtually no trace of execration marks, nor of erased legends or portraits;

only three cases of potential (not assured) massive overstrikes for political reasons exist, and none that can be strongly deduced for a general recast. This is meagre to the extreme and should not encourage us to employ the term *damnatio memoriae*. As a rule, Hellenistic kings who defeated their opponents on the battlefield never seriously pursued the impossible goal of cleaning the coin circulation from an iconographic point of view. To the contrary, such a conclusion provides additional support for the fact that monetary matters were driven first by economic financial pragmatism and only occasionally as the place for a battle of images.

And finally, it should be added that most of the relevant possible evidence in Hellenistic times concerns Roman coinage. So, in a way, those who are inclined to see republican Rome as an aggressive individualistic society, herein may see the growing power of coin images, instrumentalized on a personal level.

NOTES

1 Burnett 1987: 66.

2 On *damnatio memoriae* in Roman culture generally, see Varner 2004; Flower 2006: 17–41; and the contributions in Benoist and Daguet-Gagey 2008.

3 The best recent synthetic account for Roman coinage is Hostein 2004.

4 On Roman coins and *damnatio memoriae*, see, in chronological order: Birch 1836–7; Mowat 1901, 1902, and 1909; Regling 1904 (n.b.: in fact Roman additions to Mowat from the Berlin coin cabinet); Münsterberg 1918; Elemèr 1937–8; Berghaus 1978; Kindler 1980; Jucker 1982; Savio 2009. I am doubtful about Paschke 2007 and Arslan 2011. Hostein (2004: 224n15) stresses that no gold coins that have been erased are reported in the literature.

5 See de Callataÿ 1994a.

6 CNG, Electronic Auction (EA) 349, 22 April 2015, https://www.numisbids.com/n.php?p=lot&sid=1077&lot=398: "While such deep cuts, like those on the obverse of this sestertius, often were the result of *damnatio memoriae*, it is hard to imagine such a procedure being used on Trajan. Known as one of 'The Five Good Emperors,' he maintained cordial relations with the Senate, was admired by the general public, and his reign suffered no attempted usurpations. Trajan did, however, have an aggressive expansionist policy, highlighted by the conquest of Dacia and its absorption into the Roman Empire. It is possible, then that these marks may have been made by someone, perhaps a former Dacian prisoner or other victim of the war, to express their dissatisfaction at the subjugation of their homeland."

7 Kroll (1993: 70): "It was evidently demonetized by means of a statute forbidding sellers of goods and services from accepting it. 97h and possibly 153e

(undertype), for example, were cut with an X to void them as legal tender, and the numerous unworn specimens from the Agora had surely been thrown away as so much trash."

8 Bilbilis was the only city to have put the name of Sejanus on its coins (see Hostein 2004: 222n9). For Sejanus, see Casadò Lopez (1976: 137–40) and *RPC*, I.1: 127–30 (no. 398–9). For Geta, see the list given by Harl (1987: 151n36) and Weisser (2012).

9 Hostein 2004: 226–7.

10 As well noticed by Hostein 2004: 226.

11 *Pace* some comments in auction sale catalogues: see, e.g., *Triton* IX, 10 Jan. 2006, 41 (crescent partially erased on a hemidrachm of Boetian coinage); CNG, EA 190, 25 June 2008, 53; LHS Numismatik, 102, 29 April 2008, 229 (thunderbolt partially erased on a stater from Elis).

12 See, perhaps, also Ashton 2002, pl. 6, no. 5–6 (the name of αινητωρ has been erased on two pseudo-Rhodian drachms).

13 See Buttrey 1973, especially 11, reverse die R; there is another reverse die [S] where his name was never engraved, reinforcing the presumption of a deliberate erasing for die R.

14 An hypothesis often evoked for Roman coinages is that some countermarks could have been applied as part of an official *damnatio memoriae*, as stated by Howgego (1985: 5–6), with Nero as the best case; but compare Le Rider 1961: 84.

15 *Triton* X, 9 July 2007, 563 (10.84g), *RPC* I 398.

16 CNG, EA 327, 28 May 2014, 826 (25.99g, 35mm, 6h). There are two countermarks on the obverse (helmeted head right (?) within a circle and ΘЄΟΥ within a rectangle).

17 See the comment of Alan Walker in *Nomos* (sales catalogue), 8, 22 Dec. 2013, no. 58: "The present coin was struck during the short period when Thoinon was in power: the dies were originally produced for Hiketas' coinage but his name was carefully erased from the reverse."

18 Paris, BnF, R2993 – see Bourgey, 10 Dec. 1962, 84 (16.55g-33mm-12h) – see de Callataÿ 1997: 304n173, and pl. LII, nr. F.

19 London, BM, 1929–10–13–532 Baxter (15.93g-30mm-11h) – see de Callataÿ 1997: 304n173, and pl. LII, nr. G.

20 In recent decades, David MacDonald and I have developed a particular interest in overstrikes and have recently launched the Greek Overstrike Database (acronym: GOD), which aims to make the evidence available on the Internet.

21 Le Rider 1975: 51: "J'ai pour ma part le sentiment que les surfrappes imparfaites ont dû être plus nombreuses que les surfrappes parfaites: l'oblitération totale du type antérieur exigeait sans aucun doute des soins particuliers et, en général, l'ouvrier devait se contenter d'obtenir pour la nouvelle monnaie

une présentation convenable, sans se soucier de ces menues traces que décèle aujourd'hui le numismate."

22 See de Callataÿ forthcoming.

23 There are no cases where a tetradrachm of Mithridates Eupator is overstruck on another coin but two good cases where his tetradrachms have been overstruck later, one by a pseudo-civic coin of Maronea (de Callataÿ 1991) and another by a late posthumous Lysimachos minted at Byzantion (de Callataÿ 2013: pl. 1–2).

24 For Seleukid coinages, see Houghton, Lorber, and Hoover 2008: 209–17 (for the commentary) and 219–30 (for the catalogue). See also de Callataÿ and Iossif 2015 (about CNG, MBS 81, 20 May 2009, 206). See also CNG, 97, 17 September 2014, 287 (15.47g): a tetradrachm of Antiochos Hierax struck in Asia Minor overstruck on Seleukos II (with the comment "The identification of the issuer as Antiochos Hierax is not certain, but seems most likely, as the coin portraiture of Antiochos III is well developed, and the portrait on the present coin does not fit in this scheme. If the coin is of Hierax, it may suggest that he had a program to recoin his rival Seleukos II's coinage by overstriking it").

25 For reasons of space, I have left aside a discussion of the rich literature on these two topics.

26 See Levy 1954: pl. XII–XIII, and also Visona 1981.

27 Seleukos I did the same: see CNG 36, 5–6 Dec. 1995, 2046 (tetradrachm "Head of Zeus / Quadriga of horned elephants driven by Athena" over Alexander "Head of Herakles / Zeus *aitophoros*" struck at Tarsos).

28 See "Corpus of Seleukid overstrikes and foreign overstrikes on Seleukid hosts" in Houghton, Lorber, and Hoover 2008: 219–30. For silver, the list is short: eleven cases, not all assured, for a sample in the broad range of around ten thousand coins.

29 Le Rider (1975: 52): "L'atelier a recouru à ce procédé expéditif probablement parce qu'il fallait faire disparaître au plus vite les traces monétaires de l'usurpation, et qu'il était urgent de mettre en circulation un nouveau numéraire."

30 Le Rider (1975: 52): "À propos d'exemples de ce genre, on a employé l'expression de 'surfrappe pour raison politique [cf. K. Regling, dans *ZfN* 33, 1922, 166n5, note à l'article de H. Dressel, *Ein Tetradrachmon des Arsakiden Mithridates III*], comme si la surfrappe possédait une vertu spéciale dans les cas de *damnatio memoriae*. À mon avis, seule l'urgence de supprimer la monnaie du vaincu et de mettre en circulation une nouvelle monnaie explique le recours à la surfrappe, qui n'est pas toujours aussi efficace qu'on l'aurait voulu, puisqu'elle laisse parfois apparaître les types et le nom du proscrit sous ceux du vainqueur. La fonte aurait été bien plus sûre si l'on avait eu le loisir de procéder à une émission normale."

31 Houghton 1979. So far, only two tetradrachms are known for Ekbatana (*SC* II, 1589).
32 Houghton 1979: 216.
33 On this, see Engels 2013, pl. 1–2.
34 See CNG, MBS 64, 24 Sept. 2003, 391.
35 Erroneously described as "Overstruck on a tetradrachm of Timarchos (cf. Houghton 990)."
36 But in so doing, he may well have been satisfied to proceed to a "symbolic indictment against the usurper's regime and *an attempt* to erase it from memory by replacing it with the symbols of the legitimate Seleucid king" (Houghton, Lorber, Hoover 2008: 216; my emphasis).
37 About overstruck Parthian coins, see Allotte de la Fuÿe 1904: pl. VI.
38 See the list of the six known coins in de Callataÿ 1994b: 42–3.
39 Allotte de la Fuÿe 1904: 187–90, no. 4 and pl. VI, nos. 4–5.
40 Figure 14 = de Callataÿ 1994b, no. 250 (pl. X: D124-R4, April 25 BCE). See also no. 269 (pl. XI: D139-R2, Sept. 25 BCE); and 300 (pl. XIII: D165-R1c, March 24 BCE).
41 de Callataÿ 1994b: 43–4.
42 For other certainly identified overstruck types, see a) Classical Numismatic Group, MBS 58, 19 Sept. 2001, 763 (14.14g – Sept. 10 CE); b) Gorny & Mosch Giessener Münzhandlung, 130, 8 March 2004, 1434 (12.23g – 11 CE); c) Peus, 388, 1 Nov. 2006, 546 (13.07g – Aug. 11 CE), and d) New York Sale, XXXIV, 6 Jan. 2015, 307 (13.48g – Aug. 11 CE). For other cases where it is less clear, see also: a) Peus 372, 30 Oct. 2002, 663 (14.08g) = Peus, 374, 23 April 2003, 160 (14.05g) = Gorny & Mosch, 134, 11 Oct. 2004, 1624 (14.08g – Sept. 11 CE); Peus, 388, 1 Nov. 2006, 548 (14.26g – Sept. 11 CE); b) Peus, 388, 1 Nov. 2006, 549 (14.10g – 15 CE [likely to be over Phraatakes and Musa]); c) Spink, 9008, 19 March 2009, 344 (14.10g – 10 CE); d) *Triton* XIII, 5 Jan. 2010, 707 (13.28g); e) CNG, EA 263, 31 Aug. 2011, 197 (11.99g – 11/12 CE).
43 Constantine Cavafy, *Orophernis*, line 1–8: "The figure on this four drachma coin / who seems to have a smile on his face / his beautiful, delicate face / this figure is Orophernis, son of Ariarathis. / A child, they threw him out of Cappadocia, / out of his great ancestral palace, / and sent him to grow up in Ionia, / to be forgotten there among foreigners."
44 See Newton 1871 (six coins at least).
45 For a most fascinating case, see Lorber and Hoover 2003: pl. 15–17.
46 On the coin of Mithridates V Euergetes, see de Callataÿ 2009, especially 65 and 78–9. On the coin of Ariarathes IV, see Arslan 2000.

5

Ptolemaic Officials and Officers in Search of Fame

CHRISTELLE FISCHER-BOVET

1. Introduction

In any new imperial context, local elites have adapted their social and political attitudes in order to maintain their local power or even to reach a higher level of power by integrating the administration of this new imperial power.[1] The Hellenistic period provided such a context. This chapter examines the different strategies that the local elites serving the Ptolemaic kings developed in order to increase their social power or social capital (here used as synonyms) both at the local level and in relationship to the king or the royal family. According to Michael Mann, social power can be defined as "the ability to pursue and attain goals through the mastery of one's environment."[2] He conceives four sources of social power working together, namely "Ideology, Economy, Military and Politics" – called the IEMP model. For Nan Lin, the term "social capital" similarly expresses how an individual is able, through investment in social relations, to "gain access to embedded resources and to enhance expected returns of instrumental or expressive actions."[3] Investment goes beyond economic investments and refers also to the social, cultural, and emotional spheres. By showing how the different forces of social power were at play in producing fame, this chapter aims to contribute to a "post-structuralist" approach to fame – as described in the introduction of the present volume – in the Hellenistic period.

One obvious way of accumulating social power is through force and coercion, and through fame from military deeds, and, closely connected, from athletic victories. Yet members of the local elites and individuals serving the new power tend to develop "softer" and complementary ways to maintain their social power, whereby fame grows from investments in social relations.

Acts of benefaction (also called euergetism) toward the local communities by Ptolemaic officials and officers belonging to the Greek and Egyptian cultural spheres, which occasionally intersected, such as the examples analysed below, became essential for becoming famous in the Hellenistic period. This is clear from honours granted to such individuals by their communities, especially statues, and recorded in honorific decrees and in Egyptian autobiographical inscriptions on statues. By doing something exceptional for their local community, generally a city or a region, and sometimes by doing particularly well what was expected from their functions (called euergetism *ob honorem*), these individuals gained fame, which usually remained limited to the local environment and did not turn into international celebrity.[4] However, the fame of some of these individuals benefited from the projection of Ptolemaic power in the eastern Mediterranean.

I argue that, through minimal adjustments, the local elites who belonged to both the Greek and the Egyptian cultural spheres of the Ptolemaic empire used rather similar strategies to secure and increase their social capital or fame. They presented themselves as generous benefactors, *euergetai,* using the king as a model, which always implied wealth. They often displayed their particular connection to the monarch and acted generously within traditional cultural contexts such as local religion. Over time, euergetism and honours became more uniform within the territory of the Ptolemaic empire, although this may have been accelerated by the empire's contraction in the second century BCE. Euergetism was not a concept limited to the cultural sphere of the Greek *poleis,* and a few essential aspects of euergetism in the Greek and the Egyptian spheres converged throughout the period.

In order to understand the process toward uniformity in culture and society that occurred in the Hellenistic period, we shall compare the construction and display of fame by Greek and Egyptian elites first in the early Ptolemaic period (ca 320s–200s BCE) and then in the late Ptolemaic period (ca 120s–30 BCE). The micro-histories that follow are not unique cases, and some of them have recently been discussed in conjunction with other examples and from different points of view by Gorre, Moyer, and Fischer-Bovet.[5] The aim of this chapter is to analyse, through the interplay between individuals and communities and between statues and inscriptions, the development of the conception of fame under the Ptolemies.

2. International Fame, or How to Become a "Supra-polis Player"

The first micro-history examines how competitions between states with imperial ambitions, such as the Ptolemaic, Seleukid, and Antigonid states, allowed some members of the local elites – who until then had only a local and marginal role – to reach fame at an international level and to become supra-*polis* players (to use John Ma's expression).[6] Service as commanders in the army of one of the Hellenistic rulers, or inclusion in the group of the so-called *philoi* (friends), who formed the informal yet close council or inner court of the king, brought fame to such individuals and their families not only in their region or city of origin but throughout the empire controlled by their royal employer.[7] In contrast to prior centuries, it became possible for a wider pool of individuals to reach an international standing by demonstrating qualities in the military sphere, but also as benefactors or some sort of "saviours." They imitated kingship ideology as expressed, for instance, through Ptolemy I's royal epithet *Soter* (Saviour). In exchange for their protection and/or generosity toward cities, it became common in the third century for cities to reward kings – and their officials and officers – with the gift of citizenship, a mark of their international network.[8]

The relationship between the Ptolemies and the family of Aitos from Aspendos in Pamphylia illustrates well these mechanisms in the 260s–20s BCE. During that time, Ptolemy II, and then Ptolemy III, succeeded in controlling part of Anatolia through the creation of a network of allies among the local population, and through the integration of elite members into their army and administration.[9] The Ptolemies developed close ties with the Aspendian elite, probably with the help of Aitos, who was *strategos* (commander) in the army of Ptolemy II. He had particularly high functions, since he founded the city of Arsinoë in Cilicia, and he received citizenship from the neighbouring city of Nagidos, from which many settlers came, and probably from Arsinoë too. At the end of the Second Syrian War, he was honoured as eponymous priest of the royal cult in Alexandria (253/2 BCE) and therefore no doubt belonged to Ptolemy II's *Philoi*.[10] Aitos' son, Thraseas, who was governor of Cilicia once Ptolemy III controlled the region again, resolved disputes over land between the citizens of Nagidos and Arsinoë and refined the organization of the institutions of Arsinoë, as recorded in an inscription containing his letter to the Arsinoeans and a decree of the Nagidians.[11] The decree mentions the decision of the citizens to praise Thraseas, but the honours were probably inscribed on another stela.

The international tone of Thraseas' career as a member of the top elite serving a Hellenistic king can be grasped from several other documents. Like most of the Ptolemies, he was granted Athenian citizenship, therefore accumulating multiple honorific citizenships.[12] In or shortly after 224/3 BCE, he became a citizen of the deme of Phlya, in the new Athenian tribe called Ptolemaïs created that year. In a slightly later honorific decree (ca 215 BCE), the Athenians thanked him for his past help – he dispatched Ptolemaic grain to Athens – and the future help he promised.[13] The decree follows the usual formulaic structure of an honorific decree and reports that the council (*Boule*) suggested to the people (*Demos*) to praise Thraseas and to crown him for his love of honour (*philotimia*) and goodwill (*eunoia*) toward the Athenian people. The honours were announced during the important civic but also international festivals of the City Dionysia, the Panathenaia, and the Eleusinia (ll. 20–2 partly reconstructed). By the late third century BCE, kings' officials and other benefactors could be, like Thraseas, crowned by a golden crown. His growing international fame and functions and his past governorship of Cilicia were stepping stones for a more important position, that of governor of Syria and Phoenicia. There, in the city of Tyre, he dedicated an equestrian statue to Ptolemy IV, God Philopator, at some point between 217 and 204 BCE, no doubt to celebrate the king's victory over his rival, the Seleukid king, at the battle of Raphia.[14] Of course, to erect such a statue was a way to display his connection with the king – Thraseas mentioned only his Alexandrian citizenship in this inscription – and to increase the fame of his own family.

Fame within the family remained connected to the military domain, since Thraseas' son, Ptolemaios, was one of the leading generals at Raphia in 217 BCE during the Fourth Syrian War against the Seleukids.[15] He followed in his father's footsteps as governor of Cilicia and, from 204/3 BCE, as governor of Syria and Phoenicia, in what seems to have become a career pattern. But fame could become dangerous when successions were uncertain, such as after the premature death of Ptolemy IV and the murder of the queen, and the subsequent riot of the Alexandrian mob in 203 BCE initiated by members of the army.[16] In his account, Polybios does not mention Ptolemaios, perhaps because he was in Syria-Phoenicia. Yet the shift of allegiance of Ptolemaios and his brothers to the Seleukids during the Fifth Syrian War has to be understood within this troubled context of court intrigues while Ptolemy V was a child, and suggests that Ptolemaios had lost his influence in Alexandria.[17] He remained governor of Syria-Phoenicia by giving the province to the Seleukid king, but this action is not strictly speaking a betrayal of the Ptolemaic dynasty, as I have argued elsewhere.[18] It may rather be the result of Ptolemaios' loss of power at the court. Yet there was no defamation of the entire family, since another branch remained powerful in Egypt. Aitos III, Ptolemaios' cousin, who was governor or *strategos* of the Fayyum during the year 203/2, was granted one of the highest honorific titles, that of eponymous priesthood, in 197/6 after the Fifth Syrian War, as recorded on the Rosetta stone.[19]

Aitos' and his descendants are representative of local families that became famous through their service to the royal family over several generations.

We have dozens of statue bases – although usually no statues are preserved – and hundreds of honorific decrees mentioning the erection of statues as one of the honours granted to royal officials and officers within the empire and sometimes even outside it (e.g., Athens, Delos, Olympia). John Ma has shown recently how this development is particular to the Hellenistic period, and indeed increased during this time, whereas it was a very rare phenomenon until the fourth century – even more so for non-royal individuals.[20] Places for erecting statues were usually the sanctuaries of the *poleis,* gymnasia, or agora, transforming particular spaces of the *poleis* in "statuescapes," to use Ma's play on words.[21]

A look at the catalogue of about 350 inscriptions collected by Marquaille in her 2001 unpublished dissertation entitled "The External Image of Ptolemaic Egypt" records about fifty-two statues for Ptolemaic officers and officials.[22] Thirty per cent are dated to the third century BCE and about 70 per cent to the second century BCE. In about 30 per cent of the cases, the decisions stemmed from the *poleis,* which honoured royal officials or officers for their goodwill, often termed *eunoia,* toward the king and the *demos,* and 10 per cent were statues dedicated by kings or queens. About 50 per cent of the statues were dedicated by officers; statues dedicated by soldiers appeared slightly later.[23] The most famous people certainly were the ones who were granted a statue of themselves by the king; but such honours were the result of a specific action or function closely tied to the king and/or the royal family. Ivana Savalli-Lestrade considers that such individuals belonged to the Friends of the king.[24] For instance, Ptolemy II erected a statue of his naval architect Pyroteles in the sanctuary of Aphrodite in Old Paphos for the design of very large warships.[25] Despite their frequency, statues of officials and officers remained slightly outnumbered by those of kings and members of their families. Marquaille's appendix records about seventy-six royal Ptolemaic statues, of which approximately 25 per cent were dedicated by cities and almost 40 per cent by officials and soldiers; the rest were dedicated by other individuals (private citizens, the king himself, or people whose identities are not preserved). Royal statues also brought some social capital to individuals who, by dedicating them, displayed their relationship with the king.

To sum up, in the third-century Greek cultural context, actions that brought fame were care for the welfare of citizens in the *poleis* and for the affairs or *pragmata* of the king and his family, and thereby the claim of a close relationship with the king. Fame was constructed and displayed through the erection of honorific decrees by citizens or by individuals belonging to the same occupational groups (generally soldiers) as those granted honours and through rewards such as crowns and citizenships – if possible, granted in international contexts – and statues near local sanctuaries or in the agora.

3. Fame in the Third Century Egyptian Context: Elite Self-Representation

The second set of micro-histories serves to explore how the Egyptian local elite responded to the new imperial situation in the late fourth and the third century BCE. There is no hint that this elite pursued international careers, at least not in the third-century Aegean. The Egyptian priestly elites continued the tradition of advertising exceptional actions by erecting statues of themselves, statues usually smaller than life-size, within the temple precincts.[26] They often recorded on them their career in hieroglyphs.

Djedhor "the Saviour"

Djedhor's career probably started under the last native Egyptian pharaohs in the 340s BCE (Thirtieth Dynasty) and the second Persian occupation (343–32 BCE) and continued under Alexander and his satrap Kleomenes, and thereafter Philip Arrhideos, king of Macedonia, who was pharaoh while Ptolemy was in charge as satrap of Egypt. Djedhor was a priest with administrative functions in the temple of the falcon god Iat-Maat in Athribis (Delta).[27] His deeds were recorded, with some variations, on hieroglyphic inscriptions engraved on statues and their bases that displayed his local prestige in the temple and the necropolis (figure 5.1).[28]

In the inscriptions of an early statue that came from the necropolis, Djedhor compared himself to a deity, which was not uncommon in the Egyptian Late Period (664–332 BCE). In later inscriptions on the statue from the temple, he called himself "Saviour" because he was able to heal people of his community from poisonous venom through magical powers. The statue bases are worn, which indicate that people touched the base and used the water that was poured in the little basin at its base.[29] Djedhor concludes by saying that he himself chose the inscriptions of the two "Saviours" (i.e., the statues). Beyond the magical component of the texts, they emphasized three deeds that directly concerned the local population. First, he organized new constructions within the temple, which he did on behalf of the king. This claim attests to Djedhor's desire to show some loyalty to the new Macedonian king, but in reality there seems to have been no royal supervision.[30] Second, he was instrumental in hiding the burials of the sacred falcons from the Persians, a rare allusion to a broader historical event. Third, his most remarkable action was to expel soldiers from the temple precinct and within it to destroy their houses.[31] He compensated them with new plots of land and perhaps paid with his own money to rebuild their houses.[32] However, he had to destroy the houses a second time; thereafter, the soldiers settled down further south of the nome. Djedhor's inscriptions encapsulate how the local

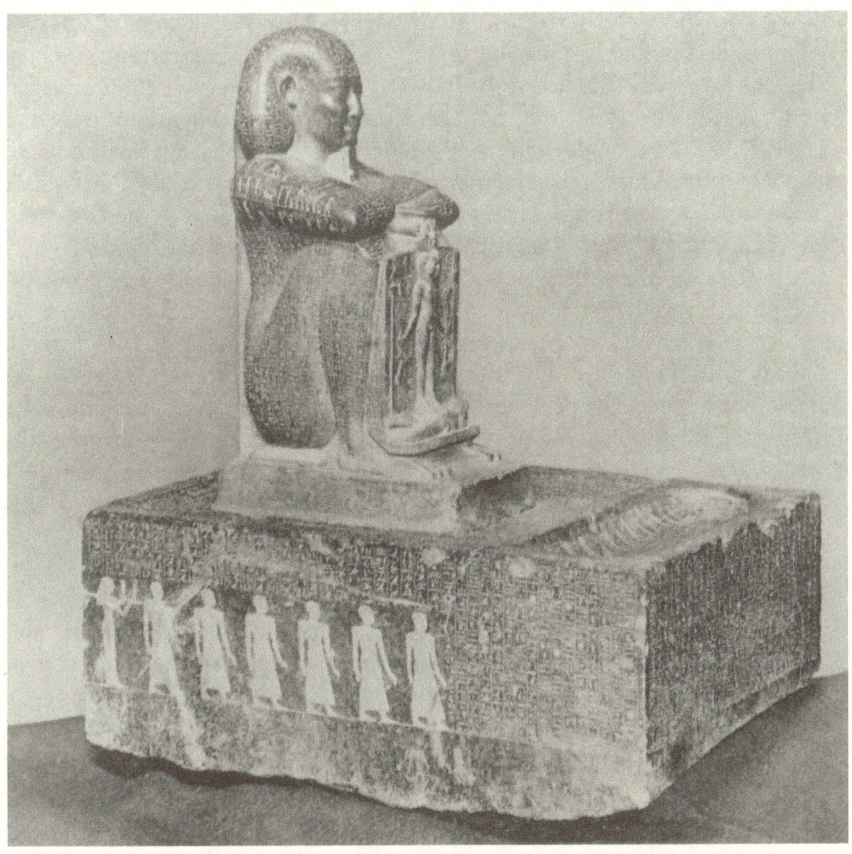

Figure 5.1 Statue of Djedhor, priest of Iat-Maat in Athribis (ca 340–330 BCE).

CGC 46341, reproduced after Jelínková-Reymond (1956), 1.

priestly elites acquired fame before the Macedonian conquest, since he was neither an official nor an officer of the king. His deeds remained local, as did their display within the local temple where he was administrator, but small adjustments were made to acknowledge the new king.

Horos of Herakleopolis

During the same troubled period of transition (340s–10s BCE) – that is, from the Thirtieth Dynasty (380–43 BCE) to the Second Achaimenid period (343–32 BCE) and the subsequent Macedonian conquest – Horos was *mr-mšʿ*,

thus a commander and perhaps a "nome governor" in Herakleopolis, south of Memphis, and probably a prophet too.[33] He belonged to a different category of benefactors than Djedhor, as he had no healing power but rather engaged in military functions as well as administrative ones inside and outside the temple. He achieved building and restoration on a large scale in the temple of Herischef in Herakleopolis. The hieroglyphic inscriptions on the dorsal pillar of his statues report that he had to destroy something during the construction work, perhaps houses belonging to soldiers (see figures 5.2 and 5.3).[34]

As in the case of Djedhor, so too Horos' protection of the local community is a *topos* that recurs on his two statues. Horos also gave land to the temple in order to cultivate wine, and he compensated the landlords with money from his household. Both Djedhor and Horos show a certain level of autonomy, which reflects the period of uncertainty before Ptolemy became king. In contrast, in the case of Thraseas' family discussed above and in the following examples, the claim of a connection with the king appears essential.

Teos I, Apries, and Teos II of Tanis

When turning to Egyptian elite families living under the Ptolemies, it is noticeable that they were still able to enjoy upward social mobility and to display achievements that generated fame. The family of Teos son of Onnophris is known through the autobiographical texts in hieroglyphs written on the statue of Teos I and his grandson or nephew Teos II found in Tanis in the oriental Delta.[35] Their dating has been debated, but Gorre plausibly has suggested about 200 BCE.[36] Teos I came from a priestly family and served in the army. Though at this still early date it was rare for Egyptians, Teos I was granted a plot of land – a well-attested allotment for Greco-Macedonian cleruchs living in Egypt.[37] His precise administrative duties remain unclear, but he served in judicial functions and he collected taxes (either for the temple or for the state, or through the temple for the state). Teos I's autobiographical inscription emphasized that he was selected by the king, had numerous cultic roles in the temple of Tanis, where he undertook large construction projects and renovations, and protected the inhabitants of his city – a significant achievement during a period of domestic revolts.[38]

The choice of a colossal (theophore) statue to honour him, even if only slightly taller than life-size (2.4 m), is remarkable because colossal statues of non-royal individuals were rare and Egyptian statuary was usually smaller than life-size (see figure 5.4).[39]

The family drew on Teos' fame, as Teos II had more important priestly functions and received the title of "great general" (*mr-mšʿ wr*) of the king. His statue is life size (left leg in the front, theophore), and the dorsal inscription also emphasizes his great care for the inhabitants of his city (see figure 5.5).

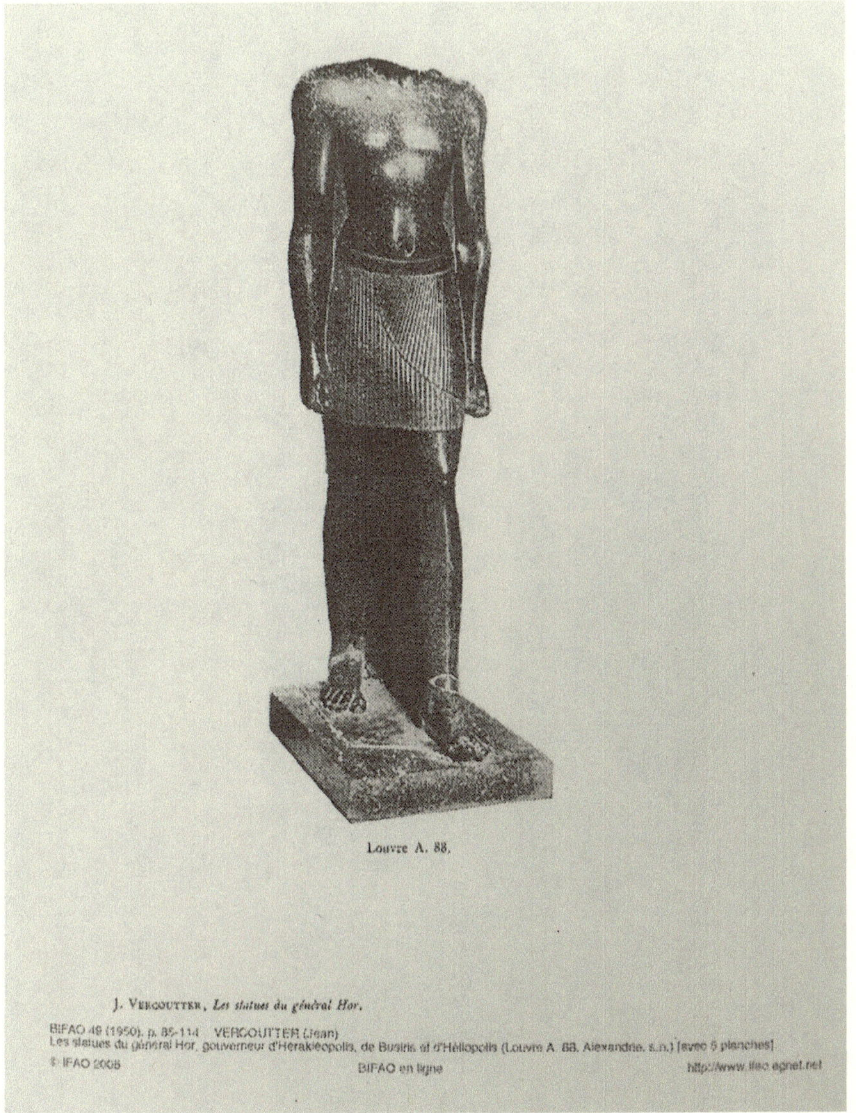

Figure 5.2 Statue of Horos of Herakleopolis (ca 340–310 BCE).

Louvre A. 88 reproduced after Vercoutter (1950), plate I.

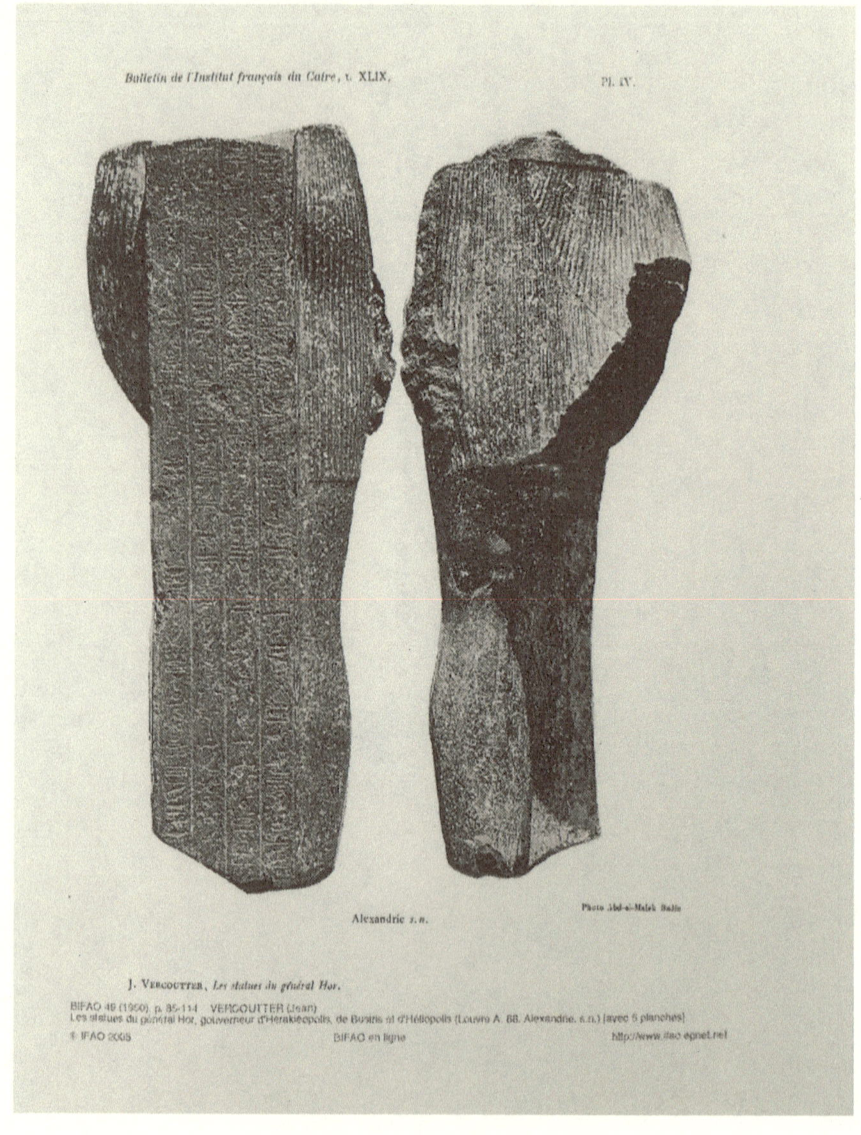

Figure 5.3 Hieroglyphic inscriptions on dorsal pillar of statue of Horos of Herakleopolis (ca 340–310 BCE).

Statue of Alexandria reproduced after Vercoutter (1950), plate IV.

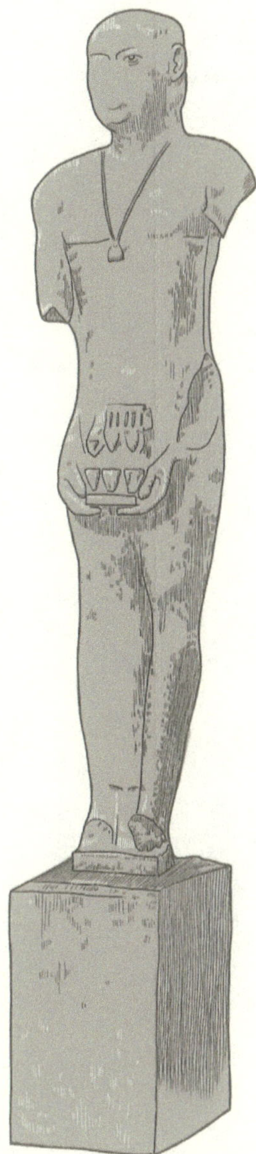

Figure 5.4 Colossal statue of Teos I.

CGC 700, line-drawing by E. Leborgne, after Zivie-Coche (1997) plate 6. Courtesy of Christiane Zivie-Coche and Philippe Brissaud, editor of the *Bulletin de la société française des fouilles de Tanis*, "cliché musée du Caire."

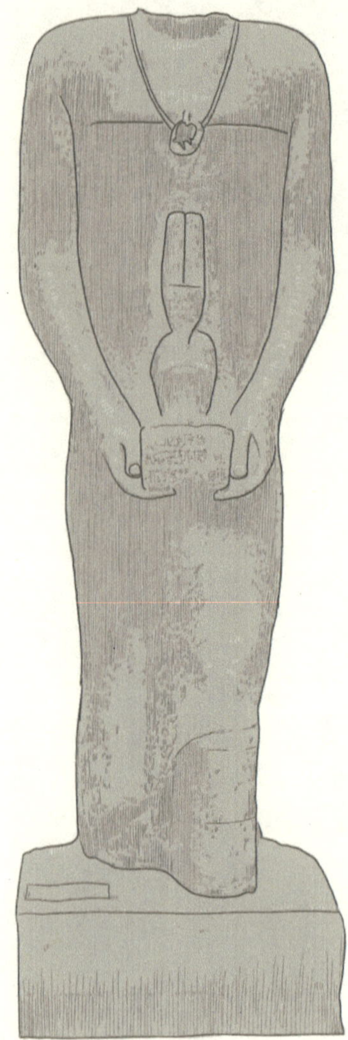

Figure 5.5 Colossal statue of Teos II.

CGC 698, line-drawing by E. Leborgne after Zivie-Coche (1997), plate 8. Courtesy of Christiane Zivie-Coche and Philippe Brissaud, editor of the *Bulletin de la société française des fouilles de Tanis,* "cliché musée du Caire."

The fame of Teos' family did not spread beyond Egypt, but Teos II's functions suggest that he was present at the court in Alexandria, if not as a member of the inner court or Friends, at least of the outer court.[40] If the dating is approximately correct, such individuals must have played a leading role during the repression of the Great Revolt and in composing trilingual decrees such as the Rosetta stone, which Egyptian priests determined.

In conclusion, the actions that generated fame in the fourth- and third-century Egyptian cultural sphere implied euergetism, as in the Greek cultural sphere.[41] In both contexts, the protection and care of the community and of the local cults were central to gaining such fame. An appeal for individuals with godlike power as "Saviour" (i.e., one who bring support) was growing not only in Egypt but was also coming forth in the Greek world with super-powerful kings, such as Ptolemy I Saviour, and even physicians.[42] But there were also a few differences. For instance, in the Ptolemaic possessions outside Egypt, the construction or restoration of temples by Ptolemaic officials and officers was not predominant, since they were not priests of these temples and their statues could be in the agora rather than near a temple.[43]

4. Fame in the Second Century: A Transition

These two cultural spheres influenced each other more than is usually thought in the context of Ptolemaic rule. Not only did the kings play with cultural overlaps, but so too did the local Egyptian priestly elites, perhaps even more after the loss of the territories outside Egypt. This occurred while the priestly elite was increasingly included in the royal administration, and while officials and officers were integrated into temple activities in the second century BCE.[44] The Greek dedication by the Alexandrian Theagenes of the statue of his father Zeno (?) son of Apollodoros, to the Egyptian god Harbaithos (Greek for "Horos of the two eyes") and to the gods who shared his temple illustrates the combination of cultural elements.[45] Since Harbaithos was the local god of the eleventh nome (Oriental delta) it is possible that the dedication took place in an Egyptian temple. The short inscription was used to display the titles and (rather low financial) functions of the father and son; yet it seems that it was the son who chose an Egyptian temple for the setting and audience. One would like to know how the statue looked in the precinct. In addition, demonstrating filial piety and enhancing the social capital, or fame, of the family by erecting statues of ancestors and displaying their careers was not limited to the Egyptian priestly families examined in section 3, although, in the Egyptian cases, the heirs did not display their own identities.

5. Fame in the First Century BCE

Panemerit and Pikas in Tanis

In Egypt during the first century BCE, care for the local population through the euergetism that was common to both the Greek and Egyptian cultural spheres continued to generate fame and, by then, closely combined aspects of each culture. This development can be explained by some shared characteristics of Egyptian and Greek euergetism(s), as analysed in the preceding sections, and by the attraction of local Egyptian religion and of some characteristics of Greek decision-making processes, such as those leading to the erection of honorific decrees and statues.

The statues of Panemerit and Pikas in Tanis allow us to explore the production and display of fame in the first half of the first century BCE on the part of royal officials who were also priests.[46] Both were chamberlains, prophets, and governors of nome (*mr-mšʿ*), with Pikas succeeding Panemerit. They bore important court titles, and their autobiographies state that they had obtained their positions from the king.[47] Above all, both were involved in reconstructing the temple of Horos of Mesen in Tanis.[48] They cared for Tanis and for its temples and gods while managing the finances of the region; therefore their euergetism can be considered partly as *ob honorem* (linked to their functions) – a phenomenon common to both the Greek and Egyptian cultural spheres. Their careers and benefactions display a similar pattern, albeit with minor differences. For instance, Panemerit expelled soldiers from the temple of Amun of Opet, as did Djedhor and Horos in Athribis and Herakleopolis in the fourth century – although, in the Tanite case, Panemerit must have received a request from a subordinate and asked the permission of the king.[49] Both Zivie-Coche and Gorre interpret the content of the inscriptions as a way to strengthen the connection between the temples of Tanis and Ptolemy XII, with Panemerit taking good care of the sanctuaries and so ensuring future stability for the king.[50]

The local fame of these individuals is not in doubt. The statues of Panemerit and Pikas were found within the temple of Amun near large private chapels that their sucessors and subordinates had erected for them, while the inscriptions record that they were blessed (Demotic *ḥsy*). Thus Panemerit and Pikas were worshipped after their death, like Djedhor in Athribis and a few other individuals who benefited from a post-mortem cult.[51] Their statues, however, do not resemble that of Djedhor but belong to a new style that appeared around 125 BCE, the so-called striding draped male figures in black basalt or granite with a dorsal pillar (see figure 5.6).[52]

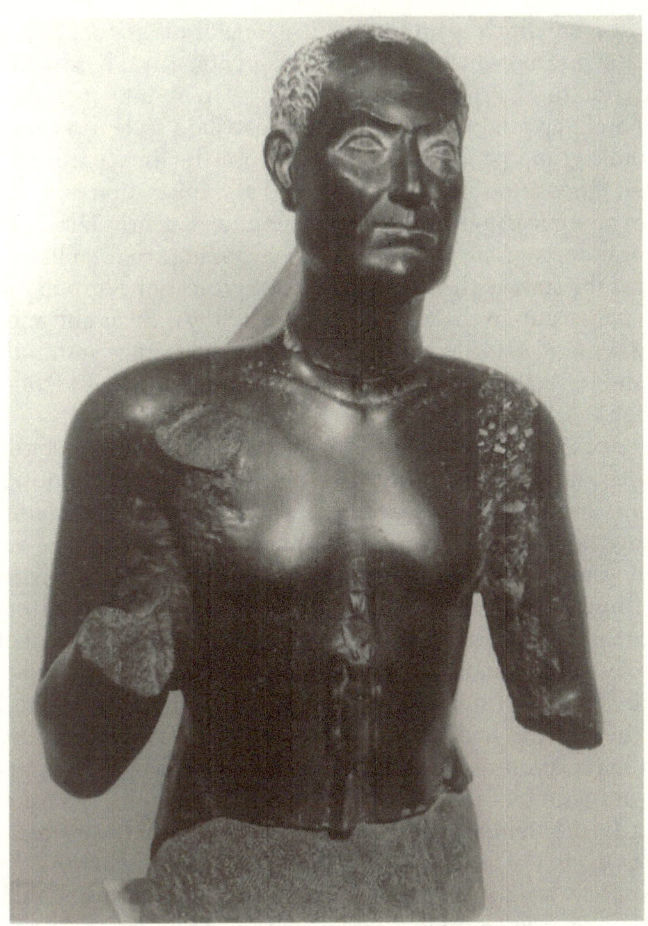

Figure 5.6 Statue of Panemerit (ca 125 BCE).

E 15683 © Musée du Louvre, Dist. RMN-Grand Palais/Pierre et Maurice Chuzeville.

When compared to other striding draped statues, those of Panemerit and Pikas are even more innovative. In his article on Egyptian elite self-presentation, Baines has emphasized their main characteristics.[53] First, the statues are about life-size, like Greek honorific statues, whereas, to that point, Egyptian statues were slightly smaller, about two-thirds of life-size, with the exception of the previously discussed statues of Teos I and Teos II, also in Tanis.[54] Second, one of the statues of Panemerit places its weight on the forward foot, which is unusual. Third, one of his statues holds its arms free from the matrix, which is unparalleled in non-royal hard-stone statues. Was such a statue Egyptian in style with a Greek influence, or Greek in style with an Egyptian influence? To try to ascribe a style to a particular culture or ethnic group no longer makes sense for the first century.[55] The elite groups that were associated with the royal administration and the temples behaved in an increasingly similar manner and evidently felt that this type of statue was appropriate.[56] It is not always possible to establish accurately who erected the statues (heirs, members of a professional group such as soldiers, or a *polis*), but, in the case of Panemerit, it was Pikas and another subordinate who decided to set up the striding draped statues within the temple complex and to establish Panemerit's cult in order to benefit from his fame and prestige.

In addition, the same individual could be represented by statues in different styles and contexts. In the case of Pikas, it is worth noting that the hieroglyphic biographical inscriptions record that the locals (*smrw*) loved him because he did useful things for them, and that a bronze statue (not preserved) was erected for him in his hometown of Sile (Tjaru), probably by the locals from Sile.[57] The same information is repeated in the lost statue of Pikas recorded by Rifaud.[58] Both Zivie-Coche and Gorre have noted that the mention of a bronze statue is unusual and that the context suggests honours similar to those usually granted by citizens and recorded on honorific decrees.[59] In fact, the text on the lost statue of Pikas (recorded by Rifaud) insists on his relation with the king and the court, while the statue now in the Cairo museum focuses more on his relationship with the local nobility;[60] consequently, it is tempting to propose that the former was erected by the Tanite priests and the latter by locals from Sile. This is what the close parallel with Kallimachos in Thebes, examined in the next section, could suggest: Kallimachos received one stone statue from the priests and two statues from the city of Thebes, one in bronze and one in stone; none of them was ever found, but the decisions to erect them have been recorded on a bilingual honorific decree.

Kallimachos in Thebes

Kallimachos (not the poet) illustrates how members of an Alexandrian family with a Hellenic background (all bearing the name Kallimachos) could become locally famous and have their fame displayed in a way similar to Panemerit and Pikas. The career of the last Kallimachos of the family took place under Cleopatra VII. He was *strategos* and responsible for the finances of the Peri-Theban nome.[61] Usually one reached such a position following a successful military career.[62] In fact Kallimachos was also *gymnasiarchos* and cavalry commander (*hipparchos*). Moreover, he bore the highest honorific title of "kinsman of the king" (*suggenes*), which did not mean that he belonged to the royal family but rather emphasized his affiliation to the court, at least the outer court. His care for the population of Thebes, which went beyond what one would expect from someone in his office, was thoroughly recorded around 39 BCE in an honorific decree following the Greek traditional structure and formulas but written in Demotic Egyptian and in Greek.[63] Kallimachos' actions, narrated in the "since clause" of the decree, were threefold. First, while he received control of Thebes after a troubled period, he supervised the maintenance of the sanctuaries and saved the lives of the people, thanks to his generous attitude (*philanthropia*) and his kindness (*euergesia*) (ll. 5–9).[64] Such actions recall the accomplishments of the Egyptian priests in the troubled period of the late fourth century BCE (discussed above) and, to some extent, the achievements of Panemerit. Second, he distributed wheat during a famine, acting "like a father for his homeland and his own children" (ll. 9–18).[65] It is possible that he did not actually pay for it himself but instead did not send the tax-grain to Alexandria.[66] Third, Kallimachos obtained the help of the god Amonrasonther (ll. 18–19). He received an oracle from the god, in public, while standing on the floor of the sanctuary. He was compared to a star and a good deity (*agathon daimon*) who shines for all (ll. 19–20). These praises may sound excessive, but Heinen has shown that there was an inflation of such terms in honorary contexts and in petitions since the Late Hellenistic period.[67] In fact, even Djedhor already had compared himself to a deity almost three centuries earlier, and Panemerit and Pikas were honoured as holy men in Tanis. Finally, Kallimachos' piety is emphasized throughout the text and associated with the generous deeds of his grandfather Kallimachos, the *epistrategos* who had re-established the royal cults (ll. 23–6).

As in the third-century Greek cultural sphere, fame was promoted by means of an honorific decree, but this time it was bilingual, and the decisions were voted by "the priests of Thebes and of Amonrasonther, the Elders (*Presbyteroi*) and all the others" (ll. 2–3), and not strictly speaking by citizens of a Greek *polis* or by the members of an occupational group. Thebes was called a *polis*, and the priests and the elders formed a sort of "council" (*Boule*), although, in the Egyptian context, the term *poleis* had developed and qualified what one could call "Greco-Egyptian cities" without the exact same institutional structure or political power as a Greek *polis*.[68] They all voted that Kallimachos be called "Saviour of the *polis*" (l. 26), which resonates with royal epithets in the Greek cultural sphere, such as Ptolemy I Saviour, but also with local saints within the Egyptian local cultural sphere, such as

Djedhor. He received three statues (*eikonas*) to be placed, on his birthday, in the most visible places of the sanctuary of the great god Amonrasonther (l. 28), while the decree was set up on the terrace (ll. 30–1). The statue from the priests was in hard stone – that is, in basalt or granite – and the two from the *polis* were in bronze and stone, respectively.[69] The bronze statue was probably Greek in appearance, but one wonders about the style of the stone statues. If a parallel may be drawn with Pikas, then the priests offered a statue with a black dorsal pillar such as the ones encountered above or that of Plato fifty years before. Plato came from a family similar to that of Kallimachos, and he had policing and judicial functions in several nomes of the Thebaid.[70] He also had oracular functions, which is less surprising than in the case of Kallimachos, since Plato was also a priest. Finally, a rare additional honour was voted for Kallimachos: the day of his birthday was to be named after him and celebrated with sacrifices for the rulers, and with crowns and banquets according to the local custom (l. 29).[71] The benevolence of Amonrasonther was to be remembered for his benefit (l. 32), the sentence leaving open whether it was for the benefit of the god or of Kallimachos.[72]

The careers of Panemerit, Pikas, and Kallimachos make salient specific various aspects of fame in late Hellenistic Egypt. First, Egyptian religion became the focus of euergetic actions on the part of officials and officers of the king, who in fact mimicked the king. Heinen has convincingly compared the section on the famine in the decree for Kallimachos in Thebes with that of the Kanopos trilingual decree, in which the priests of Egypt, gathered in a synod in 238 BCE, voted honours, among other things, to the king who had provided grain during a famine.[73] While in the case of Kanopos and the other trilingual decrees, the priests acted as a fictive *polis*, in first-century Thebes the priests and elders of one single "Greco-Egyptian *polis*" took action together to honour a common benefactor and to increase his fame.[74] Second, the erection of statues for non-royal individuals conveniently had become a tendency within both cultural spheres, and some statues combined Greek and Egyptian influences, as is evidenced by the striding draped male figures and, even more so, by the statues of Panemerit and Pikas. Similarly, granting inflated honorific titles, such as "blessed one" or "good deity," had become a common trend, symbolically acknowledging that officials and officers could act as generously as their king did and therefore could receive similar honours, so that even their birthdays could be celebrated. But this occurred as an extension of the royal cults and was locally limited, while the earlier trilingual decrees had established royal festivals throughout Egypt.

It has been assumed that the career of Panemerit shows that the temples and towns benefited from a certain autonomy, and that Kallimachos acted almost as a king or a viceroy; but such interpretations betray a perception of serious decline of royal power in the late Ptolemaic period.[75] Heinen has shown that inflated honorific terms were becoming more common and that, if the kings were represented as dependent on the gods in the trilingual decrees, as was Kallimachos in his honorific decree, it was because the text emanated from priests.[76] One can add that Kallimachos was not a threat to Cleopatra, but he acted precisely as if he were a real royal kinsman (*suggenes*) – that is, more generously than what his function required. Moreover, on the relief above the inscription for Kallimachos, the queen and the king are represented as honouring the gods according to the tradition, and they are not replaced by Kallimachos. For the Ptolemies, it was useful politically to have officials and officers who generated trust among the population by imitating the king, at times even by communicating with the local god and becoming local saints or saviours. The Ptolemies let such loyal people be famous.

6. Conclusion

This chapter has sought to explore how fame was understood by different audiences within Ptolemaic society and what their expectations were, how the connections and service to the royal family was an essential element of their fame, and to what extent the concept of fame in the Greek and Egyptian spheres overlapped or influenced each other over time. The examination of the construction and display of fame conceived as social capital – generated through investments in social relations that involved religion and the economy, as well as politics, and that could complement or even replace military deeds – has provided a framework for an analysis of an assemblage of texts and statues that initially may seem unrelated. At least two sets of arguments can be made as a way to conclude. First, investment in social relations through care for the local population was a common ground that generated fame in both the Greek and Egyptian cultural spheres, although it took different forms in the fourth and third century BCE. In Egypt, the welfare of the communities was closely related to the temples, while in the Greek world it evolved within the context of the Greek *poleis*. Yet the common principle possibly facilitated the integration of the priestly local elites into the Ptolemaic administration and army, while the role of royal officials and officers increased within the Egyptian temples – which, in turn, explains the general focus on Egyptian cults. In addition, as royal officials and officers, they all emphasized their more or less close relationship with the king in order to enhance their fame. Second, the display of fame through statues of nonroyal individuals was a new development in the Hellenistic Greek world, but it already existed among the Egyptian elites. This may be connected to the growing tendency to conceive of certain individuals achieving exceptional deeds as sharing some godlike nature. These habits conveniently converged. Egyptian temple precincts can also be perceived as "statuescapes," and in certain cases the decision-making process of voting honours through a decree was adapted outside the Greek *polis*. Some of the statues even reflected the combination of Greek and Egyptian elements and possible influences. By the late Hellenistic period, the cultural and ethnic backgrounds of the officials and officers in Egypt no longer mattered. It was felt proper to the priests and the inhabitants of Thebes, whoever they were, to compare Kallimachos to a star shining for all.

NOTES

1 E.g., the definition in Dreyer and Mittag (2011: 10–11): "The 'local' elite is a minority not necessarily homogeneous, which emerges from a politically-, socially- or ethnically-defined society. It can be composed differently depending on the criteria valid at the time. It has a decisive influence on the decisions that are to be relevant for their communities. The members of the local elite aim to monopolize the communication with the center of power and legitimize their actions among the majority of the local population long-term, and thus try to perpetuate their privileged position" (English translation by B. Dreyer in Dreyer and Gerardin, forthcoming).

2 Mann 1986: 2, 6.

3 Lin 1999: 39.

4 On euergetism *ob honorem*, see Thiers 2006: 287–9 and Veyne 1976: 214. See also the discussion of Tryphaina's euergetism by Ager, in chapter 1 in this volume, and D'Agostini's chapter on Amastris' euergetism.

5 For other similar examples, see Gorre 2009; Moyer 2011b; Moyer 2011a; and Fischer-Bovet 2014: 301–62.

6 Ma 2013: 295.

7 Thus, Rowlandson 2007; Strootman 2014: 117–35.

8 See the discussion of Aitos and his son Thraseas below. On Athenian citizenship granted to most of the Ptolemies, see note 13 below. See also, for instance, a retired Ptolemaic officer receiving citizenship in Thera, in Chaniotis 2005: 152, 154.

9 This family is very well documented over several generations; see Peremans and Van't Dack 1950–81, II/VII, 1828; and Sosin 1997 with sources and bibliography and the inscription of Arsinoë in Cilicia (*SEG* 39 1426) analysed by Habicht and Jones 1989; Chaniotis 1993; and Petzl 2002 (with corrections to the text).

10 Clarysse and Van der Veken 1983: 8.

11 *SEG* 39 1426; see further bibliography in ibid.
12 On the Ptolemies, see Osborne 1981–3: vol. 4, T101–102, PT 140, 144.
13 IG II^2 836 (only lines 1–4) = IG II^3 1185 = *SEG* 39 134; Habicht 1992: 76.
14 *SEG* 56 1881 = *SEG* 56 1877 = I.Tyr. II 28/29, no. 18; Rey-Coquais 1989: 614–17; Habicht and Jones 1989: 345–6.
15 Peremans and Van't Dack 1950–81: vol. II 2174 = vol. VI 15236.
16 On these events, see Polybios 15.25–35.
17 The exact date is debated: for 199/8 BCE instead of 202/1 BCE, see Fischer 1979; Piejko 1991.
18 For the list of betrayals and sources, see Winnicki 2001: 140–1; Fischer-Bovet forthcoming-a.
19 OGIS 90 (Rosetta) = Austin (2006) no. 283. This honorific position argues against Sosin (1997), who suggests that Aitos III lost real power and was removed from the military. But most often the *strategos* of the Fayyum had a military career, see I.Fayoum I 13 and on "nome-*strategoi*," Fischer-Bovet 2014: 323, 326.
20 Ma 2013: 4–5.
21 See, e.g., the city plans in Ma 2013: 309–25.
22 Marquaille 2001: Appendix 2.
23 Ma 2013: 295.
24 Savalli-Lestrade 1998: XIII–XIV.
25 Marquaille 2001: Appendix 2, Old Paphos (Cyprus) no. 2 = OGIS 39; Ptolemy II for the king of Sparta (Olympia no. 2 = Syll.^{3} 433) and for the Athenian Glaukon (Olympia no. 4 = Syll.^{3} 462); Ptolemy III for a king of Sparta (Olympia 5 = I.Olympia 309); a gold statue by Ptolemy VIII and the queen in Kos (no. 7 = OGIS 141) for the former tutor of their children.
26 Baines 2004.
27 According to Gorre (2009: no. 70 [c]), he is a sort of *lesônis*, or temple administrator elected by the priests, without bearing the title.
28 In Greek, translated as "Teos"; Peremans and Van't Dack 1950–80: vol. III/IX, 5825; (1) statue and base, CGC 46341 (the statue is 65 cm high and the base is 31 cm high, Cairo), provenance Tell Athribis, probably the temple; Thiers 1995: doc. 4; (2) broken naophore statue Cairo 4/6/9/1; (3) statue base OIC 10589 (Oriental Institute, Chicago); for Sherman 1981: 83–5 OIC 10589 and CGC 46341 may be dated to ca 325–3 BCE, the former being anterior and coming from the necropolis; full discussion in Gorre 2009: no. 70 and Jelínková-Reymond 1956.
29 Sherman 1981: 102 and note 40 there.
30 Gorre 2009: no. 70 (e) and Sherman 1981: 100.
31 The soldiers are Greek, since they were not called Persians; on this see Sherman 1981; Thiers 1995: 507; Gorre 2009: no. 70; Agut-Labordère and Gorre 2014: 38–9.

32 According to Gorre (2009: no. 70 [b]) about line 24, *contra* Jelínková-Reymond (1956: 103), Djedhor did not pay with his own wealth.

33 Louvre A 88 (granite, 119 cm high without head and base) and statue of Alexandria, no inventory number; Vercoutter 1950. On his possible function as nome governor, see Gorre 2009: no. 41.

34 Thiers 1995: doc. 5.

35 Zivie-Coche 1997. I thank Christiane Zivie-Coche and Philippe Brissaud for permission to use the plates as models for the drawing of figures 5.4 and 5.5.

36 Gorre 2009: nos. 80 and 81.

37 See *SB* III 6285 (229/8 BCE), first attestation of an Egyptian soldier with a five-aroura plot; for larger estates, see the discussion on Ptolemaios son of Panas, with 120 arouras of cleruchic land according to P. Haun. Inv. 406, l. 35–60 in Thompson and Vandorpe 2017.

38 On the revolts, see McGing 1997 and Véïsse 2004.

39 The few known examples are discussed by Zivie-Coche (1997: 65–6) and Baines (2004: 49–50): Haremhab of Naukratis, 3.6 m.

40 For inner and outer courts see Moyer (2011a: 20), with note 15 there for further bibliography.

41 It argues against Van Minnen (2000) that "euergetism," in the sense of standard or spontaneous expenses dispensed by a magistrate, occurred only in the Fayyum and in the case of Kallimachos.

42 Ptolemy I's epithet "Saviour" was first used by the Rhodians for thanking him for his help during Demetrios' siege. Although the context was military, its meaning is broader, referring to "the ability of the leader to provide the utmost degree of support (i.e., salvation) to a community"; see S.G. Caneva (2016: 72–7); Sherman (1981: 102) on a fourth-century Syracuse doctor.

43 In the catalogue of inscriptions collected by Marquaille 2001: Appendix 2, there are only two instances: Halikarnassos no. 2 and Xanthos no. 6. The former (= OGIS I 16) is a dedication of a temple to Sarapis, Isis and Arsinoë Philadelphos under Ptolemy II in Halikarnassos. The latter (OGIS I 91) is a dedication of a *temenos*, a temple and a statue of Artemis under Ptolemy V in Xanthos (no longer under Ptolemaic control).

44 Thus, Agut-Labordère and Gorre 2014; Fischer-Bovet 2014.

45 Thus I. Alexandrie 58, ca second century BCE; see also Ma 2013: 185–6.

46 Zivie-Coche 1987, 2001, 2004; Baines 2004: 52–5; Gorre 2009: nos. 83 and 84.
Panemerit: Peremans and Van't Dack 1950–80 vol. I 294, 988 = vol. II 2128 = vol. III 5717. Inscriptions on two statues and diverse fragments: (1) D 88 = Cairo JE 67094; (2) D 87 = Louvre E 15683; (3) D 26 = Louvre E 15685); (4) Cairo JE 27493 = CGC 27493.
Pikas: Peremans and Van't Dack 1950–80 vol. I/VIII 306 = vol. III/IX 5775, 5778a, 6207 (statue Cairo JE 67093 and a lost statue "Rifaud."

47 Zivie-Coche 2001: 428 and Gorre 2009: nos. 83, 369. They disagree on who granted favours in column 2, though Gorre (378) brings convincing arguments in favour of the king rather than the god.

48 For a detailed analysis, see Zivie-Coche 2001 and Gorre 2009. They do not seem to have belonged to the army. On this, see Gorre (2009: no. 83 [d]) *contra* Quaegeubeur in Van't Dack et al. 1989: 102, who thinks Panemerit, like Peteimouthes, belonged to the army (Gorre 2009: no. 73).

49 For this argument, see Gorre 2009: no. 83(d).

50 Zivie-Coche 2001: 425; Gorre 2009: no. 83(e).

51 References, e.g., in Gorre 2009: no. 83(b).

52 Kaiser 1999: 245–7.

53 Baines 2004: 52–5.

54 On the size, see, e.g., Ma 2013: 17.

55 It cannot be determined whether these innovations and combinations were triggered by internal developments or by Hellenic influence. Baines (2004: 51), *contra* Moyer (2011a: 31–6), rejects the term "hybrid" for the image of these statues.

56 Fischer-Bovet 2014: 308–10.

57 Cairo JE 67093; Gorre 2009: nos. 84, 381.

58 The text of the lost statue is established after J.-J. Rifaud, *Voyage en Égypte, en Nubie, et lieux circumvoisins, depuis 1805 jusqu'en 1827* (unpublished), plate 126: Pikas is said to be loved by the "nobility of the court" because he did useful things for them, but since the statue is in Sile, those who erected it must be the locals (*smrw*) who are mentioned in the statue Cairo JE 67093, who were more inclined than the nobility of the court to erect a statue in Sile. I thank Gilles Gorre for sharing his insights on these texts with me.

59 Zivie-Coche 2004: 281, 383–4; Zivie-Coche 2001: 461; Gorre 2009: nos. 84, 384–5.

60 Gorre 2009: no. 84 (b).

61 Peremans and Van't Dack 1950–81: vol. I/VIII 381 = vol. II/VIII 2216 = vol. VI 17148; Hutmacher 1965: plate 1; Mooren 1975: 0143, 0211, 00335. This Kallimachos is Kallimachos II, according to Blasius (2001: 95–8) but it is still debated whether there were two or three generations; see further Ricketts 1982–3.

62 See the introduction to this chapter and Fischer-Bovet 2014: 323, 326. On the army and the gymnasium, see Fischer-Bovet 2014: 282–4.

63 I. Prose 46 = OGIS I 194 = *SEG* 24 1217; see Blasius (2001) with partial English translation; Heinen (2006) with German translation and earlier bibliography.

64 The following analysis is based on the Greek text. For the Demotic text, the edition announced by Farid (1993: 49) has probably been abandoned, and informal discussions with Demotists confirmed that the Demotic text is hardly readable.

65 OGIS I 194, l. 12: [ὥσπερ πατὴρ ὑπὲρ] οἰκείας πατρίδος καὶ τέκνων γνησίων.

66 Van Minnen 2000: 444–5.

67 Heinen 2006: 38–9 with parallels.

68 On the meaning of the term *polis* in the Egyptian context outside Alexandria, Naukratis and Ptolemais, see Heinen 2006: 31–5 and Fischer-Bovet forthcoming-b.

69 On σκληρός as granite or basalt, see Bernand 1997.

70 Plato's father married an Egyptian, which may explain his priestly function; see Coulon 2001: 107 and plates XV–XXI; and Gorre 2009: no. 24.

71 For the other earlier example, see Boethos, founder of cities, in OGIS I 111 and Heinen 2000.

72 For αὐτῶι as a dative of benefit, see Blasius 2001: 96 and Heinen 2006: 35–6.

73 Heinen 2006.

74 On priests acting as a fictive *polis* in the trilingual decrees, see Clarysse 2000 and Moyer 2011b.

75 E.g., Bernand (1992: 114) who speaks of the "agony" of the royal power. For Panemerit, see Zivie-Coche 2001: 360–1.

76 Heinen 2006.

6

Lemnian Infamy and Masculine Glory in Apollonios' *Argonautica*

JUDITH FLETCHER

The myth of the Lemnian women offers a combination of sex and violence that was apparently irresistible to Greek poets and their audiences. Their story circulated widely in the ancient world, with variations shaped according their authors' agenda. These tales exemplify the idea that famous, or in this case infamous, people are denoted by their unusual actions and qualities. The Lemniai are notorious for their refusal to conform to societal expectations of feminine behaviour because they dared to murder their unfaithful husbands, and their mistresses, along with all the Lemnian men, and then established a gynaecocracy on the island.[1] The notable exception to their wickedness in most versions was their queen, Hypsipyle, who hid her father, Thoas, in a chest set out to sea. Interestingly, she is the only Lemnian woman whose name is well known; she is famous precisely because she is unique within her category. When Jason and the Argonauts landed on the island ruled by Hypsipyle, they had affairs with the women, impregnated some of them, and went on their way. The union between the Argonaut Euphemos of Tanairos and one of the Lemnian women produced descendants who eventually founded Cyrene in North Africa. Through generative male intervention, the infamous Lemnian disaster results in an illustrious line sired by a man whose name means "good reputation."

There were, of course, variations in the tale. According to the fragmentary remains of Euripides' *Hypsipyle*, Jason stayed with the Lemnian queen until she bore twin sons; it was *after* he left that the women murdered their husbands. Hypsipyle fled to Thebes to avoid retribution at the hands of the other Lemnian women, angered because their queen spared her father, who eventually came back to Lemnos. The play deals with the vicissitudes of her life after she is enslaved in Greece, and is eventually reunited with her sons. She may be a heroic figure herself, but her description of the other women of Lemnos (*TrGF* 5.759a.1596) makes it clear that they are the same vengeful murderers found in other accounts.[2] Only a fraction of stories about the Lemnian women survive, many just as fragments or titles, but, to judge from what remains, the consistent theme is the criminal daring of the Lemniai. This aspect of their character continues to be emphasized in Latin treatments by Statius (*Thebaid* 5.28–721) and Valerius Flaccus (*Argonautica* 2.72–427). The most extensive surviving Greek version is by Apollonios of Rhodes, whose nuanced portrait of Hypsipyle emphasizes her distinctiveness. Nonetheless the Lemnian queen includes herself among the scandalous husband-killers and endeavours to control their reputation. But while fame can be self-fashioned and controlled to a certain extent, infamy is a less malleable state. Hypsipyle's attempt to restrain the bad reputation of the Lemnian women is ultimately doomed to fail.

The purpose of this chapter is to explore the theme of fame and infamy in surviving Greek versions of the Lemnian tale, with a view to understanding how their representation in Apollonios' *Argonautica* deviates from and yet conforms to the construction of women's reputation generally and Lemnian infamy specifically. As I shall argue, historical and social changes contributed to these divergences, but stereotypes retained a certain currency with regard to women's reputation. Like all cultural products, literature about the Lemnian women reflects the ideology and values of the society that produced it. A focus on the theme of fame and infamy helps to identify what features the Greek poets selected in their deployment of the Lemnian myth and what aspects of the story were highlighted as notions about women's public identities evolved between the early classical and Hellenistic periods. Cultural norms regarding women's visibility and their relationship to power changed over the centuries that separate the earliest Lemnian stories and the one told by Apollonios, a paradigm shift that affected how the story was told.

1. The Athenian Perspective

Although Homer's original audiences were familiar with some version of the Argonauts' sojourn on Lemnos, it is impossible to determine when the Lemnian massacre became a fully developed episode in the tale.[3] The earliest references to the Lemnians are too fragmentary or obscure to allow any assessment of how the women's character was represented. Euphemos, the Argonaut whose affair with a Lemnian woman led to the Battiad dynasty, is mentioned in Hesiod's *Ehoiai* (fr. 253 Merkelbach-West). Pausanias (5.17.9) describes a famous cedar-wood chest of Kypselos (tyrant of Corinth) that depicted the victory of Euphemos in Lemnos at the chariot race in honour of Peleus. These data suggest that the story of the encounter between the Argonauts and Lemnian women went back at least to the eighth century BCE and that the foundation of Cyrene was a well-established feature in the tradition – a limb of the story that probably grew when the Greeks were expanding into North Africa.

Certainly by the early fifth century BCE, the Lemnian women had earned notoriety for killing their husbands, which suggests that their tale had been in circulation for some time. Two of the earliest surviving versions emphasize the infamy of the Lemnian women. Herodotos provides a unique coda to the myth that goes beyond the first generation of Lemnian shame, but it exemplifies the association of the Lemnians with scandal so well that it is an appropriate introduction to the topic. The historian tells how the Pelasgian inhabitants of Lemnos abducted Athenian women, who bore their captors' children on Lemnos; fearing a future uprising, the Pelasgians killed the Athenian mothers and children. This variation seems to be Athenocentric propaganda, typical of Herodotos, validating Athenian control of Lemnos in the fifth century (Evans 1963: 168–70). The important point for this discussion comes at the end of the section, when Herodotos refers to the Lemnian women's murder of their husbands, an event that occurred before the slaughter of the Athenian women and children: "Ἀπὸ τούτου δὲ τοῦ ἔργου καὶ τοῦ προτέρου τούτων, τὸ ἐργάσαντο αἱ γυναῖκες τοὺς ἅμα Θόαντι ἄνδρας σφετέρους ἀποκτείνασαι, νενόμισται ἀνὰ τὴν Ἑλλάδα τὰ σχέτλια ἔργα πάντα Λήμνια καλέεσθαι" (From this deed and one earlier than this, which the women committed when they killed their husbands, who were companions of Thoas, it has been customary throughout Greece that all cruel deeds be called Lemnian, *Histories* 6.137.4–8.4).[4] It would be difficult to say that cruel deeds were proverbially Lemnian throughout Greece, unless they actually were, but Herodotos is not necessarily telling a familiar tale when he says that the Lemnian men's crime contributed to this reputation. This is the only surviving version of that event until Zenobius (*Centuria* 4.91) repeats it five centuries later, and he is obviously influenced by the Herodotean variation. It is worth noting, however, that later sources such as the fifth-century CE paroemiographer Hesychius associated the Lemnians with bad reputations and infamy. From this brief survey, it is obvious that the Lemnian women's notoriety must have been established at least by the fifth century BCE; they became the embodiment of infamy, an association strong enough to survive for over a millennium.[5]

The second reference to Lemnian notoriety in the fifth century BCE occurs in Aeschylus, whose career was peaking only a few decades before the publication of Herodotos' *Histories*.[6] A choral ode in Aeschylus' *Choephori* substantiates Herodotos' claim about Lemnian infamy. Orestes and Elektra plot the murder of their mother, Klytemnestra, in retaliation for her murder of their father. The Chorus urges them on and offers three mythic paradigms illustrating its reflection that "surpassing all is wicked female passion whereby wedded union is weakened" (*Choephori* 599–601). The mythic *exempla* feature dangerous women killing male kin, but only one is perfectly appropriate in how it treats wives killing husbands.

There is some textual controversy about this passage, but it is clear that the Chorus of slave women offers the Lemnian paradigm as the best fit for Klytemnestra's crime.[7]

Κακῶν δὲ πρεσβεύεται τὸ Λήμνιον
λόγῳ, γοᾶται δὲ δημόθεν κατά-
πτυστον, ἤκασεν δέ τις
τὸ δεινὸν αὖ Λημνίοισι πήμασιν.
θεοστυγήτῳ δ᾽ ἄγει
βροτῶν ἀτιμωθὲν οἴχεται γένος.
σέβει γὰρ οὔτις τὸ δυσφιλὲς θεοῖς.
τί τῶνδ᾽ οὐκ ἐνδίκως ἀγείρω;

Among crimes, the Lemnian holds first place
in stories, and it is lamented by the people as
an abomination. And a person compares
any new horror to the Lemnian calamities.
Because of their god despised pollution,
the race has vanished, dishonoured by mortals.
For no one reveres what is inimical to the gods.
Which of these tales have I not cited justly?
(*Choephori* 631–8, Garvie's text)

Like Herodotos, Aeschylus manipulates the myth for his own narrative requirements. He ignores the union with the Argonauts (although the myth was in circulation, as the chest of Kypselos and other sources indicate) and instead declares that the Lemnian *genos* (race) has vanished because of the foul deeds of its women. He specifically associates their dishonour with the end of the family line. This fits well with the themes of the trilogy: the house of Atreus is in danger of extinction because Klytemnestra killed its patriarch. And, like Herodotos, Aeschylus emphasizes the infamy of the Lemnians: theirs is the most famous and abhorrent of all crimes. As we have already observed, earlier versions of the Lemnian story feature affairs with the Argonauts and their resulting offspring. Why therefore can Aeschylus say that their *genos* has vanished? Note that he is not claiming that the Lemnian women never bore children again. Since a patrilineal family had to be perpetuated through the father, he is right to say, from an Athenian perspective, that genocide has occurred. This is consistent with the argument that Apollo uses to defend Orestes in his trial: the father is the true parent of the child (*Eumenides* 657–65). In this case, with all the Lemnian men gone, the Lemnian race is extinct – a scandal – and the Lemnian women become signifiers not only of dishonour and ill repute but also of sterility.

The explicit combination of sterility and infamy in the Lemnian story is unique to Aeschylus, but it exemplifies how the myth can be tailored to emphasize certain elements of a frame story and how it reflects the prevailing patriarchal values of its original audiences.[8] He is not the only Athenian dramatist to exploit Lemnian ignominy to emphasize the dangerous potential of angry women. The mere mention of their name is enough to telegraph the repulsive possibility of women killing men. In Euripides' *Hecuba,* the former Trojan queen invokes them (along with the Danaids, *Hecuba* 886) as she persuades Agamemnon that she and her attendants have the strength and cunning required to kill the perfidious Polymestor. Euripides was drawing on a vast cultural archive shared by an audience who had only to hear the name "Lemnian" to shudder in horror. They would be familiar with the myth from the numerous treatments in Athenian tragedy and comedy. Only titles and fragments remain (the longest being Euripides' *Hypsipyle*), but the sheer number of these is evidence of the popularity of the Lemnian theme.

The fragments of tragic versions of the union between the Lemnian women and the Argonauts are sufficient to make it obvious that the dangerous qualities of the women are repeatedly emphasized in literary treatments. Not only are they deadly, but they also have a reputation for being sexually aggressive. A scholiast on Apollonios (*Argonautica* 1.769–73) notes that Aeschylus' *Hypsipyle* has the armed Lemnian women forcing the Argonauts to swear an oath to "mingle" with them. Athenian drama tends to be uncomfortable with the idea of women making men swear anything that would put them under women's control: the idea of women being able to coerce men to perform sexually is the *ne plus ultra* of this concept. According to a fragment of Sophokles' *Lemniai,* the women engaged in "fierce combat" (μαχήν ἰσχυράν) with the Argonauts first (*TrGF* 4.384–9). Violence seems to be a form of foreplay in this tale, which is preserved in Statius' version of the event in *Thebaid* 5.376–97.[9]

The Lemnian theme was also popular on the Athenian comic stage. Fragments of Aristophanes' *Lemniai* remain, and of the Lemnian plays by

Nikochares, Antiphanes, Alexis, and Diphilos. [10] Although not enough survives to reconstruct any of these treatments, it seems likely that the myth provided an opportunity to depict sex-starved women prevailing over the first men that they have seen in over a year. We have only to look at the final moments of Aristophanes' *Assemblywomen* (when three hags dispute over their sexual rights to a young citizen) to see how uncomfortably funny this could be. Aristophanes, his rivals, and successors took full advantage of the comic potential of the Lemnians' reputation for a dangerous female libido. As is so often the case, women's bad reputations include some aspect of their sexuality.

The popularity of the Lemnian theme in both tragedy and comedy attests to and perpetuates the women's notoriety. It is only by an accident of preservation that they are not as well known in contemporary culture as Medea or Klytemnestra, since they were just as prevalent in Greek drama. As Aeschylus and Herodotos indicate, the Lemnians were the very embodiment of infamy. How did this register with Athenian attitudes about women's reputations? The intended audiences of tragedy and comedy were exposed to an ideology famously summed up by Thucydides' version of Perikles' funeral speech: "Hers is the great reputation whose fame, whether for excellence or blame, is spread least among the males" (Thucydides, *Histories* 2.45.2).[11] Admittedly that sentence is decontextualized, but there are other data to support the idea that citizen women were not to be mentioned in public. Women of citizen status were not named in court (at least while they were alive) and could not appear to give testimony. The ideal is of a silent, invisible woman, although reality was much more nuanced. Forensic rhetoric illustrates how litigants could play fast and lose with these ideals to smear the reputations of their opponents' mothers and wives (Schaps 1977: 323–30).

In the calculus of citizenship, Athenian women can become bearers and signifiers of dishonour. Women's reputations were always possible subjects of gossip and scandal, providing ammunition for the constant negotiation of one-upmanship among men. Although men were also subject to rumour and scandal, gossip functioned more as a type of social control for women, who did not have the ability to counteract it in public. As Virginia Hunter put it, "Gossip penetrated into the privacy of the *oikos* to mark out women who did not conform to community standards" (1994: 116). *Hetairai* and metic women (by no means the same) could be named, and were more likely to gain a reputation in a society where having a reputation of any sort was, notionally at least, not a good thing for a woman.

It is important to consider the broader implications of fame and infamy in the context of gender when we think about the representation of the Lemnian women in Athenian drama. Anxiety about female agency in the Athenian theatre has been well studied. The landscape of tragedy is populated reassuringly by captive women (who are usually silent like Iole in Sophokles' *Trachiniai*) or become silenced (like Tekmessa in his *Ajax*); women who willingly accept death on behalf of men (such as Euripides' Alkestis); or alternately, and more disturbingly, by characters such as Klytemnestra, Medea, Phaidra, and Deianeira who have some degree of sexuality and agency.[12] Women like Alkestis may have a posthumous honour for service to their family, but the foreign witch Medea has a more insidious reputation. The chorus of her name play reflects on the bad reputation of women given by the poets (410–45), which the play ironically validates. In this context it is easy to understand that the fame of the Lemnian women goes hand in hand with their murderous agency. In Athenian tragedy, any woman who acts in anger is likely to disgrace herself, the Lemnians included. As Aeschylus put it, their crime "is preeminent in story" (*Choephori* 631).

2. Beyond Athens: The Lemnian Story in Praise Poetry

As the preceding discussion indicates, conventional attitudes about fame and gender influenced how the Lemnian women were presented and received in the civic context of classical Athens. Let us now look beyond Athens to investigate how the Lemnian story plays out in a genre that exists specifically for the purpose of celebrating male achievements in the context of an aristocratic *ethos* and hero cult.[13] Pindar's epinician poems, composed in the early fifth century BCE, were commissioned by wealthy patrons to commemorate their own (and sometimes other men's) athletic achievements. Charles Segal describes the genre as "a public voice bestowing blame and praise in a communal gathering." Pindar's masterpiece, *Pythian* 4, memorialized the chariot victory of Arkesilaos IV in 462 BCE (about four years before Aeschylus' *Oresteia*). King of the prosperous Greek colony Cyrene in North Africa, Arkesilaos traced his lineage back to Battos, its founder descended from the Argonaut Euphemos (or Euphamos, the Doric version of his name) and a Lemnian woman.[14]

In his treatment of the episode, Pindar (or his client) chose to celebrate the illustrious paternity of Arkesilaos, which inevitably meant that he had to acknowledge the unnamed Lemnian foremother of his *laudandus*. *Pythian* 4 is roughly contemporaneous with Herodotos' and Aeschylus' harsh words about Lemnian infamy, but Pindar was not obliged to make the same assessment. His treatment of the myth is determined by his client's desire for glory, which he traces back to his Argonautic and Lemnian ancestry. Cyrene in fact had a tradition of powerful women, including Arkesilaos' paternal grandmother, the formidable Pheretima (her name means "bringer of honour"), who had been responsible for a few political murders, according to Herodotos, although she came to a hideous end (Pindar, *Pythian* 4.162–200). Although Pindar does not go so far as to glorify the daring of the Lemnian women, he does not suppress their violent tendencies either.

The structure of *Pythian* 4 helps to celebrate the founding of Cyrene in a particularly brilliant way; the Lemnian women frame the story, composed as a ring composition. The first part of the poem is a prophecy in the voice of Medea, now with the Argonauts on the island of Thera. She explains the significance of a clod of earth given to Euphamos in Libya that was swept overboard, and prophesizes that it would wash up on of the island Thera, later populated by descendants of Euphamos, who, as we know, will found Cyrene.

Medea recounts how Euphamos will sleep with "foreign women" (i.e., the Lemnians – the plural here is intriguing) to found a "choice race" (*Pythian* 4.50–1) with "honour from the god," and the "noble fame" of Euphamos (whose name means "good reputation") is highlighted again in a catalogue of the Argonauts, now in the voice of the narrator (175). Toward the end of this unusually long poem, after narrating the quest for the Golden Fleece, the poem returns to the Lemnian women. Pindar's variation is to make the Lemnian encounter happen on the voyage home (which is why Medea can predict it), after the fleece has been won. Now in the voice of the narrator the poem continues:

Ἔν τ᾽ Ὠκεανοῦ πελάγεσσι μίγεν πόντῳ τ᾽ ἐρυθρῷ
Λαμνιᾶν τ᾽ ἔθνει γυναικῶν ἀνδροφόνων:
ἔνθα καὶ γυίων ἀέθλοις ἐπέδειξαν κρίσιν ἐσθᾶτος ἀμφίς,
καὶ συνεύνασθεν. καὶ ἐν ἀλλοδαπαῖς
σπέρμ᾽ ἀρούραις τουτάκις ὑμετέρας ἀκτῖνος ὄλβου δέξατο μοιρίδιον
ἆμαρ ἢ νύκτες. τόθι γὰρ γένος Εὐφάμου φυτευθὲν λοιπὸν αἰεὶ
τέλλετο …

Reaching the expanses of Ocean, and the Red Sea,
they mingled with the tribe of Lemnian women, husband-killers.
There they displayed their strength in athletic competitions
contending for the prize of a cloak,
and they went to bed with the women. In foreign fields then
the fated day, or night, received the seed of your shining prosperity;
for there the race of Euphemos was planted,
to continue forever … *(Pythian* 4.249–57)

This new order of events shifts the focus to Euphamos; Hypsipyle is not mentioned (and Medea's presence is enough to suppress that version of the story). Pindar glides over the Lemnian women's past, acknowledging that they were husband-killers, but without judgment. There is no mention of conflict between Lemnians and Argonauts, but there is an athletic competition (as depicted on the chest of Kypselos), a mirror of the victory of Arkesilaos, descendant of Euphamos.[15] What is important here is that Euphamos planted his seed in Lemnos, from which the Battiad dynasty, the rulers of Cyrene, would grow and which ends with Arkesilaos, *laudandus* of the poem. The focus is on fame, not infamy – and has shifted from the Lemnians' crime to their fertility. The ensuing glory is strictly masculine; the foremother of the Battiad dynasty is not named (although *scholia* give her various names). It is as if female notoriety can be transmuted into masculine glory.

3. Apollonios and the Hellenistic Perspective

Some two hundred years later, Cyrene was part of the Ptolemaic empire. One of its most famous women was Berenike II, wife of Ptolemy Euergetes, her second husband. She was anything but nameless or invisible; rather, she typified the celebrity of royal women of this age. As Dee Clayman puts it in her study of Berenike, "The women of the ruling class [of Cyrene] were not inhibited by the norms of behaviour that ruled their sisters on the mainland, and the islands" (2014: 29). The Athenian civic ideal of the silent, invisible woman no longer applied, at least not to the aristocratic members of Hellenistic society.

Sarah Pomeroy, in her *Women in Hellenistic Egypt*, notes an increased public visibility and economic agency of women in Ptolemaic Egypt (1985: 148–73). We find the emergence of female euergetism, wealthy women being celebrated for their public benefactions, and other evidence of women's public personae.[16] Related to this change in gender stereotypes is a shift from the androcentric poetry of classical Greece to a female subjectivity, thanks to poets such as Theokritos, who wrote with an aristocratic female patron in mind. In general, women had more access to education, as the existence of learned women poets such as Erinna and Anyte suggest. They were consumers and even producers of poetry at a time when women, at least those of the elite, could be named and celebrated publicly. Arsinoë II, for example, is celebrated as the producer of an Adonis pageant for a female audience in Theokritos' *Idyll* 15. Silence and obscurity are no longer the desiderata for women, whose reputations could be both good and bad.

Considering this context, we turn to Apollonios' *Argonautica*, which features the longest surviving version of the affair between the Lemnian women and the Argonauts thus far. Anatole Mori, in *The Politics of Apollonios' Argonautica*, considers the public identities of elite and royal women in her analysis of the Lemnian episode. Mori reads the poem as a validation of Greek expansion (especially in the context of Apollonios' *ktisis* poems that celebrate the foundation of a city or colony). She notes that Jason's interactions are characterized by diplomacy whenever possible. With regard to the Lemnian episode, she compares the mass union of Argonauts to Lemnian women with the mass marriage of Alexander's men to the women of Susa (Arrian, *Anabasis* 7.4.4–8). And she observes that the ideological roles played by the early Ptolemaic queens established "a positive, even corrective model for the traditional epic representation of women" (2008: 101). As she notes, there was a well-established tradition of women co-ruling with men, although they seldom ruled independently. Apollonios represents the Lemnians as politically astute, independent women, in keeping with this enhanced political involvement of women. In addition, Mori has done an admirable job of recuperating the character of Jason, seeing him more as a diplomat than a feminized pretty boy emasculated by the Lemnians.[17] The existence of male and female co-rulers, as she points out, would shape how audiences received the story of Jason's encounter with Hypsipyle, although of course Jason does not accept her invitation to replace her father. A new recognition of women's public activity does not entirely replace anxiety about female political agency found in Athenian drama, but it does acknowledge the possibility of competent, respectable women in the civic sphere.

Mori is reading the Lemnian episode in the general framework of royal women's public identities. Dee Clayman is more specific, and reads it as a product of the historical period of Berenike II (2014: 36–8). The epic ends in Libya with a reference to the founding of Cyrene, Berenike's birthplace, by the descendants of a Lemnian woman. Accepting a date of the composition of the *Argonautica* in or around 238 BCE, the reign of Ptolemy Euergetes and Berenike II, she sees a special applicability of the Lemnian story to Berenike, who reportedly had her first husband Demetrios the Fair killed when she discovered him in bed with her mother Apame.[18] Thus, Berenike too was a husband-killer, if Justin's lurid account (*Epitome* 26.4–8) is to be believed, who would not stand for marital infidelity. In dynastic terms, this had advantages parallel to those of her Lemnian foremother. She was able to marry her cousin Ptolemy Euergetes and become queen of Egypt. The correspondence between the Lemnians and Berenike puts a different cast on the episode. For one thing, the Lemnian story generalizes the crime of husband killing, and

Apollonios plays down the severity of the crime, as we shall see below. It is especially significant that the poem ends with the Argonauts in Libya and the promise of a future colony populated by the descendants of Euphemos and his Lemnian lover. Even if we are sceptical about the husband-murder parallel, there is adequate connection between Berenike and the Lemnian women just in terms of the foundation of Cyrene. On the other hand, Justin's account does exploit, and perhaps even creates, the element of scandal in Berenike's biography. He illustrates how receptive his audience would be to spicy details about a female public figure's ambitions.[19]

The possibility that women may not be able to control their own reputations in the still predominantly patriarchal public world is something to consider as we turn to Apollonios' treatment of the Lemnians' reputation. The episode is loaded with irony but also with pathos, especially in contrast with that of Athenian versions of the tale. On the surface, it seems that the poet is trying to rehabilitate the Lemnian reputation while still acknowledging their crimes. If we examine the episode in more detail, we see how it humanizes the women and offers their perspective of the situation, typifying Alexandrian female-centred poetry, as noted above. The *Argonautica* is unique among surviving accounts of the episode up to that point because it is focalized through Hypsipyle and her subjects, allowing us to understand their concerns, one of which is their bad reputation. This is consonant with the theme of reputation and honour within the poem itself and is, moreover, a generic feature of epic. As Fantuzzi and Hunter put it, "The fundamental purpose of epic [is] the perpetuation of men's fame, *kleos*" (2004: 93). It is the poet's role to perpetuate the glory of his subjects. In the first line of the *Argonautica*, the narrator announces that he will "recall the famous deeds of people born long ago" (παλαιγενέων κλέα φωτῶν, 1.1). Glory is what the Argonauts are after, so much so that the prophet Idmon, foreseeing his own death on the expedition, is still motivated by a desire for glory (ἐυκλείῃ, 1.447). It is not just the fame of Jason at stake here: Apollonios celebrates the glory of all the Argonauts, notably in the final lines of the poem.[20]

In the Lemnian episode, the heroic pursuit of a glorious reputation is jeopardized, as a female population endeavours to suppress its own shameful disrepute. These attempts at controlling fame and infamy, Greek and Lemnian, respectively, are not mutually exclusive, nor does one affect the other. Yet the confluence of these two agenda creates a narrative tension that remains throughout the poem. Lemnos is the Argonauts' first stop on their expedition at the end of their eventful first day. The narrator immediately recounts the murder of the Lemnian men the year before: the slaughter is a ruthless crime (*Argonautica* 1.609–10), as he observes, but he expresses some sympathy (however ironic) for the women, apostrophizing them as "unhappy" (ὢ μέλεαι, 1.616):

> Ἔνθ᾽ ἄμυδις πᾶς δῆμος ὑπερβασίῃσι γυναικῶν
> νηλειῶς δέδμητο παροιχομένῳ λυκάβαντι.
> δὴ γὰρ κουριδίας μὲν ἀπηνήναντο γυναῖκας
> ἀνέρες ἐχθήραντες, ἔχον δ᾽ ἐπὶ ληιάδεσσιν
> τρηχὺν ἔρον, ἃς αὐτοὶ ἀγίνεον ἀντιπέρηθεν
> Θρηικίην δῃοῦντες: ἐπεὶ χόλος αἰνὸς ὄπαζεν
> Κύπιδος, οὕνεκά μιν γεράων ἐπὶ δηρὸν ἄτισσαν.
> ὢ μέλεαι, ζήλοιό τ᾽ ἐπισμυγερῶς ἀκόρητοι.
> οὐκ οἶον σὺν τῇσιν ἑοὺς ἔρραισαν ἀκοίτας
> ἀμφ᾽ εὐνῇ, πᾶν δ᾽ ἄρσεν ὁμοῦ γένος, ὥς κεν ὀπίσσω
> μήτινα λευγαλέοιο φόνου τίσειαν ἀμοιβήν.
> (*Argonautica* 1.609–19)

> There all together the entire citizen body had been ruthlessly
> overpowered in the previous year by the crimes of the women.
> For the men had come to despise and reject their lawful wives,
> but developed a savage passion for the captive women
> whom they brought back after pillaging Thrace
> on the opposite shore. The terrible anger of Kypris
> afflicted them, because they had not paid her honour for a long time.[21]
> O unhappy women, sad victims of insatiable jealousy.
> Not only did they slaughter their own husbands along with the women
> for their affairs, but an entire generation of men at the same time,
> so that they would not pay any retribution later for the wretched crime.

This perspective exemplifies a characteristic of Apollonios that Andrew Morrison identifies as a "narratorial sympathy for the pathetic situation of his characters" (2007: 278).[22] Apollonios' narrator tends to be more emotionally involved with his characters than the earlier epic Homeric narrator.[23] It is important to remember that this narrative voice is a constructed persona, whose act of recounting the adventures of the Argonauts reveals a complex relationship to his story. His is a learned voice replete with allusions, especially to Homer, but one that also challenges the received tradition. Yet beyond his intricate and even contentious intertextuality we can also detect a personality who is often disturbed or vague about his sources. Note, for example, the occasional use of the particle πού ("I suppose"), an expression of uncertainty (*Argonautica* 1.536–8).[24]

For now we observe that this narrator has sympathy for the women, who have been performing men's jobs, quite happily preferring them to their traditional tasks of weaving. When the ship approaches, they don men's armour, fearing an attack by the Thracians, and throng to the shore "like flesh-eating Thyiades" (*Argonautica* 1.636). The simile is ironic but leads an educated reader to recall the tragic predecessors of this moment; in Sophokles, for example, the women engage in combat with the Argonauts. The Lemnian women in the *Argonautica*, however, watch the shoreline in "helpless distress." These are not the dangerous, sex-starved women that Athenian drama represents. Instead, combat is averted by diplomacy, persuasion, and good sense. The narrator thus subtly guides the sympathies of his audience by presenting the women as timid, cautious, and eventually sensible. He identifies a few of them by name, Iphinöe the messenger and Polyxo the old nurse, giving some humanity to this usually anonymous group.

Faced with the dilemma of receiving outsiders into this closed society, Hypsipyle calls an assembly: she recommends giving the Greeks provisions but making them remain outside the city walls for a night. Her principal concern is the Lemnian women's reputation. If the Argonauts get to know them too well, a "bad report" (κακὴ … /βάξις) will spread about the women's horrible deeds (*Argonautica* 1.661–2). She vainly hopes to thwart their future proverbial status by feeding the Argonauts and sending them on their way none the wiser. But she is no tyrant, and judiciously turns over important decisions to her democratic assembly.[25] Calling the women together, she sets out the dilemma and her plan:

> Ὦ φίλαι, εἰ δ᾽ ἄγε δὴ μενοεικέα δῶρα πόρωμεν
> ἀνδράσιν, οἷά τ᾽ ἔοικεν ἄγειν ἐπὶ νηὸς ἔχοντας,
> ἤια, καὶ μέθυ λαρόν, ἵν᾽ ἔμπεδον ἔκτοθι πύργων
> μίμνοιεν, μηδ᾽ ἄμμε κατὰ χρειὼ μεθέποντες
> ἀτρεκέως γνώωσι, κακὴ δ᾽ ἐπὶ πολλὸν ἵκηται
> βάξις: ἐπεὶ μέγα ἔργον ἐρέξαμεν, οὐδέ τι πάμπαν
> θυμηδὲς καὶ τοῖσι τόγ᾽ ἔσσεται, εἴ κε δαεῖεν.
> (*Argonautica* 1.657–3)

> Friends, let us give pleasing gifts to these men,
> such things as are suitable to take back to their ships,
> provisions, and sweet wine, so that they might remain firmly
> outside our walls, and not come among us out of need

> and get to know us too well, for an evil report might travel far and wide. We have committed a terrible deed, and it would not be pleasant for them either if they learned of it.

Hypsipyle, who includes herself among the Lemnian man-killers (μέγα ἔργον ἐρέξαμεν), is most concerned with controlling their reputations. It is an endearing but ironic counterpoint to the women's well-established reputation, of which the narrator and his narratees are well aware. As he had earlier explained, the androcides were divinely motivated (a common feature of the myth, although this is the first surviving version that mentions it), yet that does not exculpate the women. The narrator saw fit to mention the crime at the very outset of the episode; it is impossible to overlook it. Now we hear about it from Hypsipyle herself, and her attempt at damage control is an acknowledgment of the magnitude of the crime. But the cautious queen is not thinking far enough ahead to consider the implications of a women-only world.

Her aged nurse, Polyxo, reminds the assembly that, without men, there will be no next generation. Thus, for purely practical reasons, not sexual appetite (although that will come later), Hypsipyle agrees to let the Lemnian women sleep with the Argonauts. Indeed Aphrodite wants the Lemnians to mate with the Greeks as a favour to Hephaistos, so that his island will be repopulated (*Argonautica* 1.850–2); divine motivation now mirrors and validates human motivation. Of course it would hardly serve either purpose – mortal or divine – if word of the slaughter reached the Argonauts. When Hypsipyle meets with Jason, she has to come up with some plausible explanation for the absence of men on the island. The Lemnians have not acquired the reputation attributed to them by Aeschylus and others, although the narrator and his naratees know the story. Hypsipyle is aware of its damaging potential, and if the island is to be repopulated she will need to control the story. Her tale, which contradicts the narrator's version, is a well-wrought lie: the men have left the island to plough the fields of their Thracian concubines, she claims (1.793–6).[26] Like all good lies, this one does contain some truthful elements, and, as Hunter put it, "is emotionally true" (1993: 112).[27] Hypsipyle goes into considerable detail about the effect of the Lemnian men's passion for the Thracian women: the consequences were so devastating that the society started to disintegrate. While Hypsipyle dissimulates the circumstance of this neglect, her vivid description of the disruption of family life rings very true. For the first time in surviving literature, the perspective of the Lemnian wives is presented, and they are treated with some degree of understanding. Unlike Euripides' Hypsipyle, the Lemnian queen does not distinguish herself from the homicidal women. But this new version of events also contributes to the impression that there may be alternate narrative paths, as we already know from Euripides. Apollonios slyly offers the possibility that Lemnian infamy could be nipped in the bud, while simultaneously affirming its existence.

Nonetheless, within the compass of the poem, the news of the mass murder never seems to leave the island; the Argonauts never learn the truth, and it is never acknowledged explicitly again by the narrator after they leave. In addition to giving us the women's perspective, the story also suggests that they have the ability to control their own reputations. That would be a lot of narrative agency, if it were true. The irony, of course, is that Apollonios' audience knows full well that the story will circulate. The fact that it does not within the poem contributes to the sense that Jason is a poor judge of feminine character, a flaw that will serve another notorious woman very well.

It is also worth noting that there seems to be no residual miasma for the Lemnian women, a phenomenon that seems to mute the severity of the deed. The idea that homicide would create a psychic pollution was prevalent in the ancient world; both legal and religious measures were required to dispel it.[28] Note, for example, the emphasis on pollution and purification after the murder of Apsyrtos. In contrast, Apollonios makes no explicit reference to the miasma attached to the Lemnian women. Did they go through the purification ritual prescribed to Jason and Medea by Kirke (*Argonautica* 4.557–61)? If they did, there is no mention of it.

In a subtle allusion to this point, when Herakles upbraids his fellow sailors for languishing in the beds of the Lemnian women, he refers to the practice of purificatory exile for homicides:

Δαιμόνιοι, πάτρης ἐμφύλιον αἷμ᾽ ἀποέργει
ἡμέας; ἦε γάμων ἐπιδευέες ἐνθάδ᾽ ἔβημεν
κεῖθεν, ὀνοσσάμενοι πολιήτιδας; αὖθι δ᾽ ἔαδεν
ναίοντας λιπαρὴν ἄροσιν Λήμνοιο ταμέσθαι;
οὐ μὰν εὐκλειεῖς γε σὺν ὀθνείῃσι γυναιξὶν
ἐσσόμεθ᾽ ὧδ᾽ ἐπὶ δηρὸν ἐελμένοι: οὐδέ τι κῶας
αὐτόματον δώσει τις ἑλὼν θεὸς εὐξαμένοισιν.
ἴομεν αὖτις ἕκαστοι ἐπὶ σφέα: τὸν δ᾽ ἐνὶ λέκτροις
Ὑψιπύλης εἰᾶτε πανήμερον, εἰσόκε Λῆμνον
παισὶν ἐπανδρώσῃ, μεγάλη τέ ἑ βάξις ἵκηται.
(*Argonautica* 1.869–78)

Fools, does kin murder keep us from our fatherland?
Or do we need wives because we have scorned our own?

Have we decided to live here and divide up
the rich plowland of Lemnos?
We will not gain glory cooped up like this so long with foreign
women. Nor is there any fleece acting of its own accord for
some god to seize and hand over to us in answer to our prayers.
Let each one of us return to his own affairs, and leave [Jason]
to the bed
of Hypsipyle all day long, until he populates
Lemnos with his sons, and his great reputation goes forth.

Herakles' derisive suggestion that the Argonauts linger on Lemnos because they are in exile for kin murder is a reminder of the women's crimes. Hypsipyle might be able to suppress the information, but the narrator shrewdly alerts his audience that murder had been committed. The danger of remaining with the Lemnian women would be to have no fame and glory or, as Herakles sarcastically suggests, for Jason to have a reputation for producing Lemnian sons. It is interesting that he uses the same term, βάξις ("report"), that Hypsipyle used when she worried about reports of the murder circulating beyond the island. The Lemnian women not only suppress their own reputations but also have the potential to suppress those of the Argonauts, or at least to offer an alternate opportunity for βάξις, much as Hypsipyle attempts for the Lemnian story.[29] Lurking behind this statement, of course, is the possibility of a different outcome for Jason among the Lemnians, as Euripides' *Hypsipyle* suggested. Yet the Argonauts do press on, and the story follows its familiar path.

Jason and his companions do indeed take stories of the Lemnian women with them, but not the stories of their crimes. When he first encounters Lykos, Jason tells of his travels thus far, including "how they were given hospitality by the Lemnian women" (ὡς Λημνιάδεσσιν ἐπεξεινοῦντο γυναιξίν, *Argonautica* 2.764). Any report of the Lemnian women is a good one, referring only to their honourable behaviour as hosts. And we are reminded of the gifts that the Lemnian women gave to their Argonaut lovers: Polydeukes takes off a robe, a guest gift (ξεινήιον), from a Lemnian woman, when he engages in the wrestling match with the Bebrykian king Amykos (2.30–2). Jason, in preparation for his trials in Kolchis, puts on a robe given to him by Hypsipyle as "a memento of their frequent lovemaking" (3.1204–6).[30] Hypsipyle's attempts at suppressing a bad reputation have been, it seems, successful, but then how would the narrator have known the story?

Jason's naive account of the women's gracious hospitality not only suggest that he is easily duped but also reinforces a tension between what the narrator knows and the story that Hypsipyle wants to suppress. But we are not allowed to forget the Lemnian crime, since a gift of Hypsipyle's is mentioned at another critical moment. Jason deploys a "sacred purple robe from Hypsipyle" (πέπλον ... ἱερὸν Ὑψιπυλείης πορφύρεον) to entice Apsyrtos into the fatal trap set by him and Medea (*Argonautica* 4.423–4). A digressive history of the robe compels the reader to remember the Lemnians just at the point when Jason and Medea will murder the boy. Like Athena's robe gift to Jason, the subject of an extensive ekphrasis as he goes to meet Hypsipyle (1.727–61), it too possesses a seductive power, but a power that leads to an act of kin murder. The apparently civilizing aspects implied by the robe's function as a gift are obviated by the murderous purpose it serves, and it is hard not to think at that point of those fatal garments of tragedy – especially the one that Medea herself will send to the Corinthian princess before she kills her own sons. Like the tragic robes that preceded it, this one it is a symbol of treachery and deceit. And although the robe is a memento of the love affair of Jason and Hypsipyle, it seems now to carry the taint of the Lemnian crime. Thus the robe links the kin murders of the Lemnians with the murderous Medea – it looks backward to the Lemnian murder and forward to a later Medea who uses her ancestral robe as a fatal trap.

How does the robe as a symbol of danger and death relate to the topic of fame and infamy? In the surface narrative, Apollonios accepts an erasure of the Lemnian women's crime, not allowing it to be repeated by the Argonauts, who are oblivious to it and who carry news only of Lemnian hospitality. But these gifts of hospitality carry with them a reminder of a murderous group of women, and one notable gift facilitates another familial murder. The Lemnian robes carry a message that can be read only by the audience of the poem, a message that perpetuates Lemnian infamy. As they so often do in Greek poetry, textiles signify stories; for example, the great purple robe woven by Helen in Homer's *Iliad* recounts a version of the Trojan War (*Iliad* 3.125–7). Ancient audiences were familiar with such "story cloths," which made it easy for poets to conflate texts and textiles.[31] Apollonios develops this common metaphor to suggest that the robe-gifts of the Lemnian women bear the taint of their reputation. None of his characters can detect this subtext, but every time the gifts of Lemnian women are mentioned we must think of their crime. It is "pre-eminent in story," to quote Aeschylus again, and what they are best known for. Thus our awareness of their reputations comes into play when we read of the robe that entraps Apsyrtos.

Hypsipyle's robe and its role in that heinous crime is the last we hear of the Lemnian women, but the island itself and its illustrious men are celebrated at the end of the poem. After an ordeal in Libya, Jason predicts that a clod of Libyan soil – a more salutary "guest gift" than Hypsipyle's robe – will become an island where Euphemos' descendants will live, and that

Euphemos will have "great and glorious fame." The narrator reveals that indeed the sons of Euphemos, "who previously dwelled on Sintian Lemnos" (*Argonautica* 4.1758–9), will populate Thera. The infamy of the Lemnian women is safely in the mythical past, while the glory of their lovers and sons extends into history.

Apollonios inherited a tradition wherein Lemnian women were a byword for infamy, but his treatment of their encounter with Jason and the Argonauts evinces a complex notion of celebrity and notoriety specific to the Hellenistic world. Unlike Athenian dramatists, whose representations of the Lemniai are informed by ideologies of gender that tinge the story with an anxious misogyny, Apollonios plays down their aggressive sexuality and emphasizes their hospitality and good sense. With more emphasis on female subjectivity, his account of the Argonauts' sojourn with Hypsipyle and her subjects exhibits typical features of Alexandrian poetry; we get a sympathetic insight into the queen's motives and judgment. The astute leadership of Hypsipyle accords with contemporary attitudes about women's agency, especially that of aristocratic women, who were more visible and authoritative than those of classical Athens. But the Lemnian queen does not align perfectly with the powerful women of the Hellenistic world, whose status and public recognition were dependent on husbands, sons, and brothers. Jason is not inclined to remain in Lesbos as co-ruler with Hypsipyle, but, on the other hand, the Argonauts do not spread reports of the crime that preceded their arrival. If it had been left up to Jason and his crew, Hypsipyle would have navigated the Lemnian women's repute into obscurity.

Writing for a society in which fame and celebrity were carefully curated by both men and women – and royal women's conduct could still result in severe condemnation if it deviated from prescribed social roles – Apollonios offers a shrewd commentary on the politics of reputation. The specter of scandal was omnipresent in the Hellenistic world, and Hypsipyle's futile attempt to staunch Lemnian infamy resonates with the histories of noble women, who were never totally in control of their own repute, as the salacious accounts of Justin show so well. By mentioning the story at the outset of the episode, the narrator reminds us that there was nothing the otherwise laudable queen could do to prevent it from spreading.

NOTES

1 The reason for their husbands' infidelity is attributed, in some versions, to a bad smell inflicted on the women by Aphrodite, who was offended by their neglect of her rites. No allusion to the smell shows up in the texts that I discuss. Jackson 1990 surveys the tradition and speculates about its origins.

2 See Bond (1963) for a discussion of the fragments of Euripides' play. Other literary treatments of the Hypsipyle stories have been collected by Jacobson (1974: 94–108) and Dräger (2016).

3 Homer mentions the son of Jason and Hypsipyle, Euneos, who gave provisions to the Achaians when they were near Lemnos (*Il.* 7.465–7; cf. 23.747).

4 All translations of Greek texts are my own, unless noted otherwise.

5 See Dumézil (1924: 9–12) on the Lemnian reputation, although, with the exception of Herodotos and Aeschylus, his examples are from late antiquity; e.g., apothegms from Photios, Suidas, and Heschyius, in addition to *scholia* from *Lysistrata*.

6 Aeschylus wrote a play called the *Lemnioi* (The Lemnian Men), but there is no evidence that it dealt with Herodotean story of the Pelasgian massacre, as Garvie suggests (1988: 218–19); it probably treated the Philoktetes theme, and was named after a Chorus of Lemnians. For its possible position in a trilogy, see Gantz 2007: 66–7.

7 Stinton (1979) wanted to rearrange the order of strophe and antistrophe in this system because, after alluding to Klytemnestra, the Chorus turn to their third mythic *exemplum*, the Lemnians. Stinton's suggestion need not concern us overly, and no editor has taken it up, but he does make the important point that the situation of the husband killing Klytemnestra is best illustrated by the Lemnian story. See Lebeck (1967) for further discussion of the stasimon's relevance to the trilogy as a whole.

8 The analogy will work the other way in later authors. Antoniadis (2015) explores how Valerius Flaccus (*Argon.* 2. 98–241) draws on the image of Klytemnestra (via Seneca) in his representation of the Lemnian crime.

9 See Lachenaud 2010: 116.

10 In an ingenious analysis, Martin (1987: 83–6) argues that *Lysistrata* is a reworking of the Lemnian theme, with the women of Athens dominating the sexuality of the men by means of an oath (although, in their case, it's an oath of abstinence).

11 Bosworth (2000a: 2–3) argues that, since Perikles is addressing war widows here, he is advising them not to be excessive in their lamentation.

12 The anxiety has been well studied by Rabinowitz (1993) and others.

13 Segal (1986: 10) and his description of *Pythian* 4 in particular: "A meditation on the relation between cosmic and moral order" (8). For a more complex understanding of Pindaric *kleos*, which associates it with hero cults, see Currie 2005: 71–84.

14 The chariot victory is also celebrated in *Pythian* 5, but *Pythian* 4 was commissioned by a political exile, Demophilos, in order to reconcile with his cousin Arkesilaos.

15 Braswell (1988: 349) conjectures that there were funeral games for Thoas. *Olympian* 4 mentions another Argonaut, Erginos, competing in and winning Lemnian athletic games.

16 As illustrated in the chapters by Ager and D'Agostini in this volume, Cleopatra Tryphaina and Amastris exemplify female euergetism.

17 See Beye (1969) on Jason as a "love hero." Clauss (1993: 106–47) suggests that these gender inversions indicate the dangers of the Argonauts being demasculinized by the Lemnians. Cf. DeForest (1994: 57–9), who has a generally deprecatory commentary on Jason's capabilities, especially in Lemnos.

18 The murder was, of course, more than the reaction of a jealous wife: it had political motivations. Apame had disregarded Magus, her deceased husband's arrangements to have her daughter marry Ptolemy, and replaced him with Demetrios, who was unpopular with the people of Cyrene. Justin takes Demetrios' epthitet, "the Fair," literally and spins a tale of mother and daughter rivals for a handsome man. The term is actually an insult, implying that Demetrios was a homosexual prostitute. See Clayman (2014: 36–8) for further discussion.

19 On Justin's account of the Ptolemaic princess Tryphaina, whose scandalous biographical details may have been created for the purposes of Seleukid propaganda, see chapter 1 in this volume.

20 As Fantuzzi and Hunter (2004: 95) observe.

21 The *scholion* for this passage (1.609–19) attributes this preference to Aphrodite's inflicting a bad smell on the women. It also mentions that the women killed the children of the mistresses, lest they avenge their fathers when they became adults. These details do not appear in surviving literature before Apollonios, however.

22 Cf. George (1972: 62), who states that the narrator "papers over the women's crime with euphemisms," and Hunter (1993: 112), who calls the narrator's exclamation "arch" and an expression of an "ironic distance between the narrator and his tale." DeForest (1994: 90–1) contrasts the narrator's opening about the Lemnian murders with the reasonable and often "delightful" behaviour later in the episode.

23 Thus, Cuypers (2005: 52–3); she describes the general nature of Apollonios' narrator, who, like the Homeric narrator, is external, omniscient, omnipresent, and anonymous, yet who has a protean character that blends the qualities of other narrative personae, including the Pindaric, Herodotean, and Kallimachean scholar. Albis (1996: 35) notes that the narrator's appropriation of his characters' point of view can "defy logic." Cf. Goldhill (1991: 293–5) on the narrator's self-representation in the *Argonautica*.

24 See Cuypers (2005: 41–5), who suggests that the που denotes that the narrator does not want to be "pinned down."

25 Fantuzzi and Hunter (2004: 127) suggest that the political structure of Lemnos might resemble that of the Hellenistic world, albeit with women substituting for men. Yet they suggest an irony here in that the decision is "in service of

desire." Perhaps they emphasize the sexual needs of the Lemnians too much here, since the need for procreation is rational, as Polyxo suggests.

26 Holmberg (1998: 140–1) discusses the "salvational" quality of the different forms of *metis* in the Lemnian episode, which correspond to the general valence of the term in the poem.

27 Berkowitz (2004: 49) observes that Hypsipyle's account fills in gaps lacking in that of the narrator, but also suggests that her lie casts doubt on the rest of her account.

28 See Harris (2015) on the continued concern with pollution in the fourth century.

29 Clare (2002: 62) suggests that the Lemnian episode explores alternative outcomes for the Argonauts. See Barbantani's chapter in this volume regarding the term βάξις, which can be either negative or positive, depending on its context.

30 A. Rose (1985: 33–40) observes that the robe symbolizes the civilized character of Polydeukes, both because it is a guest gift and also because it contrasts with the cruder attire of Amykos. In keeping with Beye's description of Jason as a "love-hero," Hypsipyle's gift cloak reminds us of Jason's ability to charm women (cf. the long ekphrastic description of Athena's cloak). As Rose observes, the significance of clothing changes throughout the epic, from that of diplomacy, hospitality, and persuasion to that of deceit and murder. See also Byre 2002: 128–9.

31 Barber (1994: 230) discusses the evidence for story cloths.

7

The "Good" Poros and the "Bad" Poros: Infamy and Honour in Alexander Historiography

TIMOTHY HOWE

1. Introduction

Once a thought has been placed in the ether of public consciousness, it becomes "public" and begins to work its insidious magic on memory and reputation. Thus, as Plutarch (*Alexander* 60) tells us, on a dark and stormy night in the spring of 326 BCE, Alexander fought a man who became an archetype of the honourable enemy – the Indian king Poros (Howe 2016). All of the Alexander sources elevate this Poros to something other than human: he was well over six feet tall, he honoured his agreements, kept his word, continued to fight when others fled, sat his elephant even after multiple wounds, and, most important, he refused to surrender even when there was no hope of victory or even escape because to do so would have been disloyal to his kingdom and his men (see table 7.1 for the relevant passages). In fact, in many ways, the Poros we see here at the battle of the Hydaspes resembles the Alexander sources' portrayals of King Alexander himself – Alexander's enemy Poros is a good, honest, honourable, and noble king who asks no more from his men than he asks from himself.[1] But in direct contrast to this honourable, good, "famous" Poros, the Alexander sources offer to history another king, also named Poros,[2] who is cowardly, disloyally self-interested, and just plain "infamous" (see table 7.1 for the relevant passages).[3] In fact, in order to differentiate the two men, Arrian, in his history of Alexander's campaign, calls this second king, "Bad Poros"

(*Anabasis* 5.21.2).[4] Consequently, by juxtaposing these two men, the Alexander sources offer us an opportunity to explore the construction of fame and infamy.

By working backwards from the Roman-era sources, I hope to demonstrate that the polarized depiction of these two Poroses depends on an original character study of good and bad kingship penned by Ptolemy I as he was establishing and legitimating his control over Egypt during the wars of the *diadochoi*. By using the Poroses to characterize good and bad kings, Ptolemy was able to centre on disloyalty and dishonour and, in so doing, highlight Ptolemy's own proper kingship in direct contrast to those of his "bad" fellow *diadochoi* such as Kassandros.[5] While scholars such as Caneva (2016: 47–59) have noted that pro-Ptolemaic Greek historiography regularly highlighted Ptolemy's positive leadership qualities (e.g., collegiality toward his fellow *diadochoi* and concern for the Macedonian soldiers) and his *diadoch* rivals' bad ones (self-interest and greed), they have explored only the Greek and Macedonian audiences of Ptolemy's historiographic message and not probed Ptolemy's Alexander history's links (and debts) to Egyptian historiography. Indeed, Caneva places Greek and Egyptian historiographic traditions in separate realms and understands them as directed to distinctly separate audiences. In what follows, I hope to show that there are not such sharp boundaries in Ptolemaic historiography – historiography that Caneva (2016: 47–9), following Gehrke (1982), calls the "routinization of charisma." Ptolemy used all the tools at his disposal to create a wide network of support, and, whatever the original intent, the fact that the Poroses were presented as polar opposites shaped their reception – their "fame," if you will – to the present day.

2. The Roman Context

But before we can jump into the world of the Poroses and Ptolemy's presentation of kingliness, we must recognize that the first-generation sources like Ptolemy's history are no longer extant and come down to us only in Roman-era synthesis and quotation.[6] As they built their historiographies of Alexander, Roman-era authors such as Diodoros, Curtius, Plutarch, and Arrian, researched (i.e., "data-mined") the original parent narratives of Ptolemy, Aristoboulos, and Kleitarchos, to name the authors they most commonly cite. As Bosworth observes, this method of mining sources and combing their information in composite narratives was not unique to the Alexander historiographers but typical for all historical writers in antiquity: "The nature of the game was to operate with the material at one's disposal, identifying and criticizing falsehood and bias, combining details from several sources into a composite picture not paralleled in any single source, but not adding invention of one's own" (2003: 194).[7] So much is true, but it belies the complexity and the art inherent in writing history. Ancient historiographers did not simply "gloss" lost Hellenistic or classical originals. In the case of the Alexander historiographers, Arrian and his fellows were literary stylists in their own rights, with their on literary agendas, audiences, and interests (Duff 1999; Spencer 2002; Welch and Mitchell 2013; Burlinga 2013; and Howe 2015b). They carefully and meticulously *chose* not only what to put in their books, but also how to interpret what they included, and they used all of their rhetorical skills to sway the reader into accepting certain "truths" (Woodman 1988: 70–116; Kraus and Woodman 1997: 5–6; cf. Rodriquez Mayorgas 2016).

We must recognize, too, that these Roman-era authors had their own story arcs and agendas, as did the Hellenistic originals that they mined for information. Consequently, Roman authors such as Arrian chose specific Hellenistic originals *because* of their compatibility in terms of subject and tone. That is, Arrian, Plutarch, Curtius, and Diodoros chose works from their libraries (and particular passages from those works) that were compatible both in subject *and* tone to their own literary and creative agendas.[8] Baynham (1998) and Spencer (2002) have discussed this process in some detail, so we need not repeat their arguments here, but this view of the creative historiographical process means that the Poros story survives in the writings of Roman-era Alexander historians because it was already famous among and relevant for their audiences. Thus, much of the original tone and tenor of the Poros story from the original first-generation authors has been preserved because it continued to be relevant for the Romans. And yet, as Spencer (2002) notes, this information is embedded in Roman contexts and observations.

Nonetheless, we can begin to "dis-embed" (so to speak) the original Hellenistic sources by mapping the different source treatments (see table 7.1 for a graphic representation of this). Several patterns are noteworthy: 1) all accounts (except Strabo's Onesikritos fragment) have Poros' noble surrender to Alexander; 2) all accounts have Bukephalas' death – though Diodoros lists this in a different context; 3) Curtius, Diodoros, and Onesikritos, as reported by Strabo, always agree; 4) the Metz Epitome, Diodoros, and Arrian always agree; but 5) only Arrian and Diodoros mention the other king named Poros; 6) only Arrian describes the other Poros as "bad"; and 7) only Arrian recounts Ptolemy's heroism.

These correlations suggest several things. First, the story of Good Poros' surrender to Alexander, while often different in circumstantial details across the sources (i.e., with respect to who acts as emissary from Alexander to

Table 7.1 Accounts of Poros in the Alexander sources

	Plut. *Alex.* 60–2	Arrian 5.18–24	Curtius 8.14.3–46	Diodoros 17.89.1–91.4	Metz Epitome 63–8	Strabo 15.1.29–30 (Onesikritos *FGrH* 134, F 21)
"Good" Poros surrenders nobly to Alexander	X	X	X	X	X	
Brother of Taxiles (or Taxiles) attempts to bring about Poros' surrender		X	X			
Comparison between "Good" Poros and cowardly Darius		X				
Bukephalas dies and Alexander founds city after him	X	X	X	X	X	X
Alexander expresses desire to reach Okeanos	X		X	X	X	
Alexander encounters fabulous beasts and mountains			X	X		X
Alexander campaigns against Indian King Abisares		X	X		X	
Alexander campaigns against Indian king Sopeithes (neighbour of "Other" Poros)			X	X		X
"Other" Poros		X		X		
Alexander sends Hephaistion against "Other" Poros		X		X		
"Good" Poros gives advice about Indian tribes to the east		X			X	
Alexander campaigns against Indian tribes	X	X	X	X	X	X
Ptolemy wins the day against allies of "Bad" Poros		X				

Poros – Moroes or Taxiles/Taxiles' brother), contains the same main elements: Poros refuses to break even when wounded, and Alexander is impressed by his honour and his loyalty to his cause. Consequently, it seems clear that Poros' nobility and Alexander's reception of that nobility resonated with all of the Roman audiences that all of our authors appealed to. So too, it seems, did the story about Bukephalas' death and Alexander's related civic foundation. Second, and most importantly, Arrian, as he does earlier for the battle narrative of the Hydaspes, seems to blend the "Egyptian" authors Ptolemy and Kleitarchos.[9] Moreover, only Arrian preserved the whole story of the Poroses, complete from the noble surrender of the Good Poros to the battle at Sangala between the Alexander-like Ptolemy and the Bad Poros' allies, which suggests that he used Ptolemy as his source.[10] The (Egyptian) Kleitarchan and Ptolemaic focus on good and bad examples of kingship seems to have appealed to Arrian and his intended audience. [11]

Here, in Arrian and Ptolemy fragment 35, Bad Poros is "bad" because of his cowardice and ignoble self-protection (Bosworth 1995: 326). The salient points in Arrian's account are as follows: Bad Poros had agreed to support Alexander when he feared Good Poros, but later, with Alexander and Good Poros allied, Bad Poros was too cowardly to keep his word – Bad Poros could no longer remain loyal to his agreement with Alexander. In fact, as Arrian reports, he never intended to: Bad Poros would say anything to preserve his own skin. The complete Poros story as we have it in Arrian portrays this Bad Poros as a dishonest and dishonourable coward whose cowardice and self-interest plunge the area into chaos and war. He is not a good king, and as a result his people suffer chaos and war. Fortunately for the realm, Alexander (and Ptolemy) and Good Poros are present to restore harmony.

3. Ptolemy and Egypt: Fame, Infamy, and Kingliness

But why did Ptolemy choose to digress on the Good and Bad Poroses in the first place? Put another way: how might we understand the role of the Poroses in Ptolemy's history of Alexander's campaign?

Interestingly, there is little scholarly debate that Arrian's account derives from Ptolemy.[12] Because Ptolemy himself plays a major role in this section of the narrative, Jacoby argued that he must also be the source, even though Arrian does not explicitly credit the Egyptian king. Indeed, scholars since Jacoby have noticed that the elements of Ptolemy's military actions at Sangala are of a piece with Ptolemy's reports of his heroism from other campaigns in Arrian's account, such as battle at the Persian Gates in 331 BCE, the capture of Bessos in 329, and at the siege of Indian Aornos in 327.[13] In all of these actions, Ptolemy took Alexander's own elite forces, the hypaspists,

Agrianes, and the archers, and brought about victory for the Macedonians. Indeed, during the battle against the Bad Poros' allies, Ptolemy plays anvil to Alexander's hammer much as he had done at the Persian Gates and at Aornos. But can we work backwards from this to understand why Ptolemy chose to juxtapose the Poroses in his history?

The Bad Poros story does not seem to make sense as a single event. Bad Poros cannot stand alone: he can be "bad" only in comparison with the nobility of the other Poros. Moreover, since Diodoros also knows about this Poros, he cannot simply be a creation of Arrian's and must derive from an earlier source. Again, since the Bad Poros story introduces Ptolemy's heroism at Sangala, it is likely the common source is Ptolemy. This becomes even more certain when we consider who Alexander sends to deal with Bad Poros while Ptolemy fights Bad Poros' allies – Hephaistion. As Sabine Müller (2013c) has shown, Ptolemy regularly heroized both himself and Hephaistion, though Hephaistion is never given the same detailed treatment, nor the same credit, as Ptolemy. Only Ptolemy gets to be portrayed as a "second Alexander," an "almost king" worthy to take command from his leader, Alexander (Howe 2008 and 2015c).

Indeed, the wider contexts of "king" and "kingliness" make the Poroses – one famous for his nobility and kingly bearing, the other infamous for his perfidy and cowardice – a good choice for a wider character study. But there may be even more to it than that. In ancient Sankrit Purusha, पुरुष, what the Greeks heard as Poros, can, in certain connotations, mean "king" or prince." According to Prakash (1967: 35–7) another variant of the name, Paurusha, पौरुष, is well attested in Sanskrit epic as a dynastic title, meaning "one descended from the Paurava clan." In ancient Indian literature, both historiographic and epic, "Poros" is a royal epithet, not unlike the Spartan and Macedonian kings calling themselves "Heraklids." In fact, the comparison to the Heraklids is especially apt, since the Paurava clan held a similar fame in the *Mahabharata,* an ancient Sanskrit epic from the Late Bronze Age / Early Iron Age, as Herakles and his descendants do in Late Bronze Age / Early Iron Age Greek epic.[14] Hence, the preponderance of kings named Poros in the Alexander historiographies (Good Poros, Bad Poros, Good Poros' son Poros). It is certainly possible that Ptolemy, his fellow *diadochoi,* and those of Alexander's veterans who had been with the Macedonian king in India were aware of this royal and heroic context for the term "Poros," but even if they were not cognizant of such linguistic nuances, they would certainly remember the different "forms" of kingly behaviour exhibited by the different men named Poros.

And here, I think, we begin to get at the purpose behind Ptolemy's inclusion of the Poroses in his Alexander history. The opportunity presented by two dynamically different kings of the same name allowed Ptolemy to digress on the character of kingship and kingliness. As Ptolemy was moving to convert his governorship under the joint kings Philip III and Alexander IV to a kingship of his own, he had to show why he was worthy to the different stakeholders he would rule; and as he fought with his rivals, who were also attempting to carve out independent kingdoms from the shreds of Alexander's empire, Ptolemy needed a medium by which he could disseminate his message to the Greek world.[15] The Poros dichotomy could fit social, political, and military contexts especially relevant to his audience, and Ptolemy could take up Alexander's mantle. Moreover, the Poros dichotomy was safe – no Macedonian rivals were mentioned here, just Indian leaders who could serve as character studies. The Greeks could find relevance in such abstractions on kingly behaviour. Indeed, using the past to safely engage the present was a long-established Greek *and* Egyptian historiographic device.

Building on the work of Alexander,[16] Ptolemy brought the priestly elites into his royal faction.[17] Throughout his royal decrees, Ptolemy took care to curate this relationship, and it is important to note that his public texts were cultic in nature, inscribed on temples, placed in temple complexes, and invoking the delicate balance between royal rule and the will (and order) of the gods, which the priests assisted in adjudicating (Gozzoli 2009: 6; Howe 2018b: 161–3). In addition, these inscribed decrees exhibited cult-centric historiographic elements, since the Egyptians (elites and non-elites) viewed history writing as taking place in a cultic, ritualized sphere as a cultic, ritualized act – that is, history was a conversation between kings and gods mediated by powerful priests and written on temple walls (Gozzoli 2009: 3–6). Consequently, history had a cultic vocabulary and syntax:

> In Egyptian royal texts such as triumphal reliefs and military stelae, the enemy is always depicted as rebellious, while the pharaoh is the one who wins whenever he comes to the battlefield. This feature has been generically called propaganda. The term is usually interpreted in its negative aspects, as full of bombastic expressions celebrating the king and his deeds. But for an ancient Egyptian, any event was strictly bound to the concept of ritual: a king's victory against his enemies is represented as defeating the Nine Bows – his cosmic enemies. Therefore, whether he had effectively won the Nine Bows or not becomes entirely irrelevant, as the pharaoh's victories permitted the maintenance of the order of the world, represented by Maat, which the supreme god has predestined for his people. Any narrated happening stands on a double plan in the Egyptian mental horizon. The first in linear: any royal deed

follows an earlier one in chronological scale. The second plan is instead cyclical: as the Nile inundation happens every year, any space of events will return again in the future. At this point, any royal victory becomes the re-enactment of a primordial victory made by some ancestors. (Gozzoli 2009: 3–4)

Thus Ptolemy, quite literally, inscribed his new order onto the cyclical history of the Egyptian people. He was the "good" king, who with his own bow had overcome his adversaries (who metaphorically represented "The Adversary" in Egyptian lore) and in so doing "restored" the old order and law to Egypt.

We can see this cycle clearly in the so-called Satrap Stela (Cairo Museum 22181), issued by the priests of Pe and Dep at the Delta town of Buto in 311 BCE. The Satrap Stela celebrates both a gift of land to Horus and his godly "parents" Pe and Dep by Ptolemy I and Ptolemy's recent victory against Antigonos. Ladynin (2005: 102–3) argues, convincingly I think, that, in part, Ptolemy made this donation to the gods at Buto (and to similar ones at other small Delta communities) out of a general fear that Antigonos would unite the empire of Alexander under his sole rule (cf. Diodoros 19.56.2). After he provoked Antigonos and his son Demetrios by invading Syria and beating Demetrios in battle, Ptolemy needed a strong Egypt to protect him from any counterinvasion. And, as Manning (2009: 100–2) notes, the priesthood was the key to unlocking native support on a financial and military level. But to achieve such support, Ptolemy would need to speak to the priests in ways they would understand and respect; he would have to convince them that he understood his traditional kingly role to actively "do Ma'at" and thereby maintain the territorial and spiritual integrity of the two halves of Egypt.[18] The text of the Satrap Stela shows Ptolemy entering this conversation in much the same way as the Good and Bad Poros digression in F 35, and, if I am correct in dating the history to 308, then both texts may well be in conversation (Howe 2018b: 165).

In the stela, Ptolemy's understanding of his role is clear: he is introduced with traditional New Kingdom descriptors (Schäfer 2011: 66–74):

He is a youthful man, strong in his two arms, effective in plans, with mighty armies, stout hearted, firm footed, who attacks the powerful without turning his back, who strikes the face of his opponents when they fight, with precise hand, who grasps to himself the bow without shooting astray, who fights with his sword in the midst of battle, with none who can stand in his vicinity, a champion whose arms are not repulsed, with no reversal of what issues from his mouth, who has no equal in the Two Lands or the foreign countries. (Tr. Simpson, Ritner, and Tobin. 2003: 393).

After this traditional introduction, the restoration of the temples that had been plundered by the enemies of Egypt is stressed: "[Ptolemy] brought back the images of the gods found in Asia, and all the furniture and all the sacred scrolls of the temples of Upper and Lower Egypt. And he restored them to their place" (ibid.). Schäfer (2009: 143) sees these acts as a conscious negotiation with the Egyptian priests in order to earn their support for Ptolemaic kingship. Clearly it worked, since this same formula was followed by Ptolemy's successors.[19]

Next, after reporting his successes in Asia against Antigonos, also in the idiom of the New Kingdom, the stela offers a "history" of an earlier Egyptian king in which Ptolemy is being educated about good and bad rule by the Egyptian elite, perhaps again to acknowledge how important that elite was to Ptolemiac rule during the present crisis.[20] Here, Ptolemy, like his predecessor Darius I (discussed further, below), participates in the now ancient genre of royal historical fiction (*Königsnovelle*; Hoffman 2005) as he learns about the actions of the pious native king Khababash, who "walked in the path of Horos" and put down the rebellion of his impious adversary Ḫšryš (variously read as Xerxes or Artaxerxes[21]), who did not honour the gods and caused disharmony in the Two Lands of Egypt.

While little of the Khababash story is accurate by modern standards, it does much to engage Egyptian interests.[22] Through links to the Egyptian historical fiction of the Middle and New Kingdoms, such as the Story of Sinhue, the Prophecy of Neferti, and especially, the *Quarrel of Apepi and Seqenenre* (Manassa 2013: 34–9), Ptolemy's rule is presented in an Egyptian idiom, as part of a cycle of ruin and restoration (Colburn 2015: 179). At the same time, by using Xerxes (or Artaxerxes) as the "adversary," the stela also engages Greek notions of triumph over a ruinous Persian king, thus recalling Philip II and Alexander's Panhellenic campaigns to end Persian tyranny.[23] These Greek *topoi* about Persians had been well established by the late 300s by the works of Aeschylus (*Persians*), Herodotos (*Histories*), Ktesias (*Persica*), and Xenophon (*Kyropaedia*), and even the Hippocratic treatise *On Airs, Waters and Places* (Llewellyn-Jones 2012).[24] And yet, the stela does not simply advocate general hatred of Persian rule, as has often been argued (Colburn 2015). Rather, it shows the audience that the interlocutors – Ptolemy and the priests – understand good and bad kingly behaviour.[25]

It seems to have worked. Both Greeks and Egyptians invested in Ptolemy's view of the past. On the Greek side, Diodoros' first century BCE account of the Second Persian Period in Egypt echoes the language of the Satrap Stela to such a degree that it is "impossible to distinguish the influences of Ptolemaic ideology from actual memories of Achaimenid rule in the Greek historical tradition" (Colburn 2015: 168). On the Egyptian side, the contemporary Demotic Chronicle (hereafter DC),[26] a priestly text written by or on behalf of the High Priest of Harsaphes in Herakleopolis (Johnson 1983: 62, 64–5) and therefore not part of the authorized discourse of the Ptolemies, praises Ptolemy I for his proper understanding of Egyptian tradition, especially kingly behaviour, and predicts that, because of this, he will pass his sovereignty on to his descendants (Johnson 1974, 1983; Gozzoli 2009: 130–2, 283–90; Howe forthcoming). While the DC credits Ptolemy with restoring Egypt to harmony and order – high praise indeed for any Egyptian king, let alone a foreigner – it also shows some priestly teeth: a king can be considered legitimate only if he has undergone the proper coronation rituals and possesses the proper emblems of office. Again and again, as if underscoring its significance by the repetition, the DC asserts that a ruler is legitimate if he is crowned, if he is equated with the falcon (the god Horos), and if he rules according to law (*ma'at*). The threat here is that, if the king does not "walk in the path of Horos" or keep *ma'at*, he will be overthrown and for this reason will not pass his kingship on to future descendants (Johnson 1983: 66, 68). In short, the DC suggests that the Egyptian priests expected there to be continual negotiation between ruler and ruled in symbolic and ritualized contexts.

Ptolemy and the priests with whom he is negotiating his kingship are clearly participating in a literary and cultural dialogue in which kingly legitimacy and audience recognition of that legitimacy have become well developed. We can see these dynamics at work early on in the New Kingdom *Quarrel of Apepi and Seqenenre*, which like the Satrap Stela's Khababash story, comes to us nested in another document, a letter-writing manual, written by the scribe Pentaweret some 340 years after the events described.[27] The *Quarrel* appears to provide an entertaining and instructive *exempli gratia* for the manual, seemingly chosen by the scribe specifically so that it might introduce, as well as give comparative literary expressions and historical context to, the more sober contents of the didactic text. As Colleen Manassa (2013: 158) puts it, "Fictionalizing military events suggests not only a desire to seek out relevant or interesting facts within the historical record, but also the desire to choose past events that were particularly relevant to 'current events.'" Thus, Manassa argues, Pentaweret consciously deployed historiographic content (both Apepi and Seqenenre were real kings) to show that he understood the structure and nuances of royal communication and thus was an appropriate source for instruction about such themes.

For our purposes, Pentaweret's use of alternating titles for Apepi and Seqenenre is most relevant, since titles are arranged here by the author to highlight improper rule and proper execution of royal authority rather than historical reality (Manassa 2013: 34–9). The *Quarrel* text, which is Upper Egyptian in orientation, calls the Upper Egyptian Seqenenre "king" (*nswt*) while the Lower Egyptian Apepi is merely addressed as "ruler" (*wr*), even though the historical Apepi was more powerful.[28] These titles not only call into doubt Apepi's authority and actions – such as his connection to the worship of Seth, the Adversary – but at the same time stress Seqenenre's devotion to *ma'at*, right order, law, and legitimacy. In addition, in order to further demarcate the differences between the two, Apepi is referred to by his birth name while Seqenenre by his royal coronation name (recall the DC's stress on coronations and titles). This dichotomy underscores Seqenenre's proper and Apepi's improper authority as well as the populace's (and gods') reception of those different authorities. The tale concludes with a warning about the need for a divinely appointed and legitimate king, a "good" king who will free the realm from evil and restore *ma'at*. Notice that there is work for Seqenenre to perform before he can be king: he cannot assume his proper position and power until Apepi is no longer proclaiming himself "king." Seqenenre, and only Seqenenre, must remove Apepi if Egypt is to be returned to harmony.

These same themes of legitimate power, proper royal behaviour, and restoration are used to effect by the non-native rulers of Egypt, the Nubians. In the 750s, hundreds of years after Pentaweret wrote his manual, the Twenty-fifth Dynasty Nubian king Piyankhy makes similar claims in his victory stela (Cairo Museum JE 48862, 47086–7):[29]

> 1. One came to say to his majesty: "the Chief of the West, the lord and ruler in Netjer, Tefnakht, … has conquered the entire West … with the Two Lands united behind him, and the counts and rulers of domains are as dogs at his feet …" (17.) [Says King Piyankhy,] "Amun of Napata has granted me to be ruler of every foreign country. He to whom I say 'you are chief,' he is to be chief. He to whom I say, 'You are not chief,' he is not chief. Amun in Thebes has granted me to be king of Egypt … I [Piyankhy] swear, as Re loves me, as my father Amun favors me, I shall go north myself! I shall tear down (25.) his [Tefnakht's] works. I shall make him abandon fighting forever! I shall end the Pestilence in the Two Lands!" (Tr. Lichtheim 1980: 68–9)

Darius I uses a similar template, though even more than Piyankhy, he takes care to show that, although he is a foreigner, he respects and understands Egyptian traditions. The Canal Stelae, set up at Tell el-Maskhuta (Cairo Museum JE 48855), Kabret (Posener 1936: 63–81), and Suez (ibid.: 81–7) and written in Old Persian, Elamite, Akkadian, and hieroglyphics, contain "teaching" stories, like those embedded in Pentaweret's manual and the Buto Satrap Stela, that show that Darius understands the importance of history and ritual and is prepared to embrace their lessons of legitimacy, restoration, and triumph over adversaries.[30] But what is especially significant about all of these stelae (as with those of Piyankhy and Ptolemy discussed above) is that they contain iconography that communicates these legitimating themes to the non-literate (much like the images on the contemporary Behistun inscription in the Zagros).[31] In a similar fashion, Darius' images on the temple of Horos at Hibis show Darius slaying the Apophis serpent, another representation of the Adversary. According to Wasmuth (2015: 215) this imagery allows Darius to shout out his name and qualifications: "Darius, the Persian, the foreign Horos who guarantees *ma'at* by slaying his foes."

4. Conclusion

Context matters, and famous personages (especially safely dead famous personages) are always historiographically useful. Arrian chose Ptolemy's narrative because it suited his own literary agenda, and Ptolemy chose to contrast the two Poroses because doing so gave him an opportunity to make some observations about proper kingly behaviour. The wars of the Successors had created an environment in which reputations and perceptions of those reputations profoundly mattered (Caneva 2016: 2–10). Indeed, the Hellenistic monarchies of the late 300s BCE see a new type of Greek kingship emerge, which looks not to the Homeric world, or to the gods, but to the Bronze Age kings of Egypt and the Near East. For these new royals and their audiences, public performances of kingliness were important. Public representation and royal propaganda reassured the different audiences about the wholesale suitability of the king. As Manning (2009) and Caneva (2016) have shown, imperial states like Ptolemaic Egypt generated their authority through precepts of honour, loyalty, submission, kingly omniscience, and above all military prowess. And perhaps even more than actions, historiography achieves these precepts on many levels; historiography ensures that a king remained "famous" rather that infamous.

Once a thought has been placed in the ether of public consciousness, it becomes "public" and has the fame it needs to work its insidious magic. To put it another way, by engaging the Poroses as exemplars of kingship, good and bad, Ptolemy began to define Hellenistic kingship in a way that empowered the various stakeholders of the realm. And whether anyone liked Ptolemy's conceptions or not, from the moment he began writing and speaking, those conceptions entered the public discourse. Indeed, the fact that Arrian was able to employ the fame and infamy of the Good and Bad Poroses for his own ends suggests the extent to which Ptolemy had influenced ancient Mediterranean conversations about kingship. And nowhere is this shown better than in Arrian's preface, where he suggests that infamy befalls a king who is caught out in a lie – just what happened to the second Poros, who, thanks to Ptolemy's historiographic output, became famous for being "bad."

NOTES

1 While it is not the purpose of this study to trace the strands of Poros' fame, it is worth noting that the Indian king gained a notable place in the Indian literary sources – clearly, Poros' fame in the period after Alexander was significant, making him an especially suitable *topos* for the Alexander sources. In some later versions of the *Mahabharata* (*The Great Epic of Bharata*), the longest epic poem that is known and the only other major Sanskrit epic apart from the *Ramayana* to survive, the historical Poros has been merged with the epic hero Paurava (or Paurisha or Parveteya, depending on the text) in much the same way as Homeric characters accreted attributes over time. Likewise, the Brahmanical *Mudrarakshasa* (*The Signet of the Minister*), a historical drama that narrates the rise of Chandragupta, dating from the late fourth century CE, celebrates the honest and noble Parvata (or Parvatesvara in some variants) for his role in defeating the invaders (i.e., Alexander and his forces) and thereby assisting Chadragupta to the throne. See Prakash (1967) for further discussion.

2 What Alexander and his soldiers heard as "Poros" seems to have been a title rather than a personal name. See discussion, below.

3 For a discussion of the nuanced interplay between fame and infamy in ancient historiography see, e.g., the essays collected in Ash, Mossman, and Titchener (2015) as well as Faber's introduction to this volume.

4 Bosworth (1995: 326) suggests that Arrian (and probably his source) is purposely making a value judgment about the "lesser" Poros, signalling to the audience his disloyalty to Alexander.

5 For treatments of Ptolemy's propagandistic links to Alexander, see de Polignac 2000; Howe 2008, 2015b; Caneva 2016: 29–47.

6 See Howe 2018a for relevant bibliography on the Ptolemy fragments.

7 See also Atkinson 2000 and especially Bosworth 2003.

8 According to his own preface, Arrian tells us that he relied on Ptolemy, supplementing him with Aristoboulos where necessary and other authors when they provided a useful anecdote or perspective; see Bosworth 1980: 16–34 and 1995: 6–7. For his part, Curtius seems to have regularly used Kleitarchos as a backbone, which he then fleshed out with Ptolemy and many others, including Aristoboulos, Nearchos, and Chares. On this, see Atkinson (1994:

25–8); Baynham (1998: 57, esp. n. 3, and 77–85) offers a nuanced discussion of the complex *Quellenforschung* relating to Curtius. Diodoros, at least for the Alexander campaign, seems to have relied primarily on Kleitarchos; see Goukowsky 2002: xix–xxxi; cf. Prandi 1996: 66–71; 2012. The Metz Epitome seems to have derived primarily from Kleitarchos; Baynham 1995.

9 See Howe (2016) for the various sources' "coverage" of the battle at the Hydaspes.

10 Arrian *Anab.* 5.21–4 = *BNJ* 138 F 35. See Howe (2018: commentary on F 35) for further analysis of the source tradition.

11 Arrian seems to have decided, unlike his historiographic predecessors the Augustus-era Pompeius Trogus and Neronian era Q. Curtius Rufus, that this digression on the context of the Poroses – that cowardice and dishonesty lead to chaos and war – would be relevant, acceptable, and useful to his audience. These wider observations on policy and kingly character are often found in Arrian's narrative and have indicated to many that there is a specifically Roman-emperor-oriented stratum in Arrian's text (Frank 2017: 211–17).

12 See Howe (2018a: commentary on F 35) for full bibliography.

13 See Howe (2008, 2015, 2018a: commentary on F 35) for the relevant bibliography.

14 Just as in the Alexander historiography, so too this interaction between literature and history did not end with Poros' death. Prakash (1967: 96) suggests that later editors may have deepened the connections between Poros and the legendary Pauravas, weaving in details from the Indian king's battles with Alexander and retrojecting them into the epic past. In this way, they created a composite, easily comprehensible aetiology that explains Poros' heroism – he is descended from the Pauravas of the *Mahabharata* who repelled invaders – "foreshadowing" Poros' future actions. At the same time, as the ancient Paurava clan of the *Mahabharat* becomes aetiologically linked to the historical Poros, Alexander's foe is linked with the hero of the Chandragupta-centred historiographic poem *Mudrarakshasa.*

15 Howe (2018b) argues that Ptolemy published his history at the Isthmian Games of 308, at a time when he was contrasting the "true" Greek freedom he (and Antigonos) offered Greece with the "slavery" of Kassandros. His intended audience was the Greeks under Kassandros' control. If this is correct, then the other Poros would serve as a metaphor for Kassandros and other "oath-breakers."

16 For Alexander's engagement with Egyptian traditions and priestly culture, see Huß 1994b 1997; Bosch-Puche 2008, 2013, 2014; Ladynin 2014; Caneva 2016: 11–28.

17 For the close connections between the priestly elite and the Ptolemies, see Huß 1994; Lloyd 2002, 2010; Baines 2004; Gorre 2009, 2013; Agut-Labordère and Gorre 2014; Caneva 2016: 29–79, esp. 59–68.

18 See Ladynin (2014) for Ptolemy I's investment in temple infrastructure.

19 Ptolemy II will use it on the Pithom Stele in much the same way (Urk. II 91.6–94.2; Thiers 2007: 100–6). See Winnicki (1994: 149n1) for the older literature on the Satrap Stele and Ptolemaic efforts at legitimation.

20 Through the Khababash story, Ptolemy invokes the important interplay between a good king and his advisers so common in Bronze Age Egyptian historical literature. In this trope, the good and pious king, while going about his business, is alerted by his advisers (usually priests of some sort) to a problem caused by an invading impious king (often a usurper or foreigner). The legitimate ruler then devises a solution to that problem and issues the appropriate commands to implement it. By erecting this stele, the Egyptian priests seem to indicate that Ptolemy fully comprehends (and approves of) these Egyptian conceptions of pious and impious, legitimate and illegitimate kings. See Howe (2018b) for further discussion.

21 For Ḫšryš as Xerxes, see Ladynin (2005: 98n34) for the relevant literature; cf. Klingott 2007; Lloyd 2010: 84; Colburn 2015: 175. For Artaxerxes, see Spiegelberg 1907: 5–6; Schäfer 2009. Briant (2002: 1044) argues that "Xerxes" is a generic term for Persian kings. Ladynin (2005: 101) agrees and argues, convincingly, that Artaxerxes III is the real subject; however, given Ptolemy's efforts to highlight his own capture of Bessos, Artaxerxes V, it is possible that Bessos is the intended Artaxerxes here.

22 For the historicity of Khababash and the literary figure reported by the Satrap Stele, see Huß 1994a; Burstein 2000.

23 The choice of Xerxes or Artaxerxes is no accident (Ladynin 2005: 103). As Colburn (2015: 177), notes, "it does fit Ḫšryš's role as a destructive, evil force in the stela's inscription, especially if it stems from a Greek tradition that remembered Xerxes as an invader and the destroyer of Athens." Ptolemy also seems to be using these traditions to cast aspersions on Antigonos.

24 For Greek proto-orientalist prejudices, see Isaac 2004: 257–303.

25 Ptolemy also seems to be warning his Greek and Egyptian audiences that they should understand the difference between a legitimate king such the native Kababash and the now "naturalized" Ptolemy and usurpers like adversaries Xerxes and Antigonos (Schäfer 2009: 148–9).

26 For a thorough assessment of the palaeographic dating issues and textual commentary, see Felber 2002.

27 We see a similar dynamic under the Ptolemies with regard to the Assyrian and Persian invasions (Ryholt 2004, 2010, 2013).

28 Apepi is known from small scarab seals, scattered monuments, and texts to have ruled over a wide swathe of Egypt and the Levant, while Seqenenre controlled only a part of the Upper Nile valley (Manassa 2013: 35).

29 For the historical background, see Morkot 2000: 150–3; Török 1995, 2009; Kahn 2013: 23. For the texts and their literary and linguistic contexts, see Gozzoli 2009: 51–67.

30 On this, see Gozzoli 2009: 116–21; Wasmuth 2015.

31 The content of Darius' Behistun (hereafter DB) inscription has much in common with these Egyptian stelae and may have been their inspiration. Gozzoli (2009: 124) argues that there is syncretism between the dualism of *ma'at* versus chaos in the Canal Stele and truth versus lie in DB. Certainly, the texts are in conversation, though it might be impossible to reconstruct to what degree. Several points of comparison are worth mentioning, though. Darius' marginalizing of Gaumata, the "false Smerdis" as a liar and pretender in DB 11–14, are strikingly similar to both Pentaweret's Seqenenre and Piyanky's Tefnakht. Further, just as with the "Quarrel" text, in DB titles matter – Darius claims Gaumata lies to the people about being a king, for only Darius is king because Ahuramazda made him king. As many have shown (e.g., Müller 2009), the "lie" is an important motif for Darius and his descendants, and so asserting that Gaumata claimed to be king when he was not is ritualistically important. Further, the people joined Gaumata in his revolt, taken in by his lies. But Darius is careful to point out that none other than Darius himself could put an end to Gaumata or his revolt. Darius and no one else dispossessed Gaumata of the kingdom. Darius and no one else brought order and restored the prosperity that the people had in the days of old. In the end, Darius' triumph narrative would have much that would resonate with Egyptians. Perhaps for this reason he had copies made in Aramaic and circulated throughout Egypt (DB 4.91–2; Cowley 1923: 249–50; Porten and Yardeni 1993: 59–71).

8

Writing Monarchs of the Hellenistic Age: Renown, Fame, and Infamy

JACQUELINE KLOOSTER

1. Introduction

If, not so long ago, scholars held that Hellenistic poetry lacked any sort of contingent, political, or ideological element,[1] nowadays attention for its courtly context is at the heart of Hellenistic studies. The general opinion is that royal patronage of literary and scientific luminaries at the Hellenistic courts must be read as a bid for prestige, fame, and celebrity in the competition between the Successor Kings:

> The fact of patronage added to their *prestige*. By accommodating poets and scholars at his court, a king met several of the requirements for being an ideal ruler. He proved that he was hospitable, benevolent and generous. The accumulation of art and knowledge in the house of the king added to his *charisma* … Just as kings would send athletes and horses to Panhellenic Games, so too they competed with one another in poetry, scholarship and science … The intellectual and artistic competition between courts … induced kings to look for poets and philosophers whose work would *amaze the world.* (Strootman 2010: 34; my emphasis)

In the field of literature, excellent and innovative poetry (e.g., Kallimachos' *Aitia*) as well as more traditional panegyrics were commissioned to help spread the renown of royal patrons.[2] The fact that a royal name was sung of in poetry was in and of itself a sought-after aim, but the renown of the ruler seems to have been that much greater if the poet was of special stature.[3] Alexander the Great famously lamented the fact that, unlike his model and hero Achilles, he had no Homer to sing of his deeds. Indeed, we know that he had only poets and historians whose reputation did not match his own, such as the notorious Choirilos and the encomiastic historiographers Kallisthenes and Onesikritos. As a result, Arrian tells us (perhaps with the aim of emphasizing the need for his own history of Alexander), that Alexander's deeds were not as famous as they might have been:

Καὶ εὐδαιμόνισεν ἄρα, ὡς λόγος, Ἀλέξανδρος Ἀχιλλέα, ὅτι Ὁμήρου κήρυκος ἐς τὴν ἔπειτα μνήμην ἔτυχε. (2) καὶ μέντοι καὶ ἦν Ἀλεξάνδρῳ οὐχ ἥκιστα τούτου ἕνεκα εὐδαιμονιστέος Ἀχιλλεύς, ὅτι αὐτῷ γε Ἀλεξάνδρῳ, οὐ κατὰ τὴν ἄλλην ἐπιτυχίαν, τὸ χωρίον τοῦτο ἐκλιπὲς ξυνέβη οὐδὲ ἐξηνέχθη ἐς ἀνθρώπους τὰ Ἀλεξάνδρου ἔργα ἐπαξίως, οὔτ' οὖν καταλογάδην, οὔτε τις ἐν μέτρῳ ἐποίησεν· ἀλλ' οὐδὲ ἐν μέλει ᾔσθη Ἀλέξανδρος, ἐν ὅτῳ Ἱέρων τε καὶ Γέλων καὶ Θήρων καὶ πολλοὶ ἄλλοι οὐδέν τι Ἀλεξάνδρῳ ἐπεοικότες, ὥστε πολὺ μεῖον γιγνώσκεται τὰ Ἀλεξάνδρου ἢ τὰ φαυλότατα τῶν πάλαι ἔργων. (Arrian, *Anabasis* 1.12.1–2)

And Alexander pronounced Achilles fortunate, as the story goes, because he had Homer as the herald of his renown to posterity. (2) And indeed, it was fitting that Alexander should think Achilles fortunate for this reason especially; for to Alexander himself this privilege was wanting, a thing which was not in accordance with the rest of his good fortune. His achievements have, therefore, not been related to mankind in a manner worthy of the hero. Neither in prose nor in verse has any one suitably honoured him; nor has he ever been sung of in a lyric poem, in which style of poetry Hiero, Gelo, Thero, and many others not at all comparable with Alexander, have been praised. Consequently Alexander's deeds are *far less known* than the meanest achievements of antiquity. (Tr. P.A. Brunt; emphasis added)

We see then, that Alexander suffered from a very peculiar problem: his deeds were fit for fame, but he could not find a suitable herald. A generation later, Ptolemy Philadelphos, whose military feats at least were much less impressive, made sure that he was praised by the very best, Kallimachos, Poseidippos and Theokritos among them, albeit in oblique and learned terms, gaining fame as a friend of the Muses. Emperor Augustus, whose claims to fame were in no way inferior to those of both these kings, learned from their examples: he did not wish to be the topic of praise poetry, *nisi et serio et a praestantissimis* ("unless in earnest and by the most outstanding writers"), charging the praetors not to let his name be cheapened in prize declamations, as Suetonius tells us (*Augustus* 89.3).[4]

But celebration in poetry and the related patronage of poets, scholars, and scientists formed but one complex of the monarchical strategies to win fame in the Hellenistic era. We see a flurry of competitive construction of impressive palaces and temples, the founding of cities named after kings or their family members, and the proliferation of portrait statues (think of Lysippos and Apelles, artists who did measure up to Alexander's greatness) and inscriptions. Interestingly enough, however, and a new development in the Greek world at this time, a competition was also going on between the crowned heads of the Hellenistic era when it came to the fame of their libraries and of the scientists and scholars they could lure to their courts.[5]

This is a typically Hellenistic development, for although we find attestations of literary sponsorship at courts from as early as *Odyssey* Book 8, the extent to which Hellenistic dynasties engaged in literary culture, library building, and funding of literary scholarship – in particular the Ptolemies and the Attalids of Pergamum – is quite unprecedented. The curating of the Greek literary legacy and the patronizing of learned poetry and refined prose had become a source of admiration and pride. In addition, a great interest in science and nature also distinguishes the Hellenistic rulers. This interest probably needs to be seen in the context of the building of credibility as "Greek" and civilized rulers that the *diadochoi* strove for – or, in Bourdieuian terms, "cultural capital."[6] They were, moreover, trying to convincingly succeed Alexander the Great, who himself had had a reputation for an interest in Greek literature, especially the *Iliad*, but also in medicine and natural wonders, sending off curious specimens to his mentor Aristotle.[7] The young Macedonian king has gone down in tradition as something of a "philosopher on horseback," thanks mainly to his close ties with Aristotle, as becomes particularly clear from Plutarch's twin essays *de Alexandri Fortuna aut Virtute*.

The testimonies indicate that many of the Hellenistic kings were indeed looking for a very specific type of celebrity, one among the Greek *intellectual* elite and avant-garde, an aim they tried to reach by enhancing their cultural capital.[8] Poems that describe Ptolemy Philadelphos and Ptolemy IV Philopator as "Friends of the Muses" (Philadelphos: Theokritos *Idyll* 14, 17 and Herondas *Mimiamb* 1; Philopator: Eratosthenes *CA* 66) confirm that learnedness and literary connoisseurship formed an important part of the image these kings wished to broadcast. The reorganization of the *Mouseia* on Mount Helikon and the temple of Homer in Alexandria instigated by Ptolemy IV Philopator point in the same direction. Perhaps the long history of Macedonian literary patronage, which included Archelaos and Euripides, ultimately played a role in this self-portrayal.

But how far could and did a monarch go in claiming literary expertise, if he wanted to add to his fame? In this chapter, I wish to investigate whether the royal striving for an image of intellectual stature, scholarly or scientific leanings, and literary connoisseurship also meant that renown could be gained by becoming an author in one's own right, as Strootman proposes:

> Famous writers and scholars were living status symbols and by patronizing such men a ruler demonstrated wisdom, learnedness and good taste. *Better still was to write oneself* ... In Renaissance Italy the connection between rulership and the arts had a theoretical basis in the ideal of the learned prince ... The Hellenistic period likewise cherished this ideal. (2010: 34; my emphasis)[9]

As testimonia show, Hellenistic kings themselves (the Ptolemies, the Attalids, and the Seleukids in particular) in fact did write literary and scientific works of various sorts. What are the driving forces behind these writings? Do the mechanisms outlined above (enhancing prestige through cultural capital; the ideal of the "learned prince") indeed apply, or are other forces at play too (propaganda, an apologetic stance, or, indeed, genuine literary or scholarly interest)? Who were the intended audiences of these texts? And if it is indeed "true that (in)famous personages reflect something of the society in which they live and die," then we may well ask how successful the writing of literature was as a bid for royal fame and celebrity.[10] In particular, I will ask whether literary activity *per se* was considered a fitting pursuit for a king, and whether it was not notoriety, or even infamy, rather than fame, that resulted from such activities.

Leo Braudy (1986: 15) defines celebrity as being "made up of four elements: a person and an accomplishment, their immediate publicity, and what posterity has thought about them ever since." This neat parcelling serves well to bring out some of the particular elements of my investigation. Of Hellenistic kings in general we might perhaps use the *bon mot* of Shakespeare's pedant Malvolio: "Some are born great, some achieve greatness, and some have greatness thrust upon them" (*Twelfth Night*, 2.5). By virtue of their royal birth, Hellenistic kings already make some claim to "greatness," celebrity, or at least social prominence. They were famous for who they were to start with, although of course this reputation could subsequently be enhanced, obscured, or even ruined by their own actions or those of others. Certainly not all royals "achieved greatness." For instance, the "accomplishments" of the ill-reputed Ptolemy IV Philopator and their "fame" surely count for nothing when compared to those of Alexander the Great or his general and successor Ptolemy I Lagides (Soter). One likely assumption would therefore seem to be that, whereas some of these kings wrote to *enhance* the renown of their accomplishments (e.g., Ptolemy I Soter's *hypomnema* of his part in the expedition of Alexander), for others the writing of a literary work may have counted as an accomplishment in its own right by which they hoped to gain fame (an example of this might be Ptolemy Philopator's tragedy *Adonis*, as will be explained below). This leads us to the question of how famous the kings became by these writings. In the absence of contemporary documentation, it is often difficult to tell to what extent writing was successful in terms of "immediate publicity." What we can attempt is to extrapolate from later sources: "what posterity has thought about them ever since" may in many cases encapsulate at least some elements of the immediate effect such writings had, although caution is needed.

2. A Brief History of Writing Rulers

To embed these issues, I start with a very brief historical survey of the phenomenon of writing kings and statesmen in antiquity in order to sketch the outlines of some parameters determining the appreciation of literary activities in such prominent men and women.[11] To begin with, we may cite Plutarch's truism that, by virtue of their prominent position, kings and statesmen are liable to attract attention in every department:

Οὐ γὰρ ὧν λέγουσιν ἐν κοινῷ καὶ πράττουσιν οἱ πολιτευόμενοι μόνον εὐθύνας διδόασιν, ἀλλὰ καὶ δεῖπνον αὐτῶν πολυπραγμονεῖται καὶ κοίτη καὶ γάμος καὶ παιδιὰ καὶ σπουδὴ πᾶσα … Ὡς γὰρ ἐν προσώπῳ φακὸς καὶ ἀκροχορδὼν δυσχεραίνεται μᾶλλον ἢ στίγματα καὶ κολοβότητες καὶ οὐλαὶ τοῦ λοιποῦ σώματος, οὕτω τὰ μικρὰ φαίνεται μεγάλα τῶν ἁμαρτημάτων ἐν ἡγεμονικοῖς καὶ πολιτικοῖς ὁρώμενα βίοις διὰ δόξαν, ἣν οἱ πολλοὶ περὶ ἀρχῆς καὶ πολιτείας ἔχουσιν, ὡς πράγματος μεγάλου καὶ καθαρεύειν ἀξίου πάσης ἀτοπίας καὶ πλημμελείας. (Plutarch, *Moralia* 800D)

For not only are men in public life held accountable for their public words and actions, but people busy themselves with all their concerns; dinner, love affair, marriage, amusement, and every serious interest … For, just as a mole or a wart on the face is more unpleasant than brand-marks, mutilations, or scars on other parts of the body, so small faults appear great when observed in the lives of leaders and statesmen on account of the opinion which the majority has of governing and public office, regarding it as a great thing which ought to be clean of all eccentricities and errors. (Tr. H.N. Fowler)

Plutarch does not spell out here that "literary activities" could also be a category to be judged by the public (although we might understand παιδιὰ καὶ σπουδὴ πᾶσα – "amusement, and every serious interest" – to refer to these), but later on he does in fact give some parameters for the kind of eloquence and literary style acceptable in a statesman: he must be eloquent but not "smell of the lamp" or be overly literary (Plutarch *Prae. ger. reip.* 801D). In general, a similar picture arises from most ancient biographies and Princes' Mirrors; a ruler is expected to be a man of learning, culture and, indeed, preferably wisdom: some literary (certainly oratorical) skill and scientific interest befit him. However, excessive indulgence in literary trifles is usually frowned upon: a statesman or king may admire poetry as a thing of beauty that brings pleasure, but this does not mean he should seriously write poetry himself (Plutarch *Perikles* 2.1). The brief historical overview below illustrates this.

In the preliterate heroic society depicted by Homer, heroism and a kingly quality are determined by the twin parameters of physical courage and rhetorical talent, which implies *euboulia*, or intellectual talents. Ideal Homeric heroes are "speakers of words and doers of deeds" (*Iliad* 9.443); the example par excellence here is probably Odysseus.[12] The singing of Achilles by his lyre (*Iliad* 9.186–91) is a different story altogether. The fact that this prince sings of the *klea andron* underlines his own unwillingness to do "glorious" deeds at this point, precisely because he feels they would not receive their due in terms of such "glory." In *Theogony* 79–103, Hesiod establishes a close link between kings and singers, both privileged by the Muses, the eldest of whom favours especially kings with royal eloquence: "From Zeus come kings and blessed is the man whom the Muses love" (*Theogony* 96–7).[13] Solon of Athens made a name for himself both by his political wisdom and his poetry.[14] Julius Caesar is almost as celebrated for his oratorical skill and the literary style of his *Commentarii* as for his feats on the battlefield, although his poetry was apparently less admired.[15] These are mostly positive examples of the link between the prestige of a king or statesman and his musical, literary, or rhetorical activity, but negative examples equally exist. Dionysios I of Syracuse, the notorious tyrant, allegedly wrote tragedies, which, though lamentably bad according to later sources, actually won him first prize at the Lenaia in Athens.[16] Tiberius is said to have been ridiculously concerned about learned questions regarding mythology and to have written erotic elegies in the vein of Parthenios and Euphorion.[17] Claudius' scatter-brained and useless erudition did not gain him much admiration (Suetonius *Claud.* 39–40). Nero is painted as a passionate if lunatic lover of poetry, music, and the stage, who plucked his lyre by the lurid flickering of Rome's great fire.[18] Hadrian was considered *poematum et litterarum nimius studiossimus* ("especially interested in poetry and letters"), which is not counted in his praise (*Historia Augusta* 14.1).[19] Still other instances of writing emperors may be found in the highly admired Stoic writings of Marcus Aurelius and, finally, the eccentric philosophical and theological treatises of

Julian. All of the above demonstrate that writing is often among the noted and remarkable activities of monarchs and prominent statesmen, an element of their public persona that to some extent determined their fame, although it is often very hard to establish why they chose to write what they did, or for which audience.

The attention ancient biographers pay to this phenomenon demonstrates, in any case, that oratorical style and literary writing formed a high-profile tool, to be used by the monarch himself for self-fashioning, and by his biographers as a means to assess character and moral value, as we can see most clearly perhaps in the rubrics on the *studia* of the emperors in Suetonius. The maxim *talis oratio qualis vita* ("style is the man," or *le style, c'est l'homme même*) was an important heuristic device[20] that also has implications for the appreciation of genre and content. Let us highlight genre for a moment, since this in many cases is what is easiest to determine for the fragmentary *testimonia* of the writings of the Hellenistic kings. Some genres clearly were more respectable and fitting the stature of the statesman or ruler than others. The historical examples we have just considered show that it made a huge difference whether a statesman, general, king, or emperor produced a rough and ready historical *hypomnema* or even history of his own deeds (a normal and, indeed, expected activity; see, e.g., Xenophon, Thucydides, Ptolemy Soter, Julius Caesar, Demetrios of Phaleron *FGrH* 228 F4, and Aratos *FGrH* 231), a tragedy (rather unusual – see Dionysios I), or, say, an erotic elegy (unwise – see Tiberius).

Finally, an important consideration seems to be that, in any case, it is nobler to *do* great things than it is to spend time *writing* about them. This sentiment is borne out, for instance, by the young Alexander in Dio Chrysostom's *Second Oration on Kingship* (17–18), a fictional dialogue between Philip of Macedon and Alexander the Great. Philip and his son discuss the latter's great admiration of Homer. At a certain point, Philip asks:

Ἀλλὰ τὸν Ὅμηρον οὕτω σφόδρα, ὦ Ἀλέξανδρε, θαυμάζων, πῶς ὑπερορᾷς αὐτοῦ τὴν σοφίαν; Ὅτι, ἔφη, καὶ τοῦ Ὀλυμπίασι κήρυκος ἥδιστ' ἂν ἀκούοιμι φθεγγομένου μέγα καὶ σαφές, οὐ μέντοι κηρύττειν ἐβουλόμην αὐτὸς ἑτέρους νικῶντας, ἀλλὰ πολὺ μᾶλλον κηρύττεσθαι. (Dio Chrysostom *Orations* 2.17–18)

"If, then, you are so enthusiastic an admirer of Homer, how is it that you do not aspire to his poetic skill?" "Because," [Alexander] replies, "while it would give me the greatest delight to hear the herald at Olympia proclaim the victors with strong and clear voice, yet I should not myself care to herald the victories of others; I should much rather hear my own proclaimed."[21]

We know that, in reality, Alexander, like many of the royal Macedonians before and after him, was indeed very keen on having his deeds painstakingly recorded, as the many references to his letters and *ephemerides* (court journals) prove (see, e.g., Pearson 1954–5: 429–55). As we saw, tradition depicted him as lamenting the absence of his "own Homer." But even if it is likely that he had some hand in the redaction of his *ephemerides*, they are of course still something entirely different from a truly literary enterprise. The *defence* of writing as an activity worthy of admiration in the statesman can, however, also be found, famously, in the preface to Sallust's *Bellum Catilinae* and in Cicero's *De Officiis* 1–4. It may be pointed out that, arguably, these two authors eventually gained more fame through their literary achievements than their by political careers – although Cicero certainly seems to have hoped that his deeds as consul in 63 BCE with regard to the Catilinarian conspiracy would gain him eternal fame as the saviour of Rome (*Against Catiline* 4.21).[22] To this end, he even attempted to heighten the renown of his consular year by glorifying himself in an epic (*Consulatus Suus*); he wanted to have it both ways – fame for his *vita activa* and *contemplativa* – but ended up mainly annoying his contemporaries with his self-praise.[23]

3. The Evidence for Writings by Hellenistic Kings

The ancient beliefs outlined above about what kind of literary activity, if any, is fitting for a king or statesman, form the background against which we should assess the writings of the Hellenistic kings. So, what *did* they write? And, can we think of the reasons why they chose to write what they did? The surviving evidence has been gathered and arranged in table 8.1. Thereafter, I discuss in some detail the more remarkable or well-documented instances.

Some preliminary observations arise from the items in table 8.1: judging from the evidence, the Ptolemies (marked in grey) are the most productive dynasty when it comes to literature. It seems likely that there is a correlation with the similarly exceptional stimulation of literary and scientific pursuits at the Ptolemaic court. When it comes to the nature and genre of the works by Hellenistic kings, historiography stands out as the most practised genre, with the subcategory of (autobiographical) letters and official records or communications, *hypomnemata* and *ephemerides*. Another relatively widespread genre is scientific writing, including didactic poetry. Epigrams are the most frequent poetic form. The most remarkable literary production is certainly Ptolemy IV's tragedy, *Adonis*.

Table 8.1 The writings of the Hellenistic kings

King	Works	Genre	References
Alexander the Great (356–323 BCE)	Letters *Ephemerides* (kept by Euhemeros and Diodotos)	Letters Court journal	Plut. *Alex. passim*; Arrian *Anab.* 6.1.4 *FGrH* 117F3a
Antipater (397–319 BCE)	Letters History of Perdikkas' Illyrian campaigns	Letters Historiography/memoir (doubtful)	Suda A 2703; *FGrH* 114; Cic. *De Off.* 2 14.48; Plut. *Comp. Alc. et Cor.* 3; Ael. *VH* 14.1
Pyrrhus (319–272 BCE)	*Hypomnemata* *Tactica*	Memoirs Military treatise	Dion. Hal. *AR* 20.10; Plut. *Pyrrh.* 21.12; Paus. 1.12.2; *FGrH* 229; Cic. *Fam.* 9.25.1; Aelian. *Tact.* 1.2; *FrGrH* 603 T2
Ptolemy Soter (367–283 BCE), Alexandria	History of Alexander Letters	Memoirs Letters	1) *FGrH* 138; *PP* VI 16 942; Arr. *Anab.* 1.2.7; 6.2.4) 2) Luc. *pro laps. in salut.* 10
Ptolemy II Philadelphos (308–246 BCE), Alexandria	Epigrams? *Idiophye*	Elegy Treatise/epigrams(?)	*Suppl. Hell.* 7.12 = *Vit. Arat.* 1.10 4–7, *FGE* 84
Philip V of Macedon (238–179 BCE), Pella	Epigrams against Alkaios of Messene	Elegy	Plut. *Vit. Tit. Flamin.* 9. *FGE* p. 79; *Anth. Pal.* 9.520 = *HE anon.* lx
Ptolemy III Euergetes I (284–222 BCE), Alexandria	Description of entry into Seleukia and Antioch 245 BCE (doubtful authorship)	Personal narrative / official war bulletin	*PPetr.* 2.52; 3.144; *FGrH* 160
Attalos I (269–197) BCE, Pergamon	*Kale peuke*	Scientific horticultural treatise	Strab. XIII 603
Ptolemy IV Philopator (244–204 BCE), Alexandria	*Adonis*	Tragedy	*Schol.* Ar. *Thesm.* 1059 = *TGrF* 119 cf. Or. Gr. 51

Ptolemy VIII (182–116 BCE) and Euergetes II (Physkon) (145–116 BCE), Alexandria	1) Memoirs, 24 books 2) Treatise on Homer?	1) Historiography 2) Philological treatise(?)	*FGrH* 234; 11 frgs all quoted by Athenaios Steph. Byz. *Anchiale*
Attalos III (170–133 BCE), Pergamon	On herbs/antidotes Official letters	Learned treatises Letters	Plut. *Dem.* 20, Gal. *Ant.*1.1, *Comp. Med.* 1,13–14; Orib. *Syn. Eustath.* 3, 4; Plin. *HN* 32.87; Cels. *De med.* 5, 19.11; Var. *Agric.*, 1.1.8; Colum. *Agric.* 1.1.7–8; *Pomp. Trog.* 36.4.3; Marc Emp. *De Medic.* 22.20 RC nos 66–7; RC 273–6 no. 68; RC 276–9 no. 69
Antiochos VIII Philometor (?–96 BCE), Antiochia	"On herbs/antidotes"	Didactic poetry	Plin. *HN* 20.264; Gal. *Ant.* 14. 185. 201
Cleopatra (69–30 BCE), Alexandria	A number of works on cosmetics and weights and measures (probably pseudo-epigraphic)	Scientific treatises(?)	Cf. Plut. *Ant.* 25 *Metr. Script.* i 218 p 767K, p. 253; *anecd. Oxon.* iii p. 164l 14

4. Historiography

It is no surprise that prose histories, letters, *hypomnemata, ephemerides*, and the like should dominate, for the obvious reasons of political justification, propaganda, and intrinsic interest. Historiographical memoirs, especially of military exploits, long had been the genre of choice for statesmen, rulers, and former generals, underlining as they did the active achievements of such great men.[24] They were often, though certainly not always, written *after* a political or military career. While it was not a fully recognized literary genre, the existence of the terms *hypomnema* and *commentarius* nevertheless imply that there was a certain *Erwartungshorizont* when it came to the first-person reports of kings, generals, and statesmen. The original understanding was that such writings were makeshift, to be enhanced and elaborated on by a professional historiographer. Yet, this often was not the way things turned out, and there thus came to exist something of a *hypomnemata* tradition on which later writers of political autobiography could base their own accounts. An interesting question, therefore, is to what extent the character of the *hypomnema* as a rough and unpolished (and hence by implication unpremeditated and truthful) account played a role in the choice of this genre. It would seem that a *hypomnema* represented a safe way to publicize one's deeds without necessarily pretending to achieve a literary accomplishment – this is probably what appealed to war-like generals and tough politicians. In table 8.1 are listed the examples of Antipater, Pyrrhus, and Ptolemy I, III, and VIII. In what follows, the careers of Ptolemy I and VIII are treated.

5. Ptolemy I Soter's History of Alexander the Great

A general of Alexander, and later the first Macedonian pharaoh of Egypt, Ptolemy I Soter wrote a history of Alexander's conquest.[25] We cannot establish how widely it was read or, in light of the theme of this volume, how famous it may have made its author; but the fact that Arrian could still obtain a copy proves its success. When and why did Ptolemy write this account? It seems likely that he stood to gain fame by linking himself to the most famous man of his own day, portraying himself as Alexander's right-hand general, and so to undergird his claims, and possibly those of his son, to the Egyptian throne, when those were still contested.[26]

If we look at the fragments, the picture emerges of an account that is factual and dry, concerned mainly with military matters, and that represented Alexander in a moderate, human light, unlike the numerous fantastic Alexander biographies, some of which were written by contemporaries.[27]

There are no traces of open boastfulness on the part of the author in these preserved fragments; but we must remember that they represent only a part of the story. Ancient opinions varied on the reliability of Ptolemy's self-representation and his motives.

Arrian, our main ancient testimony, claims to be completely convinced of Ptolemy's truthfulness. This may well be a rhetorical ploy to vouch for the truthfulness of his own account, but it is enlightening to see his arguments. Ptolemy (like Aristoboulos, who is also a source for Arrian), he claims, was an eyewitness to what he recounts, and wrote after Alexander died, so not as propagandist or flatterer of a living ruler and therefore without bias (αὐτοῖς ἤ τε ἀνάγκη καὶ ὁ μισθὸς τοῦ ἄλλως τι ἢ ὡς συνηνέχθη ξυγγράψαι ἀπῆν, Arrian *Anabasis* 1.2–3). Most interesting is Arrian's argument that Ptolemy was, moreover, a *king* and would, therefore, never tell a lie (Πτολεμαῖος δὲ πρὸς τῷ ξυστρατεῦσαι ὅτι καὶ αὐτῷ βασιλεῖ ὄντι αἰσχρότερον ἤ τῳ ἄλλῳ ψεύσασθαι ἦν, Arrian *Anabasis* 1.2).[28] This view may hark back to ancient Persian kingship ideals, which Alexander and his successors came to adopt, that made "truthfulness" a central value,[29] and it is of course entirely possible that Ptolemy himself said something to this effect. This "truthfulness," moreover, pertains to the record of *Alexander*'s deeds. But we may wonder how truthful and unbiased Ptolemy was regarding his own part in history. Indeed, other ancient sources hint that there was a self-aggrandizing tenor to the memoir – for instance, in the passing remark of Quintus Curtius Rufus (9.5.21). In describing the (apparently glorious) expedition mounted to punish the Indi held responsible for the wounding of Alexander, Curtius states that some historians believe Ptolemy to have been present. Ptolemy himself, however, does not make this claim in his memoir, even though he was "certainly not inclined to depreciate his own glory," in Curtius' words.[30]

Modern scholarly opinion is divided. While Tarn (1948: vol. 2) believed that Ptolemy was completely trustworthy, Badian (1961) holds that he represents himself in an overly positive light. This latter view is now mostly accepted and is also supported by records showing that Ptolemy is trying to wriggle himself into the royal bloodline by claiming that Philip II was his real father (Curtius 9.8.22; Pausanias 1.6.2; Aelian fr. 285), by trying to marry Alexander's half-sister Cleopatra (Diodoros 20.37.3–6; Parian Marble, *FGrH* 239 B 19), and by hijacking Alexander's body and prominently displaying it in a mausoleum in Alexandria.[31] Bosworth, moreover, argues that Ptolemy was involved in the falsification of Alexander's will, the enigmatic ancient document known as the *Liber de Morte*, in order to promote his own claims to kingship in the struggles following Alexander's death.[32] It seems attractive to read Ptolemy's *hypomnema* of the campaign of Alexander, the world's most famous king and his previous commander and friend, in this light too. The existence of Ptolemy's memoir may make us wonder whether Ptolemy's adversaries also used this tool of propagandistic *hypomnemata* (next to more common political tools like diplomacy and military actions) to establish their positions. If they did, we can only say that these attempts were apparently not as successful and authoritative as Ptolemy's.

6. Ptolemy VIII Euergetes II's Memoirs

The other royal history that is substantially extant is that of Ptolemy VIII Euergetes II. This king had a reign troubled by fierce dynastic struggles, and he receives very negative press in the ancient sources, as a debauched, negligent, and extremely cruel ruler.[33] The twenty-four books of his autobiographical *hypomnemata,* though equally historiography, are entirely different from Soter's writings. Athenaios, who quotes extensively from the king's works, calls them *poluthrulētoi* ("notorious"), an epithet they gained presumably because of their content and their author. Indeed, from what glimpses we get, our first impression might be that of a rather frivolous *chronique scandaleuse*. To cite Fraser's paraphrase,

> [they concern] the exotic birds kept in the Palaces' area of the city ...; an account of the mistresses of his ancestor Philadelphos; and, as indicative of his interest in his fellow monarchs, his very highly coloured description of the buffoonery of Antiochos Epiphanes in Rome, and his reference to the luxuries of the court of Massanassa. Other fragments refer to his own life during his long years of exile in Cyrene.[34]

Yet, a closer look reveals that maybe the summing up of exotic animals and the gossip about predecessors and fellow monarchs was not as insignificant as it might seem, nor indeed entirely representative of the gist of the account. As Peter Nadig has shown, it is possible to read many of the anecdotes with a political slant. Nadig sees a condemnation rather than celebration of Ptolemaic *tryphe* in the anecdotes about Philadelphos, and notes a Rome-friendly attitude throughout. This seems likely, since Euergetes II courted support from these quarters in his domestic power struggles. Nadig further discerns Euergetes II's fashioning of himself as a "good king," beloved by his soldiers and interested in the wonders of the natural world – something of a new Alexander, perhaps.[35] Moreover, it seems likely that the king also treated more explicitly political topics, which left no trace in Athenaios' sample, weighted toward the curious and the culinary as it is. In all likelihood, then, the exiled king used his *hypomnemata* to justify himself, and to ingratiate himself with possible Roman allies. We may wonder what, if anything, the memoirs said about the bloody dynastic struggles in which he killed his nephew and his own son, among others, but we may guess that, if they were featured, they would have exonerated him.[36] In any case, the combination of Euergetes II's reputation in other sources and the evaluation of his work in Athenaios suggest that his work may have been avidly read, and hence made him famous, but not for the intended reasons.

7. Scientific Treatises and Scholarly Works

Somewhat unexpectedly, perhaps, we observe that a remarkable number of Hellenistic monarchs composed natural scientific treatises, didactic poetry, and works of scholarship. It is well known that science was highly appreciated at the Hellenistic courts and flourished to an unprecedented extent. Research in medicine and the establishment of zoological gardens at courts, such as the menagerie of Ptolemy Philadelphos mentioned by Ptolemy Euergetes II, held out the promise of mastery over the known world and was therefore considered a suitable kingly interest.[37] The keeping of exotic animals showed the extent of the royal dominions, while the mastery over medicine and the curing of friends and subjects has a tradition that goes back to Achilles, and was revived (perhaps looking toward this model) by Alexander.[38] However, even though medicine took flight in Cos and Alexandria under luminaries such as Praxagoras, Herophilos, and Erasistratos, it was rather unusual that kings should study and practise medicine on a professional level.

8. Attalos III: "On Antidotes"

A passage in Plutarch's *Life of Demetrios Poliorketes* suggests interesting parameters for the evaluation of various kingly "hobbies" (*paidia, banausia*), scientific and botanical research among them, and how they reflect on the king's dignity and hence reputation, in this case the reputation of Attalos III of Pergamon.

Εὐφυὴς γὰρ ὢν καὶ θεωρητικός, οὐκ εἰς παιδιὰς οὐδ' εἰς διαγωγὰς ἀχρήστους ἔτρεψε τὸ φιλότεχνον, ὥσπερ ἄλλοι βασιλεῖς αὐλοῦντες καὶ ζωγραφοῦντες καὶ τορεύοντες. Ἀέροπος γὰρ ὁ Μακεδὼν τραπέζια μικρὰ καὶ λυχνίδια τεκταινόμενος ὁπότε σχολάζοι διῆγεν. Ἄτταλος δ' ὁ Φιλομήτωρ ἐκήπευε τὰς φαρμακώδεις βοτάνας, οὐ μόνον ὑοσκύαμον καὶ ἐλλέβορον, ἀλλὰ καὶ κώνειον καὶ ἀκόνιτον καὶ δορύκνιον, αὐτὸς ἐν τοῖς βασιλείοις σπείρων καὶ φυτεύων, ὀπούς τε καὶ καρπὸν αὐτῶν ἔργον πεποιημένος εἰδέναι καὶ κομίζεσθαι καθ' ὥραν. Οἱ δὲ Πάρθων βασιλεῖς ἐσεμνύνοντο τὰς ἀκίδας τῶν βελῶν χαράττοντες αὐτοὶ καὶ παραθήγοντες. Ἀλλὰ μὴν Δημητρίου καὶ τὸ βάναυσον ἦν βασιλικόν, καὶ μέγεθος ἡ μέθοδος εἶχεν, ἅμα τῷ περιττῷ καὶ φιλοτέχνῳ τῶν ἔργων ὕψος τι διανοίας καὶ φρονήματος συνεκφερόντων, ὥστε μὴ μόνον γνώμης καὶ περιουσίας, ἀλλὰ καὶ χειρὸς ἄξια φαίνεσθαι βασιλικῆς. (Plutarch, *Life of Demetrios Poliorketes* 20.2–5)

For [Demetrios] had good natural talents and was given to investigation, and did not apply his ingenuity to things that would afford useless pleasure or diversion, like other kings who played on the flute, or painted, or chased metals. Aeropus, king of Macedon, spent his hours of leisure in making little tables and lamps. Attalos III surnamed Philometor, amused himself with planting poisonous (or medicinal) herbs, not only henbane and hellebore, but hemlock, aconite, and *dorycnium*. These he cultivated in the royal gardens, and besides gathering them at their proper seasons, made it his business to know the qualities of their juices and fruit. And the kings of Parthia took a pride in forging and sharpening heads for arrows. But the mechanics of Demetrios were of a princely kind; there was always something great in preparation. Together with a spirit of curiosity and love of the arts, there appeared in all his works *a grandeur of design and dignity of intention, so that they were not only worthy of the genius and wealth, but of the hand of a king.* (Tr. B. Perrin; my emphasis) [39]

What Plutarch implies here is that, in and of itself, it was not automatically considered a good thing for a king to display serious interest in sciences or arts that were not readily associated with the tasks of a ruler. The same thought, as we have seen above, occurs in *Perikles* 2.1, where it is stated that a gifted young man might admire the works of a sculptor or a poet but should not strive to be a Phidias or an Archilochos: the objects and works of art that they make might give pleasure, but that does not mean they are great men. Only moral ἀρετή should be imitated. Similarly, we see that, despite the fact that it was apparently prestigious to function as a patron of the sciences, posing as a scientist, scholar, or artist in one's own right was not always the right way to gain fame as a ruler (contrast Strootman 2010: 34). The hobbies described here clearly incurred the odium of oddity and frivolity. If so, why did kings engage in them and publicize their interests?

The interest in toxicology, which is well attested for late Hellenistic courts and continues into the Roman empire, was driven by at least the following considerations: 1) that a king could in this way defend himself against attempted assassinations and harm his enemies (and would not hesitate to let this be known);[40] and 2) that, by inventing remedies against various illnesses and noxious animals, the king might pose and be known as a protector and saviour of his people.[41]

As Plutarch signals (*Demetrius* 20.2–5), Attalos III was a dedicated botanist. He wrote numerous treatises on botanical themes (as cited by Varro and Columella) and on pharmacology and toxicology (Galen and others frequently and respectfully cite him on this).[42] Indeed, the king was so well known and respected for this knowledge that certain remedies were called "Attalids" after him. He was clearly a serious and innovative researcher in the field, and famous as such (Scarborough 2008). Like Attalos I, Attalos III attracted professional authors to write on his favourite themes: that Nikander of Kolophon, as court poet of the Attalids, wrote his *Theriaka* and *Alexipharmaka* for the pleasure of these kings is well known. Even if it is not entirely clear for which of the Attalid monarchs his poems were written, modern consensus favours Attalos III.[43] Clearly there was a traditional interest in toxicology and medical science at Pergamon, which may have started with the world-famous fourth-century Asklepieion. We may remember that Galen, too, came from this same tradition.

Nevertheless, in some quarters Attalos III's interest was apparently deemed excessive and sinister. It was suggested that he had come to the study of toxicology after his despair at the death of his mother, Stratonike, and his wife, Berenike, whom he (mistakenly) believed to have been murdered, and that he took his revenge by poisoning the presumed murderers (Justin *Epitome* 36.4.1). We also hear that he tested his poisons on convicted criminals,[44] and sent poisonous plants to his friends, a strange gift.[45] It seems likely that these anecdotes, which depict the king as deranged, resulted from the public awareness of his notorious botanical interests rather than the other way around; they may plausibly be understood as examples of biographical interpretation of his writings, fuelled by a dislike of his politics.

Something similar might also apply to the less-well-documented Seleukid king Antiochos VIII Epiphanes Philometor (Grypos), who likewise studied toxicology. This monarch apparently wrote a didactic poem on a toxicological theme from which a sixteen-line fragment in elegiac distichs is cited by Galen. The poem opens with a *sphragis*, which proudly emphasizes empirical research (probably to signify his distance from the Alexandrian "rationalist" school which followed Herophilos): Ἴησιν μάθε τήνδε πρὸς ἑρπετά, ἣν Φιλομήτωρ/Νικήσας, πείρᾳ κέκρικεν Ἀντίοχος ("Learn of this remedy against snakes, which Antiochos Philometor gained, by empirical analysis"; *Antidotes* 14.185).[46] In his case, too, a biographical anecdote was recounted that related to attempted poisoning (by his own mother), which he turned against the culprit, so killing her (Justin *Epitome* 39.2.1). In both cases, then, the writings of these kings harmed rather than helped their reputation.

9. Ptolemy VIII Euergetes II's Treatise on Homer

Despite his eventual reputation for driving away the scholars from his court (the *fautores pueri* – that is, the partisans of his nephew; Justin *Epitome* 38.8), Ptolemy VIII Euergetes II, whom we just encountered as the author of a notorious memoir, was in fact reputed to have been something of a scholar himself. This interest in learning seems to come up in the *hypomnemata* too, with mention of the names of rare birds and other natural wonders (Fr. 9, 2–3, 6, 10, 11 Nadig). Indeed, as a student of Aristarchos, he is even credited by Athenaios with a conjecture on a Homeric verse concerning the nature of the vegetation on Kalypso's island (*Odyssey* 5.72); scholars have presumed that this was part of a larger work on Homer. The king read σίου (water parsnip) instead of ἴου (violet), arguing that the latter plant does not grow in watery meadows, whereas the former does. This conjecture suggests an interest not only in Homer, then, but also in the natural world. We might even ask whether the suggested emendation, concerning as it does an edible plant (a water parsnip), also reveals something about the king's gastronomic inclinations. He was, after all, called *Physkon* (pot-belly), and many fragments quoted by Athenaios equally concern gastronomic pleasures. Then again, this might be a representation of the work that is skewed by Athenaios' own culinary interests. An anecdote in Plutarch *Adulator* 17 about courtiers flattering the king (probably Euergetes II) by engaging him in philological discussions deep into the night,[47] and the testimony of a fourth-century CE inscription (*Epiph. Mens.* Z 338) that calls him *philologos*, would support the likelihood of a treatise on Homer. Indeed, it is not unimaginable that Euergetes II's attempts at Homeric scholarship were embarked upon as a means to rehabilitate him in the eyes of the intelligentsia after alienating them by chasing many of their number away. That this Ptolemy was interested in scholarship to the extent of writing on Homeric glosses is perhaps not surprising in the context of the Alexandrian library and its famous scholars, and certainly if we remember that Aristarchos was his teacher.

10. Cleopatra's Remedies

Finally, we reach the various treatises ascribed to Cleopatra VII, the last Ptolemaic pharaoh, concerning metrics and weights, cosmetics, and hair care.[48] Aetius claims that the remedies stem from Queen Cleopatra (Cleopatra VII Philopator), but is unlikely that she truly was the author of these writings. In the first place, the weight standard she employs came into use only as late as 64 CE; but, besides, it seems unlikely that the queen would have found time to write on such mundane topics as hair care. So why was she credited with these treatises?

In antiquity, Cleopatra enjoyed a considerable reputation for intellectual prowess. Plutarch in his *Life of Antony* speaks glowingly of her stunning linguistic achievements and general intelligence; according to him, she was the only pharaoh to master demotic Egyptian (as well as Arabic, Aramaic, and the language of the troglodytes, among others).[49] But, of course, she was equally known for her exquisitely luxurious lifestyle, her physical grace, and her legendary charm. It is not hard to imagine that someone attempting to sell his own beauty routine would select the name of the fabled queen, or even that a namesake came to be confused with her without any disingenuous intent. Moreover, in medieval times, Cleopatra's famed intelligence gained her an afterlife as a female sage and alchemist, concerned with the philosopher's stone and remedies for eternal youth.[50]

11. Poetry

Finally, we turn to poetry. The first thing to be noted here is the predominance of epigrams. It is not hard to see why epigrams were favoured as poetical means of expression by royals: they flourish in a convivial and impromptu context. As such, they are a comparatively risk-free genre of poetry that, lacking success, could easily be brushed away as *parerga*, and, if successful, served to demonstrate a ready wit, a trait universally admired in antiquity, as the numerous aphorism and *chreiai*-collections attest.[51] Their brevity, moreover, made them ideal as "catch-phrases" to be spread widely and so gain their author fame.

12. Ptolemy's Epigram on Aratos

It is doubtful whether the epigram in praise of Aratos of Soloi, cited in his biography (*Suppl. Hell.* 712 = *Vita Arati* 1.10.4–7) should be attributed to Philadelphos.[52] Ascribing the poem to him has the benefit of connecting it to two contemporary epigrams in praise of this poet, by Leonidas of Tarentum and Kallimachos (Leonidas *Anth. Pal.* 9.25; Kallimachos *Anth. Pal.* 9.507). Indeed, Alan Cameron (1995) suggests that all three epigrams were composed in a competitive context at court. If so, the epigram would have made an excellent showcase for the wit, taste, and literary acumen of King Philadelphos, who is praised on all sides by poets and others for his love of the Muses, and is generally known for his patronage of the Alexandrian Library and the Mouseion and their authors.[53] It is especially tantalizing to imagine that the king would engage in such an exchange with famous authors of his own time, a royal amateur among the professionals. What would the stakes have been? Could one attempt to be a wittier poet than the king? What also remains to be explained is why all these Alexandrians sang the praises of an author working at the court of the Macedonian Antigonos Gonatas, who was intermittently on hostile terms with the Ptolemies. Could it have been a bid to win over Aratos to come and stay at the Alexandrian Mouseion?[54]

13. Philip V's Epigrams against Alkaios of Messene

Another poetic "competition," though of a much grimmer character, allegedly took place in the exchange between the epigrammatist Alkaios of Messene and Philip V of Macedon, as recounted by Plutarch (*Flamininus* 9). After the battle of Kynoskephalae (197 BCE, between Philip V and Titus Flamininus), five thousand Macedonians were left unburied on the field, according to Plutarch. In an epigram that enjoyed great popularity, Alkaios of Messene voiced the great indignation this caused among the Greeks. It began thus: Ἄκλαυστοι καὶ ἄθαπτοι, ὁδοιπόρε, τῷδ' ἐπὶ τύμβῳ ... ("un-lamented and unburied, wayfarer, in this tomb we lie ...").[55] Plutarch says that Philip retorted in kind with a distich threatening to have Alkaios impaled, closely echoing the opening words of his poetic critic: Ἄφλοιος καὶ ἄφυλλος, ὁδοιπόρε, τῷδ' ἐπὶ νώτῳ / Ἀλκαίῳ σταυρὸς πήγνυται ἠλίβατος ("Barkless and leafless, wayfarer, this steep cross is fastened to Alkaios' backside").

Of course, Philip's epigram does not so much aim at poetic excellence as on savage rebuttal and a show of power and ruthlessness. Plutarch's formulation, that Philip simply made fun of Alkaios (ὁ μὲν γὰρ ἀντικωμῳδῶν τὸν Ἀλκαῖον τῷ ἐλεγείῳ, παρέβαλλεν, "for he, in his own turn making fun of Alkaios with the distich, responded," *Vit. Tit. Flam.* 9.3), makes us doubt the reality of his intention of killing Alkaios in the first place.[56] Nevertheless, the fact that Philip responded thus suggests how powerful a weapon poetic invective could be when it came to making or breaking a reputation.[57] Indeed, Plutarch implies that Philip easily got rid of his anger this way, whereas *Titus Flamininus* was annoyed by Alkaios' epigram, which apparently gained great currency (λεγόμενον δὲ πολλαχοῦ καὶ ὑπὸ πολλῶν, "often repeated by many," *Vit. Tit. Flam.* 9.3). This epigram, in passing, ascribes the victory to the *Aitolians* rather than to the Romans. Of course, as with so many of the *bon mots* and *apophthegmata* attributed to various famous personages of the ancient world, we may wonder whether Philip's epigram is authentic or not. In any case, it was apparently something that Philip "could plausibly have said" and that gained currency enough for Plutarch to include it in his biography of Philip and spawned other variations besides (cf. *Anth. Pal.* 9.520).

14. Ptolemy IV's Tragedy Adonis

Most intriguing of the literary productions of the Hellenistic monarchs, but unfortunately also most obscure, is the tragedy written by Ptolemy IV Philopator entitled *Adonis*, according to a *scholion* on Aristophanes' *Thesmophoriazusae* 1059:

Ἐπεὶ εἰσήγαγε κακοστένακτον τὴν Ἠχὼ ὁ Εὐριπίδης ἐν τῇ Ἀνδρομέδᾳ, εἰς τοῦτο παίζει. ἐζήλωσε δὲ αὐτὸν Πτολεμαῖος ὁ Φιλοπάτωρ ἐν ᾗ πεποίηκε τραγῳδίᾳ Ἀδώνιδι, περὶ ἧς ὁ ἐρώμενος αὐτῷ Ἀγαθοκλῆς γέγραφεν, ὁ ἀδελφὸς τῆς ἐρωμένης αὐτοῦ πάλιν Ἀγαθοκλείας ...

Because Euripides had brought on stage in his *Andromeda* a lamenting Echo, he (Aristophanes) parodies this. Ptolemy Philopator strove to imitate him in the tragedy which he wrote, *Adonis*, about which his lover Agathokles had written for him, who was in turn the brother of his lover Agathokleia.

The difficult *scholion*, after commenting on a parodic imitation by Aristophanes of a Euripidean poetic feature in the *Andromeda*, apparently states that Ptolemy Philopator emulated this same feature of Euripides' (lost) *Andromeda* in his tragedy *Adonis*, "about which wrote his lover Agathokles, the brother of Agathokleia who was also his lover." What can we make of this mysterious affirmation? We know that Euripides in his *Andromeda* composed some kind of wailing lament, which involved an echoed response. Ptolemy IV apparently imitated this particular literary invention in another lamenting scene in his tragic *Adonis*. It is unclear how Agathokles and Agathokleia fit in – although the closeness of these echoing names to a remark about "echoes" is tantalizing. The implication, however, seems to be that Agathokles (Philopator's lover, commander, and palace co-conspirator) wrote a commentary on the tragedy (περὶ ἧς ὁ ἐρώμενος αὐτῷ Ἀγαθοκλῆς γέγραφεν, "about which his lover Agathokles wrote [for him?]"). There is no other evidence to this effect. Perhaps the information is garbled, and Agathokles really was the *dedicatee* of the tragedy. This seems reasonable if it was a love story, which the Adonis myth of course warrants.[58] In any case, there appears to be a sense that the (erotic) life and the literary ventures of the king were somehow intertwined, a common feature in appraisals of literary works of rulers, as we saw in the case of Attalos and Antiochos.

It is hard to make more of the evidence; we do not know whether Philopator wrote before or after his accession to the throne, whether his tragedy was ever staged, and why he chose to write a tragedy rather than, say, an elegy. He probably wrote more than just the one tragedy, however, since a contemporary inscription apparently names him among contemporaries as a "tragedian."[59] It may be worthwhile to speculate a bit about the choice of theme, Adonis. Although other dramas on the same theme existed, it is important that the Adonis festival had a special ideological significance for the Ptolemies (cf. Theokritos *Idyll* 15).[60] Perhaps, then, the tragedy was composed as a special high-profile part of a festival organized at court by the royal family? Was Philopator attempting to give new emphasis to the literary profile inherited from his Ptolemaic predecessors? We also hear that he founded a temple for Homer and was praised in an epigram by his teacher Eratosthenes (Powell *CA* 66) for his love of the Muses.

It is a pity we know so little of this literary work and how it may have influenced its author's reputation. It was highly unusual for a king to compose something as poetically demanding as a tragedy.[61] Most anecdotes featuring monarchs dabbling in drama underline the dangers of such practice: distraction from affairs of state, tyrannical misapprehensions about one's own talents, and impersonation of despicable characters (Dionysios I, Nero). This in fact fits well with what we hear of Philopator in the sources, which generally describe him as a would-be philologist but also as "debauched" and "inattentive to his reign," and a matricide to boot, who ends up being killed in a palace revolution (Josephus *AJ* 12.130–1; Polybios 2.51; 15.25–34; Justin *Epit.* 30.1–2).[62]

15. Conclusion

As we have seen, it might have been more dignified simply to do great deeds rather than to write. But if one did choose the latter, prose treatises and political/military memoirs were, next to epigrams, the genres of choice for kings to write in. It is worth noting that the choices of the Hellenistic monarchs correspond neatly to the type of literature or science fostered at their courts. The likely assumption is that a trend was established by the founder of a dynasty who invited experts on his topic of choice to court. Subsequently, his descendants honoured this interest as a matter of dynastic prestige.

In some cases, writings helped the king gain fame as a creditable ruler, an expert scientist, or a connoisseur. One may think, respectively, of Soter's *hypomnema,* Attalos III's toxicological treatises, and Philadelphos' epigram. But literary profiling could, and did, backfire, whether indiscrete, like the memoirs of Philometor, or frivolous or sinister, like the toxicological studies of Antiochos VIII and Attalos III. What the Greeks thought of Philip's savage retort to Alkaios, or of Philopator's tragic *Adonis,* is hard to establish, but the contexts suggest that they were not wholly enthusiastic. All in all, the path of literature was an uneasy one to tread for a king; it was much safer to stick to great deeds, or literary patronage, as many praised monarchs had done before and have done since, in the race for undying renown.

NOTES

1 See, e.g., Howald 1926: 137; Snell 1946: 284; Lesky 1971: 788; Schwinge 1986: 76.

2 For the fragments of such panegyric elegies, see in particular Barbantani 2001. Previously Ziegler 1966 had speculated about the existence of many lost Hellenistic panegyric epics.

3 See, e.g., Strootman 2013: 33.

4 For the importance of being *laudatus a laudato viro* ("praised by a man of praise"), see also Cicero *Fam.* 5.12.7.

5 See, e.g., *Letter of Aristeas*; Josephus *AJ* 12.20. On the idea that compiling an encompassing library was a bid for cultural hegemony, see especially Too 2010: 83–115.

6 On this topic, see, e.g., Too 2010: 83–116; Klooster 2011: 15–21.

7 For Alexander's love of literature, see Plutarch *Alex.* 7; 8; *Mor.* 327A–328A, Dio Chrysostom *Or.* 2. For his interest in natural wonders and philosophy and his financial support of Aristotle and other philosophers, see, e.g., Athenaios 398, Plutarch *Alex.* 8.

8 See Pfeiffer 1970: 114–286 on Alexandria and 286–306 on Pergamon; Fraser 1972: ch. 10 with notes on Alexandria; Weber 1993: passim on Alexandria; Strootman 2013.

9 Strootman (2013: 30–45) goes on to mention the examples of Alexander the Great, "philosopher in arms" (Onesikritos *FGrH* 134 F17a = Str. 15.1.64), Ptolemy Soter (to whom he erroneously attributes the tragedy *Adonis*, which is the work of Ptolemy IV Philopator; see below), Antiochos VIII, Ptolemy II Philadelphos, Ptolemy III Euergetes, and Philip V of Macedon. The naming of both Ptolemy II Philadelphos and Ptolemy III Euergetes as epigrammatists is another unfortunate mistake, presumably stemming from the doubt in scholarship about who wrote the epigram *Suppl. Hell.* 712 (see below).

10 Faber, p. 4, this volume; see also Braudy 1986: 6.

11 This topic forms the focus of an on-going project I am currently pursuing, entitled "A Portrait of the Statesman as an Artist. The Evaluation of Writing Rulers in Antiquity," supported by a Marie Curie–Pegasus grant at Ghent University in 2012.

12 Cf. Solmsen 1954; Schofield 1986; and Klooster 2018.

13 See Stoddard 2003.

14 See, e.g., Plato *Ti.* 21a-c; Plutarch *Sol.* 1–4.

15 Suetonius *Iul.* 55: *Eloquentia militarique re aut aequavit praestantissimorum gloriam aut excessit.* Cf. Cicero *Brut.* 252; Quintilian *Inst.* 10.114; Tacitus *Ann.* 13.3.4, *Dial.* 21.5 and 25.3; Fronto p. 181 ed. Rom.; Plutarch *Caes.* 3.2.

16 Cf. Diodorus Siculus 14.109.2; see further Duncan 2012.

17 Suetonius *Tib.* 70: *Maxime tamen curavit notitiam historiae fabularis usque ad ineptias atque derisum.* On this see Klooster 2017.

18 See Suetonius *Ner.* 20–8; Tacitus *Hist.* 1–4; *Ann.* 13–16; Josephus *BJ* 2–6; *AJ* 20; Dio 61–3; Philostratus *Vit. Ap. Tyan.* 4–5.

19 See Klooster 2017 on Tiberius and Hadrian, and Klooster forthcoming on the styles of the Caesars in Suetonius.

20 For this expression, see in particular Seneca *Ep.* 114 for the Latin version (here used with reference to Maecenas and his poetry), and George Louis Leclerc, count of Buffon (1707–88), for the French expression, in his *Discours sur le Style* (1753). The phenomenon is analysed for antiquity by Möller 2004.

21 We should read this dialogue as ironic with regards to Alexander's youthful enthusiasm (thus, e.g., Gangloff 2006: 260–3), but the thought expressed here is common; see, e.g., Plutarch *De glor. Ath., passim;* Plutarch. *Per.* 2.1; Pliny *Ep.* 1.10.

22 Cicero's actions of self-promotion are impressive in their assiduity. They contain, among others, a public letter in Latin dedicated to Pompey (*Fam.* 5.7.3); a Greek *hypomnema* commissioned from Atticus (*Att.* 2.1.1–2; cf. Nepos *Att.* 18.6.); a request for a Greek epic by poet Archias (not finished; see *Att.* 1.16.13); *Hypomnema/Commentarius* in Greek by Cicero himself in 60 BCE (Plutarch *Crass.* 13.4; *Caes.* 8.4; *Cic.* 15.1–3; Dio 46.2.4); a request to Poseidonios (historian) to base a monograph on Cicero's own *hypomnema* (politely declined; *Att.* 1.20.6; 2.1.1–2); *Consulatus Suus* (in three books, 59 BCE?; *Div.* 1.17); a letter in 56 BCE to Lucceius (*Fam.* 5.12) requesting a historical monograph; *De Temporibus Meis* in 55 BCE (three books; see, e.g., *Fam.* 1.9.23); "Secret history": *De Consiliis Suis,* to be released after his death (see, e.g., *Att.* 2.6.2, 2.8.1, 14.17.6, 16.11.3; Dio 39.10.2–3).

23 See Seneca *Brev. Vit.* 5.1; Plutarch *Cic.* 24; Quintilian *Inst.* 11.1.17.

24 On this in general, see Marasco 2011.

25 On the histories of Ptolemy Soter, see, e.g., Jacoby *FGrH* 138; Kornemann 1935; Tarn 1948; Pearson 1960; Badian 1961; Errington 1969; Roisman 1984; Ellis 1994: 20–2.

26 Ameling (*BNP* s.v. "Ptolemy Soter") mentions the following possibilities: "During the dispute over the legacy of Alexander? After his assumption of the royal title? During the – questionable – co-regency after 285?"

27 See the remarks of Plutarch with regard to Onesikritos' credibility in *Alex.* 46.

28 Equally interesting is the fact that, despite the availability of Ptolemy's reliable eyewitness account, Arrian nevertheless felt called upon to write a history of Alexander himself, because he did not think previous accounts were up to standard (Arrian *Anab.* 1.12). On this anecdote, see also the chapter by Howe in this volume.

29 Cf. Herodotos 1.136; Xenophon *Cyr.* 8.8.3.

30 Q. Curtius Rufus 9.5.21: *Ptolomaeum, qui postea regnavit, huic pugnae adfuisse auctor est Clitarchus et Timagenes: sed ipse scilicet gloriae suae non*

refragatus, afuisse se, missum in expeditionem, memoriae tradidit ("Clitarchus and Timagenes are our authorities for the statement that Ptolemy, who was later king, was present at this battle, but he himself who was certainly not inclined to depreciate his own glory, has written that he wasn't there, since he had been sent on an expedition").

31 See Parian Marble, *FGrH* 239 B 11; Pausanias 1.7.1; Curtius 10.10.20; Diodoros 18.28.3–6; Strabo 17.1.8 (794); *Heidelberg Epit., FGrH* 155 F2.1. Pausanias 1.7.1 attributes the move to Philadelphos.

32 The *Liber de Morte* forms the end of the ancient *Alexander Romances.* Although it is believed to be a falsification, it is held to be ancient, probably stemming from the period of the struggles for succession after Alexander's death. Ptolemy is a likely candidate for its authorship, since he clearly stands to gain by its contents. On this, see Bosworth 2000b and, further, Ellis 1994: 21.

33 See, e.g., his sobriquet *kakergetes* (Menekles of Barka *FGrH* 234), and *physkon,* apparently a reference to the Lesbian tyrant Pittakos, surnamed thus by Alkaios. The story of his misdeeds is told in bloody detail by Justin in his *Epitome of Pompeius Trogus* 38.8, who notes that the people hated and feared him (*territus populus,* 38.8.6), and the Romans thought him ridiculous and despicable (*sed quam cruentus civibus, tam ridiculus Romanis fuit,* "and just as much as he was covered with the blood of the Roman people so too was he derided by them," 38.8.9), on account of his unappealing appearance and see-through dress. The ancient testimonies are conveniently gathered by Nadig 2007.

34 Fraser 1972, 2: 515.

35 See the reading of Nadig 2007: 18–23 of, respectively, Fr. 7, 8, where he sees Ptolemy VIII deprecating the *tryphe* of his Ptolemaic ancestors and posing as Rome-friendly, and Fr. 9, 2–3, 6, 10, 1 where he believes the king to be profiling himself as good, generous, intellectually interested, and courageous. In Fr. 4 and 5, Nadig again finds criticism of *tryphe* of the Ptolemaic predecessors and a generally Rome-friendly attitude.

36 See Nadig 2007: 17 on Philometor's reputation. We may compare emperor Claudius' memoirs, and his history of the civil wars, which he was hindered from finishing by his grandmother and mother, presumably for reasons of discretion (Suetonius *Claud.* 41).

37 See Müller-Wollermann 2003.

38 According to tradition, Achilles was taught medicine by Chiron; see, e.g., Schol. bT Il. 9.443a, and Alexander by Aristotle (Plutarch *Alex.* 8).

39 On this passage, see T.C. Rose 2015: 199–201.

40 See Jacques 2002: xiv–xx.

41 For the idea that knowledge of remedies against poisons could serve the populace, see, e.g., Nikander *Ther.* 1–5.

42 Celsus 5.19.11, Pliny *HN* 32.8, and Galen *De compos. med. per genera* 1.12 cite him on various plasters; Galen *De compos. med. sec. locos* 8.3 cites his diet for problems of the digestive tract; Galen *De simpl. medicam temper. ac facult.* 10 cites his investigations of the therapeutic properties of the secretions of animals.

43 See, on this problem, the introduction of Gow and Schofield (1997: 7–8).

44 See Galen *De ant.* 1.1, and, on compound drugs, 1.14.

45 Cf. Justin *Epit.* 36.4.3: *Omissa deinde regni administratione hortos fodiebat, gramina serebat et noxia innoxiis permiscebat, eaque omnia veneni suco infecta velut peculiare munus amicis mittebat* ("Afterwards, having abandoned the administration of the kingdom, he ploughed his gardens, sowed seeds and mixed poisonous and inoffensive plants together, and these latter ones, infected by the venomous saps, he sent to his friends as peculiar gifts"). It remains unclear what the intention of such gifts may have been: were they meant as a threat, or even attempts at murder, or perhaps rather to allow the friends of the king to defend themselves from possible enemies?

46 Interestingly, Galen first cites the versified recipe of Antiochos and then gives a prose account, showing that such poetry was considered completely accurate when it came to ingredients and amounts. This gives us reason to pause when discussing the presumed "literariness" of the *Theriaka* and *Alexipharmaka* of Nikander, although it must be admitted that Antiochos' style and vocabulary are far less literary than Nikander's.

47 It is unclear whether the "Ptolemy'" referred to by Plutarch (*Adulat.* 17) is Ptolemy VIII Euergetes II or Ptolemy IV Philopator, whom we shall encounter below; each is known for "posing as lover of learning," and as a cruel and violent tyrant. The gist of the anecdote is as follows: "[Flatterers] would contend with him about an obscure word or a trifling verse or a point of history, and keep it up till midnight; but when he indulged in wanton cruelty and violence, played the cymbals and conducted his initiations, not one of all these people opposed his course" (Tr. C. Babbitt).

48 See Plant 2004: 135–44 for translations of the extant fragments; further Fraser (1972: II.548306), who cites Usener (1873: 412–13); Fr. Hultsch 1866: I.218–33, and especially 233 [P 767K]. The titles are: ἐκ τῶν Κλεοπάτρας κοσμητικῶν περὶ σταθμῶν καὶ μέτρων (*From Cleopatra's Cosmetics, on Measures and Weights*); anecd. Oxon. iii p. 164 l.14: κομμωτικὴ τέχνη (*The Art of Haircare*); Paul. Aeg. iii 2CMG ix i p. 132: οὐλοποιὰ καὶ βάμματα τριχῶν (*Setting of Curls and Hair Dyes*).

49 See, e.g., Plutarch *Ant.* 25–7. Everyone had heard of her legendary baths in the milk of donkeys and her feat of dissolving an immensely costly pearl in acid and drinking it, to impress Antony (Pliny *HN* IX.119).

50 References in Plant 2004: 145–7. A curious falsification datable to the seventeenth century by the maverick Swiss humanist Melchior Goldast,

furthermore, attributed to her a spurious and chronologically impossible correspondence with the physician Soranos (fourth century CE), concerning remedies for her priapism; on this see A.E. Hanson 2008. Based on her reputation (especially in Latin literature; see, e.g., Horace *Carm.* 1.37) of debauchment and lechery, these letters aim mainly at titillating a male readership.

51 See Plutarch *Apophthegmata regum*; see also the metrical one-liner pronounced as a retort to Demosthenes by Philip I (Plutarch *Dem.* 20.3), and see the section "Epigrams by Imperial Romans" in Page (1981), featuring Tiberius, Germanicus, and Hadrian, among others.

52 The text in the *Vita Arati* speaks of "Ptolemy Physkon" (i.e., Ptolemy VIII), but that may be a mistake. Against attribution: Gabathuler 1937: 94; Fraser 1972: I.780, II.841n305, 1090n459. Page *FGE* 84 thinks the attribution may be correct. Cameron (1995: 83; 322–3n 106) thinks the poem must be by Philadelphos.

53 Theokritos *Id.* 14, 17; Herodas 1 (Tzetzes, *CGF* i 1899, Kaibel, p. 19 Pb 4ff.) calls Philadelphos "*philologōtatos.*"

54 Cf. the stories that recount the various manoeuvres Hellenistic kings undertook to get famous literary men (to remain) at their court. Cf. Strootman 2010: 35, who refers to Vitruvius 7 Prologue 5–7 on the imprisonment of Aristophanes of Byzantion after his attempt to join the Attalid court.

55 Plutarch *Flam.* 9.3: λεγόμενον δὲ πολλαχοῦ καὶ ὑπὸ πολλῶν. The epigram reads as follows: Ἄκλαυστοι καὶ ἄθαπτοι, ὁδοιπόρε, τῷδ' ἐπὶ τύμβῳ / Θεσσαλίας τρισσαὶ κείμεθα μυριάδες, / Αἰτωλῶν δμηθέντες ὑπ' Ἄρεος ἠδὲ Λατίνων, / οὓς Τίτος εὐρείης ἤγαγ' ἀπ' Ἰταλίης / Ἠμαθίῃ μέγα πῆμα· τὸ δὲ θρασὺ κεῖνο Φιλίππου / πνεῦμα θοῶν ἐλάφων ᾤχετ' ἐλαφρότερον ("Unwept, O wayfarer, unburied we lie on this Thessalian hillock, the thirty thousand, brought down by the war feats of the Aetolians and the Latins, whom Titus led forth out of broad Italia, a great woe to Macedonia; and nimbler than fleet-footed deer, fled that dauntless spirit of Philip") (*Anth. Pal.* 7.247, tr. W.R. Paton, adapted). For the attestations, apart from Plutarch, see Page 1981: 79.

56 The other epigram on Alkaios attributed to the king, though not by Plutarch, is another faux epitaph (*Anth. Pal.* 9.520). It seems less topical, if more savage, and there is even more reason to think that it is spurious. For other exchanges of epigrams between leaders and civilians, see *FGE* 564 (9.137); Hadrian III; and *Scriptores Historiae Augustae* 16.3–4.

57 A chilling example of the physical response an epigram could elicit is the anecdote told about a certain Daphidas of Telmessos, said to have been crucified on Mount Thorax near Magnesia on the Maeander because he had ridiculed the Attalids in an epigram: "Purpled with bruises, mere scraps of the treasure of Lysimachos, you rule the Lydians and the Phrygians." Cf. Strabo 14.1.39; Suda s.v. "Daphidas," and Hansen 1967: 144n5. One may think also of Philip of Macedon and his response to Demosthenes (Plutarch *Dem.* 20).

58 See Kotlińska-Toma 2014: 146.

59 *TrGF 119* (with notes 114–15, pp. 282–3): in an inscription from Menshijeh, datable to 270–246 BCE, a certain "Ptolemaios" is named as "*sunagonistēs tragikos*." We may contrast, for instance, Augustus who attempted to write a tragedy entitled *Aias*, but threw his drafts away because he was dissatisfied with his own style (Suetonius *Aug.* 85).

60 This was a religious festival in honour of Adonis, which was held in Alexandria and celebrated in a poem by Theokritos. Cf. Reed (2000) on the ideological importance of Adonis for the Ptolemies.

61 See, in particular, the anecdotes mentioned above referring to Dionysios I of Syracuse (Diodoros 14) and Nero (Suetonius *Ner.*, *passim*).

62 Josephus *AJ* 12.130–1; Polybios 2.51; 15.25–34; Justin *Epit.* 30.1–2.

9

Creating Alexander: The "Official" History of Kallisthenes of Olynthos

WALDEMAR HECKEL

Καὶ ἐν τούτῳ ἀγγέλλεται τὸ Ὀρφέως τοῦ Οἰάγρου τοῦ Θρᾳκὸς ἄγαλμα τὸ ἐν Πιερίδι ἱδρῶσαι ξυνεχῶς· καὶ ἄλλοι ἄλλα ἐπεθείαζον τῶν μάντεων, Ἀρίστανδρος δέ, ἀνὴρ Τελμισσεύς, μάντις, θαρρεῖν ἐκέλευσεν Ἀλέξανδρον· δηλοῦσθαι γάρ, ὅτι ποιητειν ἐπῶν τε καὶ μελῶν καὶ ὅσοι ἀμφὶ ᾠδὴν ἔχουσι πολὺς πόνος ἔσται ποιεῖν τε καὶ ᾄδεν Ἀλέξανδρον καὶ τὰ Ἀλεξάνδρου ἔργα.

Arrian, *Anabasis* 1.11.2

Meanwhile, it was reported that the statue of Orpheus, son of Oeagros the Thracian, in Pieria, had sweated continuously; the seers interpreted this variously, but Aristander of Telmissos encouraged Alexander by saying that it meant that makers of epics and choric songs and writers of odes would be hard at work on poetry and hymns honouring Alexander and his exploits. (Tr. P.A. Brunt)

Ἐπεὶ δὲ ὥρμησε πρὸς τὴν στρατείαν, ἄλλα τε δοκεῖ σημεῖα παρὰ τοῦ δαιμονίου γενέσθαι, καὶ τὸ περὶ Λείβηθρα τοῦ Ὀρφέως ξόανον (ἦν δὲ κυπαρίττινον) ἱδρῶντα πολὺν ὑπὸ τὰς ἡμέρας ἐκείνας ἀφῆκε. Φοβουμένων δὲ πάντων τὸ σημεῖον, Ἀρίστανδρος ἐκέλευσε θαρρεῖν, ὡς ἀοιδίμους καὶ περιβοήτους κατεργασόμενον πράξεις, αἳ πολὺν ἱδρῶντα καὶ πόνον ὑμνοῦσι ποιηταῖς καὶ μουσικοῖς παρέξουσι.

Plutarch, *Alexander* 14.8–9

Moreover, when he set out upon his expedition, it appears that there were many signs from heaven, and, among them, the image of Orpheus at Leibethra (it was made of cypress wood) sweated profusely at about that time. Most people feared the sign, but Aristander bade Alexander be of good cheer, assured that he was to perform deeds worthy of song and story, which would cost poets and musicians much toil and sweat to celebrate. (Tr. B. Perrin)

With the gift of hindsight, it was easy for those who shaped Alexander's image to speak of omens of greatness and the promise of heroic fame (*kleos*).[1] Diodoros offers a similar "prediction," although this applied to the events immediately following Alexander's visit to Ilion – that is, to the upcoming battle at the Granicus River:

Τοῦ δὲ βασιλέως ἀναζεύξαντος ἐκ τῆς Τρῳάδος καὶ καταντήσαντος πρὸς τὸ τέμενος τῆς Ἀθηνᾶς ὁ μὲν θύτης Ἀλέξανδρος κατανοήσας πρὸ τοὺ νεὼ κειμένην εἰκόνα χαμαὶ τοῦ Φρυγίας ποτὲ σατραπεύσαντος Ἀριοβαρζάνου καί τινων οἰωνῶν αἰσίων ἄλλων ἐπιγενομένων προσῆλθε τῷ βασιλεῖ καὶ νικήσειν αὐτὸν ἱππομαχίᾳ μεγάλῃ διεβεβαιοῦτο καὶ μάλιστ', ἂν τύχῃ περὶ τὴν Φρυγίαν ἀγωνισάμενος·προσετίθει δὲ καὶ διότι ταῖς ἰδίαις χερσὶν ἀποκτενεῖ μαχόμενος ἐν παρατάξει στρατηγὸν ἐπιφανῆ τῶν πολεμίων·. (Diodoros 17.17.6)

As the king began his march out of the Troad and came to the sanctuary of Athena, the sacrificant named Alexander[2] noticed in front of the temple a statue of Ariobarzanes, a former satrap of Phrygia, lying fallen on the ground, together with some other favourable omens that occurred. He came to the king and affirmed that he would be victor in a great cavalry battle and especially if he happened to fight within the confines of Phrygia; he added that the king with his own hands would slay in battle a distinguished general of the enemy. (Tr. C. Bradford Welles)

But it is clear that Alexander left nothing to chance and enlisted in his entourage various writers who would create his image and promulgate his achievements in the Greek world. One of them, alas, proved an embarrassment to the king: Choirilos of Iasos, a hack poet who celebrated Alexander's deeds in an epic poem in which the king appeared as Achilles. Alexander famously remarked: "I would rather be Homer's Thersites than the Achilles of Choirilos."[3] As his official historian, however, Alexander chose a man who had already made his reputation by writing a *History of Greece* (*Hellenika*) and who was a kinsman of his own tutor, Aristotle. This was Kallisthenes of Olynthos, an enigmatic man who, in his writing, inclined to sycophancy but in his personal life showed an independence of spirit that led to his downfall and death.

Source criticism has been preoccupied with trying to determine the source of each piece of information found in the writings of the extant historians. For more than seventy-five years of *Quellenforschung*, all roads have led to Jacoby (1923). This has had some unfortunate consequences: some have sought to characterize the works of lost historians on the basis of fragments,[4] and it has become all too common for scholars to conclude that negative depictions of Alexander derive from "bad sources."[5] But, although the primary historians have not survived, we have a wealth of information in the extant historians, supplemented by material found in the writers of stratagems, geographers, and those who merely collected anecdotes.[6] Thus we are left with a mosaic formed from diverse sources from different periods that offer conflicting images. Although we attempt to sort out which information is credible and which is not, we often ignore one important fact: namely, that the image of Alexander was not formed at the same time by these primary sources. We seek the "truth" about Alexander, but we tend to forget that what people said about him during his lifetime is very different from what they thought after his death. And, since five hundred years separate the life of the Macedonian king from Arrian, the last of the extant Alexander historians, a great deal of contamination and embellishment took place.[7] That has not stopped scholars from regarding Arrian as the most reliable source. In fact, he is no more to be trusted than the others, though his crime is often not one of commission but rather of omission. At any rate, his claim to be doing Alexander justice is tantamount to an admission that he took pains to create a positive image of him.

Καὶ εὐδαιμόνισεν ἄρα, ὡς λόγος, Ἀλέξανδρος Ἀχιλλέα, ὅτι Ὁμήρου κήρυκος ἐς τὴν ἔπειτα μνήμην ἔτυχε. Καὶ μέντοι καὶ ἦν Ἀλεξάνδρῳ οὐχ ἥκιστα τούτου ἕνεκα εὐδαιμονιστέος Ἀχιλλεύς, ὅτι αὐτῷ γε Ἀλεξάνδρῳ, οὐ κατὰ τὴν ἄλλην ἐπιτυχίαν, τὸ χωρίον τοῦτο ἐκλιπὲς ξυνέβη οὐδὲ ἐξηνέχθη ἐς ἀνθρώπους τὰ Ἀλεξάνδρου ἔργα ἐπαξίως, οὔτ' οὖν καταλογάδην, οὔτε τις ἐν μέτρῳ ἀλλ' οὐδὲ ἐν μέλει ᾔσθη Ἀλέξανδρος, ἐν ὅτῳ Ἱέρων τε καὶ Γέλων καὶ Θήρων καὶ πολλοὶ ἄλλοι οὐδέν τι Ἀλεξάνδρῳ ἐπεοικότες, ὥστε πολὺ μεῖον γιγνώσκεται τὰ Ἀλεξάνδρου ἢ τὰ φαυλότατα τῶν πάλαι ἔργων·. (Arrian, *Anabasis* 1.12.2)

Alexander, so the story goes, blessed Achilles for having Homer to proclaim his fame to posterity. Alexander might well have counted Achilles happy on this score, since, fortunate as Alexander was in other ways, there was a great gap left here, and Alexander's exploits were never celebrated as they deserved, either in prose or verse; there were not even choral lyrics for Alexander as for Hiero, Gelo, Thero and many others not to be compared with him, so that Alexander's exploits are far less known than very minor deeds of old times. (Tr. P.A. Brunt)[8]

In short, Arrian believes that the attempts of the primary sources, including the official version of his campaign, had missed their mark.

What was it, then, that established Alexander's fame? The first step was, of course, to win fame (*kleos*) through his own actions, and this was more easily done through overcoming enemies by force rather than by negotiation. One had to be bad in order to be "Great." Effective, and even brutal, treatment of the enemy got people's attention, and the success of future action owed a great deal to reputation, in this case *terror nominis.* That was something Alexander did not give the Celts who lived beyond the Ister (Danube) an opportunity to learn.[9] And even the Thebans in 335 BCE, despite the alleged *kataplexis* ("shock") and *phobos* ("awe") that accompanied the arrival of the Macedonian army in the previous year, did not end their resistance. By contrast, the Athenians found it easy and expedient to learn from the fate of the very Thebans they had themselves incited to rebellion. From the security of the *bema,* Demosthenes could fulminate against, and even deride, the Macedonian king, but the destruction of Thebes called for sober reflection.

Yet a reputation for brutality would take Alexander only so far. Were it not for a contrived image of the king as a man who performed noble acts on behalf of the Greek world, Alexander would have been remembered as a butcher, along the lines of Genghis Khan. Nevertheless, Matthew White (2012), in a book that has appeared under various titles, including *The Great Big Book of Horrible Things* and *Atrocities,* ranks Alexander's campaigns as only the seventieth worst atrocity, far behind Genghis Khan, who comes in at number 2.[10] That has not stopped several modern scholars from classifying Alexander as a monster and comparing him with Hitler and Stalin.[11] The statistics for enemy casualties during Alexander's campaigns, although it is difficult to verify the numbers given by the sources, leave little doubt that the man credited with a vision of Brotherhood of Mankind killed a very large number of people, military and civilian. And, indeed, Alexander was most brutal on the occasions when he himself suffered a physical wound. Not for nothing did Justin (Trogus) say of Philip that, after losing an eye at Methone, "the injury did not make him ... *more savage in his treatment of his enemies.*"[12]

But how do we get from the man whom David Lonsdale (2004), in the subtitle of one of his books, called "killer of men" to Plutarch's portrait of the philosopher king who brought the greatest benefit to the world?[13] The answer is, of course, the deliberate creation of an image, one that appealed so greatly to W.W. Tarn.[14] That image was crafted by Kallisthenes of Olynthos, the so-called official historian of the campaign. Within a short time, it found its way into the works of other primary authors, some of which idealized Alexander,[15] while others depicted him as oscillating between noble and base actions. About Kallisthenes so much has been written, despite the fact that so little is known. I wish to add to that discussion some speculation of my own – for *speculation* is all that the evidence will allow.

I

Kallisthenes was, of course, in a position to know how events unfolded. But even more, he was able to shape the history of the campaign and the image of the king. Lionel Pearson writes, "So long as he remained in favour, he had the opportunity to know how Alexander himself wanted his exploits recorded and interpreted to the Greek world" (1960: 22).[16]

It is generally agreed – although there is no explicit evidence – that Kallisthenes' history was sent to Greece in installments, probably at the end of each campaigning season. David Golan, for no compelling reason, thought that "rather than follow events closely, he allowed an interval – or rather, perspective – of approximately two years before moulding his notes into history" (1988: 22). Pearson leaves open the possibility that, after his death, Kallisthenes' manuscript was "taken over and prepared for publication by someone else; but there is no indication who this editor may have been" (1960: 23). A similar view is taken by Jona Lendering, whose website about Kallisthenes' history claims that "it is certain that the work *was not published in yearly installments* to inform those remaining at home ... It was published as a unity, which can be shown from the fact that it consistently portrayed Alexander's right hand man Parmenion as over-prudent" (my emphasis).[17] But an extended interval or a publication date after 327 BCE would, to my mind, defeat the purpose of having a propagandist historian who wrote for a Greek audience of not entirely willing allies in order to highlight victories without end and the brilliance of the young king, and also to bolster Greek support for the campaign.[18]

If we base our assumptions on the fragments in Jacoby, then the remark about the portrayal of Parmenion would have to be regarded as grossly exaggerated. Only one fragment of Kallisthenes (124 F37) mentions Parmenion, and this suggests neither repeated criticism nor over-prudence. Plutarch writes:

Ὅλως γὰρ αἰτιῶνται Παρμενίωνα κατ᾽ ἐκείνην τὴν μάχην νωθρὸν γενέσθαι καὶ δύσεργον, εἴτε τοῦ γήρως ἤδη τι παραλύοντος τῆς τόλμης, εἴτε τὴν ἐξουσίαν καὶ τὸν ὄγκον, ὡς Καλλισθένης φησί, τῆς Ἀλεξάνδρου δυνάμεως βαρυνόμενον καὶ προσφθονοῦντα.

There is general complaint that in that battle [i.e., Gaugamela] Parmenion was sluggish and inefficient, either because old age was now impairing somewhat his courage, or because he was made envious and resentful *by the arrogance and pomp*, to use the words of Kallisthenes, of Alexander's power. (*Alexander* 33.10; my emphasis)

From this fragment it is clear that many writers criticized Parmenion's performance in the battle – although they disagreed on the reason for this – and that Kallisthenes attributed it to his resentment of Alexander's "arrogance and pomp." Nevertheless, it may in fact have been Kallisthenes who was responsible for the initial negative portrayal of Parmenion. There are numerous passages in the extant historians that show Alexander and Parmenion at odds on matters of tactics or policy, and generally these cast the old soldier in a bad light. But not all "disagreements" redound to Alexander's credit, and clearly not all are the work of a single author (Bearzot 1987: 89–104).[19] But even if Kallisthenes' work contained a number of actual and implied criticisms of Parmenion, this does not support the view that it was published after Parmenion's death. Lendering supposes that Kallisthenes created a negative portrait of Parmenion after the Philotas affair in order to justify the execution of father and son. Earlier instances of friction between Alexander and his general (which is surely what Lendering means by "*consistent*" portrayal of Parmenion as "over-prudent") would thus have been created retroactively.

Ernst Badian, in his article "The Death of Parmenio" took the opposite view: "The next few years saw the decline of his [Parmenio's] influence and the increase in Alexander's stature *in the army's eyes*. Not *all* our stories of the occasions on which Alexander ignored Parmenio's advice will be true. But some go back to *good sources* (*Ptolemy or even Kallisthenes*) and show that this kind of interpretation was *meant* to be spread" (1960: 328; my emphasis). But the problem with Badian's thesis is that Ptolemy did not write until long after the events (whatever date one assigns to him), and, if one attributes the negative portrait of Parmenion to Kallisthenes, these stories would not have reached the audience for whom Badian thinks they were intended.[20] And this brings me to one of my main points. Although Kallisthenes would have needed Alexander's approval before "publishing" his history (or rather installments of it), the work was not meant for the Macedonian army – assuming that the common soldier could even read[21] – but for the Greeks on the other side of the Aegean. Indeed, if it were made available to the army, ongoing denigration of Parmenion – even if its main purpose was to enhance Alexander's reputation – would have caused dissension in the ranks of the officers and possibly open rebellion among the soldiery.[22] The question is not what image Kallisthenes was creating, but rather *for whom*.

At this point, I should like to return to my earlier observation about the original form of fame (*fama*), when actions lead to reports and rumours that spread by word of mouth, by messengers, perhaps by refugees, and almost certainly by travellers, especially merchants who moved from city to city.

These reports spread primarily eastward and only briefly anticipated the arrival of the Macedonian army. Though some areas would have welcomed Alexander as a liberator, most viewed his advance with alarm. By contrast, the earliest written accounts of Alexander's achievements and character moved westward, since there was effectively no audience for Greek history in the East. Hence, there was a difference between *terror nominis* and the positive image of the king.

Marian Plezia (1972) noted that the title of Kallisthenes' work, *Praxeis Alexandrou* ("The Deeds of Alexander"), was rarely used in the period down to the fourth century, and that it had a philosophical purpose: to present Alexander as a *politikos* and a benefactor of Hellenism. Hence, the work had a biographical flavour. Alexander is presented as the avenger of the Greeks against the hereditary enemy. His military actions were, naturally, depicted as beneficial to the Greeks as a whole, and particularly those who had lost their homeland.[23]

II

What, then, can we assume that Kallisthenes' "official" history contained? To begin with, it is highly likely that, when extant historians spoke of Alexander's policies vis-à-vis the Greek world such as the punishment of Greek mercenaries who were regarded as traitors because they served the Persian king, this was reported originally (and deliberately) by Kallisthenes. In this case, it justified the treatment of the mercenaries – Alexander sent them to hard labour camps in Macedonia and, until 331, would not release them or mitigate their sentences – a warning to other mercenaries, of whom there was an abundance in Greece and Asia Minor, that opposition to the king (and to the Panhellenic Crusade) promised death or imprisonment.[24] The fragments do not tell us this, but common sense does.

Kallisthenes was the only truly contemporary historian and was hired, in effect, as the propaganda minister.[25] What form the *Praxeis Alexandrou* took is not entirely clear, if one resorts to Jacoby's collection, which contains only eleven fragments (Fragments 28–38) that can be attributed with certainty to that work and a few others that may come from the work (Fragments 41–2, 44, 53–4). The largest fragment is, of course, Polybios' detailed criticism of Kallisthenes' talents as a military historian, using as an example his account of the battle of Issus.[26] But other fragments show that Kallisthenes commented on places from Greek mythology and saga, thus forming a link, as he undoubtedly intended, between the Macedonian army's crossing into Asia and the Trojan War.[27] Alexander's sacrifice at the Hellespont was probably a conscious (but, in this case, successful) imitation of Agesilaos at Aulis, who was himself imitating Agamemnon. But one of the difficulties is that much of Kallisthenes' positive portrayal of Alexander was probably incorporated into the accounts of Ptolemy and Aristoboulos, the writers who were least critical of Alexander and most trusted by Arrian. Does this then mean that, when Arrian introduces stories that do not come from these two authors (the *logoi* or *legomena*), they are not from Kallisthenes (on the assumption that Kallisthenes was for the most part subsumed in the apologetic historians)? I believe so. Hence, Kallisthenes cast Alexander more in the role of an Agamemnon than an Achilles. As I have argued elsewhere, it was not Kallisthenes' intention to depict Alexander as a latter-day Achilles.[28] Bernadotte Perrin, in an article published in 1895, demonstrated that the inspiration for these Alexander-Achilles/Hephaistion-Patroclus stories came from the sudden death of Hephaistion in 324 BCE, and Alexander's own death soon afterwards.[29] None of this was known to Kallisthenes, who, if he was not executed in connection with the Pages' conspiracy in 327 BCE, was imprisoned and died soon afterwards.[30] I would argue that Kallisthenes depicted Alexander as he wished to be, certainly in the early years of the campaign – as the descendant and imitator of Herakles.[31] The evidence for *imitatio Herculi* is in fact impressive and undeniable.

Two important aspects of Kallisthenes' portrayal of Alexander (the foreshadowing of his Asian kingship and his recognition as, if not a god, at least the son of one) I must postpone briefly, for they raise questions about the historian's integrity. But there is one other episode (or, rather, series of episodes) for which Kallisthenes must surely have been the original source. This is the account that begins with Alexander's attack on the Persian Gates and culminates in the destruction of Persepolis. Again, this is something that I discussed many years ago (Heckel 1980)[32] – although, in my younger days, I fell into the trap of assigning all things sensational and rhetorical to Kleitarchos of Alexandria. Curtius and Pompeius Trogus may have found the account of these events in Kleitarchos, or in another source that used Kleitarchos, but I now believe that the story was crafted originally by Kallisthenes.

Alexander reached the Persian Gates (located between Susa and Persepolis)[33] and failed to dislodge the defenders. Like Xerxes at Thermopylae,[34] Alexander ran the risk of having his mission thwarted by a gallant defensive stand in the pass. But, like Xerxes, he was helped by a local herdsman who showed him a path around the Gates.[35] This secured the approach to the most important of Persia's cities, Persepolis. Curtius writes:

Postero die convocatos duces copiarum docet nullam infestiorem urbem Graecis esse quam regiam veterum Persidis regum; hinc illa immensa agmina infusa, hinc Dareum prius, dein Xerxem Europae impium intulisse bellum; excidio illius parentandum esse maioribus.

Alexander told his men that no city was more hateful *to the Greeks* than Persepolis, the capital of the old kings of Persia, the city from which troops without number had poured forth. To appease the spirits of *their forefathers* they should wipe it out! (*History of Alexander* 5.6.1; my emphasis added)

Notice that Alexander, who would have been addressing a predominantly Macedonian army, nevertheless emphasized the *Greek* experience. But in order to hammer home the message, we are told that, just before the taking of the city, Alexander encountered a pitiful band of mutilated Greeks.[36] These were victims of Persian atrocities in the past – though it would be hard to find a historical context, or at least one in their lifetimes, in which they would have suffered such mutilation at Persian hands. They numbered eight hundred, according to Diodoros and Justin; four thousand, if we follow Curtius. When they saw Alexander, they threw their hands (if they had them) in the air and rejoiced that "Zeus the avenger of Greece" (*ultor Graeciae*) had brought retribution upon Persia. The mutilated Greeks also engage in a debate over whether they should remain in Asia or allow Alexander to repatriate them. The leaders of the debate bear the names Euktemon and Theaitetos, and they conduct a philosophical dialogue, something appropriate to a rhetorical writer and amateur philosopher. The names appear only in Curtius' account but are probably not his own invention. Thereafter, Alexander conducted a sack of Persepolis, a torch-lit *komos* instigated by the Athenian courtesan, Thaïs, providing the occasion for the burning of the palace. The destruction of Athenian temples was thus avenged.

If we believe, as Badian did, that Kallisthenes' work was read by the troops, we would wonder why Alexander chose to advertise the end of the Panhellenic War, when in fact the contest was far from finished as long as Darius lived – indeed, as long as anyone claiming to be the legitimate Achaimenid ruler (as Bessos later did) continued to rally opposition – and all troops, Greek and Macedonian, were eager for demobilization. But the answer is, once again, to be found in the audience. This was written for the Greeks in the West, not for the grumbling allied troops who were required to soldier on. Jona Lendering does not provide a satisfactory reason for delaying this account for two more years. Furthermore, he suggests that Kallisthenes ended his account with the death of Bessos (the man who assumed the upright tiara and the name Artaxerxes), but by that time the forces of the League of Corinth had all been dismissed, and the purpose of the work (entitled *Praxeis Alexandrou* but ending long before the king's labours were over) seems unclear. If the work was sent to Greece in its complete form at this point, many will have found the ending either anticlimactic or premature, whichever way one looks at it.[37] If the work was not complete but never published in installments, then one must ask: how did the work of a traitor who died in Alexander's camp come to be known to the Greek world?

To argue that the "Persian Gates to Persepolis" story does not come from Kallisthenes requires us to believe that, later, when the mandate of the League of Corinth was no longer an issue, and when the Greeks had again showed themselves unfaithful to their Macedonian masters (in the Lamian War), some later writer such as Kleitarchos revived the very propaganda that Kallisthenes was hired to promulgate but did not.[38] Once again, what was viewed by the victims in the East as a wave of doom and destruction rolling over the Persian Empire was promoted in Greece as the successful (indeed, brilliant) execution of policy and long-desired revenge by the Macedonian king, his army, and the allied contingent.

More personal elements were added, all intended to cast Alexander in a favourable light. He showed restraint in his dealings with Persian women (even though, in truth, he took Barsine as his mistress and may very well have had sexual relations with the wife of Darius – the denials, which allegedly satisfied Darius himself, do not ring true).[39] The story of the cutting of the Gordian knot also puts a brave face on a fiasco; for, even if we allow that Alexander cheated, it was nevertheless unlikely that he sliced through the knot with one clean motion. He must either have whacked the entire knot off the wagon's pole or else hacked away at it in a way that was embarrassing and unbecoming. No wonder Aristoboulos (*FGrH* 139 F7) changed the story and said that the king merely extracted a pin that held the coils of the rope together.

III

But what about Kallisthenes the man? In 1923, W.K. Prentice noted that earlier scholars had remarked in disbelief on "the contradictions between certain statements made by ancient writers about Kallisthenes and … the implications of certain passages actually quoted from Kallisthenes himself" (74–5).[40] For example, in Fragment 31 (*FGrH* 124), Kallisthenes describes the receding sea at Mount Climax as aware of the king's presence and moving accordingly "so that in withdrawing it might somehow seem to make obeisance to him" (that is, προσκυνεῖν).[41] Similarly, Plutarch (*Alexander* 17.6) says that several historians imply that, by some great and heaven-sent good fortune, the sea retired to make way for Alexander, although at other times it always came rolling in with violence.[42] And Plutarch quotes Menander, making fun of Alexander and saying, "If I clearly must pass through some place by sea, this will lie open to my step" (*Alex.* 17.7). Kallisthenes' inspiration was probably Xenophon's *Anabasis*, where the crossing of the Euphrates at Thapsakos is described in similar terms:[43]

Ταῦτα δὲ ποιήσας διέβαινε συνείπετο δὲ καὶ τὸ ἄλλο στράτευμα αὐτῷ ἅπαν. Καὶ τῶν διαβαινόντων τὸν ποταμὸν οὐδεὶς ἐβρέχθη ἀνωτέρω τῶν μαστῶν ὑπὸ τοῦ ποταμοῦ … <u>Ἐδόκει δὴ θεῖον εἶναι καὶ σαφῶς ὑποχωρῆσαι τὸν ποταμὸν Κύρῳ ὡς βασιλεύσοντι</u>.

After this [Cyrus] crossed the river, and the whole of the rest of the army followed. In the crossing no one got wet from the river-water above the nipples … *It seemed certain that there was something supernatural about it, and that the river had undoubtedly made way for Cyrus, as he was destined to be king*. (Xenophon, *Anabasis* 1.4.17–18; my emphasis)

Here the word is ὑποχωρῆσαι, but the reference to *proskynesis* is obvious, since at 1.6.10 Xenophon describes the practice. It seems remarkable, then, that the man who is famous for his refusal to perform *proskynesis* (in 328/7 BCE) should describe this natural phenomenon in this way. But the episode at Mount Climax is meant to foreshadow Alexander's kingship of Asia, not his divinity. Similarly, it is noted that Kallisthenes described Alexander's visit to Siwah and confirmed his recognition as the son of Zeus Amun – something that he reiterated (perhaps tongue-in-cheek) in his description of the preliminaries to the battle of Gaugamela, and yet he later objected to the flatterers who spoke of the king's divinity. Once again, the *Ammonssohnschaft* was in origin political, designed to strengthen Alexander's position in Egypt: like the pharaohs over the ages, he was son of Re.[44] Kallisthenes, in promoting the "miraculous" journey and the pronouncement of the high priest, had to take into account the sensibilities of his Greek audience, who would have understood that the young king had followed in the footsteps of his mythical ancestors, Perseus and Herakles. In fact, Arrian says that "Alexander sought to rival Perseus and Herakles, as he was descended from them both; and in addition he himself traced his birth in part to Ammon, just as the legends traced that of Herakles and Perseus to Zeus" (*Anabasis* 3.3.2, tr. P.A. Brunt). The underlying source for this is clearly Kallisthenes.[45]

Kallisthenes' fall from grace was described by various writers: clearly he made himself unpopular for his failure to perform *proskynesis* – an experiment that was proceeding tolerably well[46] – alienating, in the process, also Hephaistion (whose influence with Alexander can hardly be underestimated);[47] for giving a speech – in order to display his rhetorical skills – disparaging the Macedonians; and for his association with Pages (*paides basilikoi*), some of whom plotted against the king's life.[48] These episodes have been discussed at length by scholars. The question that remains to be asked is: what accounts for the dramatic change in Kallisthenes' behaviour? A change there certainly must have been, since the sources do not comment on his behaviour before 328 BCE.

It was said that "Kallisthenes in his history deified Alexander but opposed the making of obeisance to him."[49] But the paradox of Kallisthenes – the idea that a man would write in one way and act in another – can nevertheless be explained. To begin with, we are told that Kallisthenes was eloquent in his rhetoric (and thus also in his writing) but boorish in his own manners (*FGrH* 124 T4 and T8). He was perhaps even somewhat naive, taking the bait when Alexander asked him to give an anti-Macedonian argument (Plutarch, *Alexander* 53.5–6).[50] To this we might add the likelihood that he believed that he was responsible for creating Alexander's image: indeed, he is said to have remarked that "he had not come to borrow fame from Alexander, but to make him renowned in the world."[51] Yet by 328/7 BCE he found himself in an unexpected position. His propaganda bulletins to the Greek world were no longer relevant and thus were unnecessary.[52] The hero of his *Praxeis* had abandoned much of his "Greekness," adopting the manners and practices of the barbarian, whom Aristotle thought fit to be a slave.[53] Kallisthenes depicted Alexander as a son of Zeus, like Herakles and Perseus, but it is doubtful that he truly considered him a god. Indeed, his Alexander had actually made light of his *Ammonssohnschaft* at Gaugamela.[54] And, finally, the man who had come to regard himself as an intimate of Alexander by sacrificing his integrity, for which he was justly denounced as a flatterer (*kolax*),[55] now found himself ousted by vile creatures such as Anaxarchos, Kleon of Argos, and Agis the Sicilian, and even Choirilos (*poeta pessimus*) and the greasy wrestler Dioxippos.[56] He was, in the end, nothing more than the "hired help." Once asked why he did not bring Alexander out of his conceit, Kallisthenes replied, "Because, while I was building singlehanded, many were those who were tearing down" (*FGrH* 124 T15).

In the face of competition from these abject flatterers, men who took his praise of Alexander to absurd lengths, Kallisthenes regained a sense of his old self, but unfortunately he had forgotten what it meant to incur the anger of the powerful. Aristotle is alleged to have recognized this failing[57] and remarked that his kinsman "had kept his superfluous wits but had thrown away his common sense."[58] That he was not actually involved in the plot hatched against the king by Hermolaos and his fellow Pages is virtually certain. They did not confess to his participation, and Ptolemy's claim that he was tortured before he was executed suggests very strongly that Alexander sought to justify his elimination of a man whose arrogance and defiance had made him hated by the king and his courtiers.[59] T.S. Brown rightly comments, "It is possible that as the student of Aristotle he had already come to know Alexander, but the sequel was to show that he did not know him well enough" (1973: 125).

NOTES

1 On the role of poets who composed epic verse and hymns in honour of Alexander, see the discussion in the chapter by Klooster in this volume.

2 Almost certainly an error for Aristander. If the emendation is correct, as I think it must be, then there is a very strong likelihood that all three passages come originally from Kallisthenes' history. See Robinson 1929.

3 Horace *Ars P.* 357 = *FGrH* 153 F10a: *poeta pessimus fuit Choerilus, qui Alexandrum secutus opera eius descripsit ... cui Alexander dixisse fertur, multum malle se Thersiten iam Homeri esse quam Choerili Achillen.* Cf. F11a = Curtius 8.5.7–8.

4 See, e.g., Pearson 1960; Brown 1949a, 1949b, and 1950.

5 See Tarn 1948 and most of Hammond's published work but especially 1983.

6 Particularly, Polyainos; Frontinus; Strabo; Pliny *HN*; Plutarch *Mor.*; Athenaios; and also Aelian *VH* and *NA*.

7 On Arrian, see especially the introduction to Bosworth 1980 and Bosworth 1988.

8 See the comments of Bosworth 1980: 104–5, and also the discussion of this passage in the chapter by Klooster in this volume.

9 During one of Alexander's earliest campaigns at the Danube, the king "enquired of the Celts what mortal thing they most dreaded, hoping his own great name (μέγα ὄνομα τὸ αὐτοῦ) had reached the Celts and gone farther" (Arrian *Anab.* 1.4.7–8). As it turned out, the Celts were far from impressed and responded that their only fear was that the sky would fall upon them. When the delegation of Celts had left, Alexander was said to have remarked: "What braggarts these Celts are!" They, no doubt, had similar thoughts about him.

10 Most of this "definitive chronicle" is based on secondary works of questionable worth.

11 Among others, see Badian 2000 and V.D. Hanson 2001: 83–90. For a useful corrective, see Rogers 2004: 280–3, and also Heckel and McLeod 2015. If Kallisthenes was responsible for inflated numbers of enemy casualties, this exaggeration was meant to enhance the conqueror's reputation.

12 Justin *Epit.* 7.6.14–15: *Cum Mothonam urbem oppugnaret, in praetereuntem de muris sagitta iacta dextrum oculum regis effodit. Quo vulnere nec segnior in bellum nec iracundior adversus hostes factus est.* On this, see Heckel and McLeod 2015.

13 See Plutarch *De Alex. Fort.* I–II.

14 Especially, Tarn (1933), criticized effectively (though somewhat excessively) by Badian (1958).

15 Two of these, Ptolemy and Aristoboulos, were used extensively by Arrian (*Anab.*, proem. 1–2) who nevertheless thought that even they did not do him justice. On Arrian's use of Ptolemy, see the chapter by Howe in this volume.

16 Pearson 1960: 22. For Kallisthenes as propagandist, see also Devine 1994. Pearson (1960: 22) adds that Kallisthenes had access to "official records maintained in the king's headquarters." This may explain why, in the described events of the years 328–3 BCE, very few Macedonians are named with patronymics. In Arrian alone there are about 130 cases of name and patronymic up to 328 BCE (the last of these at 4.12.2) but only 35 more in the rest of the work, the bulk of these coming from three lists: the members of the Pages' conspiracy (8); the names of the Somatophylakes in 324 (8); and the names of the bridegrooms at Sousa (7). The only other extensive list for the later period comes from Arrian's *Indica* 18, based on Nearchos and clearly from an official document, where 32 patronymics (including those of non-Macedonians) are given. The same imbalance applies to the years before the beginning of the campaign, where Arrian names only two Macedonians with patronymic, in addition to Ptolemy son of Lagos, which is his normal way of referring to the historian – not surprising, since Kallisthenes began his history with the crossing into Asia (cf. Devine 1994: 92n6). But official records did not help Kallisthenes with his understanding of military terminology. Devine draws attention to the differences in the use and understanding of such terms between Kallisthenes and Ptolemy.

17 Jona Lendering, "Callisthenes of Olynthus" (2004), Articles on Ancient History, https://www.livius.org/articles/person/callisthenes-of-olynthus/

18 In mid-330 BCE, the Greek allies, including the Thessalian cavalry (whom Kallisthenes appears to have given a very positive treatment), were dismissed. Nor was the continuation of the campaign entirely appealing to the Macedonian troops.

19 One example of Parmenion's good advice is reported by Arrian *Anab.* 3.18.11, and it is noteworthy that Arrian omits the details of how Alexander ignored this advice (e.g., on the destruction of Persepolis).

20 As I noted in Heckel 1977: 11.

21 But, of course, in most cases works of this sort were read aloud to larger audiences, and this is even more unimaginable in the setting of the Macedonian camp.

22 Alexander showed his concern for such negative reaction by creating the ἄτακτοι, the so-called disciplinary unit, under the command of Leonidas (for references, see Heckel 2006: 147 "Leonidas [2]").

23 Plezia 1972: 266: "Als Vorkämpfer der Hellenen musste er zwar als Bezwinger ihres Erbfeindes, der Achämenidenmonarchie, dargestellt werden, wozu ihn schon seine Stellung als Oberbefehlshaber des Korinthischen Bundes bestimmte, aber seine militärischen Erfolge im Kampfe gegen Persien mussten wohl in Kallisthenes' Meinung von der positive Förderung des Griechentums begleitet werden, in erster Linie wahrscheinlich von der Lösung der akuten Frage der anwachsenden Menge der Heimatlosen, deren Bedeutung schon Isokrates nachdrücklich betont hatte."

24 Arrian *Anab.* 1.16.6 and 3.6.2 with Bosworth 1980: 278.

25 Justin *Epit.* 12.6.17 = *FGrH* 124 T9: "Callisthenes … was on intimate terms with Alexander because they had both been pupils of Aristotle, and he had also been invited by the king to be the author of the latter's chronicles." One might compare Kallisthenes with the embedded journalists who accompanied the U.S. forces on their campaigns in the Middle East: their reports came out quickly but only after being censored by those in power.

26 Discussed by Devine 1994: 93–4.

27 For the view that, in 348 or 347 BCE, Kallisthenes accompanied Aristotle to the court of Hermias of Atarneos, where his interest in Homer was further stimulated by the nearby site of Troy, see Brown 1949a, esp. 227–8. See also Pearson 1960: 41–6.

28 Heckel (2015), against the view of Stewart (1993: 78–86), who follows uncritically the views of Ameling (1988). Pearson (1960: 41–4) argues that Kallisthenes stressed Alexander's Trojan ancestry but does not attribute to Kallisthenes the Alexander-Achilles parallel; for the claims of the Molossian royal house to be descended from Neoptolemos and Andromache, see Heckel (1981, with earlier literature).

29 Chugg (2006: 84) rejects Perrin's views as "19th century opinion." The date of Perrin's article has no bearing on the validity of the argument. The deaths, following closely upon one another, perhaps inspired Ephippos of Olynthos as well (*FGrH* 126: *On the Deaths of Alexander and Hephaistion*). On the other hand, Ephippos is quoted by Athenaios 13.538b as saying that Alexander used to wear the lion skin of Herakles and carry a club. Cf. Luschy (1968: 121): "Er [Alexander] wird den Tod Hephaistions als eine Art Omen betrachtet haben: *stirbt Patroklos, so stirbt auch bald Achill*" (my emphasis).

30 For the different versions of Kallisthenes' death, see Arrian *Anab.* 4.14.3 and Plutarch *Alex.* 55.9. Ptolemy said that he was tortured and crucified. The use of torture must have been intended to extort an admission of complicity in the Pages' conspiracy. Bosworth (1980: 100) notes that crucifixion was used primarily for traitors and rebels, and he accepts Ptolemy's version as the correct one, adding, "The drastic and ignominious punishment … is a measure of the magnitude of Callisthenes' offence in Alexander's eyes." But the apologists

Aristoboulos and Chares both mention that he was imprisoned (caged) and died of a disease of lice before his case could be presented to the Greeks. See Chares, *FGrH* 125 F15; Ptolemy, 138 F17; and Aristoboulos 139 F33.

31 Kallisthenes was responsible for noting that Alexander's desire to visit the oasis of Siwah was in emulation of his ancestors Perseus and Herakles (*FGrH* 124 F14a = Strabo 17.1.43), discussed below.

32 For other source questions, see now Howe 2015c. The events leading up to, and including, the controversial motivation for (and enactment of) the burning of Persepolis are given exhaustive treatment by Seibert (2004–5). Whatever one makes of the author's conclusions, the study constitutes a parsing of the extant historians, an overview of the archaeological evidence, and an informative *Forschungsbericht*. Seibert (2004–5: 99) sees Kallisthenes as the underlying source, which was nevertheless reconfigured by Kleitarchos: "Die nüchterne Darstellung des Kallisthenes / Ptolemaios gestaltete Kleitarch aus Alexandrien im Stile eines modernen Journalisten der Regenbogenpresse um" (100). I thank Dr Richard Hazzard for bringing this paper to my attention and Professor Sabine Müller for obtaining a copy for my use.

33 On the precise location, see now Speck 2002 and Moritani 2014.

34 Cf. Burn 1963: 121.

35 The herdsman was, allegedly, a captive Lykian. On the significance of the Lykian, see Zahrnt 1999. I am not sure which primary source was responsible for the story that a wolf (*lykos*) led Alexander into Persia (Plutarch *Alex*. 37.2; cf. Polyainos 4.3.27).

36 See Yardley and Heckel (1997: 174–5) with references and literature.

37 Lane Fox 1973: 328: "Callisthenes would have finished his *Deeds of Alexander* down to the ending of the Greek allies' service, the natural place for the panegyric to stop."

38 According to Athenaios 13.576d–e, Kleitarchos mentioned the role of Thaïs in the burning of Persepolis. Nevertheless, the story probably came originally from Kallisthenes, who would not have been troubled by the fact that Thaïs, at some point, became Ptolemy's mistress (see Heckel 2006: 262). Athenaios knew Kleitarchos' history, but the only three quotations from Kallisthenes come from his earlier work on Greek history and the Sacred War.

39 See Bosworth 1980: 221 and Yardley and Heckel 1997: 160–1.

40 See also Corssen 1917.

41 Ὅπου γε Καλλισθένης τὸ Παμφύλιον πέλαγος Ἀλεξάνδρου παριόντος εἰ καὶ μὴ γηθόσυνον διαστῆναι, ὡς ἐν Ὀδοποιίᾳ ἀλλ' ἐξυπαναστῆναι λέγει αἰσθόμενον οἷον τῆς ἐκείνου πορείας καὶ οὐδ' αὐτὸ ἀγνοῆσαι τὸν ἄνακτα, ἵνα ἐν τῷ ὑποκυρτοῦσθαι πως δοκῇ προσκυνεῖν.

42 Ἡ δὲ τῆς Παμφυλίας παραδρομὴ πολλοῖς γέγονε τῶν ἱστορικῶν ὑπόθεσις γραφικὴ πρὸς ἔκπληξιν καὶ ὄγκον, ὡς θείᾳ τινὶ τύχῃ παραχωρήσασαν Ἀλεξάνδρῳ τὴν

θάλασσαν, ἄλλως ἀεὶ τραχεῖαν ἐκ πελάγους προσφερομένην, σπανίως δέ ποτε λεπτοὺς καὶ προσεχεῖς ὑπὸ τὰ κρημνώδη καὶ παρερρωγότα τῆς ὀρεινῆς πάγους διακαλύπτουσαν.

43 Noted by J. Rufus Fears in his commentary on E. Badian's paper at the Center for Hermeneutic Studies at Berkeley ("The Deification of Alexander the Great," *Colloquy* 21 [1976] 28).

44 See, e.g., Malek 2003: 99–100. I avoid the thorny problem of whether Alexander was actually crowned as pharaoh, on which see Burstein 1991. I do not, however, endorse Burstein's conclusion that Alexander's failure to be crowned Pharaoh

has important implications for our understanding of Alexander himself since it suggests that, contrary to the view maintained by Ulrich Wilcken and others, the greeting of Alexander at Siwah by the priest of Amon as Son of Zeus was not merely the formal welcome normally accorded a visiting Pharaoh and already familiar to the king from his coronation at Memphis, but a genuine surprise which must have, as the ancient sources indicate, greatly impressed Alexander precisely because he had not previously experienced it. (Burstein 1991: 145)

It is hard to believe that either Kallisthenes or Alexander was ignorant of the Egyptian practice. It was in all probability known also to Kambyses, whose envoys to the Ammonium (doubtless sent for political purposes) are translated by Herodotos (3.26) – accepting the lies of his Egyptian sources – into a hostile army bent of the oracle's destruction. That has not, however, stopped at least one archaeological team from combing the desert with metal-detectors in search of "the lost army."

45 See Bosworth 1980: 269–70.

46 Cf. Lane Fox 1973: 323.

47 On Hephaistion, see Heckel 2016: 93.

48 For *proskynesis* and the conspiracy of the Pages, see Curtius 8.5.5; Arrian *Anab.* 4.9.7–8; Plutarch *Alex.* 54.3–6; Justin *Epit.* 12.7.1–13; Valerius Maximus 7.2 ext. 11, 9.5 ext. 1; Ammianus Marcellinus 18.3.7; and Tatianus, *Ad Gr.* 2, p. 2, 25.

49 *FGrH* 124 T21: ἐν μὲν γὰρ ταῖς ἱστορίαις ἀπεθέου τὸν Ἀλέξανδρον, ἀντέκο[ψε δ'] αὐτοῦ ταῖς προσκυνήσεσι.

50 Brown 1949a: 247: "Callisthenes rose like a trout to the fly," to which Brown adds that "the episode does not place Alexander in an attractive light."

51 Arrian *Anab.* 4.10.2: Οὔκουν αὐτὸς ἀφῖχθαι ἐξ Ἀλεξάνδρου δόξαν κτησόμενος, ἀλλὰ ἐκεῖνον εὐκλεᾶ ἐς ἀνθρώπους ποιήσων.

52 If the role of Aristander is indeed ascribable to Kallisthenes (Robinson 1929), then there is some support for the view that he was still writing in the winter of 328/7 BCE (i.e., not long before the Pages' conspiracy). He appears in Arrian *Anab.* 4.4.3–9 and 4.15.8; cf. Plutarch *Alex.* 50.3–5. He is mentioned in the

context of 323 by Aelian *VH* 12.64 and Appian *Syr.* 64 [338], but the latter is clearly a case of confusion with Peithagoras of Amphipolis, and the former may be as well. See Heckel 2006: 45–6.

53 Lane Fox 1973: 323: "As a 'flatterer who tried to make a god out of Alexander,' he would have been the very last person at court to have spoken against divine honours for a living man, but as a Greek who had worked with Aristotle, he saw this social custom as a different matter. To pay *proskynesis* to a man had long seemed slavish, at least to the Greeks, and whatever else, Kallisthenes had been brought up to believe in the values of Greek culture." On Greek and Persian values, see also Momigliano 1979.

54 Plutarch *Alex.* 33.1 = *FGrH* 124 F36.

55 Kallisthenes as *kolax*: Polybios 12.12 = *FGrH* 124 T20.

56 Curtius 8.5.7–8: *Nec Macedonum haec erat culpa ... sed Graecorum, qui professionem honestarum artium malis corruperant moribus. Agis quidem Argivus, pessimorum carminum post Choerilum conditor, et ex Sicilia Cleo.* Dioxippos was said to have likened Alexander's blood to the ichor of the immortal gods (Aristoboulos *FGrH* 139 F47 = Athenaios 6.251a).

57 *FGrH* 124 T6 = Diog. Laert. 5.4–5.

58 *FGrH* 124 T5: Ὁ Ἀριστοτέλης τὸν Καλλισθένην ἀπέσκωψεν εἰπὼν τὸν μὲν περιττὸν νοῦν ἔχειν, τὸν δὲ ἀνθρώπινον ἀποβεβληκέναι.

59 See especially Arrian *Anab.* 4.14.1; cf. Plutarch *Alex.* 55.9. For Ptolemy's claim that he was tortured: Arrian *Anab.* 4.14.4. The accounts of his death given by various other authors (*FGrH* 124 T18a-f) are worthless. Hamilton (1969: 156) attempts to reconcile the accounts of Ptolemy and Chares, who says that Kallisthenes was carried around in chains for seven months, by assuming that he was executed thereafter, but fails to note that Chares places Kallisthenes' death after Alexander's wounding in the Mallian town (late 326 BCE), which only raises new questions about the date and reason for Kallisthenes' arrest. Strabo 11.11.4 C517 says Kallisthenes was arrested in Baktria at Kariatai and this must have occurred no later than the end of spring 327 BCE. Perhaps Chares meant to write "a year and seven months."

REFERENCES

Ager, S.L. 2017. "Symbol and Ceremony: Royal Weddings in the Hellenistic Age." In A. Erskine, L. Llewellyn-Jones, and S. Wallace (eds), *The Hellenistic Court: Monarchic Power and Elite Society from Alexander to Cleopatra*, 165–88. Swansea, UK.

– 2020. "'He Shall Give Him the Daughter of Women': Ptolemaic Queens in the Seleukid House." In R. Oetjen and F. Ryan (eds), *New Perspectives in Seleucid History, Archaeology and Numismatics in Honor of Getzel M. Cohen*, 183–201. Berlin.

Ager, S.L., and C. Hardiman. 2016. "Female Seleukid Portraits: Where Are They?" In Coşkun and McAuley, 143–72.

Agut-Labordère, D., and G. Gorre. 2014. "De l'autonomie à l'intégration. Les temples égyptiens face à la couronne des Saïtes aux Ptolémées (VIe-IIIe siècle AV. J.-C.)." *Topoi* 19.1: 17–55.

Albis, R.V. 1996. *Poet and Audience in the Argonautica of Apollonius*. Lanham, MD.

Allotte de la Fuÿe, Fr.-M. 1904. "Monnaies arsacides surfrappées." *Revue Numismatique*, series 4, 8: 174–96.

Ameling, W. 1988. "Alexander und Achilleus: Ein Bestandsaufnahme." In W. Will (ed.), *Zu Alexander der Grosse*. Volume 2: 657–92. Amsterdam.

Antoniadis, T. 2015. "Scelus Femineum: Adultery and Revenge in Valerius Flaccus' *Argonautica* Book 2 (98–241) and Seneca's *Agamemnon*." *Symbolae Osloenses* 89: 60–80.

Arslan, M. 2000. "A Unique Tetradrachm of Ariarathes, King of Cappadocia, from a Hoard Found at Kotyora (Ordu)." In B. Kluge and B. Weisser (eds), *Proceedings of the 12th International Numismatic Congress, Berlin 1997*, 230–2.

– 2011. "Un cas de *damnatio* pour des motifs religieux sur une monnaie d'or de l'empereur Dioclétien." *Cercle d' Études Numismatiques* 48.3: 385–8.

Ash, R., J. Mossman, and F.B. Titchener (eds). 2015. *Fame and Infamy: Essays for Christopher Pelling on Characterization in Greek and Roman Biography and Historiography*. Oxford.

Asheri, D. 1996. "Colonizzazione e decolonizzazione." In C. Settis (ed.), *I Greci: Storia cultura arte società*, 73–115. Turin.

Ashton, R. 2002. "Opuscula Anatolica. 6. *Damnatio Memoriae* in Second-Century BC Karia or Lykia?" *Numismatic Chronicle* 162: 30–1.

Atkinson, J.E. 1994. *A Commentary on Q. Curtius Rufus' Historiae Alexandri Magni: Books 5 to 7,2*. Amsterdam.

– 2000. "Originality and Its Limits in the Alexander Sources of the Early Empire." In Bosworth and Baynham, 307–25.

– 2009. *Curtius Rufus: Histories of Alexander the Great. Book 10*. Oxford.

Austin, M.M. 2006. *The Hellenistic World from Alexander to the Roman Conquest: A Selection of Ancient Sources in Translation*. 2nd ed. Cambridge.

Badian, E. 1958. "Alexander the Great and the Unity of Mankind." *Historia* 7: 287–306.

– 1960. "The Death of Parmenio." *TAPA* 91: 324–38.

– 1961. "Review of L. Pearson, *The Lost Histories*." *Gnomon* 33: 660–7.

– 2000. "Conspiracies." In Bosworth and Baynham, 51–2.

Baines, J. 2004. "Egyptian Elite Self-Presentation in the Context of Ptolemaic Rule." In W.V. Harris and G. Ruffini (eds), *Ancient Alexandria between Egypt and Greece*, 33–61. Columbia Studies in the Classical Tradition 26. Leiden, NL.

Ballesteros Pastor, L. 2014. "Mithridates, God-King? Iranian Kingship in a Greek Context." In Gnoli and Muccioli, 179–92.

Barbantani, S. 1993. "I poeti lirici del canone alessandrino nell'epigrammatistica." *Aevum Antiquum* 6: 5–97.

– 2001. Φάτις νικηφόρος, *Frammenti di elegia encomiastica nell'età delle guerre galatiche*: *Supplementum Hellenisticum*. Milan.

– 2005. "Goddess of Love and Mistress of the Sea: Notes on a Hellenistic Hymn to Arsinoe-Aphrodite (*P.Lit. Goodsp*. 2, I–IV)." *Ancient Society* 35: 133–63.

– 2007. "The Glory of the Spear: A Powerful Symbol in Hellenistic Poetry and Art. The Case of Neoptolemus 'of Tlos' (and other Ptolemaic Epigrams)." *SCO* 53: 67–138.

– 2011. *Callimachus on Kings and Kingship*. In B. Acosta-Hughes, L. Lehnus, and S. Stephens (eds), *The Brill Companion to Callimachus*, 178–200. Leiden, NL.

– 2012. "Hellenistic Epinician." In C. Carey, R. Rawles, and P. Agocs (eds), *Receiving the Komos: Ancient and Modern Reception of the Victory Ode*. Supplement Bulletin of the Institute of Classical Studies 112: 37–55. London.

– 2014. "'Déjà la pierre pense où votre nom s'inscrit': Identity in Context in Verse Epitaphs for Hellenistic Soldiers." In R. Hunter, A. Rengakos, and E. Sistakou (eds), *Hellenistic Studies at a Crossroads: Exploring Texts, Contexts and*

Metatexts. Trends in Classics Supplementary Volume 25: 301–34. Berlin and New York.

– 2016. "'Simplify Me When I Am Dead': War Heroes in Hellenistic Funerary Epigrams." *Aevum Antiquum* 16: 183–239.

– 2017. "'His σῆμα Are Both Continents.' Alexander the Great in Hellenistic Poetry." *Studi Ellenistici* 31: 51–127.

– 2018. "'Fui buon poeta e buon soldato': *Kleos* militare e *paideia* poetica negli epigrammi epigrafici ellenistici." *Eikasmos* 29: 283–312.

– 2019. "Hellenistic and Roman Military Epitaphs on Stone and on Papyrus: Questions of Authorship and Literariness." In C. Carey, I. Petrovic, and M. Kanellou (eds), *Greek Literary Epigram: From the Hellenistic to the Byzantine Era*, 154–75. Oxford.

Barber, E. 1994. *Women's Work: The First 20,000 Years. Women, Cloth, and Society in Early Times*. New York.

Bartlett, B. 2016. "The Fate of Kleopatra Tryphaina, or: Poetic Justice in Justin." In Coşkun and McAuley, 135–42.

Baynham, E. 1995. "An Introduction to the Metz Epitome. Its Traditions and Value." *Antichthon* 29: 60–77.

– 1998. *Alexander the Great: The Unique History of Quintus Curtius*. Ann Arbor, MI.

Bearzot, C. 1987. "La Tradizione su Parmenione negli Storici di Alessandro." *Aevum* 61: 89–104.

– 2011. "Royal Autobiography in the Hellenistic Age." In G. Marasco (ed.), *Political Autobiographies and Memoirs in Antiquity*, 37–86. Leiden, NL.

Becher, I. 1966. *Das Bild der Kleopatra in der griechischen und lateinischen Literatur*. Berlin.

Bellinger, A.R. 1949. "The End of the Seleucids." *Transactions of the Connecticut Academy of Arts and Sciences* 38: 51–102.

Bennett, C. n.d. *The Ptolemaic Dynasty*. www.tyndalehouse.com/Egypt/ptolemies/genealogy.htm. Accessed 12 September 2015.

Benoist, S., and A. Daguet-Gagey (eds). 2008. *Un discours en image de la condamnation de mémoire*. Metz, DE.

Benveniste, E. 1969. *Les vocabulaires des institutions Indo-Européennes*. Paris.

Berenson, E., and E. Giloi (eds). 2010. *Constructing Charisma: Celebrity, Fame, and Power in Nineteenth-Century Europe*. New York.

Berghaus, P. 1978. "Erasionen auf Münzen von Pergamon in der Sammlung Th. Bieder der westfälischen Wilhelms-Universität." In S. Şahin, E. Schwertheim, and J. Wagner (eds), *Festschrift für Friedrich Karl Dörner*. Volume 1: 158–62. Leiden, NL.

Berkowitz, G. 2004. *Semi-Public Narration in Apollonius'* Argonautica. Leuven, Paris, and Dudley, MA.

Bernand, A. 1992. *La prose sur pierre dans l'Egypte hellénistique et romaine*. Paris.
– 1997. "Sur le 'marbre' du Phare d'Alexandrie." *ZPE* 118: 131–8.
Bevan, E.R. 1902. *The House of Seleucus*. Volume 2. London.
– 1927. *The House of Ptolemy: A History of Hellenistic Egypt under the Ptolemaic Dynasty*. London.
Beye, C.R. 1969. "Jason as Love-Hero in Apollonios' *Argonautika*." *GRBS* 10: 31–55.
Bielman Sánchez, A. 2003. "Régner au féminin: Réflexions sur les reines attalides et séleucides." In F. Prost (ed.), *L'Orient méditerranéen de la mort d'Alexandre aux campagnes de Pompée: Cités et royaumes à l'époque hellénistique*, 41–61. Rennes, FR.
Bigwood, J.M. 2004. "Queen Mousa, Mother and Wife (?) of King Phraatakes of Parthia: A Re-evaluation of the Evidence." *Mouseion* 4: 35–70.
Billows, R.A. 2015. "Nymphis (432)." In I. Worthington (ed.), *Brill's New Jacoby Online*. http://referenceworks.brillonline.com/browse/brill-s-new-jacoby
Bingen, J. 2007. "Ptolemy I and the Quest for Legitimacy." In R.S. Bagnall (ed.), *Hellenistic Egypt: Monarchy, Society, Economy, Culture*, 15–30. Edinburgh.
Birch, S. 1836–7. "Researches on the Coins of Caracalla and Geta Having the Head of the Latter Erased." *Proceedings of the Numismatic Society* 194–7.
Bittner, A. 1998. *Gesellschaft und Wirtschaft in Herakleia Pontike: Eine Polis zwischen Tyrannis und Selbstverwaltung*. Bonn.
Blasius, A. 2001. "Army and Society in Ptolemaic Egypt: A Question of Loyalty." *APF* 47: 81–98.
Boddez, T. 2016. "Entre le roi et la cite: Remarques sur le développement des cultes héroïques entre 336 et 150." *Erga/Logoi* 4: 75–116.
Boedeker, D. 1995. "Simonides on Plataea: Narrative Elegy, Mythodic History." *ZPE* 107: 217–29.
Bond, G., (ed.). 1963. *Euripides: Hypsipyle*. Oxford.
Bond, S. 2014. "Altering Infamy: Status, Violence, and Civic Exclusion in Late Antiquity." *CA* 33: 1–30.
Boorstin, D. 1961. *The Image: A Guide to Pseudo-events in America*. New York.
Bosch-Puche, F. 2008. "L'autel du temple d'Alexandre le Grand Bahariya retrouv." *BIFAO* 108: 29–44.
– 2013. "The Egyptian Royal Titulary of Alexander the Great, Part 1: Horus, Two Ladies, Golden Horus, and Throne Names." *JEA* 99: 131–54.
– 2014. "The Egyptian Royal Titulary of Alexander the Great, Part 2: Personal Name, Empty Cartouche, Final Remarks, and Appendix." *JEA* 100: 89–109.
Bosworth, A.B. 1980. *A Historical Commentary on Arrian's History of Alexander*. Volume 1. Oxford.
– 1988. *From Arrian to Alexander*. Oxford.
– 1995. *A Historical Commentary on Arrian's History of Alexander*. Volume 2. Oxford.

– 1996. *Alexander and the East: The Tragedy of Triumph*. Oxford.

– 2000a. "The Historical Context of Thucydides' Funeral Oration." *JHS* 120: 1–16.

– 2000b. "Ptolemy and the Will of Alexander." In Bosworth and Baynham, 207–41.

– 2002. *The Legacy of Alexander: Politics, Warfare, and Propaganda under the Successors*. Oxford.

– 2003. "Plus ça Change … Ancient Historians and Their Sources." *Cl. Ant.* 22.2: 167–98.

Bosworth, A.B., and E.J. Baynham (eds). *Alexander the Great in Fact and Fiction*. Oxford.

Bouvier, D. 2002. *Le sceptre et la lyre: L'Iliade ou les héros de la mémoire. Collection Horos*. Grenoble.

Bradford-Welles, C. 1963. "The Reliability of Ptolemy as an Historian." In E. Rostain (ed.), *Miscellanea di Studi Alessandrini in Memoria di A. Rostagni*, 101–17. Turin.

Braswell, B. 1988. *A Commentary on the Fourth Pythian Ode of Pindar*. Berlin.

Braudy, L. 1986. *The Frenzy of Renown: Fame and Its History*. New York.

Briant, P. 1998. "Colonizzazione ellenistica e popolazioni del Vicino Oriente: dinamiche sociali e politiche di acculturazione." In C. Settis (ed.), *I Greci: Storia cultura arte società*. Volume 3: 309–33. Turin.

– 2002. *From Cyrus to Alexander: A History of the Persian Empire*. Winona Lake, IN.

Briant, P., W.F.M. Henkelman, and M. Stolper (eds). 2008. *L'archive des fortifications de Persépolis: État des questions et perspectives de recherches. Actes du colloque organisé au Collège de France par la "Chaire d'Histoire et Civilisation du Monde Achéménide et de l'Empire d'Alexandre" et le "Réseau International d'Études et de Recherches Achéménides" (GDR 2538 CNRS), 3–4 novembre 2006* (Persika 12). Paris.

Bringmann, K. 1986. "Geschichte und Psychologie bei Poseidonios." In I.G. Kidd (ed.), *Aspects de la philosophie hellénistique*, 29–66. Geneva.

– 1997. "Die Rolle der Königinnen, Prinzen und Vermittler." In M. Christol and O. Masson (eds), *Actes du x*[e] *Congrès International d'Épigraphie Grecque et Latine*, 169–74. Paris.

Brosius, M. 1996. *Women in Ancient Persia*. Oxford.

– 2016. "No Reason to Hide: Women in the Neo-Elamite and Persian Periods." In S.L. Budin and J. Macintosh Turfa (eds), *Women in Antiquity: Real Women across the Ancient World*, 156–74. London and New York.

Brown, T.S. 1949a. "Callisthenes and Alexander." *AJP* 70: 225–48.

– 1949b. *Onesicritus: A Study in Hellenistic Historiography*. Berkeley and Los Angeles.

– 1950. "Clitarchus." *AJP* 71: 134–55.

– 1973. *The Greek Historians*. Lexington, MA.

Budin, S.L. 2003. *The Origin of Aphrodite*. Bethesda, MD.

Bulloch, A. 2006. "Jason's Cloak." *Hermes* 134: 44–68.

Burlinga, B. 2013. *Arrian's Anabasis: An Intellectual and Cultural Story. Akanthina* 6. Gdańsk.

Burn, A.R. 1963. *Alexander the Great and the Middle East.* Harmondsworth, UK.

Burnett, A. 1987. *Coinage in the Roman World.* London.

Burstein, S.M. 1974. *Outpost of Hellenism: The Emergence of Heraclea on the Black Sea.* Berkeley.

– 1991. "Pharaoh Alexander: A Scholarly Myth." *Anc. Soc.* 22: 139–45.

– 2000. "Prelude to Alexander: The Reign of Khababash." *AHB* 14: 149–54.

Burton, R.W.B. 1962. *Pindar's Pythian Odes.* Oxford.

Buttrey, T.V. 1973. "The Morgantina Gold Hoard and the Coinage of Hicetas." *Numismatic Chronicle* 7.13: 11–15.

Byre, C. 2002. *A Reading of Apollonius Rhodius' Argonautica: The Poetics of Uncertainty.* Lewiston, NY.

Cairns, D. 1993. *Aidos: The Psychology and Ethics of Honour and Shame in Greek Literature.* Oxford.

Cameron, A. 1995. *Callimachus and His Critics.* Oxford.

Caneva, S. 2012. "Queens and Ruler Cults in Early Hellenism: Festivals, Administration, and Ideology." *Kernos* 25: 75–101.

– 2013. "La face cachée des intrigues de cour: Prolégomènes à une étude du role des femmes royales dans les royaumes hellénistiques." In S. Boehringer and V. Sebillotte Cuchet (eds), *Des femmes en action: L'individu et la function en Grèce antique,* 133–51. Paris and Athens.

– 2014a. "Courtly Love, Stars, and Power: The Queen in Third-Century Royal Couples, through Poetry and Epigraphic Texts." In M.A. Harder, R.F. Regtuit, and G.C. Wakker (eds), *Hellenistic Poetry in Context,* 25–57. Leuven, BE, Paris, and Walpole, MA.

– 2014b. "Ruler Cults in Practice: Sacrifices and Libations for Arsinoe Philadelphos, from Alexandria and Beyond." In Gnoli and Muccioli, 85–116.

– 2016. *From Alexander to the Theoi Adelphoi: Foundation and Legitimation of a Dynasty.* Studia Hellenistica 56. Leuven.

Capdetrey, L. 2007. *Le pouvoir Séleucide: Territoire, administration, finances d'un royaume hellénistique (312–129 avant J.-C.).* Rennes.

Carney, E. 1988. "Eponymous Women: Royal Women and City Names." *AHB* 2: 134–42.

– 2000. *Women and Monarchy in Macedonia.* Norman, OK.

– 2011. "Being Royal and Female in the Early Hellenistic Period." In A. Erskine and L. Llewellyn-Jones (eds), *Creating a Hellenistic World,* 195–220. Swansea, UK.

– 2013. *Arsinoë of Egypt and Macedon. A Royal Life.* Oxford.

Carroll, M. 2011. "*Memoriae* and *Damnatio Memoriae*: Preserving and Erasing Identities in Roman Funerary Commemoration." In M. Carroll (ed.), *Living through the Dead: Burial and Commemoration in the Classical World*, 69–90. Oxford.

Casadò Lopez, P.M. 1976. "Las 'damnatio memoriae' en las monedas bil-bilitanas de Sejano." *Numisma* 26: 138–43.

Chamoux, F. 1958. "Epigramme de Cyrène en l'honneur du roi Magas." *BCH* 82: 571–87.

Chaniotis, A. 1993. "Ein diplomatischer Statthalter nimmt Rücksicht auf den verletzten Stolz zweier hellenistischer Kleinpoleis (Nagidos und Arsinoe)." *Epigraphica Anatolica* 31: 33–42.

– 2005. *War in the Hellenistic World: A Social and Cultural History*. Oxford.

– 2009. "Lament for a Young Man: A New Epigram from Aphrodisias." In Á. Martínez Fernández (ed.), *Estudios de Epigrafía Griega*. Serie investigación 1: 469–78. La Laguna, ES.

Chugg, A. 2006. *Alexander's Lovers*. Private publication.

Clare, R.J. 2002. *The Path of the Argo: Language, Imagery and Narrative in the Argonautica of Apollonius Rhodius*. Cambridge.

Clarysse, W. 2000. "Ptolémées et temples." In D. Valbelle and J. Leclant (eds), *Le décret de Memphis: colloque de la Fondation Singer-Polignac à l'occasion de la célébration du bicentenaire de la découverte de la Pierre de Rosette*, 41–65. Paris.

Clarysse, W., and G. Van der Veken. 1983. *The Eponymous Priests of Ptolemaic Egypt: Chronological Lists of the Priests of Alexandria and Ptolemais with a Study of the Demotic Transcriptions of Their Names*. Leiden, NL.

Clauss, J. 1993. *The Best of the Argonauts: The Redefinition of the Epic Hero in Book 1 of the Argonautica*. Berkeley and Oxford.

Clayman, D. 2014. *Berenice II and the Golden Age of Ptolemaic Egypt*. Oxford.

Clément-Tarantino, S. 2016. "Wanderings of Fama and 'Fame's Narratives' in the *Aeneid*." In S. Kyriakidis (ed.), *Libera Fama: An Endless Journey*, 55–70. Newcastle upon Tyne, UK.

Cohen, G.M. 1995. *The Hellenistic Settlements in Europe, the Islands, and Asia Minor*. Berkeley.

Colburn, H.P. 2015. "Memories of the Second Persian Period in Egypt." In J.M. Silverman and C. Waerzeggers (eds), *Political Memory in and after the Persian Empire*, 165–202. Atlanta.

Corssen, P. 1917. "Das angebliche Werk des Olynthiers Kallisthenes." *Philologus* 74: 1–57.

Coşkun, A., and A. McAuley (eds). 2016. *Seleukid Royal Women: Creation, Representation, and Distortion of Hellenistic Queenship in the Seleukid Empire*. Stuttgart.

Coulon, L. 2001. "Quand Amon parle à Platon (La statue Caire JE 38033)." *RdE* 52: 85–111.

Cowley, A.E. 1923. *Aramaic Papyri of the Fifth Century B.C.* Oxford.

Cudjoe, R.V. 2010. *The Social and Legal Position of Widows and Orphans in Classical Athens*. Athens.

Currie, B. 2005. *Pindar and the Cult of Heroes*. Oxford.

Cuypers, M.J. 2004. "Apollonius of Rhodes." In I. De Jong, R. Nünlist, A. Bowie (eds), *Narrators, Narratees, and Narratives in Ancient Greek Literature*, 35–69. Leuven, BE.

D'Agostini, M. 2013. "La strutturazione del potere seleucidico in Anatolia: Il caso di Acheo il Vecchio e Alessandro di Sardi." *Erga/Logoi* 1: 87–106.

– 2016. "Representation and Agency of Royal Women in Hellenistic Dynastic Crises: The Case of Berenike and Laodike I." In A. Bielman-Sánchez, I. Cogitore, and A. Kolb (eds), *Femmes influentes dans le monde hellénistique et à Rome, IIIe s. av. J.-C.–Ier s. ap. J.-C.*, 35–60. Grenoble.

de Callataÿ, F. 1991. "Un tétradrachme de Mithridate surfrappé à Maronée." *Numismatica e Antichità Classiche* 20: 213–26.

– 1994a. "Les écus de Louis XV et de Louis XVI à la lumière du trésor de Châtelet (Belgique)." *Revue Numismatique* 6.36: 303–5.

– 1994b. *Les tétradrachmes d'Orodès II et de Phraate IV: Étude du rythme de leur production à la lumière d'une grande trouvaille*. Studia Iranica 14. Paris.

– 1997. *L'histoire des guerres Mithridatiques vue par les monnaies.* Louvain-la-Neuve, BE.

– 2004. "Le premier monnayage de la cité d'Amastris (Paphlagonie)." *SchwNumRu* 83: 57–80.

– 2009. "The First Royal Coinages of Pontos (from Mithridates III to Mithridates V)." In J. Munk Høtje (ed.), *Mithridates VI and the Pontic Kingdom*, 53–94. Aarhus, DK.

– 2012. "Les fabuleuses richesses des rois hellénistiques: Monnayages et Weltmachtpolitik." In V. Penna (ed.), *Les mots et les monnaies*, 91–101. Ghent, BE.

– 2013. "Byzantion over Mithradates Eupator: How the Pontic King Paid His Thracian Mercenaries after the Treaty of Dardanos (85 BC)." *Notae Numismaticae* 8: 95–101.

– forthcoming. "What Does the Dense Network of Thracian and Macedonian Overstrikes on Late Hellenistic Tetradrachms Reflect?" In U. Peter (ed.), *Thrace: Local Coinage and Regional Identity. Numismatic Research in the Digital Age*. Berlin.

de Callataÿ F., and P. Iossif. 2015. "Un tétradrachme de Lysimaque surfrappé sur une pièce d'Antiochos Ier à Sardes." *Revue Numismatique* 172: 235–42.

DeForest, M. 1994. *Apollonius'* Argonautica*: A Callimachean Epic*. Leiden, NL.

de Polignac, F. 2000. "The Shadow of Alexander." In C. Jacob and F. de Polignac (eds), *Alexandria, Third Century BC: The Knowledge of the World in a Single City*, 32–41. Alexandria, VA.

Derderian, K. 2001. *Leaving Words to Remember: Greek Mourning and the Advent of Literacy*. Mnemosyne Supplement 209. Leiden.

Desideri, P. 1967. "Studi di storiografia Eracleota, I, Promathidas e Nymphis." *SCO* 16: 366–416.

Devine, A.M. 1994. "Alexander's Propaganda Machine: Callisthenes as the Ultimate Source for Arrian, *Anabasis* 1–3." In I. Worthington (ed.), *Ventures into Greek History*, 89–103. Oxford.

Dillery, J. 2015. *Clio's Other Sons: Berossus and Manetho*. Ann Arbor, MI.

Dmitriev, S. 2007. "The Last Marriage and Death of Lysimachus." *GRBS* 47: 135–49.

Dörner, F.K. 1996. "Epigraphic Analysis." In D.H. Sanders (ed.), *Nemrud Dağı: The Hierothesion of Antiochos I of Commagene*. Volume 1: 361–77. Winona Lake, IN.

Dräger, P. 2016. "Lemnian Women, Hypsipyle." In *Brill's New Pauly Online*. http://referenceworks.brillonline.com/cluster/New%20Pauly%Online?s.num=0

Dreyer, B., and P.F. Mittag. 2011. *Lokale Eliten und hellenistische Könige: Zwischen Kooperation und Konfrontation*. Oikumene. Studien zur Antiken Weltgeschichte 8. Berlin.

Dreyer, B., and F. Gerardin. Forthcoming. "Antiochos III and the Local Elites: Politics of Deals at Its Peak." In C. Fischer-Bovet and S. von Reden (eds), *Comparing the Ptolemaic and Seleucid Empires*.

Duff, T. 1999. *Plutarch's Lives: Exploring Virtue and Vice*. Oxford.

Dumézil, G. 1924. *Le crime des Lemniennes*. Paris.

Dumitru, A.G. 2016. "Kleopatra Selene: A Look at the Moon and Her Bright Side." In Coşkun and McAuley, 253–72.

Duncan, A. 2012. "A Theseus outside Athens: Dionysius I of Syracuse and Tragic Self-Presentation." In K. Bosher (ed.), *Theatre outside Athens: Drama in Greek Sicily and South Italy*, 137–55. Cambridge.

Eamon, W. 1991. "Court, Academy, and Printing House: Patronage and Scientific Careers in Late-Renaissance Italy." In B. Moran (ed.), *Patronage and Institutions*, 25–50. Woodbridge, UK.

Ecker, U. 1990. *Grabmal und Epigramm: Studien zur fruhgriechischen Sepulkraldichtung*. Stuttgart.

Ehling, K. 2008. *Untersuchungen zur Geschichte der späten Seleukiden (164–63 v. Chr.)*. Stuttgart.

Elemèr, J. 1937–8. "The Use of *damnatio memoriae* on a Dupondius of Caligula." (In Hungarian). *Numizmatikai Közlöny* 36/37: 89–91.

Ellis, W. 1994. *Ptolemy of Egypt*. London and New York.

Enenkel, K.A.E., and I.L. Pfeijffer (eds). 2005. *The Manipulative Mode: Political Propaganda in Antiquity. A Collection of Case Studies*. Leiden, NL.

Engels, D. 2013. "A New Frataraka Chronology." *Latomus* 72: 39–80.

Erçiyas, D.B. 2003. "Herakleia Pontica-Amastris." In D.V. Grammenos and E.K. Petropoulos (eds), *Ancient Greek Colonies in the Black Sea*, 1403–31. Thessaloniki.

– 2006. *Wealth, Aristocracy, and Royal Propaganda under the Hellenistic Kingdom of the Mithradatids in the Central Black Sea Region of Turkey*. Leiden and Boston.

Errington, R.M. 1969. "Bias in Ptolemy's History of Alexander." *CQ* 19: 233–42.

– 2008. *A History of the Hellenistic World, 323–30 BC*. Malden, MA.

Evans, J. 1963. "Note on Miltiades' Capture of Lemnos." *CP* 58: 168–70.

Evans Grubbs, J. 2002. *Women and the Law in the Roman Empire*. London and New York.

Fantuzzi, M., and R. Hunter. 2004. *Tradition and Innovation in Hellenistic Poetry*. Cambridge.

Farid, A. 1993. *Die demotischen Inschriften der Strategen*. Volumes 1 and 2. Varia Aegyptiaca, Supplement 4, pts 1–2. San Antonio. TX.

Felber, H. 2002. "Die Demotische Chronik." In A. Blasius and B.U. Schipper (eds), *Apokalyptik und Ägyten: Eine kritische Analyse der relevanten Texte aus dem griechisch-römischen Ägypten*, 66–111. Leuven, NL.

Fenster, T., and D.L. Smail (eds). 2003. *Fama: The Politics of Talk and Reputation in Medieval Europe*. Ithaca, NY, and London.

Fernández-Galiano, E. 1987. *Posidipo de Pela*. Madrid.

Finkelberg, M. 1986. "Is κλέος ἄφθιτον a Homeric Formula?" *CQ* 36: 1–5.

Fischer, T. 1979. "Zur Seleukideninschrift von Hefzibah." *ZPE* 33: 131–8.

Fischer-Bovet, C. 2014. *Army and Society in Ptolemaic Egypt*. Armies of the Ancient World 1. Cambridge.

– forthcoming-a. "Ptolemaic Imperialism in Southern Anatolia (Lycia, Pamphylia and Cilicia)." In M. Munn (ed.), *Building a New World Order: Hellenistic Monarchies in the Ancient Mediterranean World*.

– forthcoming-b. "Reassessing Hellenistic Settlement Policies: The Seleucid Far East, the Ptolemaic Red Sea Basin and Egypt. 2b. Reassessing Ptolemaic Settlement Policies: Another look at the *poleis*." In C. Fischer-Bovet and S. von Reden (eds), *Comparing the Ptolemaic and Seleucid Empires: Integration, Communication and Resistance*, Cambridge.

Flower, H.I. 2006. *The Art of Forgetting: Disgrace and Oblivion in Roman Political Culture*. Chapel Hill, NC.

Flower, R. 2013. *Emperors and Bishops in Late Roman Invective*. Cambridge.

Franco, C. 1993. *Il Regno di Lisimaco: Strutture amministrative e rapporti con le città*. Pisa.

Frank, R. 2017. "The Hero vs. the Tyrant: Legitimate and Illegitimate Rule in the Alexander-Caesar Pairing." In T. Howe, S. Müller, and R. Stoneman (eds), *Ancient Historiography on War and Empire*, 210–25. Oxford.

Fraser, P.M. 1972. *Ptolemaic Alexandria*. Volumes 1–3. Cambridge.

– 1996. *Cities of Alexander the Great*. Oxford.

Gabathuler, M. 1937. *Hellenistische Epigramme auf Dichter*. St Gallen, CH.

Gallotta, S. 2014. "Appunti su Memnone di Eraclea." *Erga/Logoi* 2: 65–77.

Gangloff, A. 2006. *Dion Chrysostome et les mythes: Hellénisme, communication et philosophie politique*. Grenoble.

Gantz, T. 2007. "The Aeschylean Tetralogy: Attested and Conjectured Groups." In M. Lloyd (ed.), *Oxford Readings in Classical Studies: Aeschylus*, 40–71. Oxford.

Garland. R. 2006. *Celebrity in Antiquity: From Media Tarts to Tabloid Queens*. London.

Garulli, V. 2008. "L'epigramma longum nella tradizione epigrafica sepolcrale greca." In A.M. Morelli (ed.), *Epigramma longum: Da Marziale alla tarda Antichità. Atti del Convegno Internazionale, Cassino, 29–31 maggio 2006*. Volume 2: 623–62. Cassino.

– 2012. *Byblos lainee: Epigrafia, letteratura, epitafio*. Bologna.

Garvie, A.F. 1988. *Aeschylus: Choephori*. Oxford.

Gavrilov, A. 2005. "Der Bosporaner Apollonius und sein Dichter (CIRB 119).Teil I." *Hyperboreus* 11.1: 60–85; Teil II, *Hyperboreus* 11.2: 215–41.

Gehrke, H. 1982. "Der siegreiche König: Überlegungen zur hellenistischen Monarchie." *AKG* 64: 247–77.

George, E.V. 1972. "Poet and Characters in Apollonius Rhodius' Lemnian Episode." *Hermes* 100: 47–63.

Gnoli, T., and F. Muccioli (eds). 2014. *Divinizzazione, culto del sovrano e apoteosi: Tra antichità e medioevo*. DiSCi, Storia antica 1. Bologna.

Golan, D. 1988. "The Fate of the Court Historian Callisthenes." *Athenaeum* 66: 99–120.

Goldhill, S. 1991. *The Poet's Voice: Essays on Poetics and Greek Literature*. Cambridge.

Gonella, R. 1995. "Ein überprägtes Tetradrachmon des Vonones I (8 bis 12 n. Chr.)." *Schweizer Münzblätter* 178: 29–32.

Gorini, G. 2002. "L'immagine del potere nelle emissioni delle regine ellenistiche." *RIN* 103: 307–18.

Gorre, G. 2009. *Les relations du clergé Égyptien et des Lagides d'après les sources privées*. Studia Hellenistica 45. Leuven, BE.

– 2013. "A Religious Continuity between the Dynastic and Ptolemaic Periods? Self-Representation and Identity of Egyptian Priests in the Ptolemaic Period (332–30 BCE)." In E. Stavrianopoulou (ed.), *Shifting Social Imaginaries in the Hellenistic Period*. Mnemosyne Supplements 340: 99–114. Leiden, BE.

Goukowsky, P. 2002. *Diodore de Sicile: Bibliothèque historique, Tome XII, Livre XVII*. Paris.

Gow, A.S., and A.F. Schofield. 1953. *Nicander: The Poems and Poetical Fragments*. Cambridge.

Gozzoli, R.B. 2009. *The Writing of History in Ancient Egypt during the First Millennium BC (ca. 1070–180BC)*. London.

Grainger, J.D. 2010. *The Syrian Wars*. Leiden, NL, and Boston.

– 2015. *The Fall of the Seleukid Empire, 187–75 BC*. Barnsley, UK.
Green, P. 1990. *Alexander to Actium. The Historical Evolution of the Hellenistic Age*. Berkeley and Los Angeles.
Greenfield J.C., and B. Porten. 1982. *The Bisitun Inscription of Darius the Great: Aramaic Version, Corpus Inscr. Iran., Pt. I, Vol. V: Texts I*. London.
Greindl, M. 1938. "Κλέος, κῦδος, εὖχος, τιμή, φᾶτις, δόξα: Eine bedeutungsgeschichtliche Untersuchung des epischen und lyrischen Sprachgebrauches." Dissertation, Munich.
Guastella, G. 2017. *Word of Mouth: Fama and Its Personifications in Art and Literature from Ancient Rome to the Middle Ages*. Oxford.
Habicht, C. 1992. "Athens and the Ptolemies." *Classical Antiquity* 11: 68–90.
Habicht, C., and C.P. Jones. 1989. "A Hellenistic Inscription from Arsinoe in Cilicia." *Phoenix* 43: 317–46.
Hafsaas-Tsakos, H. 2009. "The Kingdom of Kush: An African Centre on the Periphery of the Bronze Age World System." *NAR* 42.1: 50–70.
Hamilton, J.R. 1969. *Plutarch, Alexander: A Commentary*. Oxford.
Hammond, N.G.L. 1983. *Three Historians of Alexander the Great*. Cambridge.
Hanaway, W.L., Jr. 1982. "Anāhitā and Alexander." *JAOS* 102: 285–95.
Hansen, E.V. 1967. *The Attalids of Pergamon*. 2nd ed. Ithaca, NY.
Hanson, A.E. 2008. "The Correspondence between Soranus, M. Anthony, and Cleopatra." In V. Boudon-Millot, V. Dasen, B. Maire, and D. Gourevitch (eds), *Femmes en medécine: Actes de la journée internationale d'étude organisée à l'université René-Descartes-Paris V, 17 mars 2006: En l'honneur de Danielle Gourevitch*, 1–29. Paris.
Hanson, V.D. 2001. *Carnage and Culture*. New York.
Hardie, P. 2012. *Rumour and Renown: Representations of* Fama *in Western Literature*. Cambridge.
Harl, K. 1987. *Civic Coins and Civic Politics in the Roman East A.D. 180–275*. Berkeley and Los Angeles.
Harris, E. 2015. "The Family, Community, and Murder: The Role of Pollution in Athenian Homicide Law." In C. Ando and J. Rüpke (eds), *Public and Private in Ancient Mediterranean Law and Religion*, 11–35. Berlin.
Hazzard, R.A. 2000. *Imagination of a Monarchy: Studies in Ptolemaic Propaganda*. Toronto.
Head, B.V. 1911. *Historia Numorum: A Manual of Greek Numismatics*. Oxford.
Heckel, W. 1977. "The Conspiracy against Philotas." *Phoenix* 31: 9–21.
– 1980. "Alexander at the Persian Gates." *Athenaeum* 58: 168–174.
– 1981. "Polyxena, the Mother of Alexander the Great." *Chiron* 11: 79–86.
– 1992. *The Marshals of Alexander's Empire*. London.
– 2006. *Who's Who in the Age of Alexander the Great*. Oxford and Malden, MA.

– 2015. "Alexander, Heracles and Achilles: Between Myth and History." In P. Wheatley and E. Baynham (eds), *East and West in the Empire of Alexander: Essays in Honour of Brian Bosworth*, 21–33. Oxford.

– 2016. *Alexander's Marshals: A Study of the Makedonian Aristocracy and the Politics of Military Leadership*. London.

Heckel, W., and J.L. McLeod. 2015. "Alexander the Great and the Fate of the Enemy: Quantifying, Qualifying and Categorizing Atrocities." In W. Heckel, S. Müller, and G. Wrightson (eds), *The Many Faces of War in the Ancient World*, 233–67. Newcastle upon Tyne, UK.

Heinemann U. 2010. *Stadtgeschichte im Hellenismus: Die lokalhistoriographischen Vorgänger und Vorlagen Memnons von Herakleia*. Munich.

Heinen, H. 2000. "Boéthos, fondateur de poleis en Égypte ptolémaïque (OGIS I 111 et un nouveau papyrus de la collection de Trèves)." In L. Mooren (ed.), *Politics, Administration and Society in the Hellenistic and Roman World*. Proceedings of the International Colloquium, Bertinoro, 19–24 July 1997: 123–53, 3 pl. Studia Hellenistica 36. Leuven, BE.

– 2006. "Hunger, Not und Macht: Bemerkungen zur herrschenden Gesellschaft im ptolemäischen ägypten." *AncSoc* 36: 13–44.

Herrmann, P. 1995. "Γέρας θανόντων: Totenruhm und Totenehrung im städtischen Leben der hellenistischen Zeit." In M. Wörrle and P. Zanker (eds), *Stadtbild und Bürgerbild im Hellenismus*, 189–97. Munich.

Hofmann, B. 2005. *Die Königsnovelle: Strukturanalyse am Einzelwerk*. Ägypten und Altes Testament 62. Wiesbaden, DE.

Hölbl, G. 2001. *A History of the Ptolemaic Empire*. London and New York.

Holmberg, I. 1998. "*Metis* and Gender in Apollonius Rhodius' *Argonautica*." *TAPA* 128: 135–59.

Hoover, O.D. 2007. "A Revised Chronology for the Late Seleucids at Antioch." *Historia* 56: 280–301.

Hostein, A. 2004. "Monnaie et *damnatio memoriae* (Ier–IVe siècle ap. J.-C.): problèmes méthodologiques." *Cahiers Glotz* 10: 219–36.

Houghton, A. 1979. "Timarchus as King in Babylonia." *Revue Numismatique* 21: 213–17.

– 1987. "The Double Portrait Coins of Antiochus XI and Philip I: A Seleucid Mint at Beroea?" *Schweizerische numismatische Rundschau* 66: 79–85.

– 1988. "The Double Portrait Coins of Alexander I Balas and Cleopatra Thea." *Schweizerische numismatische Rundschau* 67: 85–95.

– 1993. "The Reigns of Antiochus VIII and Antiochus IX at Antioch and Tarsus." *Schweizerische numismatische Rundschau* 72: 87–111.

Houghton, A., and W. Müseler. 1990. "The Reigns of Antiochus VIII and Antiochus IX at Damascus." *Schweizer Münzblätter* 40: 57–62.

Houghton, A., C. Lorber, and O. Hoover (eds). 2008. *Seleucid Coins: A Comprehensive Catalogue. Part II. Seleucus IV through Antiochus XIII.* New York, Lancaster, and London.

Howald, E. 1926. *Ethik des Altertums.* Munich.

Howe, T. 2008. "Alexander in India: Ptolemy as Near Eastern Historiographer." In T. Howe and J. Reames (eds), *Macedonian Legacies: Studies in Ancient Macedonian History and Culture in Honor of Eugene N. Borza*, 215–34. Claremont, CA.

– 2015a. "Alexander and 'Afghan' Insurgency: A Reassessment." In T. Howe and L.L. Brice (eds), *Brill's Companion to Insurgency and Terrorism in the Ancient Mediterranean*, 151–82. Leiden, NL.

– 2015b. "Arrian and 'Roman' Military Tactics. Alexander's Campaign against the Autonomous Thracians." In T. Howe, E. Garvin, and G. Wrightson (eds), *Greece, Macedon and Persia: Studies in Social, Political and Military History in Honour of Waldemar Heckel*, 87–93. Oxford.

– 2015c. "Introducing Ptolemy: Alexander and the Persian Gates." In W. Heckel, S. Müller, and G. Wrightson (eds), *The Many Faces of War in the Ancient World*, 166–95. Newcastle upon Tyne, UK.

– 2016. "Plutarch, Arrian and the Hydaspes: An Historiographical Approach." In F. Landucci Gattinoni (ed.), *Alexander's Legacy*. Monografie del Centro Ricerche di Documentazione sull'Antichità Classica, 39: 25–39. Rome.

– 2018a. "Ptolemy 138." In I. Worthington (ed.), *Brill's New Jacoby Online*. http://referenceworks.brillonline.com/browse/brill-s-new-jacoby

– 2018b. "Kings Don't Lie: Truthtelling, Historiography and Ptolemy I Soter." In T. Howe (ed.), *Ptolemy I Soter: A Self-Made Man*, 155–84. Oxford.

Howgego, C.J. 1985. *Greek Imperial Countermarks.* London.

Hughes-Hallett, L. 1990. *Cleopatra: Histories, Dreams and Distortions.* New York.

Hultsch, Fr. 1866. *Metrologicorum Scriptorum Reliquiae.* Leipzig.

Hunter, R. 1993. *The* Argonautica *of Apollonius: Literary Studies.* Cambridge.

– 2003. *Theocritus. Encomium of Ptolemy Philadelphus.* Hellenistic Culture and Society 19. Berkeley, Los Angeles, and London.

Hunter, V. 1994. *Policing Athens: Social Control in the Attic Lawsuits, 420–320 B.C.* Princeton, NJ.

Huß, W. 1994a. *Der makedonische König und die ägyptischen Priester.* Stuttgart.

– 1994b. "Der rätselhäfte Pharao Chababasch." *SEL* 11: 97–112.

– 1997. "Ägyptische Kollaborateure in persischer Zeit." *Tyche* 12: 131–43.

– 2001. *Ägypten in hellenistischer Zeit, 332–30 v. Chr.* Munich.

Hutmacher, R. 1965. *Das Ehrendekret für den Strategen Kallimachos.* Beiträge zur Klassischen Philologie 117. Meisenheim am Glan, DE.

Imhoof-Blumer, F. 1883. *Monnaies Greques.* Paris.

Iossif, P. 2014. "The Apotheosis of the Seleucid King and the Question of High-Priest/Priestess: A Reconsideration of the Evidence." In Gnoli and Muccioli, 129–48.

Iossif, P., and C. Lorber. 2007. "Laodikai and the Goddess Nikephoros." *AC* 76: 63–88.

Isaac, B. 2004. *The Invention of Racism in Classical Antiquity*. Princeton, NJ.

Isager, S. 1998. "The Pride of Halikarnassos." *ZPE* 123: 1–23.

Jackson, S. 1990. "Myrsilus of Methymna and the Dreadful Smell of the Lemnian Women." *Illinois Classical Studies* 15: 77–83.

– 1993. *Creative Selectivity in the* Argonautica *of Apollonius*. Amsterdam.

Jacobs, B. 2000. "Die Reliefs der Vorfahren des Antiochos I. von Kommagene auf dem Nemrud Dağı – Versuch einer Neubenennung der Frauendarstellungen in den mütterlichen Ahnenreihen." *MDAI(I)* 50: 297–306.

Jacobson, H. 1974. *Ovid's Heroides*. Princeton, NJ.

Jacoby, F. 1923. *Die Fragmente der griechischen Historiker*. Berlin.

Jacques, J.M. 2002. *Nicandre, Oeuvres, Tome II*. Paris.

Jelínková-Reymond, E. 1956. *Les inscriptions de la statue guérisseuse de Djed-her-le-Sauveur*. Bibliothèque d'Étude 23. Cairo.

Johnson, J. 1974. "The Demotic Chronicle as an Historical Source." *Enchoria* 4: 1–17.

– 1983. "The Demotic Chronicle as a Statement of a Theory of Kingship." *JSSEA* 13.2: 61–72.

Jucker, H. 1982. "Die Bildnisstrafen gegen den Toten Caligula." In B. Von Freytag, D. Mannsperger, and F. Prayon (eds), *Praestant Interna: Festschrift für Ulrich Haussmann*, 110–18. Tübingen, DE.

Kahn, D. 2013. "The History of Kush: An Outline." In F. Jesse and C. Vogel (eds), *The Power of Walls: Fortification in Ancient Northeastern Africa. Proceedings of the International Workshop Held at the University of Cologne 4th–7th August 2011*, 17–32. Cologne.

Kaibel, G. 1878. *Epigrammata Graeca ex Lapidibus Conlecta*. Berlin.

Kaiser, W. 1999. "Zur Datierung Realistischer Rundbildnisse Ptolemäich-römischer Zeit." 55 *MDAIK*: 237–63.

Keaveney, A., and J.A. Madden. 2015. "Memnon (434)." In I. Worthington (ed.), *Brill's New Jacoby Online*. http://referenceworks.brillonline.com/browse/brill-s-new-jacoby

Kent, R.G. 1943. "Old Persian Texts." *JNES* 2: 302–6.

Kindler, A. 1980. "The 'damnatio memoriae' of Elagabal on City-Coins of the Near East." *Schweizer Münzblätter* 117: 3–7.

Klingott, H. 2007. "Xerxes in Ägypten: Gedanken zum negativen Perserbild in der Satrapenstele." In St Pfeiffer (ed.), *Ägypten unter fremden Herrschern: Von der persischen Satrapir bis zur römischen Provinz*, 34–53. Frankfurt.

Klooster, J.J.H. 2011. *Poetry as Window and Mirror: Positioning the Poet in Hellenistic Poetry*. Leiden, NL.

– 2017. "Tiberius and Hellenistic Poetry." *Aitia* 7.1 21 March 2017. https://aitia.revues.org/1766 DOI 10.4000/Aitia.1766. Accessed 16 August 2018.

– 2018. "A Doer of Deeds and a Speaker of Words: The Cultural Reception of Phoenix' Educational Ideal." In J. Klooster and B. van den Berg (eds), *Homer and the Good Ruler: The Reception of Homeric Epic as Princes' Mirror through the Ages*, 65–85. Leiden, NL.

– forthcoming. "*Qualis Oratio, Talis Princeps:* The Styles of the Caesars in Suetonius' *Vita Caesarum.*"

Kornemann, E. 1935. *Die Alexandergeschichte des Königs Ptolemaios I von Ägypten: Versuch einer Rekonstruktion*. Leipzig and Berlin.

Kosmin, P.J. 2014. *The Land of the Elephant Kings: Space, Territory, and Ideology in the Seleucid Empire*. Cambridge, MA and London.

Kotlińska-Toma, A. 2014. *Hellenistic Tragedy: Texts, Translations and a Critical Survey*. London.

Kraus, C.S., and A.J. Woodman. 1997. *Latin Historians*. Oxford.

Kroll, J.H. 1993. *The Athenian Agora. XXVI: The Greek Coins*. Princeton, NL.

Kyriakidis, S. (ed.). 2016. *Libera Fama: An Endless Journey*. Newcastle upon Tyne, UK.

Lachenaud, G. 2010. *Scholies à Apollonios de Rhodes Fragments 9*. Paris.

Ladynin, I.A. 2005. "Adversary Ḫšryš(3): His Name and Deeds According to the Satrap Stela." *CdE* 80: 87–113.

– 2014. "The Argeadai Building Program in Egypt in the Framework of Dynasties' XXIX–XXX Temple Building." In V. Grieb, K. Nawotka, and A. Wojciechowska (eds), *Alexander the Great and Egypt: History, Art, Tradition*, 221–40. Wiesbaden, DE.

Landucci Gattinoni, F. 1992. *Lisimaco di Tracia nella prospettiva del primo ellenismo*. Milan.

– 2014. "La divinizzazione del sovrano nella tradizione letteraria del primo ellenismo." In Gnoli and Muccioli, 71–84.

Lane Fox, R. 1973. *Alexander the Great*. London.

Lebeck, A. 1967. "The First Stasimon of Aeschylus' *Choephori*: Myth and Mirror Image." *CP* 62: 182–5.

Le Bohec-Bouhet, S. 2006. "Réflexions sur la place de la femme dans la Macédoine." In A.-M. Guimier-Sorbets, M.B. Hatzopoulos, and Y. Morizot (eds), *Rois, cités, nécropoles: Institutions, rites et monuments en Macédoine*, 187–98. Athens and Paris.

Le Rider, G. 1961. "Les ateliers monétaires de la côté syrienne, phénicienne, palestinienne, égyptienne et cyrénéenne." *VI Congresso Internazionale di Numismatica*, 67–109. Rome.

– 1965. *Suse sous les Séleucides et les Parthes: Les trouvailles monétaires et l'histoire de la ville*. Paris.

– 1975. "Contremarques et surfrappes dans l'Antiquité grecque." In J.-M. Dentzer, Ph. Gauthier, and T. Hackens (eds), *Numismatique antique: Problèmes et méthodes*, 27–56. Nancy and Louvain, BE.

– 1986. "L'Enfant-roi Antiochos et la reine Laodice." *Bulletin de correspondance hellénique* 110: 409–17.

Leschhorn, W. 1984. *Gründer der Stadt: Studien zu einem politisch-religiösen phänomen der griechischen Geschichte.* Stuttgart.

Lesky, A. 1971. *Geschichte der Griechischen Literatur*. Bern.

Levin, D. 1971. *Apollonius'* Argonautica *Re-Examined*, I: *The Neglected First and Second Books.* Leiden, NL.

Levy, B.E. 1954. "The Overstruck Coinage of Ptolemy I." *ANS Museum Notes* 6: 69–84.

Lichtheim, M. 1980. *Ancient Egyptian Literature: The Late Period.* Berkeley.

Lin, N. 1999. "Building a Network Theory of Social Capital." *Connections* 22: 28–51.

Llewellyn-Jones, L. 2012. "The Great Kings of the Fourth Century and the Greek Memory of the Persian Past." In J. Marincola, L. Llewellyn-Jones, and C. Maciver (eds), *Greek Notions of the Past in the Archaic and Classical Eras: History without Historians*, 317–48. Edinburgh.

Lloyd, A.B. 2002. "The Egyptian Elite in the Early Ptolemaic Period: Some Hieroglyphic Evidence." In D. Ogden (ed.), *The Hellenistic World: New Perspectives*, 117–36. Swansea, UK.

– 2010. "From Satrapy to Hellenistic Kingdom: The Case of Egypt." In A. Erskine and L. Llewellyn-Jones (eds), *Creating a Hellenistic World*, 83–105. Swansea, UK.

Lonsdale, D. 2004. *Alexander the Great: Killer of Men*. New York.

Lorber, C.C., and O.D. Hoover. 2003. "An Unpublished Tetradrachm Issued by the Artists of Dionysos." *Numismatic Chronicle* 163: 59–68.

Luschy, H. 1968. "Der Löwe von Ekbatana." *Archäologische Mitteilungen aus Iran* 1: 115–22.

Ma, J. 2005. "The Many Lives of Eugnotos of Akraiphia." In B. Virgilio (ed.), *Studi ellenistici* 16: 141–91.

– 2013. *Statues and Cities: Honorific Portraits and Civic Identity in the Hellenistic World*. Oxford.

Macurdy, G.H. 1932. *Hellenistic Queens: A Study of Woman-Power in Macedonia, Seleucid Syria, and Ptolemaic Egypt*. Baltimore, MD.

Mahaffy, J.P. 1895. *The Empire of the Ptolemies*. London.

– 1898. *A History of Egypt under the Ptolemaic Dynasty*. London.

Malek, J. 2003. "The Old Kingdom (c. 2686–2125 BC)." In I. Shaw (ed.), *The Oxford History of Ancient Egypt*, 89–117. Oxford.

Malitz, J. 1983. *Die Historien des Poseidonios*. Munich.

Manassa, C. 2013. *Imaging the Past: Historical Fiction in New Kingdom Egypt*. Oxford.

Mann, M. 1986. *The Sources of Social Power*. Cambridge.

Manning, J. 2009. *The Last Pharaohs: Egypt under the Ptolemies, 305–30 BC.* Princeton, NJ.

Marasco, G. 1983. "Alessandro, i diadochi e il culto dell'eroe eponimo." *Prometheus* 9: 57–62.

– (ed.). 2011. *Political Autobiographies and Memoirs in Antiquity.* Leiden, NL.

Marquaille, C. 2001. "The External Image of Ptolemaic Egypt." PhD dissertation, London.

Martin, R. 1987. "Fire on the Mountain: *Lysistrata* and the Lemnian Women." *CA* 6: 77–105.

Martínez Fernández, Á. 2006. *Epigramas Helenísticos de Creta.* Madrid.

Masciadri, V. 2008. *Eine Insel im Meer der Geschichten: Untersuchungen zu Mythen aus Lemnos.* Stuttgart.

Mathisen, R.W. 1978. "The Activities of Antigonos Gonatas 280–277 BC and Memnon of Herakleia, Concerning Herakleia." *AncW* 1: 71–4.

McGing, B. 1997. "Revolt Egyptian Style. Internal Opposition to Ptolemaic Rule." *APF* 43/2: 273–314.

Meeus, A. 2014. "The Territorial Ambitions of Ptolemy I." In H. Hauben and A. Meeus (eds), *The Age of the Successors and the Creation of the Hellenistic Kingdoms (323–276 B.C.)*: 263–306. Leuven, BE.

Meister, K. 1963. "Autobiographische Literatur und Memoiren (Hypomnemata) (*FGrHist* 227–238)." In H. Verdin, G. Schepens, and E. De Keyser (eds), *Purposes of History: Studies in Greek Historiography from the 4th to the 2nd Centuries BC*, 83–91. Leuven, BE.

Merkelbach, R., and M.L. West. 1967. *Fragmenta Hesiodea.* Oxford.

Merkelbach, R., and J. Stauber. 2005. *Jenseits des Euphrat: Griechische Inschriften. Ein epigraphisches Lesebuch.* Munich and Leipzig.

Meyer, M. 1992/3. "Mutter, Ehefrau und Herrscherin: Darstellungen der Königin auf seleukidischen Münzen." *Hephaistos* 11/12: 107–32.

Michel, P.M. 2017. "De la dénomination des reines en Babylonie séleucide." *Nouvelles Assyriologiques brèves et utilitaires* 1: 32–3.

Misch, G. 1949–50 [1907]. *Geschichte der Autobiographie. Bd. 1. Das Altertum.* Bern.

Möller, M. 2004. *Qualis Oratio, Talis Vita: Zu Theorie und Praxis Mimetischer Verfahren in der Griechisch-römischen Literaturkritik.* Heidelberg.

Momigliano, A. 1979. "Persian Empire and Greek Freedom." In A. Ryan (ed.), *The Idea of Freedom: Essays in Honour of Isaiah Berlin*, 139–51. Oxford.

Mooren, L. 1975. *The Aulic Titulature in Ptolemaic Egypt: Introduction and Prosopography.* Verhandelingen van de Koninklijke Academie voor Wetenschappen, Letteren en Schone Kunsten van België. Brussels.

Moretti, L. (ed.). 1967. *Iscrizioni storiche ellenistiche: Testo critico, traduzione e commento.* Volume 1. *Attica, Peloponneso, Beozia.* Florence.

– 1975. *Iscrizioni storiche ellenistiche: Testo critico, traduzione e commento.* Volume 2. *Grecia centrale e settentrionale.* Florence.

– 2001. *Iscrizioni storiche ellenistiche: Testo critico, traduzione e commento.* Volume 3. *Supplemento e indici, a cura di Filippo Canali de Rossi.* Florence

Mori, A. 2008. *The Politics of Apollonius' Argonautica.* Cambridge.

Moritani, K. 2014. *A Historical and Topographical Study of Alexander's Expedition in Iran.* Tokyo.

Mørkholm O. 1991. *Early Hellenistic Coinage.* Cambridge.

Morkot, R.G. 2000. *The Black Pharaohs: Egypt's Nubian Rulers.* London.

Morrison, A.D. 2007. *The Narrator in Archaic Greek and Hellenistic Poetry.* Cambridge.

Mowat, R. 1901. "Martelage et abrasion des monnaies sous l'Empire romain." *Revue Numismatique* 443–71.

– 1902. "Martelage et abrasion des monnaies sous l'Empire romain." *Revue Numismatique* 286–90 and 464–7.

– 1909. "Martelage et abrasion des monnaies sous l'Empire romain." *Revue Numismatique* 500–2.

Moyer, I. 2011a. "Court, Chora, and Culture in Late Ptolemaic Egypt." *AJP* 132: 15–44.

– 2011b. "Finding a Middle Ground: Culture and Politics in the Ptolemaic Thebaid." In P.F. Dorfman and B.M. Bryan (eds), *Perspectives on Ptolemaic Thebes: Papers from the Theban Workshop 2006.* Studies in Ancient Oriental Civilization 65: 115–45. Chicago.

Muccioli, F. 2003. "Cleopatra Thea, una regina tolemaica nella dinastia dei Seleucidi." In N. Bonacasa, A.M. Donadoni Roveri, S. Aiosa, and P. Mina (eds), *Faraoni come Dei, Tolomei come Faraoni,* 105–16. Turin and Palermo.

– 2011. "Il culto del sovrano di epoca ellenistica e i suoi prodromi. Tre casi paradigmatici: Ierone I, Lisandro, la Tirannide di Eraclea Pontica." In G.A. Cecconi and C. Gabrielli (eds), *Politiche religiose nel mondo antico e tardoantico: Poteri e indirizzi, forme del controllo, idee e prassi di tolleranza. Atti del convegno internazionale di studi,* 97–132. Bari, IT.

– 2013. *Gli epiteti ufficiali dei re ellenistici.* Historia Einzelschriften 224. Stuttgart.

– 2016. "Poteri ereditari o sacralizzati nelle monarchie ellenistiche." In F. De Luise (ed.), *Legittimazione del potere, autorità della legge: Un dibattito antico,* 199–222. Trento, IT.

Müller, S. 2009. "Das antike Perserreich im Ausnahmezustand. Dareios I. im Kampf gegen die 'Lüge.'" In O. Ruf (ed.), *Ästhetik der Ausschließung, Ausnahmezustände in Geschichte, Theorie, Medien und literarischer Fiktion,* 21–50. Würzburg, DE.

– 2013a. "The Female Element in the Political Self-Fashioning of the Diadochoi: Ptolemy, Seleucus, Lysimachus and Their Iranian Wives." In V. Alonso Troncoso and E. Anson (eds), *After Alexander: The Time of the Diadochi,* 199–214. Oxford.

– 2013b. "Ptolemaios und die Erinnerung an Hephaistion." *Anabasis* 3: 75–92.

– 2013c. Review of Thomas R. Martin and Christopher W. Blackwell, *Alexander the Great: The Story of an Ancient Life. AHB Online Reviews* 3: 77.
– 2016. "Visualizing Political Friendship, Family Ties, and Links to the Argead Past in the Time of the Successors." In C. Bearzot and F. Landucci (eds), *Alexander's Legacy*, 121–40. Milan.
Müller-Wollermann, R. 2003. "Zoologische Gärten als Mittel der Herrschaftslegitimation im Alten Ägypten." *Die Welt des Orients*, 33: 31–43.
Münsterberg, R. 1918. "*Damnatio memoriae*": *Monatsblatt der numismatischen Gesellschaft in Wien* 11: 32–7.
Murray, J. 2014. "Anchored in Time: The Date in Apollonius' *Argonautica*." In M.A. Harder, R.F. Regtuit, G.C. Wakker (eds), *Hellenistic Poetry in Context*, 247–84. Leuven, BE.
Nadig, P. 2007. *Zwischen König und Karikatur: Das Bild Ptolemaios' VIII. im Spannungsfeld der Überlieferung.* Munich.
Nagy, G. 1979. *The Best of the Achaeans: Concepts of the Hero in Archaic Greek Poetry*. Baltimore, MD, and London.
– 1981. "Another Look at *kleos aphthiton*." *WJA* N.F. 7: 113–16.
Natzel, S.A. 1992. *Klea gunaikon: Frauen in den "Argonautica" des Apollonios Rhodios.* Trier, DE.
Nenci, G. 1963. "Il segno regale e la taumaturgia di Pirro." In E. Rostain (ed.), *Miscellanea di Studi Alessandrini in Memoria di A. Rostagni*, 152–61. Turin.
Newton, C.T. 1871. "On an Inedited Tetradrachm of Orophernes II, King of Cappadocia." *Numismatic Chronicle*, n.s. 11: 19–27.
Obryk, M. 2012. *Unsterblichkeitsglaube in den griechischen Versinschriften*. Berlin and Boston.
Ogden, D. 1999. *Polygamy, Prostitutes and Death: The Hellenistic Dynasties*. London.
Olbrycht, M.J. 2016. "Alexander the Great at Susa (324 B.C.)." In C. Bearzot and F. Landucci (eds), *Alexander's Legacy*, 61–72. Milan.
O'Neil, J.L. 2002. "Iranian Wives and Their Roles in Macedonian Royal Courts." *Prudentia* 34 (2): 159–77.
Oppel, H. 1937. *Kanon: Zur Bedeutungsgeschichte des Wortes und seiner Lateinischen Entspruchungen* (*regula-norma*). Philologus Supplementband 30, Heft 4. Leipzig.
Osborne, R. 1981–3. *Naturalization in Athens: A Corpus of Athenian Decrees Granting Citizenship*. 4 volumes. Akademie voor Wetenschappen, Letteren en Schone Kunsten van België. Volumes 81, 101, 109. Brussels.
Otto, W., and H. Bengtson. 1938. "Zur Geschichte des Niedergangs des Ptolemäerreiches." *Bayerische Akademie der Wissenschaften: Philosophisch-historische Klasse. Sitzungsberichte* 17. Munich.
Paganoni, E. 2015. "Bithynia in Memnon's Perì Herakleias: A Case Study for a Reappraisal of Old and New Proposals." *AHB* 29: 57–79.

Page, D. 1981. *Further Greek Epigrams*. Cambridge.

Paschke, B.A. 2007. "Das verunstaltete Münzportrait des Nero: Spuren einer privaten *damnatio memoriae?*" *Mitteilungen der österreichischen numismatischen Gesellschaft* 47.1: 16–24.

Payne, T. 2009. *Fame: From the Bronze Age to Britney*. London.

Pearson, L. 1954–5. "The Diary and the Letters of Alexander the Great." *Historia* 3: 429–55.

– 1960. *The Lost Histories of Alexander the Great*. New York.

Perassi, C. 2014. "*Similitudinem Quidem Immense Reputatio Est* (NH VII, 52). Evocazione, assimilazione, sovrapposizione nella ritrattistica monetale antica." *NAC* 43: 169–202.

Peremans, W., and E. Van't Dack. 1950–81. *Prosopographia Ptolemaica*. Studia Hellenistica 6, 8, 11–13, 17, 20–21, 25. Leuven.

Peristiany, J.G. (ed.). 1966. *Honour and Shame: The Values of Mediterranean Society*. Chicago.

Perrin, B. 1895. "Genesis and Growth of an Alexander-Myth." *TAPA* 26: 56--68.

Petzl, G. 2002. "Das Inschriftendossier zur Neugründung von Arsinoë in Kilikien: Textkorrekturen." *ZPE* 139: 83–8.

Pfeiffer, R. 1970. *Geschichte der klassischen Philologie: Von den Anfängen bis zum Ende des Hellenismus*. Hamburg.

Piejko, F. 1991. "Antiochus III and Ptolemy Son of Thraseas: The Inscription of Hefzibah Reconsidered." *AC* 60: 245–59.

Piras, A. 2004. "Mesopotamian Sacred Marriage and Pre-Islamic Iran." In A. Panaino and A. Piras (eds), *Schools of Oriental Studies and the Development of Modern Historiography.* Melammu Symposia 4: 249–59. Milan.

Pirenne-Delforge, V. 2005. "Des épiclèses exclusives dans la grèce polythéiste? L'exemple d'Ourania." In N. Belayche, P. Brulé, G. Freyburger, Y. Lehmann, L. Pernot, and F. Prost (eds), *Nommer les Dieux: Théonymes, épithètes, épiclèses dans l'antiquité*. Recherches sur les Rhétoriques Religieuses 5: 271–90. Rennes.

Pironti, G. 2005. "Aphrodite dans le domaine d'Arès: Éléments pour un dialogue entre mythe et culte." *Kernos* 18: 167–85.

Pitt-Rivers, J. 1966. "Honour and Social Status." In J.G. Peristiany (ed.), *Honor and Shame: The Values of Mediterranean Society*, 19–77. Chicago.

Plant, I.M. 2004. *Women Writers of Ancient Greec and Rome: An Anthology*. London.

Plezia, M. 1972. "Der Titel und der Zweck von Kallisthenes' Alexandergeschichte." *Eirene* 60: 263–8.

Pomeroy, S. 1985. *Women in Hellenistic Egypt: From Alexander to Cleopatra*. New York.

Porten, B., and A. Yardeni. 1993. *Textbook of Aramaic Documents from Egypt*. Volume 3. *Literature, Accounts, Lists.* Winona Lake, IN.

Posener, G. 1936. *La première domination perse en Égypte*. Cairo.
Prakash, B. 1967. *A History of Poros*. Patiala, IN.
Prandi, L. 1996. *Fortuna e realtà dell'opera di Clitarco*. Stuttgart.
– 2012. "New Evidence for the Dating of Cleitarchus (POxy LXXI.4808)?" *Histos* 6: 15–26.
Prentice, W.K. 1923. "Callisthenes, the Original Historian of Alexander." *TAPA* 54: 74–85.
Prettejohn, E. 2012. *The Modernity of Ancient Sculpture: Greek Sculpture and Modern Art from Winckelmann to Picasso*. London.
Primo, A. 2009. *La storiografia sui Seleucidi: da Megastene a Eusebio di Cesarea*. Pisa and Rome.
Quadrino, D. 2010. "Note su un epigramma funerario di età ellenistica da Sikinos (IG XII, suppl. 183)." In E. Dettori, C. Braidotti, and E. Lanzillotta (eds), *Ou pan ephemeron: Scritti in memoria di Roberto Pretagostini* II, 1127–44. Rome; reprinted in A. Inglese, V. Foderà, and D. Quadrino (eds), *Epigraphica cicladica*, 47–71. Tivoli.
Rabinowitz, N. 1993. *Anxiety Veiled: Euripides and the Traffic in Women*. Ithaca, NY.
Ramsey, G. 2016a. "The Diplomacy of Seleukid Women: Apama and Stratonike." In A. Coşkun and A. McAuley, 87–104.
– 2016b. "Hellenistic Women and the Law: Agency, Identity, and Community." In S.L. Budin and J. Macintosh Turfa (eds), *Women in Antiquity: Real Women across the Ancient World*, 726–38. London and New York.
Reed, J.D. 2000. "Arsinoe's Adonis and the Poetics of Ptolemaic Imperialism." *TAPA* 130: 319–51.
Regling, K. 1904. "Zur griechischen Münzkunde. III. Erasionen." *Zeitschrift für Numismatik* 24: 134–44.
Rey-Coquais, J.-P. 1989. "Apport d'inscriptions inédites de Syrie et de Phénicie aux listes de divinités ou à la prosopographie de l'Égypte hellénistique ou romaine." In L. Criscuolo and G. Geraci (eds), *Egitto e storia Antica: Atti del Colloquio Internazionale. Bologna, 31.8–2.9.1987*, 609–19. Bologna.
Richter, H.-D. 1987. *Untersuchungen zur hellenistischen Historiographie: Die Vorlagen des Pompeius Trogus für die Darstellung der nachalexandrischen hellenistischen Geschichte (Iust. 13–40)*. Frankfurt.
Ricketts, L.M. 1982–3. "The Epistrategos Kallimachos and a Koptite Inscription: *SB* V 8036 Reconsidered." *AncSoc* 13–14: 161–5.
Robert, L. 1984. "Pline VI 49, Demodamas de Milet et la reine Apame." *BCH* 108: 467–72.
Robinson, C.A., Jr. 1929. "The Seer Aristander." *AJP* 50: 195–7.
Rodriguez Mayorgas, A. 2016. "History and Memory in Roman Thinking of the Past: *Historia* and *Memoria* in Republican Literature." *Quaderni di Storia* 83: 51–76.

Rogers, G.M. 2004. *Alexander: The Ambiguity of Greatness*. New York.

Roisman, J. 1984. "Ptolemy and His Rivals in His History of Alexander the Great." *CQ* 34: 373–85.

Rojek, C. 2001. *Celebrity*. London.

Rose, A. 1985. "Clothing Imagery in Apollonius' *Argonautica*." *QUCC* 50: 29–44.

Rose, T.C. 2015. "A Historical Commentary on Plutarch's Life of Demetrius." PhD dissertation, Iowa.

Rowlandson, J. 2007. "The Character of Ptolemaic Aristocracy: Problems of Definition and Evidence." In T. Rajak, S. Pearce, and J. Aitken (eds), *Jewish Perspectives on Hellenistic Rulers*, 29–49. Hellenistic Culture and Society 50. London.

Roy, J. 1998. "The Masculinity of the Hellenistic King." In L. Foxhall and J. Salmon (eds), *When Men Were Men: Masculinity, Power and Identity in Classical Antiquity*, 111–35. London and New York.

Ryholt, K. 2004. "The Assyrian Invasion of Egypt in Egyptian Literary Tradition: A Survey of the Narrative Source Material." In J.G. Dercksen (ed.), *Assyria and Beyond: Studies Presented to Mogens Trolle Larsen*, 484–510. Leiden, NL.

– 2010. "A Sesostris Story in Demotic Egyptian and Demotic Literary Exercises (O. Leipzig UB 2217)." In H. Knuf, Chr. Leitz, and D. von Recklinghausen (eds), *Honi soit qui mal y pense: Studien zum pharaonischen, griechisch-römischen und spätantiken Ägypten zu Ehren von Heinz-Josef Thissen*. Orientalia Lovaniensia Analecta, 194: 429–37. Leuven, BL.

– 2013. "*Imitatio Alexandri* in Egyptian Literary Tradition." In T. Whitmarsh and S. Thomson (eds), *The Romance between Greece and the East*, 59–78. Cambridge.

Saprykin, S.J. 1997. *Herakleia Pontica and the Tauric Chersonesus before Roman Domination VI–I Centuries B.C.* Amsterdam.

Savalli-Lestrade, I. 1994. "Il ruolo pubblico delle regine ellenistiche." In S. Alessandrì (ed.), *'Ιστορίη studi offerti dagli allievi a Giuseppe Nenci in occasione del suo settantesimo compleanno*, 415–32. Galatina, IT.

– 1998. *Les Philoi royaux dans l'Asie hellénistique*. Geneva.

– 2003. "La place des reines à la cour et dans le royaume à l'époque hellénistique." In R. Frei-Stolba, A. Bielman, and O. Bianchi (eds), *Les femmes antiques entre sphère privée et sphère publique*, 59–76. Bern.

– 2015. "Les adieux à la Basilissa: Mise en scène et mise en intrigue de la mort des femmes royales dans le monde hellénistique." *Chiron* 45: 187–219.

Savio, A. 2009. "L'effetto della damnatio memoriae sulle Monete dell'alto Impero." In L. Travaini (ed.), *Valori e disvalori simbolici delle monete: I trenta denari di Giuda*, 105–17. Rome.

Scarborough, J. 2008. "Attalos III: Research Toxicologist." In L. Cilliers (ed.), *Asklepios: Studies on Ancient Medicine*, 138–56. Bloemfontein, ZA.

Schäfer, D. 2009. "Persian Foes – Ptolemaic Friends? The Persians on the Satrap Stela." In P. Briant and M. Chauveau (eds), *Organisation des pouvoirs et contacts culturels dans les pays de l'empire achéménide: Actes du colloque organisé au Collège de France par la "Chaire d'histoire et civilisation du monde achéménide et de l'empire d'alexandre" et le "Réseau international d'études et de recherches achéménides" (GDR 2538 CNRS), 9–10 Novembre 2007* (Persika 14): 143–52. Paris.

– 2011. *Makedonische Pharaonen und hieroglyphische Stelen: Historische Untersuchungen zur Satrapenstele und verwandten Denkmälern*. Studia Hellenistica 50. Leuven, BE.

Schaps, D. 1977. "The Woman Least Mentioned: Etiquette and Women's Names." *CQ* 27: 323–30.

Schmitt, H.H. 1991. "Zur Inszenierung des Privatlebens des hellenistischen Herrschers." In J. Seibert (ed.), *Hellenistische Studien: Gedenkschrift für H. Bengtson*, 75–86. Munich.

Schofield, M. 1986. "*Euboulia* in the *Iliad*." *CQ* 36: 6–31.

Schwinge, E. 1986. *Künstlichkeit von Kunst: Zur Geschichtlichkeit der alexandrinischen Poesie*. Munich.

Segal, C. 1986. *Pindar's Mythmaking: The Fourth Pythian Ode*. Princeton, NJ.

Seibert, J. 1967. *Historische Beiträge zu den dynastischen Verbindungen in hellenistischer Zeit*. Wiesbaden, DE.

– 2004–5. "Alexander der Groβe in Persepolis (Taḵt-e Jamšīd)." *Iranistik* 6: 5–105.

Selden, D.L. 1998. "Alibis." *CA* 17.2: 289–412.

Sherman, E.J. 1981. "Djedḥor the Saviour Statue Base OI 10589." *JEA* 67: 82–102, pl. XIII–XIV.

Sider, D. 2011. Review of A. Petrovic, *Simonideischen Versinschriften*. *ExClass* 15: 331–4.

Simpson, W.K., R.K. Ritner, and V.A. Tobin. 2003. *Literature of Ancient Egypt: An Anthology of Stories, Instructions, Stelae, Autobiographies, and Poetry*. New Haven, CT.

Smith, C., and R. Covino (eds). 2011. *Praise and Blame in Roman Republican Rhetoric*. Swansea, UK.

Snell, B. 1946. *Die Entdeckung des Geistes: Studien zur Entstehung des europäischen Denkens bei den Griechen*. Hamburg.

– 1971. *Tragicorum Gaecorum Fragmenta*. Volume 1. Göttingen, DE.

Solmsen, F. 1954. "The Gift of Speech in Homer and Hesiod." *TAPA* 85: 1–15.

Sosin, J.D. 1997. "P. Duk. inv. 677: Aetos, from Arsinoite Strategos to Eponymous Priest." *ZPE* 116: 141–56.

Speck, H. 2002. "Alexander at the Persian Gates: A Study in Historiography and Topography." *AJAH* n.s. 1:1–234.

Spencer, D. 2002. *The Roman Alexander: Reading a Cultural Myth*. Exeter, UK.

Spiegelberg, W. 1907. *Papyrus Libbey: An Egyptian Marriage Contract*. Toledo, OH.

Stecher, A. 1981. *Inschriftliche Grabgedichte auf Krieger und Athleten: Eine Studie zu griechischen Wertprädikationen*. Innsbrück, AT.

Stephens, S.A. 2003. *Seeing Double: Intercultural Poetics in Ptolemaic Alexandria*. Hellenistic Culture and Society 37. Berkeley.

Stewart, A. 1993. *Faces of Power: Alexander's Image and Hellenistic Politics*. Berkeley.

Stinton, T. 1979. "The First Stasimon of Aeschylus' *Choephori*." *CQ* 29: 252–62.

Stoddard, K. 2003. "The Programmatic Message of the 'Kings and Singers' Passage: Hesiod, 'Theogony' 80–103." *TAPA* 133: 1–16.

Strootman, R. 2005. "Kings against Celts: Deliverance from Barbarians as a Theme in Hellenistic Royal Propaganda." In K.A.E. Enenkel and I.L. Pfeijffer (eds), *The Manipulative Mode: Political Propaganda in Antiquity: A Collection of Case Studies*, 101–41. Leiden, NL.

– 2010. "Literature and the Kings." In J.J. Clauss and M. Cuypers (eds), *A Companion to Hellenistic Literature*, XX—XX. Oxford.

– 2011. "Hellenistic Court Society: The Seleukid Imperial Court under Antiochos the Great, 223–187 BCE." In J. Duindam, T. Artan, and M. Kunt (eds), *Royal Courts in Dynastic States and Empires: A Global Perspective*, 63–89. Leiden, NL, and Boston.

– 2013. "Literature and the Kings." In J. Clauss and M. Cuypers (eds), *A Companion to Hellenistic Literature*: 30–45. 2nd ed. Malden, MA, and Oxford.

– 2014. *Courts and Elites in the Hellenistic Empires: The Near East after the Achaemenids, c. 330–30 BCE*. Edinburgh.

– 2016. "'The Heroic Company of My Forebears': The Ancestor Galleries of Antiochos I of Kommagene at Nemrud Dağı and the Role of Royal Women in the Transmission of Hellenistic Kingship." In Coşkun and McAuley, 209–29.

Sullivan, R. 1990. *Near Eastern Royalty and Rome, 100–30 BC*. Toronto.

Syson, A. 2013. *Fama and Fiction in Vergil's Aeneid*. Columbus, OH.

Taietti, G. Forthcoming. "The Poets at Alexander's Court: How Flat Is Flattery?" In B. Cartlidge, J. Kwapisz, M. Perale, and G. Taietti (eds), *The Lost Generations: Hellenistic Poetry before Callimachus*.

Tarn, W.W. 1933. "Alexander the Great and the Brotherhood of Mankind." *PCPS* 19: 123–66.

– 1948. *Alexander the Great*. Volumes 1 and 2. Cambridge.

Thalmann, W.G. 2011. *Apollonius of Rhodes and the Spaces of Hellenism: Classical Culture and Society*. Oxford.

Thiers, C. 1995. "Civils et militaires dans les temples: Occupation illicite et expulsion." *BIFAO* 95: 493–516.

– 2006. "Égyptiens et Grecs au service des cultes indigènes: Un aspect de l'évergétisme en Égypte lagide." In M. Molin (ed.), *Les régulations sociales dans l'Antiquité*, 275–301. Rennes.

– 2007. *Ptolémée Philadelphe et les prêtres d'Atoum de Tjékou: Nouvelle édition commentée de la "stèle de Pithom" (CGC 22183)*. Montpellier, FR.

Thomas, J.-F. 2002. *Gloria et Laus: Étude sémantique*. Leuven, BE.

Thompson, D., and K. Vandorpe. 2017. *The Edfu Nome Surveyed*. Cambridge.

Thonemann, P. 2015. *The Hellenistic World: Using Coins as Sources*. Oxford.

Tondriau, J. 1948. "La Tryphè: philosophie royale ptolémaïque." *Revue des études anciennes* 50: 49–54.

Too, Y.L. 2010. *The Idea of the Library in the Ancient World*. Oxford.

Török, L. 1995. *The Birth of an Ancient African Kingdom: Kush and Her Myth of the State in the First Millennium BC*. Cahier de recherches de l'Institut de papyrologie et égyptologie de Lille, Supplement 4. Lille, FR.

– 2009. *Between Two Worlds: The Frontier between Ancient Nubia and Egypt, 3700 BC–500 AD*. Probleme der Ägyptologie 29. Leiden, NL.

Tsagalis, C.C. 2008. *Inscribing Sorrow: Fourth-Century Attic Funerary Epigrams*. Trends in Classics – Supplementary Volume 1. Berlin.

Usener, H. 1873. "Vergessenes." *Rheinisches Museum* 28: 391–435.

Van Bremen, R. 2003. "Family Structures." In A. Erskine (ed.), *A Companion to the Hellenistic World*, 313–30. Oxford.

Van Minnen, P. 2000. "Euergetism in Graeco-Roman Egypt." In L. Mooren (ed.), *Administration and Society in the Hellenistic and Roman World: Proceedings of the International Colloquium, Bertinoro 19–24 July 1997*, 437–69. Studia Hellenistica 36. Leuven, BE.

Van't Dack, E., W. Clarysse, G. Cohen, J. Quaegebeur, and J.K. Winnicki (eds). 1989. *The Judean-Syrian-Egyptian Conflict of 103–101 B.C.: A Multilingual Dossier Concerning a "War of Sceptres."* Collectanea Hellenistica 1. Brussels.

Varner, E.R. 2004. *Monumenta Graeca et Romana: Mutilation and Transformation. Damnatio Memoriae and Roman Imperial Portraiture*. Leiden, NL.

Vatin, C. 1970. *Recherches sur le manage et la condition de la femme mariée à l'époque hellénistique*. Paris.

Véïsse, A.-E. 2004. *Les "révoltes Égyptiennes": Recherches sur les troubles intérieurs en Egypte du règne de Ptolémée III Evergète à la conquête romaine*. Studia Hellenistica 41. Leuven, BE.

Vercoutter, J. 1950. "Les statues du général Hor, gouverneur d'Hérakléopolis, de Busiris et d'Héliopolis (Louvre A. 88, Alexandrie, sans numéro d'inventaire)." *BIFAO* 49: 85–114.

Veyne, P. 1976. *Le pain et le cirque: Sociologie historique d'un pluralisme politique*. Paris.

Visona, P. 1981. "An Unusual Ptolemaic Overstrike in Ann Arbor." *Numismatic Circular* 89.6: 199.

Volk, K. 2002. "Κλέος ἄφθιτον Revisited." *CP* 97: 61–8.

Von Aulock, H. 1967. *Sylloge Nummorum Graecorum Deutschland: Sammlung v. Aulock. Heft 15. Nachträge I, Pontus. Armenia Minor. Paphlagonien. Bithynien*. Berlin.

Von Müller, A. 1977. *Gloria Bona Fama Bonorum: Studien zur Sittlichen Bedeutung des Ruhmes in der Frühchristlichen und Mittelalterlichen Welt.* Husum.

Walker, S. 2001. "Cleopatra's Images: Reflections of Reality." In S. Walker and P. Higgs (eds), *Cleopatra of Egypt: From History to Myth*, 142–7. Princeton, NJ.

Wasmuth, M. 2015. "Political Memory in the Achaemenid Empire: The Integration of Egyptian Kingship into Persian Royal Display." In J.M. Silverman and C. Waerzeggers (eds), *Political Memory in and after the Persian Empire*, 203–38. Atlanta.

Weber, G. 1993. *Dichtung und höfische Gesellschaft: Die Rezeption von Zeitgeschichte am Hof der ersten drei Ptolemäer.* Stuttgart.

Weisser, B. 2012. "Erasionen des Porträts von Geta auf Münzen Kleinasiens." In B. Pferdewirt and M. Scholz (eds), *Bürgerrecht und Krise: Die Constitutio Antoniniana 212 n. Chr. und ihre innenpolitischen Folgen*, 28–9. Mainz, DE.

Welch, K., and H. Mitchell. 2013. "Revisiting the Roman Alexander." *Antichthon* 47: 80–100.

Wheatley, P. 2015. "Diadoch Chronography after Philip Arrhidaeus: Old and New Evidence." In P. Wheatley and E.J. Baynham (eds), *East and West in the World Empire of Alexander: Essays in Honour of Brian Bosworth*, 241–58. Oxford.

Whitby, M. (ed.). 1998. *The Propaganda of Power: The Role of Panegyric in Late Antiquity*. Leiden, NL.

White, M. 2012. *The Great Big Book of Horrible Things: The Definitive Chronicle of History's 100 Worst Atrocities*. New York.

Whitehorne, J. 2001. *Cleopatras*. London and New York.

Widmer, M. 2008. "Pourquoi reprendre le dossier des reines hellénistiques? Le cas de Laodice V." In F. Bertholet, A. Bielman Sánchez, and R. Frei-Stolba (eds), *Egypte – Grèce – Rome: Les différents visages des femmes antiques. Travaux et colloques du séminaire d'épigraphie grecque et latine de l'IASA 2002–2006, Avant-propos de M. Corbier*, 63–92. Bern.

– 2016. "Apamè: Une reine au cœur de la construction d'un royaume." In A. Bielman-Sánchez, I. Cogitore, and A. Kolb (eds), *Femmes influentes dans le monde hellénistique et à Rome, IIIe s. av. J.-C.–Ier s. ap. J.-C.*, 17–34. Grenoble, FR.

– 2019. "Translating the Seleucid *Basilissa*: Notes on the Titulature of Stratonike in the Borsippa Cylinder." *G&R* 66: 264–79.

Will, E. 1979. *Histoire politique du monde hellénistique 323–30 av. J.C.* Volume 1, 2nd ed. Nancy, FR.

– 1982. *Histoire politique du monde hellénistique*. Volume 2, 2nd ed. Nancy, FR.

Winder, S. 2017. "The Hands of Gods? Poison in the Hellenistic Court." In A. Erskine, L. Llewellyn-Jones, and S. Wallace (eds), *The Hellenistic Court: Monarchic Power and Elite Society from Alexander to Cleopatra*, 373–407. Swansea, UK.

Winnicki, J.K. 1994. "Carrying Off and Bringing Home the Statues of the Gods: On an Aspect of the Religious Policy of the Ptolemies towards the Egyptians." *JJP* 24: 149–90.

– 2001. "Die letzten Ereignisse des vierten syrischen Krieges: Eine Neudeutung des Raphiadekrets." *JJurP* 31: 133–45.

Woodman, A.J. 1988. *Rhetoric in Classical Historiography*. London.

Wypustek, A. 2013. *Images of Eternal Beauty in Funerary Verse Inscriptions of the Hellenistic and Greco-Roman Periods*. Leiden, NL, and Boston.

Yardley, J.C. 2003. *Justin and Pompeius Trogus: A Study of the Language of Justin's Epitome of Trogus*. Toronto.

Yardley, J.C., and R. Develin. 1994. *Justin: Epitome of the Philippic History of Pompeius Trogus*. Translated by J.C. Yardley, with introduction and explanatory notes by R. Develin. Atlanta.

Yardley, J.C., and W. Heckel. 1997. *Justin: Epitome of the* Philippic History *of Pompeius Trogus*. Volume 1, *Books 11–12: Alexander the Great*. Oxford.

Yavetz, Z. 1974. "*Existimatio, Fama*, and the Ides of March." *HSCP* 78: 35–65.

Zahrnt, M. 1999. "Alexander der Grosse und der Lykische Hirt. Bemerkungen zur Propaganda Während des Rachekrieges (334–330 v. Chr.)." *Archaia Makedonia* 6: 1381–7.

Zecchini, G. 1990. "La storiografia lagide." In H. Verdin, G. Schepens, E. De Keyser (eds), *Purposes of History: Studies in Greek Historiography from the 4th to the 2nd Centuries BC*, 213–33. Leuven, BE.

Ziegler, K. 1966. *Das hellenistische Epos: Ein vergessenes Kapitel der griechischen Dichtung*. Leipzig.

– 1988. *L'epos ellenistico: Un capitolo dimenticato della poesia greca*, 2nd ed. with appendix, *Ennio poeta epico ellenistico*, edited by F. De Martino. Bari, IT.

Zivie-Coche, C. 1987. "Les travaux de Panemerit et Pikhaâs à Tanis." *Cahiers de Tanis* 1: 177–86.

– 1997. "Teos et Teos: Autobiographies." *Bulletin de la Société Française des Fouilles de Tanis* 11: 63–81.

– 2001. "Les statues de Panemerit, prince de Tanis Sous le règne de Ptolémée Aulète." In P. Brissaud and C. Zivie-Coche (eds), *Tanis: Travaux récents sur le tell Sân el-Hagar 2, 1997–2000*. 349–439. Paris.

– 2004. *Statues et autobiographies de dignitaires: L'époque ptolémaïque à Tanis. Travaux récents sur le tell Sân el-Hagar* 3. Paris.

CONTRIBUTORS

Sheila L. Ager, professor, Department of Classical Studies, University of Waterloo; Dean of Arts, University of Waterloo; area editor, Hellenistic world, *Encyclopedia of Ancient History* (Wiley-Blackwell). Publications: *Interstate Arbitrations in the Greek World, 337–90 B.C.* (Berkeley, 1996); "Marriage or Mirage? The Phantom Wedding of Cleopatra and Antony," *CP* 108 (2013): 139–55; "Peaceful Conflict Resolution in the World of the Greek Federal States," in H. Beck et al. (eds), *Greek Federal States* (Cambridge, 2015).

Silvia Barbantani, professor, Istituto di Filologia Classica e Papirologia, Università Cattolica del Sacro Cuore, Milan; editor, *Aevum Antiquum*. Publications: Φάτις νικηφόρος, *Frammenti di elegia encomiastica nell'età delle guerre galatiche: Supplementum Hellenisticum 958, 969* (Milan, 2001); "Callimachus on Kings and Kingship," in B. Acosta-Hughes et al. (eds), *The Brill Companion to Callimachus* (Leiden, NL, 2011); "Hellenistic and Roman Military Epitaphs on Stone and on Papyrus: Questions of Authorship and Literariness," in C. Carey et al. (eds), *Greek Literary Epigram: From the Hellenistic to the Byzantine Era* (Oxford, 2016).

Monica D'Agostini, instructor, Istituto di Filologia Classica e Papirologia, Università Cattolica del Sacro Cuore, Milan; post-doctoral fellow, Waterloo Institute for Hellenistic Studies (2015). Publications: "The Shade of Andromache: Laodike of Sardis between Homer and Polybios," *AHB* 28 (2014): 37–60; "The Multicultural Ties of the Mithridatids: Sources, Tradition and Promotional Image of the Dynasty of Pontus in 4th–3rd Centuries B.C.," *Aevum* 90 (2016): 83–95.

François de Callataÿ, professor, Department of History and Archaeology, Université libre de Bruxelles, Brussels; curator, Royal Library of Belgium. Publications: "Control Marks on Hellenistic Royal Coinages: Use, and Evolution towards Simplification?," *Revue belge de Numismatique* 158 (2012): 39–62; "Royal Hellenistic Coinages: From Alexander to Mithradates," in W. Metcalf (ed.), *The Oxford Handbook of Greek and Roman Coinage* (Oxford, 2012); (ed.), *Quantifying the Greco-Roman Economy and Beyond* (Bari, IT, 2014); *Cléopâtre, usages et mésusages de son image* (Brussels, 2015).

Riemer A. Faber, professor, Department of Classical Studies, University of Waterloo. Publications: "The Ekphrasis in Naevius' *Bellum Punicum* and Hellenistic Literary Aesthetics," *Hermes* 140 (2012): 417–27; (ed., with S. Ager), *Belonging and Isolation in the Hellenistic World* (Toronto, 2013); "Nonnus and the Poetry of Ekphrasis in the *Dionysiaca*," in D. Accorinti (ed.), *Brill's Companion to Nonnus of Panopolis* (Leiden, NL, 2016); "Ekphrasis, Emasculation, and Epic Tradition in the *Thebaid* of Antimachus," *AJP* 138 (2017): 435–60; "The Hellenistic Origins of Memory as Trope for Literary Allusion in Latin Poetry," *Philologus* 161 (2017): 77–89; *Erasmi Annotationes ad Galatas, ad Ephesios: Collected Works of Erasmus* Volume 58 (Toronto, 2017).

Christelle Fischer-Bovet, associate professor, Department of Classics, University of Southern California Dornsife. Publications: "Counting the Greeks in Egypt: Immigration in the First Century of Ptolemaic Rule," in C. Holleran et al. (eds), *Demography and the Graeco-Roman World* (Cambridge, 2011); "Ethnicity, Greco-Roman Egypt," in R. Bagnall et al. (eds), *Encyclopedia of Ancient History* (Oxford, 2012); *Army and Society in Ptolemaic Egypt, 323–30 BC* (Cambridge, 2014); "Un aspect des conséquences des réformes de l'armée lagide: Soldats, temples Egyptiens et inviolabilité (asylia)," in A.-E. Véïsse et al. (eds), *L'armée en Égypte aux époques saïte, ptolémaïque* (Paris, 2014); "Towards a Translocal Elite Culture in the Ptolemaic Empire," in M. Lavan et al. (eds), *Cosmopolitanism and Empire: Universal Rulers, Local Elites and Cultural Integration in the Ancient Near East Mediterranean* (Oxford, 2016).

Judith Fletcher, professor, Department of History, Wilfrid Laurier University, Waterloo. Publications: (ed.), *Virginity Revisited: Configurations of the Unpossessed Body* (Toronto, 2007); *Performing Oaths in Classical Greek Drama* (Cambridge, 2012); "Weapons of Friendship: Props in Sophocles' *Philoctetes* and *Ajax*," in V. Liapos et al. (eds), *Opsis: Greek and Roman Stagecraft and Spectacle* (Leiden, NL, 2013); *Oaths and Swearing in Ancient Greece* (Berlin, 2014); *Myths of the Underworld in Contemporary Culture: The Backward Gaze* (Oxford, 2019).

Waldemar Heckel, professor, Department of Classical Studies, University of Calgary. Publications: *The Conquests of Alexander the Great: Key Conflicts of the Ancient World* (Cambridge, 2008); (ed., with L. Tritle), *Alexander the Great: A New History* (Oxford, 2009); (ed., with J. Yardley and P. Wheatley), *Justin: Epitome of the Philippic History of Pompeius Trogus,* volume 2 (Oxford, 2011); "The Three Thousand: Alexander's Infantry Guard," in B. Campbell et al. (eds), *The Oxford Handbook of Warfare in the Classical World* (Oxford, 2013).

Timothy Howe, professor, Department of History, St Olaf College, Minnesota. Editor, *Ancient History Bulletin.* Publications: *Pastoral Politics: Animals, Agriculture and Society in Ancient Greece* (Claremont, CA, 2008); (ed.), *Traders in the Ancient Mediterranean* (Chicago, 2015); (ed., with L. Bryce), *Brill's Companion to Insurgency and Terrorism in the Ancient Mediterranean* (Leiden, NL, 2015); (ed., with S. Müller, H. Bowden, and R. Rollinger), *The History of the Argeads: New Perspectives* (Wiesbaden, DE, 2017); (ed., with S. Müller and R. Stoneman), *Ancient Historiography on Politics and Empire: Classical Greece, Achaemenid Persia, and the Empire of Alexander the Great* (Oxford, 2017); (ed.), *Ptolemy I Soter: A Self-Made Man* (Oxford, forthcoming).

Jacqueline Klooster, lecturer, Department of Classical Studies, University of Groningen. Publications: *Poetry as Window and Mirror: Positioning the Poet in Hellenistic Poetry* (Leiden, NL, 2011); "Time, Space, and Ideology in the Aetiological Narratives of Apollonius Rhodius' *Argonautica,*" in C. Reitz et al. (eds), *Von Ursachen sprechen: Eine aitiologische Spurensuche* (Berlin, 2015); "Apollonius of Rhodes," in K. de Temmerman et al. (eds), *Characterization in Ancient Greek Literature* (Leiden, NL, 2017); (ed., with B. Van den Berg), *Homer and the Good Ruler: The Reception of Homeric Epic as Princes' Mirror through the Ages* (Leiden, NL, 2018).

INDEX

Achaimenid, 13, 73–4, 82, 86n7, 117, 164, 207
Achilles, 7–8, 38, 46, 53, 62nn2, 4, 65n23, 173, 177, 185, 195n38, 200, 201, 206, 213
Adonis, 143, 176, 179, 180, 190–2, 193n9, 198n60
Aelian, 180, 183, 215–16n52
Aelius Sejanus, 92, 95
Aeneas, 70
Aeropus, 186
Aeschylus, 137–9, 140–1, 148, 151, 153nn5, 6, 164
Agamemnon, 139, 206
Agathokleia, 191
Agathokles, 191
Agesilaos, 205
Agis, 210
Aitos (of Aspendos in Pamphylia), 113
Aitos III, 114, 131n19
Ajax (Aias), 46, 51, 62, 68n54, 141, 198n59
Alexander IV, 162
Alexander the Great, 7–9, 13, 15–17, 70–5, 79, 86n6, 88n28, 98, 144, 156–64, 168nn1, 2, 4, 5, 168–9n8, 169nn14, 16, 172–5, 178–80, 182–3, 193nn7, 9, 194nn21, 26, 28, 195nn32–8, 199–211, 211n1, 212nn19, 22, 214n35, 216nn56, 59
– and Achilles, 7, 38, 173, 200, 201, 206, 213n28
– and Herakles, 38, 206, 213n29
– and Siwah, 214n31, 215n44
– and the Celts, 202, 211n9
– and the Persians, 116, 183, 206
– appearance of, 8
– association with Ammon, 209–10
– association with Pages, 206, 209–10, 212n16, 213n30
– at the Danube, 202, 211n9
– reputation of, 17
– use of propaganda, 8–9, 98, 172–3, 178–9, 193n7, 199–201, 203
Alexander Zabinas, 20, 34n50
Alexandria, 33n34, 58, 98, 114, 120, 123, 134n68, 185
– and Alexander, 7, 53
– and the Egyptians, 21–2, 39, 113, 123, 126–7
– and the Ptolemies, 19, 21–2, 28, 114, 174, 180–1, 183, 188
– culture in, 12, 55, 145, 152, 180–1, 187–9, 198n60, 206

Alexis, 140
Alkestis, 141
Amastris (city), 13, 78–9, 81–5, 88n32
Amastris (person), 13, 70–1, 73–80, 82–6, 87n24, 88n32, 89n47, 154n16
ambitio, 5
Ammianus Marcellinus, 215n48
Ammonios, 58
Amykos, 150, 155n30
Anahita, 80, 82, 84
Anaxarchos, 210
Andromache, 25, 213n28
Antigonos, 75, 76, 163–4, 169n15, 170nn23, 25, 189
Antileon of Rhodes, 41–2
Antioch, 22, 33n28, 34n51, 79, 180
Antiochos I (Theos), 29, 36nn63, 66
Antiochos II, 31
Antiochos III, 29, 34n50, 60, 109n24
Antiochos IV (Epiphanes), 184
Antiochos VII (Sidetes), 25, 87n21
Antiochos VIII (Grypos), 12, 18–31, 32n19, 32–3n24, 33nn26, 28, 34nn46, 49, 50, 35n55, 36n60, 181, 187, 191–2, 193, 196n46
Antiochos IX (Kyzikenos), 12, 22–5, 27–8, 32–3n24, 33nn26, 28, 36, 34n50, 35n55
Antiochos X, 33–4n24
Antiochos XI, 29, 32n16
Antiochos XIII, 32n16
Antiochos Hierax, 109n24
Antipater, 48, 75, 180, 182
Antiphanes, 140
Antony, 94
Anyte, 50, 61, 143
Aornos, 160–1
Apame, 74–6, 78, 144, 154n18
Apameia, 23, 78
Apepi, 165–6, 170n28
Aphrodite, 80–2, 84–5, 88nn34, 35, 37, 38, 115, 148, 152n1, 154n21
Apollo, 39, 139
Apollonios of Pantikapaion, 40–2
Apollonios of Rhodes, 15, 135, 136, 139, 143–6, 149, 151–2, 154nn21, 23
ἀποφθέγματα (*apophthegmata*), 190
Apries, 118
Apsyrtos, 149, 151
Aratos of Soloi, 189
Archelaos, 174
Archias, 194n22
Archilochos, 60, 186
Archos (of Sikinos), 50–1
ἀρετή (*arete*), 40–1, 43, 45–8, 50, 51, 54–5, 59–61, 63n8, 66nn28, 32, 69n61, 186
Ariarathes IV, 106, 110n46
Ariobarzanes, 200
Aristander, 199, 211n2, 215n52
Aristion, 94
Aristoboulos, 157, 168, 183, 206, 208, 212n15, 213–14n30, 216n56
Aristophanes, 139–40, 190–1, 197n54
Aristotle, 174, 193n7, 195n38, 200, 210–11, 213nn25, 27, 216n53
Arkesilaos, 63n10, 141, 143, 153n14
Arrhideos, 116
Arrian, 15, 73, 80, 144, 156–61, 167–9, 173, 180, 182, 183, 194n28, 199, 201, 206, 209, 211nn7, 9, 212nn15, 16, 19, 216n59
Arruns, 24
Arsinoë II, 23, 78, 84, 87n21, 88nn34, 43, 88–9n45, 89n48, 113, 130n9, 132n43, 143
Artaxerxes, 164, 170nn21, 23, 207
Asklepiades, 51
Asklepiodotos, 61, 69n61
Athena, 92, 151, 200

Athenaios, 80, 180, 184–5, 188, 193n7, 213n29, 214n38
Attalids, 16, 63n10, 98, 174–5, 180–1, 191–2, 197nn54, 57; remedies called Attalids, 185–7, 192, 195n41
Attalos I, 180, 187, 191
Attalos III (Philometor), 181, 185–7, 192
Atticus, 194n22
auctoritas, 6
Augustus, 169n11, 173, 198n59
authority, 5, 15, 21, 71, 73, 76–7, 83, 85, 165–6
ἀξίωμα (*axioma*), 5, 49, 67n43, 176, 186

Bacchylides, 47, 63n8
βάξις (fame), 42–3, 147, 149, 150, 155n29
Bagadat, 100
Barsine, 86, 208
βασιλεύς (*basileus*), 37, 39, 41, 85
βασίλισσα (*basilissa*), 21, 32n18, 70, 79–80, 83–4, 86, 87n18
Behistun Inscription, 167, 171n31
βῆμα (*bema*), 202
benefaction, 14, 36n62, 112, 114, 128, 143
– benefactor, 61, 62n5, 113–14, 118, 205
– forms of, 36n62, 118, 124
– purpose of, 112
Berenike, 15, 31, 143–5, 187
Berenike II, 15, 35, 143–4
Berenike Syra, 20, 35
Bessos, 15, 160, 170n21, 207
Bukephalas, 158–60

Canal Stela, the, 166, 171n31
Caracalla, 94
Catilinarian conspiracy, 179
celebritas, 5–6
celebrity, 3–11, 14, 16, 70, 90, 112, 143, 152, 172, 174–5
– celebrated events, 9, 12, 16, 27–30, 37–9, 42, 44, 54, 66n29, 82, 84, 114, 128, 141–5, 153n14, 162–3, 168n1, 173, 177, 184, 198n60, 200, 201
– celebrities, 4, 7, 18
censorship, 6, 213n25
Chairippos, 49
Chares, 168–9n8, 213–14n30, 216n59
charisma, 5, 11, 28, 157, 172; χάρισμα (*charisma*), 43
Choirilis, 173
Choirilos of Iasos, 200, 210
χρεῖαι (*chreiai*), 188
Cicero, 179, 180, 193n4, 194n22
claritas, 5
Cleopatra II, 19–21, 26, 30, 32n18, 35n54
Cleopatra III, 19, 22, 26, 28–9, 32n18, 35nn54, 57
Cleopatra IV, 12, 22–4, 26–30, 31nn5, 8, 32–3n24, 33n28, 34n46, 35n54
Cleopatra VII, 7, 8, 126, 129, 181, 188–9
Cleopatra Selene, 28, 30, 31n8
Cleopatra Thea, 20–2, 25, 27–9, 32n16, 35n54
Cleopatra Tryphaina, 12, 18–30, 31n3, 32n19, 33nn28, 36, 34nn45, 46, 49, 35n54, 57, 59, 36nn60, 62, 63, 66, 67, 154n16
cleruch, 118, 132n37
coinage, 9–10, 13, 76, 90–102, 104–7, 109n28
– Athenian, 93, 96–7
– Hellenistic rulers portrayed on, 13–14, 21, 29, 32n16, 34n51, 70, 79–85, 98, 99–101, 104–6, 108n17, 109nn23, 24, 110n46
– Ptolemaic, 20–1, 30, 32n16, 98

Columella, 181, 186
Corinth, 137, 151
Corinth, League of, 207–8
Curtius, 157–9, 168–9n8, 169n11, 183, 206, 207
Cyrene, 15, 39, 135, 137, 141–5, 154n18, 184

Damagetos, 53, 61
damnatio memoriae, 13–14, 90–1, 94, 99, 106–7, 107nn2, 4, 6, 108n14, 109n30
Darius I, 164, 166–7, 171, 207–8
Darius III, 15, 32n17, 73, 79–80
Deianeira, 25, 141
Demetrios I (Poliorketes, Besieger), 53, 83, 99–102, 163, 185–6
Demetrios II, 20, 25
Demetrios of Phaleron, 178
Demodamas, 74
Demosthenes, 197nn51, 57, 202
Demotic Chronicle, 165–7
δέσποινα (*despoina*), 13, 76–7
diadochos (*diadochoi*), 72, 74–7, 80, 88n43, 157, 161, 174
Dido, 70
dignitas, 6
dignity, 185–6
Diodoros, 73, 75, 80, 157, 158–9, 161, 163, 164, 167, 168–9n8, 183, 198n61, 200, 207
Diomedes, 59
Dionysios, 72, 75–7, 83
Dionysios I (tyrant of Syracuse), 13, 177–8, 192, 198n61
Dionysios Halicarnassus, 79
Dionysos, 38, 73
Dioxippos, 210, 216n56
Diphilos, 140
divinization, 84, 89n47
– comparison to deity, 37–8, 82, 84, 116, 123, 127, 130, 206, 209–10, 216nn53, 56
– deification, 209–10
Djedhor, 116–17, 124, 127–8, 132n32
Dolon, 51
δόξα (*doxa*), 5, 39–40, 46, 54, 63n8, 176, 215n51
Drypetis, 73

ἔκδοσις (*ecdosis*), 22, 29, 76–7
Egypt, 14, 15, 22, 28–9, 38, 58, 75, 84, 98–9, 112, 114–16, 118, 123–30, 134n68, 143–4, 157, 160, 162–7, 169n16, 170nn20, 28, 171n31, 182, 188, 209, 215n44
Elektra, 138
encomium, 8, 9, 12, 37–9, 42, 44, 48, 51–2, 54, 63n8, 64n20, 66n29, 173
ἐντάφιον (*entaphion*), 45
envy, 7, 58, 203
Ephippos of Olynthos, 213n29
ἐπιγαμία (*epigamia*), 75, 77
Epigonoi, 71, 79
Epigonos, 46, 50
ἐπικλεές (*epikles*), 41
ἐπιφανεία (*epiphaneia*), 5, 200
epitaph, 12, 37, 39, 41–51, 53–4, 56, 59–61, 63n8, 65n24, 67n39, 68nn54, 55, 197
Erasistratos, 185
Eratosthenes, 174, 192
Erinna, 143
Eros, 80–2
εὐβουλία (*euboulia*), 177
euergetism, 14, 36n62, 37, 40, 69n61, 112, 123–4, 127–8, 130n4, 132n41, 143, 154n16
euergetism *ob honorem*, 112, 124, 130n4
Eugnotos (of Akpraipha), 52–3
Euktemon, 207
Eumenes, 75
Eumenes II, 105
Euneos, 153n3
εὔνοια (*eunoia*), 39, 114–15

Euphemos (also as Euphamos), 141–3, 145, 151–2
Euphorion, 177
Euphrates, 209
Euripides, 25, 135, 139, 141, 148–50, 153n2, 174, 191
execration, 14, 91, 94, 106
existimatio, 6

fama, 4–6, 17nn1, 6, 18, 27–8, 31n4, 48, 70, 82, 204
fame, 3–14, 17, 37–9, 41–3, 45–7, 49–50, 54–9, 61, 63nn7, 8, 64n12, 65n23, 66n35, 67n38, 68n54, 70–1, 77, 83–5, 90–1, 129, 161, 204
– and gender, 37, 70, 141, 151–2
– conveyance of (*see* propaganda)
– creation of, 70, 111–15, 117–18, 123–4, 129, 136, 157, 172, 201, 208
– eternal fame, 37, 39, 42–3, 45, 50, 57, 61, 62n4, 65n23, 69n61
– posthumous, 83–4
– pursuit of, 7, 9, 175–6, 178–9, 182, 186
– role of, 7, 57, 128, 140, 167, 168n1, 174
Frontinus, 211

Galatians, 39
Galen, 34, 186–7, 196nn42, 46
Gaugamela, battle at, 17, 203, 209–10
Gelo, 173, 201
γέρας (*geras*), 37, 39, 40, 58
Germanicus, 197n51
Geta, 94–5, 108
gloria, 5, 193n15, 194–5n30
glory, 6–7, 37, 63n8
– and gender, 7, 15, 135–55, 177
– by association, 40–1, 56–7, 64n15
– celebrated in literature and art, 38–40, 42, 45, 49, 51–6, 59–60, 62n4, 68–9n47, 141, 145, 177
– desire for, 65n23, 145, 150, 183
– due to military achievement, 12, 41–3, 46–7, 51–4, 56–9, 61, 64n19, 66n32, 113–14, 183, 201
– eternal glory, 53, 64n22, 66n28
– of a city or a governor, 38, 54, 56, 152
– propagandized in coinage (*see* propaganda)
Granicus River, battle at, 200
Greeks
– and gender, 25, 37–8, 63n7, 70, 79, 86n7, 88n42, 135
– art of, 125–6, 128–9
– as creators of celebrity, 4–5, 13, 16, 53, 115, 126–7, 129, 145, 174, 204–5
– association with, 7, 36n62, 38, 63n7, 79–80, 112, 123, 148, 162, 202–3, 210
– culture of, 13, 33n36, 38, 72, 123–4, 126–7, 129–30, 133n55, 169n15, 170nn23, 24, 174, 207, 209, 216n53
– Greek myth, 25, 79, 205
– importance of language and literature of, 7, 37, 50, 60, 127, 131n28, 136, 140, 144–5, 151, 157, 161, 174, 194n22, 200

Hadrian, 177, 194n19, 197n56
heir, 29, 38, 57, 123, 126
Hektor, 46, 53, 66nn28, 35, 67n47, 68n48
Helen, 151
Helios, 80–3
Hephaistion, 73, 159, 161, 206, 209, 213n29
Hephaistos, 148
Herakleia, 13, 70–3, 75–8, 80, 83–4, 88nn32, 40, 43, 88–9n45
Herakleopolis, 117–20, 124, 165
Herakles, 25, 38, 46, 72–3, 149–50, 161, 206, 209–10, 213n29, 214n31
Hermias of Atarneos, 67n39, 213n27
Hermolaos, 210

hero, 43, 45
– cult of, 55, 58, 87n27, 141, 153n13
– founder-heroes, 37, 79
– heroic deeds, 37, 41, 44, 48, 50–1, 56, 58, 67n43, 79, 145, 158, 160–1, 169n14, 173, 200, 210
– Homeric, 7, 38–9, 66nn28, 35, 68n48, 177
– in literature and tradition, 62n2, 79, 154n17, 155n30, 168n1, 169n14
– in war, 41, 51, 53, 59
– of the *polis*, 38, 48, 53
Herodes, 39, 41
Herodotos, 137–8, 140–2, 153n5, 164, 215n44
heroine, 136
Herondas, 174
heroon, 67n41
Herophilos, 185
Hesychius, 137
Hieron (of Syracuse), 38
Hiketas, 94–6, 108n17
Hitler, 202
Homer, 16, 38–9, 43–4, 46, 48, 53, 55–6, 61, 63n8, 65n24, 66nn28, 35, 68n54, 79, 136, 146, 151, 153n3, 154n23, 167, 173–4, 177–80, 187–8, 192, 200–1, 213n27
honour, 5–7, 38, 42, 47, 54, 82, 129, 137, 141–2, 145, 156, 160, 164, 167
– dishonour, 6, 138–40, 157, 160, 198n60, 199
– divine honours, 82, 129, 216n53
– honorific decrees and titles, 10, 14, 74, 112–15, 124–9, 131n19
– honourable deeds, 25, 150
– honours granted, 14, 37, 39–41, 48–51, 59, 62n2, 63n7, 80, 112–13, 115, 118, 126, 128, 130, 146, 173, 192, 211n1
– of a city, 39, 82
Horos (Egyptian god), 117–18, 123–4, 164–5, 167
Horos of Herakleopolis, 117, 119–20, 124
Hydaspes, battle of, 156, 160, 169n9
Hypsipyle, 15, 135–6, 143, 145, 147–8, 150–1, 155nn27, 30
– and Berenike II, 15
– and Jason and the Argonauts, 15, 144, 148, 150–2
– and women, 152
– described by Apollonios of Rhodes, 136
– play by Euripides, 135, 139, 150, 153nn2, 3
– robe of, 150–1, 155n30

iconography, 10, 13, 80, 82, 84, 167
immortality, 38, 43, 44, 62n6, 64n12, 66n29, 69n61
– granting of, 13, 44, 91
– of fame, 50, 53, 57
– state of, 42, 62n2, 216n56
infamia, 6, 12, 18, 31n4
infamy, 3, 5–6, 9, 11–12, 18, 70, 90–1, 140, 143, 152, 157, 168n3
– and gender, 25, 30, 34n44, 70, 135–7, 139–40
– and kingliness, 160, 168, 175
– control of, 15, 136–7, 145, 167
– infamous deeds, 17, 25, 29
– Lemnian infamy (*see also* Lemnos), 135–55
– means of recording, 10
– social function of, 4, 6–7, 8, 11, 14, 70, 135
inscriptions, 8–10, 12–13, 34n51, 39, 42, 44, 115, 117–18, 130n9, 132nn43, 46, 167, 170n23, 171, 174, 188, 191, 198n59
– Egyptian, 14, 30, 112, 116, 120, 123–4, 126

- erasures of, 94
- for self-promotion, 70, 114, 129
- funerary, 48, 53, 67n39
- in religious contexts, 83
Iphinoë, 147

Jason, 15, 144–5, 149–52, 153n3, 154n17, 155n30; and the Argonauts, 135, 150, 152
jealousy, 19, 22, 25–6, 154n18
Josephus, 192
Julius Caesar, 177–8
Justin, 12, 19, 21–7, 32, 33n29, 33–4n37, 34, 34n39, 35n54, 49, 144–5, 152, 154nn18, 19, 187, 192, 195n33, 196n45, 202, 207, 211n12, 213n25; *Epitome* of, 19, 23, 35n54, 144, 187, 195n33

Kallimachos (poet), 16, 39, 56, 66n35, 172–3, 189
Kallimachos (*strategos*), 126–30, 132n41, 133n61
Kallisthenes of Olynthos, 16–17, 173, 200, 202–10, 211nn2, 11, 212nn12, 16, 18, 213nn23, 25, 27–8, 30, 214nn31, 38, 215nn44, 52, 216nn53, 55, 59
Kambyses, 213n44
Kanopos, trilingual decree of, 128
Karia, 48, 55
Kassandros, 78, 157, 169n15
κατάπληξις (*kataplexis*), 202
Khababash, 164–5, 168–9n8, 206, 208, 214nn32, 38
Klearchos, 76, 88, 88nn40, 43
Kleitarchos, 157, 160, 168n8, 206, 208, 214nn32, 38
Kleodemos, 56–7
Kleomenes, 116
Kleon (of Argos), 210
κλέος (*kleos*), 5, 7, 13, 38–9, 41, 43–5, 47–8, 51–2, 54–61, 62n4, 63n8, 64n12, 65n23, 66nn28, 29, 68nn52, 54, 69n61, 145, 153n13, 200–1
Klytemnestra, 138, 140–1, 153nn7, 8
κόλαξ (*kolax*), 210
Krateros, 13, 73, 75, 77, 86n5
Kromna, 78–9
Ktesias, 164
κῦδος (*kudos*), 39, 47, 49, 54, 59, 63n8, 66n32
Kynoskephalae, 190
Kypselos, 137, 138, 143
Kyría/Kyreia, 75, 87n14
κύριος (*kyrios*), 75, 77, 87n13
Kytaros, 13, 78

Lamian War, 208
Laodike, 14, 35n54, 99–101
Laodike III, 29, 80, 88n35
Laodike IV, 21, 32n16
Laodike V, 21, 25
Laodike Thea, 29, 36n66
Laodikeia, 46, 78
laudandus, 38, 63n8, 141, 143
laudatio, 6
laus, 5, 193n4
Lemnos, 15, 136–7, 143, 145, 150, 152, 153n3, 154n17, 154–5n25
- Apollonios and, 136, 149
- legends of, 15, 137–40, 148, 150, 152, 153nn5, 7, 10
- women of (also as *Lemniai*), 15, 25, 34n44, 135–55
Leonidas, 45
Leonidas of Tarentum, 189, 212n22
library, 16, 174, 193n5; of Alexandria, 38, 188–9
Libya, 142, 144–5, 151
Livy, 24–5, 33n37, 34n40, 35n54
Louis XV, 91

Louis XVI, 91–2
Lucian, 180
Lucius Tarquinius Superbus, 24
Lykos, 150
Lysimachos, 13, 76–8, 83–5, 87n24, 88nn29, 43, 44, 88–9n45, 109n23, 197n57
Lysippos, 10, 39, 174

ma'at, 38, 162, 166
Macedonians, 57, 80, 161–2, 174, 190, 197n55, 202, 204–5, 212nn16, 18
– and Alexander, 7, 72–3, 179, 201–2, 204, 207–10
– and Philip, 178, 197n57
– generals and conquests of, 75, 117–18, 182
– interactions with Greeks, 20, 83, 174
– interactions with Persians, 74
– rule of, 74–5, 78
– successor ruler of, 78, 98, 116, 157, 180, 189–90, 193n9
Mahabharata, 161, 168n1, 169n14
μάντις (*mantis*), 47
marriage, 19, 24, 26, 28–9, 31, 35, 74–5, 77, 86n6, 87nn13, 24, 138; and fame, 22, 144; as means
to obtaining status, 20, 31n8, 74–5, 80
Maxentius, 94
Medea, 25, 140–3, 149, 151
media, 4, 8–11, 29–30, 71
– architecture as medium, 9, 13, 59, 79, 82, 116, 118, 123–4, 173–4
– coinage as medium, 9–10, 13–4, 20, 29–30, 70, 76, 82–4, 90–1, 98, 107, 107n4
– other forms of media, 47, 170nn19, 20, 22, 171n31
– poetry as medium, 4, 12–13, 16, 37–9, 42–6, 48, 50, 51, 56, 60–1, 62nn2, 4, 63n8, 65n24, 67n38, 141, 143–5, 151, 168n1, 172–4, 189, 190, 192, 194n22, 199–200, 211n1
– statuary as medium, 9, 14, 39, 44, 49, 53, 59, 69, 112, 114–16, 118, 123–6, 128–30, 174
– *stele* as medium, 12, 37, 39, 41–51, 53–4, 56–7, 59–61, 63n8, 65nn23, 24, 68nn54, 55, 113, 162–7, 170nn19, 20, 23, 171n31, 190, 197n56
Megistias, 47
Memnon (of Herakleia), 13, 71–2, 78, 80–1, 84, 86nn3, 4, 88n43
memory, 9, 13–14, 43–8, 50, 59, 61, 65n25, 66nn27, 29, 69n61, 82, 84, 91, 98, 105, 110n36, 141, 156, 165; art, 10, 30, 38
Menander, 42, 208
Menecharmos, 47
Menelaos, 66n35
Menodoros, 567
Mithridates I (of Parthia), 29
Mithridates V (Euergetes), 105–6, 110n46
Monument, 6, 9–10, 13, 30, 36nn63, 66, 44, 46, 50, 53, 59, 62–3n6, 67n45, 69n61, 170n28
Moroes, 160
Mudrarakshasa, 168n1, 169n14
Musa (queen), 98, 102, 104–5

Nearchos, 86n6, 168n8, 212n16
Neon, 47–8, 50
Neoptolemos, 213n28
Neoptolemos (Ptolemaic general), 39, 63n8
Nero, 108n14, 177, 192, 198n61
Nikander, 187, 195n41, 196n46
Nikasichoros, 55–6
Nike, 80–2, 85
Nymphis of Herakleia, 71–2

οἰκιστής (*oikistes*), 13, 78–9, 82, 85
ὄλβος (prosperity), 37
Onesikritos, 158–9, 173, 194n27
Orestes, 138–9
Orophernes, 105, 106, 110n43
Orpheus, image of, 199
overstrikes (of coins), 14, 91, 97–103, 107, 108n20, 109nn23, 24, 28, 110 nn35, 37, 42
Oxathres, 73, 76, 79–8, 83

panegyric, 10, 16, 172, 193n2
Panemerit, 123–8, 132n46, 133n48, 134n75
πάρεργα (*parerga*), 189
Parmenion, 17, 203–4
Parthenios, 177
Parthians, 20, 25, 98, 102, 110n37, 186
patronage, 38, 172–4, 189, 192
Paurava, clan of, 161
Paurava, epic hero, 168n1, 169n14
Pausanias, 34n52, 63n8, 136–7, 183, 195n31
Peithagoras of Amphipolis, 215–16n52
Pentaweret, 165–6, 171n31
Perdikkas, 72–3, 180
Perikles, 87n13, 140, 153n11
Persepolis, 74, 206–8, 214nn32, 38
Perseus, 209–10, 214n31
Persian Gates, battle at, 17, 160–1, 206, 208
Persians, 13, 17, 72, 80, 86, 88n42, 116, 164, 166, 170n21, 183, 205, 207–8
– customs of, 74, 83
– headdress of, 80–1, 85
– princess of, 76
– queen of, 13
– values of, 216n53
– women, 70, 73–4, 76, 79
Phaedra, 141
Phanias, 48
Pheretima, 141
Phidias, 186
Phila, 75–6, 80, 83
Philetairos, 98
Philip I, 21, 29, 32n16, 197n51
Philip II (of Macedon), 79, 164, 178, 183, 197n57
Philip III, 162
Philip V, 180, 190, 193n9
Philippi, 162
Philoktetes, 153n6
Philometor, 27, 34nn51, 52, 181, 185–7, 192, 195n36
φίλοι (friends), 39
φιλόμουσος (lover of the Muses), 39
φιλονεικίᾳ (*philoneikia*), 5
Philopoimen, 47, 63n8
φιλοτιμίᾳ (*philotimia*), 5, 114
φόβος (*phobos*), 202
Photios, 71–2, 153n5
Phraatakes, 102, 104–5, 110n42
Phraates IV, 102–3
piety, 27, 84, 123, 127
Pikas, 124–8, 133n58
Pindar, 38–9, 44, 64n12, 141–3
Pittakos, 195n33
Piyankhy, 166–7
Plataia, 44, 62n2
Plato, 128
Plato (Egyptian), 134n70
Pliny, 34n50, 181
Plutarch, 87n13, 156–9, 174, 176–7, 180–1, 185, 186, 188, 190, 196n47, 197nn51, 55–6, 199, 202–3, 208, 210, 214–15n30
πόλις (*polis*), 14, 47, 49, 53, 55–6, 60, 72, 112–13, 115, 126–9, 130, 134nn68, 74
πολυανδρία (*polyandria*), 44
πολυθρύλητοι (*poluthrulētoi*), 184
Polybios, 114, 131n16, 192, 205

Polydeukes, 150, 155n30
Polymestor, 139
Polyxo, 147–8, 155–6n25
Pompeius Trogus, 23–5, 27, 33nn32, 33, 34, 37, 34nn41, 49, 35n54, 169n11, 195n33, 202, 206, 208
Porphyry, 78
Poseidippos, 39, 51, 55, 173
Poseidonios of Apameia, 23–4, 27, 32n17, 33nn34, 36, 51, 194n22
posterity, 6, 42–4, 48, 50–1, 64, 65nn23, 25, 66nn27, 35, 173, 175–6, 201
Praxagoras, 41, 185
prestige, 16, 53, 73, 126, 172, 175, 177, 192
πρόνοια (*pronoia*), 39
προσκύνησις (*proskynesis*), 17, 209, 215n48, 216n53
propaganda, 9–11, 38, 42, 50, 71, 79 112, 114, 116, 126–7, 143, 157, 162, 167, 175, 184, 210
– and truth, 15–16, 183
– art as, 9
– coins as mode of, 13, 90–2
– historical writing and, 137, 145, 154n19, 173, 182, 189, 203, 205, 208, 212n16
Ptolemies, 16, 20, 36n68, 41, 113, 130n8, 165, 169n17, 189
– and fame, 112, 118, 129
– as patrons of culture, 38, 61, 174, 175, 179
– association with Adonis festival, 191, 198n60
– infamy of, 18
– interaction with the Seleukids, 20, 31
– self-representation of, 30
Ptolemy I (Soter), 15, 34n52, 78, 98, 113, 123, 127, 132n42, 157, 163–5, 170nn18, 20, 175, 179–80, 182–4, 194nn25–6, 195n32
Ptolemy II (Philadelphos), 31, 37–9, 71, 84, 113, 115, 131nn25, 132n43, 170n19, 173–4, 180, 184–5, 189, 192, 193n9, 195n31, 197nn52–3
Ptolemy III (Euergetes I), 15, 30, 35n54, 72, 113, 131n25, 143–4, 180, 193n9
Ptolemy IV (Philopator), 30, 38, 114, 174–6, 180, 185, 188, 190–2, 193n9, 196n47
Ptolemy V, 114, 132n43
Ptolemy VI, 20, 21, 31n10
Ptolemy VIII (Euergetes II), 19–22, 26, 28, 30–1, 34n49, 35n54, 132n25, 180, 184, 187–8, 195n35, 196n47, 197n52
Ptolemy IX, 22, 28, 30, 34n52
Ptolemy X, 22, 28, 33n26
Ptolemy Keraunos, 23, 87n21
Pyroteles, 115
Pyrrhus, 180, 182
Pytheas, 64n12

Quintus Curtius Rufus, 157–8, 168–9nn8, 11, 183, 194n30, 206–7, 215n48, 216n56

Raphia, battle of, 114
recognition, 77, 152, 165, 206, 209
renown, 4–7, 11, 172; kinds of, 5, 56, 63n8; ways of obtaining or spreading, 6, 16, 59, 173, 175, 179, 193, 210
reputation, 8, 31, 145, 147–52, 185, 190, 192, 200, 202
– bad, 15, 136–7, 140–1, 187
– good, 41, 46, 135, 188
– of artists, 10
– of rulers, 8, 13–14, 16–18, 27–8, 41, 173, 175, 202, 204, 211n11
– of women, 12, 29, 70, 136, 139–41, 143
– social function of, 4, 7, 156, 167

Rhodogoune, 25
rumor, 5
rumour, 6, 18, 28, 42, 70, 85, 140, 204

Sacred War, 213n38
Sallust, 179
Sangala, battle of, 160–1
Sappho, 38, 50
Sardis, 77
satrap, 44, 66n27, 74–5, 116, 200
Satrap Stela, the, 163–6, 170nn19, 22
satrapy, 13, 76, 78, 82
Saviour (*Soter*), 113, 116, 123, 127, 129, 132n42, 179, 186
Sejanus, 92, 94–5, 108n8
Seleukeia, 14, 33n26, 79, 99–101, 104–5
Seleukids, 12, 16, 18–25, 31, 35n57, 36n62, 80, 98, 106, 109n24, 114, 175
Seleukos I, 74, 78–9, 86n6, 109n27
Seleukos II, 109n24
Seleukos V, 20
Sesamos, 13, 78–9
Sextus Tarquinius, 24
σῆμα (*sema*), 43–6, 49, 61, 66n35
shame, 6–7, 18, 47, 137, 141, 145
Simonides, 38, 44–7, 53, 61, 62n2, 66nn28, 32
Sophokles, 25, 46, 139, 141, 147
Sopolis, 60–1, 68n57
Soranos, 196–7n50
Stalin, 202
Stateira, 73
stater, 72–3, 80–2, 85, 94, 96, 108n11
Statius, 136, 139
status, 8–9, 21, 26, 29, 44, 46, 59, 68n43, 77, 83, 140, 147, 152, 175
Strabo, 79, 80, 158–9, 180–1, 216n59
στρατηγός (*strategos*), 113–14, 126–7, 131n19
Stratonike, 76, 80, 87n18, 88n35, 187
Stratonikeia, 48
Suetonius, 173, 177–8, 193n15, 194n17, 194n19
συγγενεῖς (relatives), 39

Tanis, 118, 121, 124–5, 127
Taxiles, 159, 160
Teleutia, 50
Teos I, 118, 121, 125, 131n28
Teos II, 118, 122–3, 125
terror nominis, 202, 205
tetradrachm, 14, 80, 94, 96–7, 99–106, 109nn23–4, 27, 30, 110nn31, 35
Thaïs, 207, 214n38
Thapsakos, 209
Tharsymachos, 48–9
Theagenes, 123
Theagenidas, 54–5
Theaitetos, 207
Thebes in Egypt, 30, 126–8, 130
Thebes in Greece, 135, 202
Themistokles, 72
Theokritos, 37–40, 62nn2, 4, 63n8, 143, 173–4, 191, 198n60
Thera, 130n8, 142, 152
Thermopylae, battle of, 44–5, 206
Thero, 173, 201
Thoas, 51, 134, 137, 153n15
Thraseas, 113–14, 118, 130n8
Thucydides, 140, 178
Tiberius, 94, 177–8, 194n19, 197n51
Tigranes, 98
Timagenes, 33n34, 194–5n30
Timarchos, 14, 98–100, 102, 110n35
Timeas, 57
τιμή (*time*), 38, 42, 57, 82
Timotheos, 72
Tios, 78–9, 84, 87n26
Tiridates, 98, 102–3
Trajan, 92–3, 107n6
Trojan War, 151, 213n27, 213n2

Tryphon, 30, 36n71
Tullia, 24–5, 35n54
Tyrtaios, 48–9, 53–4, 66n29, 67n46, 48

ὑπόμνημα (*hypomnema*), 175, 178–80, 182–4, 188, 192, 194n22

Valerius Flaccus, 136, 153n8
Varro, 6, 17n6, 186
Vitruvius, 197n54
Vonones, 98, 102, 104–5

Wars of the Successors, 71, 167

Xenophon, 164, 178, 209
Xerxes, 164, 170nn21, 23, 25, 206

Zamaspos, 44
Zenobius, 137

PHOENIX SUPPLEMENTARY VOLUMES

1 *Studies in Honour of Gilbert Norwood* edited by Mary E. White
2 *Arbiter of Elegance: A Study of the Life and Works of C. Petronius* Gilbert Bagnani
3 *Sophocles the Playwright* S.M. Adams
4 *A Greek Critic: Demetrius on Style* G.M.A. Grube
5 *Coastal Demes of Attika: A Study of the Policy of Kleisthenes* C.W.J. Eliot
6 *Eros and Psyche: Studies in Plato, Plotinus, and Origen* John M. Rist
7 *Pythagoras and Early Pythagoreanism* J.A. Philip
8 *Plato's Psychology* T.M. Robinson
9 *Greek Fortifications* F.E. Winter
10 *Comparative Studies in Republican Latin Imagery* Elaine Fantham
11 *The Orators in Cicero's* Brutus*: Prosopography and Chronology* G.V. Sumner
12 Caput *and Colonate: Towards a History of Late Roman Taxation* Walter Goffart
13 *A Concordance to the Works of Ammianus Marcellinus* Geoffrey Archbold
14 *Fallax opus: Poet and Reader in the Elegies of Propertius* John Warden
15 *Pindar's* Olympian One*: A Commentary* Douglas E. Gerber
16 *Greek and Roman Mechanical Water-Lifting Devices: The History of a Technology* John Peter Oleson
17 *The Manuscript Tradition of Propertius* James L. Butrica
18 Parmenides of Elea *Fragments: A Text and Translation with an Introduction* edited by David Gallop
19 *The Phonological Interpretation of Ancient Greek: A Pandialectal Analysis* Vít Bubeník

20 *Studies in the Textual Tradition of Terence* John N. Grant
21 *The Nature of Early Greek Lyric: Three Preliminary Studies* R.L. Fowler
22 Heraclitus *Fragments: A Text and Translation with a Commentary* edited by T.M. Robinson
23 *The Historical Method of Herodotus* Donald Lateiner
24 *Near Eastern Royalty and Rome, 100–30 BC* Richard D. Sullivan
25 *The Mind of Aristotle: A Study in Philosophical Growth* John M. Rist
26 *Trials in the Late Roman Republic, 149 BC to 50 BC* Michael Alexander
27 *Monumental Tombs of the Hellenistic Age: A Study of Selected Tombs from the Pre-Classical to the Early Imperial Era* Janos Fedak
28 *The Local Magistrates of Roman Spain* Leonard A. Curchin
29 Empedocles *The Poem of Empedocles: A Text and Translation with an Introduction* edited by Brad Inwood
30 Xenophanes of Colophon *Fragments: A Text and Translation with a Commentary* edited by J.H. Lesher
31 *Festivals and Legends: The Formation of Greek Cities in the Light of Public Ritual* Noel Robertson
32 *Reading and Variant in Petronius: Studies in the French Humanists and Their Manuscript Sources* Wade Richardson
33 *The Excavations of San Giovanni di Ruoti, Volume 1: The Villas and Their Environment* Alastair Small and Robert J. Buck
34 *Catullus Edited with a Textual and Interpretative Commentary* D.F.S. Thomson
35 *The Excavations of San Giovanni di Ruoti, Volume 2: The Small Finds* C.J. Simpson, with contributions by R. Reece and J.J. Rossiter
36 The Atomists: Leucippus and Democritus *Fragments: A Text and Translation with a Commentary* C.C.W. Taylor
37 *Imagination of a Monarchy: Studies in Ptolemaic Propaganda* R.A. Hazzard
38 *Aristotle's Theory of the Unity of Science* Malcolm Wilson
39 Empedocles *The Poem of Empedocles: A Text and Translation with an Introduction, Revised Edition* edited by Brad Inwood
40 *The Excavations of San Giovanni di Ruoti, Volume 3: The Faunal and Plant Remains* M.R. McKinnon, with contributions by A. Eastham, S.G. Monckton, D.S. Reese, and D.G. Steele
41 *Justin and Pompeius Trogus: A Study of the Language of Justin's* Epitome *of Trogus* J.C. Yardley
42 *Studies in Hellenistic Architecture* F.E. Winter
43 *Mortuary Landscapes of North Africa* edited by David L. Stone and Lea M. Stirling

44 Anaxagoras of Clazomenae *Fragments and Testimonia: A Text and Translation with Notes and Essays* by Patricia Curd
45 *Virginity Revisited: Configurations of the Unpossessed Body* edited by Bonnie MacLachlan and Judith Fletcher
46 *Roman Dress and the Fabrics of Roman Culture* edited by Jonathan Edmondson and Alison Keith
47 *Epigraphy and the Greek Historian* edited by Craig Cooper
48 *In the Image of the Ancestors: Narratives of Kinship in Flavian Epic* Neil W. Bernstein
49 *Perceptions of the Second Sophistic and Its Times – Regards sur la Seconde Sophistique et son époque* edited by Thomas Schmidt and Pascale Fleury
50 *Apuleius and Antonine Rome: Historical Essays* Keith Bradley
51 *Belonging and Isolation in the Hellenistic World* edited by Sheila L. Ager and Riemer A. Faber
52 *Roman Slavery and Roman Material Culture* edited by Michele George
53 *Thalia Delighting in Song: Essays on Ancient Greek Poetry* Emmet I. Robbins
54 *Stymphalos: The Acropolis Sanctuary, Volume 1* Gerald Schaus with contributions by Sandra Garvie-Lok, Christopher Hagerman, Monica Munaretto, Deborah Ruscillo, Peter Stone, Mary Sturgeon, Laura Surtees, Robert Weir, Hector Williams, Alexis Young
55 *Roman Literary Cultures: Domestic Politics, Revolutionary Poetics, Civic Spectacle* edited by Alison Keith and Jonathan Edmondson
56 Fides *in Flavian Literature* edited by Antony Augoustakis, Emma Buckley, and Claire Stocks
57 *Maternal Conceptions in Classical Literature and Philosophy* edited by Alison Sharrock and Alison Keith
58 *Celebrity, Fame, and Infamy in the Hellenistic World* edited by Riemer A. Faber